Painting Texas History to 1900

AMERICAN STUDIES SERIES

WILLIAM H. GOETZMANN, EDITOR

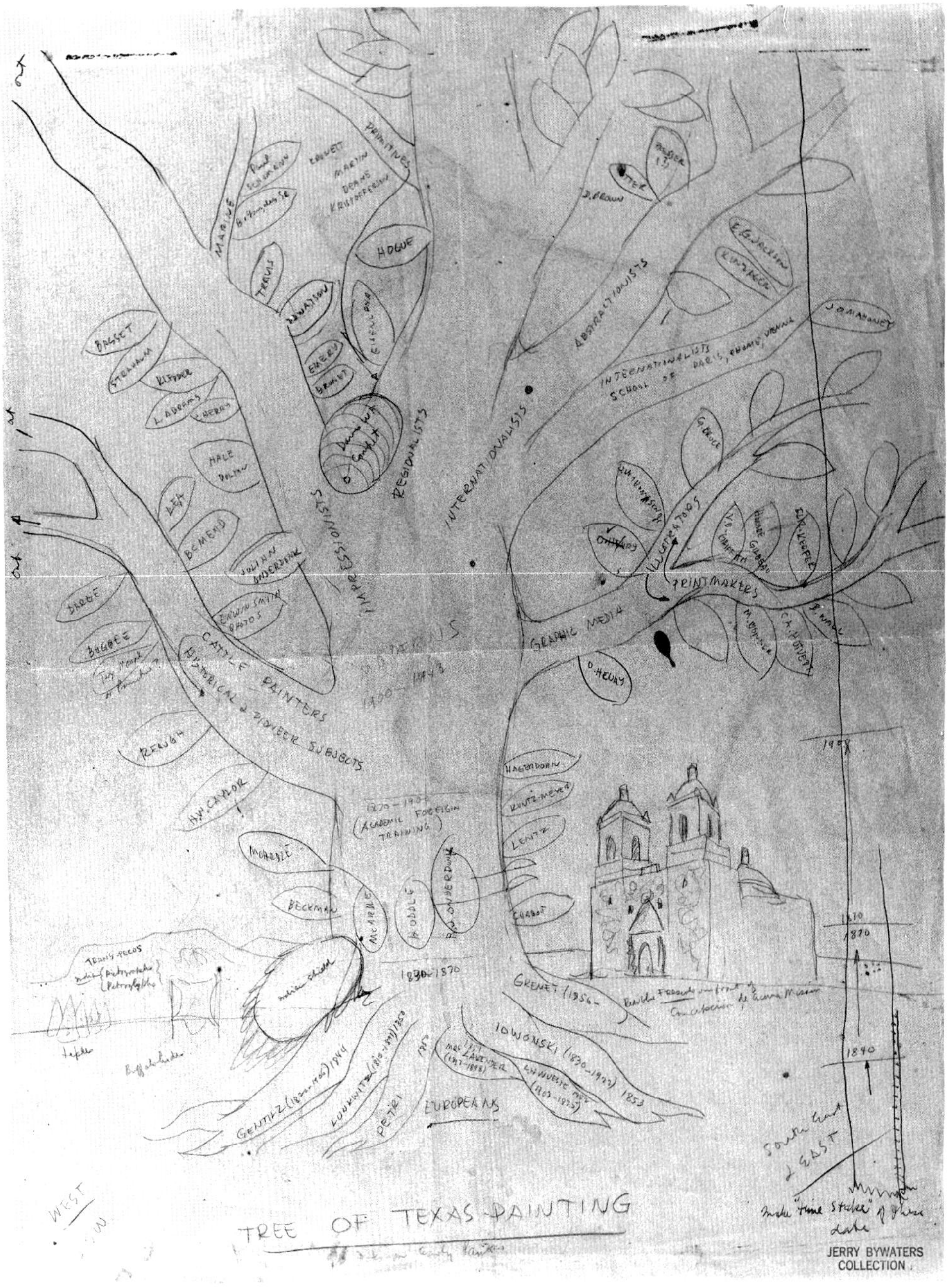

Jerry Bywaters (1906–1989), *Tree of Texas Painting,* n.d. Pencil. This sketch traces the progression of Texas painting, beginning with Indian pictographs (lower left corner) and continuing through the mid-twentieth century. Artists mentioned include Theodore Gentilz, William Henry Huddle, Carl G. von Iwonski, Henry Arthur McArdle, Robert Jenkins Onderdonk, Friedrich Richard Petri, and Frank Reaugh. Bywaters also incorporated into the sketch a time line along the right-hand border as well as depictions of artifacts of Indian life and of Mission Concepción. Jerry Bywaters Collection on Art of the Southwest, Hamon Arts Library, Southern Methodist University, Dallas, Texas.

PAINTING TEXAS HISTORY TO 1900

Sam DeShong Ratcliffe

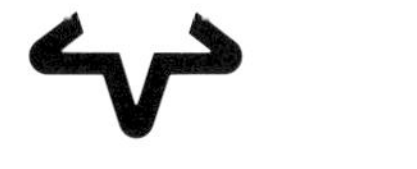

UNIVERSITY OF TEXAS PRESS, AUSTIN

FOR CRISTI,
WITH ALL MY LOVE

Requests for permission to reproduce material from this work should be sent to Permissions, University of Texas Press, Box 7819, Austin, TX 78713-7819.

∞ The paper used in this publication meets the minimum requirements of American National Standard for Information Sciences—Permanence of Paper for Printed Library Materials, ANSI Z39.48-1984.

The color reproductions in this book were made possible, in part, through the generous assistance of the Hoblitzelle Foundation and The Summerlee Foundation of Dallas.

LIBRARY OF CONGRESS
CATALOGING-IN-PUBLICATION DATA

Ratcliffe, Sam DeShong, 1952–
    Painting Texas history to 1900 / by Sam DeShong Ratcliffe.—
1st ed.
        p.   cm.—(American studies series)
    Includes bibliographical references and index.
    ISBN 0-292-78113-X (alk. paper)
    1. Texas in art.   2. Art, American.   3. History in art.
    I. Title.   II. Series.
    N8214.5.U6R38   1992
    758'.99764—dc20   92-9752

Portions of chapter 1 were published previously in *Southwestern Historical Quarterly* 94 (April 1991): 506–534. Reprinted with the permission of the Texas State Historical Association.

Contents

Illustrations

COLOR PLATES

BLACK-AND-WHITE FIGURES

Acknowledgments

A FEW YEARS AGO, I embarked upon an adventure into two territories that overlapped. I had some familiarity with one of these, the history of Texas and the Southwest, and what I regarded as a nodding acquaintance with the other, American art history. The following expressions of gratitude are directed to a few of the host of "guides" I encountered along the trail of piecing together the many fragments of a story that proved to have as many facets as the Southwestern landscape. Thanking them gives me more pleasure than anything else connected with this project.

As I began researching this subject for a doctoral dissertation at the University of Texas at Austin, Professor William H. Goetzmann furnished more aid than I can possibly acknowledge here. His ideas, motivation, and capacity for looking at history and art through a variety of lenses have served me well throughout a graduate program and beyond. Professor John E. Sunder also has offered invaluable aid and encouragement in enabling me to better practice the craft of writing. Professor L. Tuffly Ellis offered encouragement and turned me toward several valuable sources in the field of Texas history. William H. Truettner of the National Museum of American Art provided indispensable background on the development of American history painting that furnished a context for my research.

A multitude of other individuals have assisted greatly in the completion of this work through contributing their knowledge of sources and otherwise assisting my research. Although many are mentioned in the notes, I also wish to acknowledge their aid here. No one can write on the history of nineteenth-century Texas art without having the pleasure of encountering Cecilia Steinfeldt at San Antonio's Witte Museum. Her knowledge of the field is staggering, and I thank her for sharing it. In the same city, Martha Utterback of the Daughters of the Republic of Texas Library at the Alamo has gone far beyond the call of duty in assisting me, especially in introducing me to the wondrous mysteries of the James T. DeShields and Theodore Gentilz collections and in patiently sorting through my many research requests. The late James Patrick McGuire of the Institute of Texan Cultures made numerous valuable comments on many aspects of the direction of my research and the progress of the manuscript. Another San Antonian, Mrs. Venora DeShields Arthur, has graciously shared knowledge of her father's career. At Baylor University, Ellen Brown of the Texas Collection provided valuable information on the career of Henry McArdle. Dr. Brian W. Dippie of the University of Victoria, British Columbia, read the entire manuscript, and I profited from his insights and encouragement.

In Austin, Dr. Ron Tyler, director of the Texas State Historical Association, and Becky Duval Reese of the University of Texas Huntington Art Gallery, now director of the El Paso Museum of Art, were of tremendous help, especially in the early stages of my research. Jean Carefoot and John Anderson of the Texas State Archives have unfailingly expedited my research on Henry McArdle, often tracking down the most arcane of questions. Book and art dealer Dorothy Sloan's well-documented energy and initiative concerning *The Destruction of Mission San Sabá* helped to fire my interest in this work, and I am grateful to her for sharing a wealth of material on it.

At Southern Methodist University, I owe thanks beyond adequate individual mention but will attempt to do so. Dr. Eugene Bonelli, dean of the Meadows School of the Arts, provided a faculty development grant to defray the expense of obtaining illustrations. Art History graduate student Marú Cueto provided invaluable aid in translation of many Spanish language sources. Ginger Strand, student assistant in the Hamon Arts Library, furnished assistance in compiling and typing the index. DeGolyer Library Director Dr. David Farmer has been a source of encouragement and a valuable sounding board for ideas. Individuals who read parts of the manuscript included Fine Arts Librarian Thomas Gates and Dr. David J. Weber, and I have profited greatly from their thoughts. I also benefited from the ideas of the late Suzanne Comer, senior editor of the SMU Press and formerly of the University of Texas Press, whose expertise and joy in writing are remembered by so many. Finally, a word of thanks to Dr. Ronald L. Davis, who, many years ago, sparked my

interest in the study of the American West and has played a crucial role in my pursuit of that interest. It is a rare pleasure to be able to serve as a colleague alongside an individual who has meant so much to my growth in this profession. And, of course, I thank my students at the University of Texas and, now, at SMU, whose interest challenges me and helps to fuel my own curiosity about the West.

I also owe many words of thanks to the staff of the University of Texas Press and to my copy editor, Christine Gilbert, who aided in matters of style and wording. They and the other individuals named here have contributed to the strengths of this book; I, of course, take responsibility for any errors.

I began this rather extended "thank-you" note by likening the writing of this book to an overland trek across the western prairies, and I close by expressing my deepest gratitude to the only person who has accompanied me every step of the way. She has spent hours listening to ideas, reading chapter drafts, and encouraging me when I sometimes felt that the destination was unreachable. For all this and for her patience and love, this book is dedicated to my wife, Cristi. Quite simply, she believed.

A Story to Burn upon the Canvas

IF, AS ONE OBSERVER has noted, Texas has recently become a "media-made mental map," then an examination of how painters depicted its history before the advent of electronic media in the twentieth century also constitutes a study of the delineation of early boundaries that enabled later popular culture to get its bearings.[1] Yet, despite increasing study of how the history of pre-twentieth-century Texas has been portrayed by historians, writers of fiction, and filmmakers, scholars have yet to examine comprehensively its numerous depictions by painters. Biographies of Texas artists, exhibition catalogs, and the few attempts that have been made to survey particular periods or fields of Texas art yield considerable information concerning paintings of Texas history up to 1900.[2] For the most part, though, historians and art historians, reluctant to venture into what members of each discipline usually have regarded as an unfamiliar, tangential subject, have shied away from devoting an entire study to this aspect of the state's cultural history.

As Alamo scholar Susan Schoelwer has observed, historians traditionally have used visual materials strictly for purposes of illustration instead of endeavoring to extract historically useful information from these images.[3] Although true, this observation does not address the root of this neglect, which is that historians, with a few exceptions, are tentative or even fearful at the prospect of evaluating the visual arts, especially painting and sculpture. They usually regard such analysis as falling within the realm of "art criticism," reserved for those scholars who have had extensive education and/or training in art or art history. Conversely, until recently, most

art historians have felt most comfortable in defining "art criticism" as aesthetic analysis. Furthermore, they have lumped paintings of Texas historical scenes, when they considered them at all, with "western art," often regarding this genre as lying outside the pale of academic respectability. Those art historians who have taken a more interdisciplinary approach by including substantial historical study in their work usually have focused on regions other than Texas.[4]

This study makes no attempt to resolve the differences or to decide the relative merits between analyzing a painting as a historical document or on aesthetic grounds. It does seek to focus on how paintings executed before the twentieth century by artists living in, as well as outside of, Texas serve as a visual narrative of the state's history up to 1900. Rather than intensively analyzing the stylistic elements of a finished canvas or the artistic development of individual painters, this study concentrates on factors contributing to a painting's creation and on assessing the cultural and historical significance of these works. This entails delving into available biographical information concerning the artist, exploring such questions as education, research methods, goals and motives for executing a particular work, and the artist's personal vision behind his or her work. Such exploration also reveals something of the interaction between artist, subject, and audience, the development of conventions in depicting a historical event, and how a particular vision of an event gained acceptance.

Despite differences in time of execution and artistic goals, all of the paintings included in this study are bound together by their artists' intent for them to function as historically evocative documents. This common characteristic was manifested in two general categories. Its most obvious manifestation was the desire of some painters to preserve a way of life in visual form, a desire sometimes tinged with nostalgia. Some of these artists also attempted to state and convey the culture, common behavior, and, on occasion, beliefs of a particular group. This large group of paintings is exemplified by works ranging from Indian cave paintings to canvases of European immigrant artists depicting Indian and Mexican life during the second half of the nineteenth century.

Other artists took a different, though related, approach in this quest to interpret the past or a past event. Seeking to express communal experiences and beliefs, they saw painting as a way to validate or justify what many Texans regarded as their national experience by infusing it with significance and tradition. To do so, many of them took on the role of the artist as educator, striving to communicate what they perceived to be the lessons of history. Performance of this role was linked closely to capturing in their art past triumphs or failures in Texas history. These painters became iconographers, attempting to fulfill what cultural historian John G. Cawelti has termed "the vital cultural function [of] embodying in visual images . . . the myths and images that float through the culture."[5] This function of the artist is exhibited most strikingly in paintings of the Texas Revolution and of other episodes of armed conflict in Texas.

Certainly, there was overlap and interplay between these two groups or types of painting, and works of some painters fall in both camps. In fact, a single work sometimes served more than one of these neatly delineated purposes. In attempting to reconcile these efforts at "objective" and "subjective" historical painting, reference to nineteenth-century British immigrant artist Thomas Moran's concept of "pictorial Nature" is helpful. In recalling his method of composition for the monumental *Grand Canyon of the Yellowstone,* which he completed in 1872, Moran freely admitted that he "place[d] no value upon literal transcripts from Nature" but instead strived to "convey its true impression." The artist went on to explain how he altered the position of the rocks, canyon walls, and the waterfall itself in his canvas to be "strictly true to pictorial Nature," creating a fictional scene that proved so convincing that "every member of the expedition with which I was connected declared that he knew the exact spot that had been produced."[6] Similarly, many of the painters whose works are included here undertook detailed research and strived to assemble historical facts

that would be true to, in Moran's terminology, "pictorial history."

The function of these paintings as evocations of history is also bound up with their function as reflectors and shapers of cultural perceptions of the events that they depicted. An effective way to understand this dual function is to examine any relationship that might exist between a painting and written narratives of its subject. During the creation of each of these paintings, with very few exceptions, the artist either witnessed the event or had access to at least one written account of it. In a few instances, the artist recorded the event as an eyewitness in written as well as in visual form. Other painters, notably many of those who executed battle scenes, often were forced to choose between several versions of their subjects. Considering this relationship between visual and written narrative involves not only addressing the issue of whether an artist was striving primarily for factual accuracy in his or her work but also assessing the painting in terms of the narrative tradition concerning the subject, a tradition that may embrace works of fiction and folklore as well as history.

Mexican poet Octavio Paz, winner of the 1990 Nobel Prize in literature, has opined that "a painting . . . presents a reality while a poem tells a story . . . a painting is static [while] a poem elapses."[7] But Paz does not regard painting as incompatible with storytelling, for he goes on to note that some painters and poets have followed "the same principles . . . the juxtaposition of fragments destined to present a pictorial reality."[8] Grouping and examining pre-twentieth-century paintings, or "fragments," of Texas history in chapters according to their respective subjects, as though in a gallery with several rooms, reveals a visual procession of progress. This procession resembles historian Frederick Jackson Turner's vision of "waves" of migrating hunters, traders, stock raisers, and farmers in his analysis of American westward expansion.[9] Regardless of the validity of Turner's interpretation of American history, it is noteworthy that many of these paintings are populated by some of the same representative figures that Turner cast as historical types. Such placement of these works in the historical contexts within which they were executed and in which their subjects occurred brings their full significance into sharper focus.

As a body of work, these paintings defy simple classification, cutting across the traditional art historical categories of "documentary," "genre," "history," and "narrative" painting and encompassing works from each of these classifications. The recently coined term of *western*

American narrative painting comes closest of any existing label to describing these works, since several of them are "narrative" or "genre" paintings that portray a general experience, such as farming or cattle driving.[10] But others are "history" paintings, created in order to memorialize a specific historical event. Therefore, I have chosen to employ the term *historical narrative painting* to refer more precisely to the works included in this study. This term can include traditional art historical categories while emphasizing that these artists used history to recount the various elements of a story; in their entirety, these images narrate a process that is the sum total of these elements.

The earliest paintings to depict Texas history were painted not on canvas or paper but on cavern walls of rocky bluffs. Pictographs painted by Indian tribes at various locations in the western areas of the state, dating from late prehistoric times, served as a form of visual narrative of the daily life of these tribes. Also termed *rock art* by anthropologists, these paintings depicted their artists' preoccupation with family life, hunting, and religious ceremonies. Later pictographs contain evidence of contact with the Europeans who began entering Texas in the sixteenth century. The earliest of these intruders, Spaniards Alvar Núñez Cabeza de Vaca and Fray Marcos de Niza, returned to Mexico during the 1530s with the first in a long line of exaggerated tales about New Spain's northern frontier, stories that soon were included in written accounts. However, only a handful of professional artists of the sixteenth and seventeenth centuries exploited this material, executing "exotic genre" scenes that reflected Europeans' "primitivist nostalgia" and desire for "vicarious exploration" of a distant frontier.[11] Since almost all of these depictions are found in maps and woodcuts, studying the earliest European images of the Southwest necessitates venturing outside the field of easel painting.

The earliest painting by a professional artist devoted to depicting a particular historical event in Texas is *The Destruction of Mission San Sabá,* executed in the early 1760s. Although the painting functions as a narrative of a pivotal event in Spain's efforts to bring Texas under effective control, it is also a propaganda piece that implicitly accuses France, Spain's eighteenth-century rival for the region, of treachery and murder. Although the history of the mission, which was destroyed in 1758, has been well-documented, information concerning this extremely important painting is so scarce that the few scholars who have researched the work cannot conclusively determine its authorship. It has an art historical significance that also has been neglected: along with Benjamin West's 1770

canvas, *The Death of General Wolfe,* it is one of the first historical paintings to depict its human subjects in contemporary, as opposed to classical, dress.[12]

The Destruction of Mission San Sabá was an anomaly in a period when painters exhibited little interest in Texas history from the time that Spain settled the province in the early eighteenth century until the influx of Anglo settlers in the 1820s and 1830s. Even more curiously, no paintings of the battles of the Texas Revolution of 1836 were executed until forty years after Texas had gained its independence from Mexico. During these four decades, painters instead contributed to the visual narration of the state's history by concentrating on other, less dramatic aspects of Texas life. Travelers, European immigrants, and American military officers chronicled such everyday activities as cattle raising, farming, and surveying. In portraying a way of life centered around a distinctively American common man, the subject matter of their works paralleled that of artists in other parts of the United States, such as George Caleb Bingham, Francis Guy, John Krimmel, and William Sidney Mount.[13]

Painters' neglect of the Texas Revolution is especially striking in light of the fact that this conflict attracted extensive attention in the American and European popular press. As did many publications during the 1830s and 1840s, the *New York Mirror* newspaper had praised Texas, referring to it as the "Eldorado of modern hopes," while *Holden's Dollar Magazine* declared that "next to the French Revolution, there is no subject so replete with romantic interest as Texan adventures."[14] However, not until later in the nineteenth century did painters begin to "mine" the events of 1836 for iconographic subject matter. By the 1870s and 1880s, artists and audiences had come to regard the war as the zenith of Texas history, a time when raw frontiersmen had delivered the region from political despotism so that their own and subsequent generations could, in turn, deliver it from the wilderness. This interest in paintings of the Texas Revolution produced a volume of artists' correspondence and reviews exceeding that devoted to any other single subject of pre-twentieth-century Texas historical narrative paintings.

Despite this abundance of subject matter, several factors had mitigated against its earlier exploitation by American artists. One of the most critical of these factors was the lack of demand for paintings in mid-nineteenth-century Texas. As did most frontier areas, Texas attracted individuals who, for the most part, did not have a great deal of what a later age would term "discretionary income" or, in many instances, any income at all. The small percentage of Texans who could afford to patronize the arts did so on a limited basis. Again, as was the pattern on the frontier, these relatively few individuals preferred to purchase "mainstream" American painting, or its imitations, instead of supporting resident Texan artists.[15]

Comparing the development of an artistic tradition in Texas to analogous historical situations, such as that of nineteenth-century California, is helpful in gaining an understanding of this process and the reasons for its slowness. In California, the prosperity generated by the 1849 gold rush sparked the wholesale transplantation of developed artistic traditions and numerous professional artists from other parts of the United States and from Europe; within a few years after the discovery of gold at Sutter's Mill, French influence was strongly evident in the architecture of San Francisco. Also, this city's rapid growth gave the California frontier a far more urban flavor than was present in Texas. These factors meant that California artists had a rather more sophisticated, well-financed, art-conscious audience than did their Texas colleagues. For example, the San Francisco Art Association mounted annual exhibitions throughout the 1870s, at least two decades before similar organizations and events existed in Texas.[16]

Outside of Texas, many artists were either ignorant of the state's history or indifferent to it as potential subject matter because of artistic training that had emphasized an attitude that only subjects from classical and European history were appropriate for historical paintings. Of course, during the 1830s, 1840s, and 1850s, many artists did paint scenes depicting the American frontier; Bingham and Emanuel Leutze were just two of the many painters whose work demonstrated that the West could furnish acceptable and even popular subject matter. The success of these and other painters of frontier life, such as Charles Deas, William Tylee Ranney, and Arthur Fitzwilliam Tait, makes American artists' neglect of Texas scenes all the more intriguing.[17]

Painters' neglect of Texas also can be explained in part by placing it within the context of the question that polarized the United States in the quarter-century following the Texas Revolution: slavery. During these years, Americans in both the North and the South equated Texas with the expansion of the "peculiar institution." By the 1850s, many painters, such as Leutze, had become preoccupied with America's intensifying sectional conflict and skewed their art so as to present a genuinely "United" States. Even New Yorker William Ranney, who had served in the Texas army during the Texas Revolution, executed no depictions of the conflict after he had returned home and become a well-known painter of Western genre

scenes. Undoubtedly, the increasingly explosive issue of slavery turned many American painters away from executing works that might have been construed as glorifying Texas, a place described in an 1844 Whig campaign broadside as a "valley of rascals."[18]

In Texas, the Civil War and Reconstruction drastically altered the equation of audience demand and artist motivation. Of all the defeated Southern states, only Texas had successfully fought a war against a foreign power. The events of 1836 provided Texans, especially Anglo-Texans, with a separate, usable past that could be celebrated in counterpoint to the defeat of 1865 and subsequent military occupation. Within a few years after the state's first post-Reconstruction government took office, this celebration began to take tangible form as the state legislature commissioned the execution of works of statuary for the grounds of the state capitol. These statues memorialized Texans who had fought in the Texas Revolution as well as in the more recent conflict, thus incorporating participants in both struggles into a pantheon of Texas heroes.[19]

The career of James T. DeShields epitomized this upsurge of historical interest that began in the state during the 1870s and 1880s. DeShields, who owned general merchandising stores in several towns in the eastern half of Texas, wrote a number of articles and books that celebrated various aspects of Texas history. By the early twentieth century, these works had attained great popularity as well as a high status among the general public concerning historical questions. They also played an important role in determining how subsequent generations of Texans would view the events of the years of the Revolution and the Republic of Texas. Although DeShields certainly did not have a monopoly on the writing of Texas history during the late nineteenth and early twentieth centuries, he did express Texans' predominant view of that history. His writings had the "feel" and texture of campfire tales that exalted the exploits of what had been and, to a certain extent, still was a warlike culture. DeShields employed several prominent Texas artists, notably Louis Eyth, Henry Arthur McArdle, and Robert Onderdonk, either to illustrate his works or to fulfill commissions for paintings. This association touched all facets of these artists' careers, as several of their canvases not executed under DeShields's patronage conveyed the tenor of his writings, portraying Texas history in an unfailingly triumphant fashion, and, as were the writings of DeShields, these painters' works were warmly received by Texans. This interest in paintings by these and other artists concerning the Texas Revolution generated a volume of reviews and other discussion that far exceeded that devoted to other Texas historical narrative paintings.[20]

At least two of these artists had been part of a general postwar migration to Texas by Southerners. Henry McArdle, who had served as a topographical artist on the staff of General Robert E. Lee, became intrigued with Texas history after taking a position on the art faculty of Baylor Female College in Independence, Texas, in 1867. While painting portraits of Texan Civil War veterans, he soaked up his subjects' tales of the battles of the Alamo and San Jacinto. In one of the clearest instances of a painter finding inspiration from an oral tradition, McArdle soon immersed himself in Texas history with an almost religious zeal. Another of DeShields's artists who helped to awaken Texans to the artistic possibilities of their past, Marylander Robert Onderdonk, might be considered a mild version of a "carpetbagger." At the invitation of Maryland friends residing in Texas, he moved to San Antonio in the 1870s in hopes of earning money from painting portraits of wealthy ranchers in order to finance art study in Europe. But drouth financially wiped out most of the area's cattle raisers, and Onderdonk, broke and stranded, remained in Texas, becoming the patriarch of the state's premier family of painters. As for Louis Eyth, aside from the fact that he was trained as a daguerrotypist in Galveston, very little is known about this artist who executed numerous illustrations for DeShields.[21]

In addition to the Texas legislature's commissioning of works of art for the Capitol following Reconstruction, lawmakers also engaged the services of a de facto state painter, Virginian William Henry Huddle. Huddle had lived in Texas (Paris) before riding in General Nathan Bedford Forrest's cavalry during the war. In the late 1870s, he began painting the portraits of Texas governors and presidents, canvases purchased by the state a decade later for display in the Capitol. Even though he never was employed by DeShields and was a less meticulous student of Texas history than was McArdle, Huddle's portraits and his *The Surrender of Santa Anna* gained immense popularity.[22]

Several questions arise concerning the choice of subject matter by these painters. The history of Texas up to the post-Reconstruction period had borne out the truth of one observation made a century later that "much of what unfolded on the frontier could be considered sources for epic historical paintings."[23] Certainly, the Texas Revolution was the logical place to begin for an artist wishing to portray heroic aspects of Texas history. But why did these painters dwell on the events of 1836 to the exclusion of so many other potential subjects, such as the Mexican War, the cowboy, Texas Rangers, or the Civil War?

Unfortunately, these artists did not leave lengthy explanations specifically addressing this question. However, since Huddle, McArdle, and Onderdonk had all received formal art education in the United States, they undoubtedly were aware of the prevailing attitudes that had governed the selection of historical subjects among American artists before the Civil War. Following the American Revolution, citizens of the new nation had begun to assemble tangible evidences of a history that would compare favorably with that of any European nation. The "grand style" of history painting exerted a tremendous appeal by combining high art with patriotism; in its early national period, America could legitimize itself both culturally and historically through paintings by John Trumbull and other artists. Between 1820 and 1860, Americans began to develop an "allegorical state of mind," desiring symbols that would enable them to affix upon the nation some kind of general, overall identity.[24] Paintings of historical subjects became an integral part of an art of American nationalism that valued the ability of a work of art to inspire patriotic sentiment over its inherent aesthetic worth. Artists such as Bingham, Leutze, and others had emphasized patriotism while simultaneously creating visual standards for the average American's self-definition as a citizen of the nation. By the time of the Civil War, American artists had fixed in their minds the notion that a historical painting had to be didactic, had to teach some kind of moral lesson.[25]

The late nineteenth-century preoccupation of Texas's most prominent artists with battles between Texas and Mexico and, to a lesser degree, Indian-white conflicts becomes understandable when seen in this light. In terms of creating a specifically Texan series of triumphant images, the Civil War and Mexican War had several common characteristics that relegated them to an inferior status when artists and writers began to draw on Texas history for subject matter. Both wars were fought almost totally outside the boundaries of Texas, were national wars in which Texans were part of a larger overall effort, and both wars left a certain bitter taste in the mouths of Texans. Obviously, the outcome of the Civil War was more difficult for the majority of Texans to accept. However, the intense opposition of antislavery and abolitionist Northerners to the Mexican War also had rankled Texans, who had welcomed the United States' victory as providing a long-sought solution to the problems of invasion from Mexico and Indian attacks on frontier settlements.

As for the cowboy and the Texas Ranger, their activities were actually too familiar to Texans of the late 1800s for painters to begin to treat them in a heroic light. In addition, cowboys especially had a rather unsavory reputation in the popular mind well into the 1880s. During the first quarter-century following Reconstruction, professional Texas painters, with the exception of Dallas's Frank Reaugh, avoided the cowboy as a subject. Serious American writers did the same until the publication of Andy Adams's *Log of a Cowboy* and Owen Wister's *The Virginian* shortly after the turn of the century. Even though the figure of the heroic cowboy has roots in the late nineteenth-century dime novel and Buffalo Bill's Wild West show, his widespread acceptance and glorification by Texans in visual media is essentially a twentieth-century phenomenon.[26]

Film and television have ensured the cowboy's place in the pantheon of Texas heroes while also treating the themes of the Texas Revolution, white-Indian conflicts, and pioneer settlement, continuing a process established during the late nineteenth century, when a Texas historical consciousness began to take visual form in paintings of these subjects. In 1886, the fiftieth anniversary of independence from Mexico sparked a statewide celebration, though on a less grandiose scale than subsequent commemorations of the Centennial and Sesquicentennial. At approximately the same time, public school textbooks began to present the state's history in a fashion similar to DeShields's writings, albeit in a more subdued tone.[27] Centered on a frontier past, this budding historical consciousness and its visual manifestations were becoming widespread during the years when the railroad was opening Texas to the rest of the United States, hastening the erosion of frontier life and folkways. While Texans gloried in their frontier past, they strived to assure themselves and the rest of the nation that it was, indeed, past and that the state was able and eager to be homogenized into the American cultural mainstream. A new century and the discovery of oil would mean more than a demographic shift to urban areas; increasingly linked to the rest of the United States economically and technologically, most Texans came to regard paintings of their state's frontier, rural history as exercises in visual nostalgia.

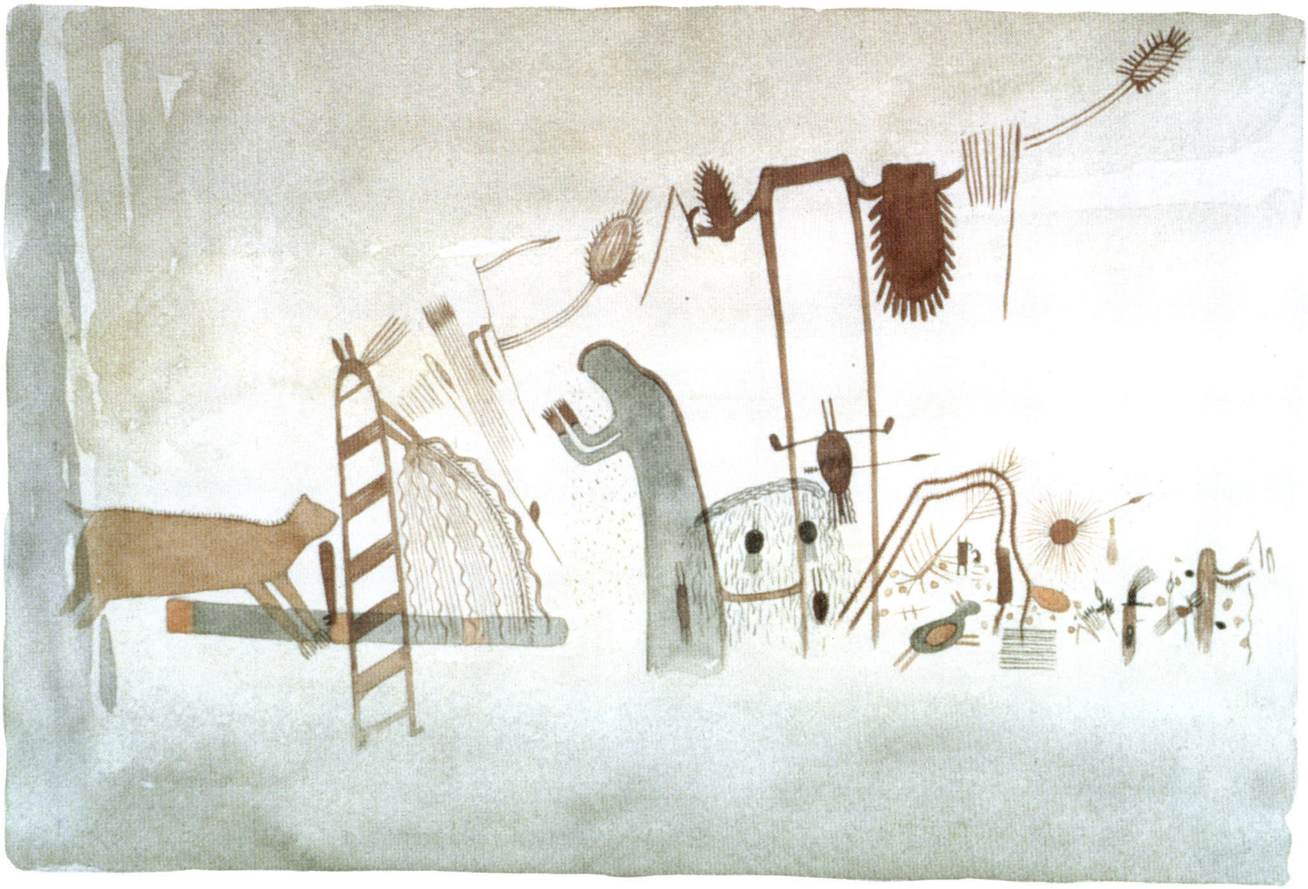

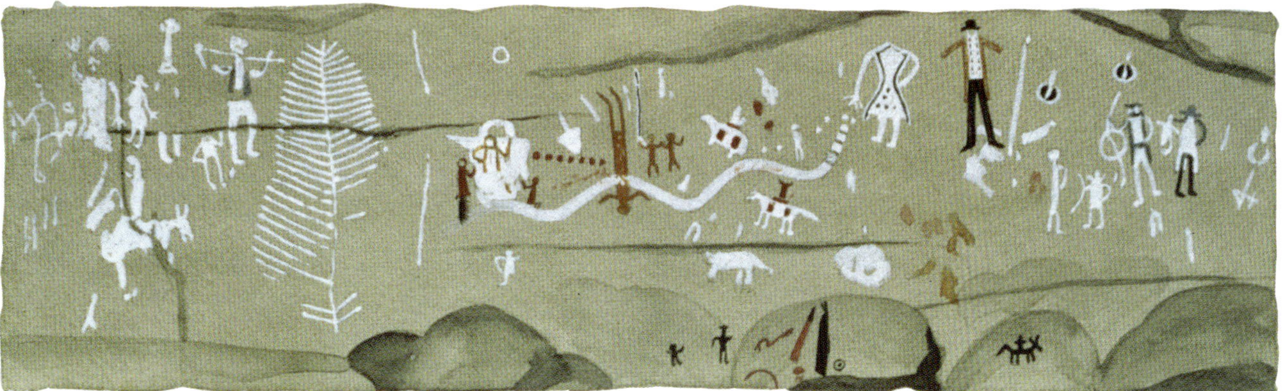

PLATE 1. *Cougars and Shaman,* Panther Cave, Lower Pecos River, n.d. Indian pictograph, watercolor copy by Forrest Kirkland. Courtesy of the Texas Memorial Museum, Austin, Texas. TMM no. 2261-160.

PLATE 2. *Nineteenth-century European,* Hueco Tanks, n.d. Indian pictograph, watercolor copy by Forrest Kirkland. Courtesy of the Texas Memorial Museum, Austin, Texas. TMM no. 2261-123.

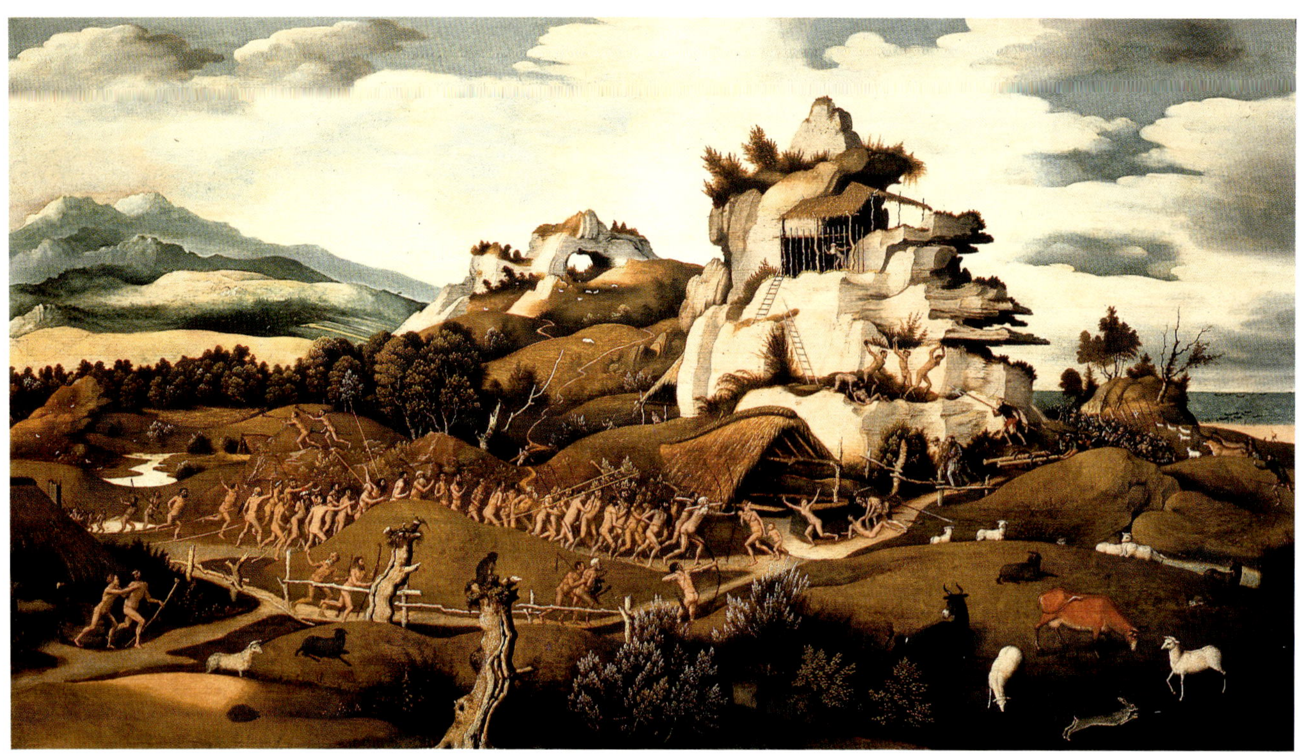

PLATE 3. Jan Mostaert, *An Episode of the Conquest of America* or
A West Indian Scene, ca. 1540–1550. Oil. Frans Hals Museum,
Haarlem, The Netherlands. Lent by Rijksdienst Beeldende Kunst,
The Netherlands.

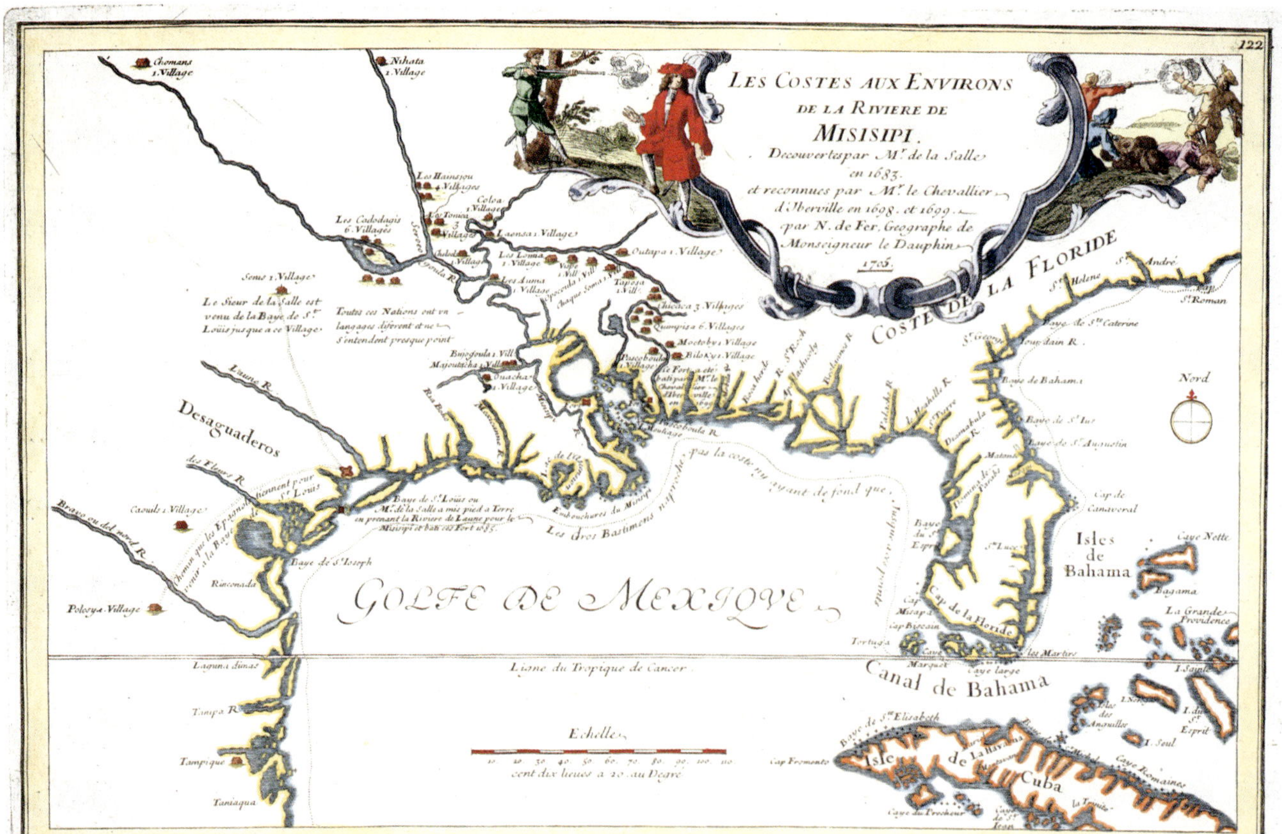

PLATE 4. Nicolas de Fer, *Les Costes aux Environs de la Riviere de
Misisipi,* 1705. Special Collections Division, The University
of Texas at Arlington Libraries.

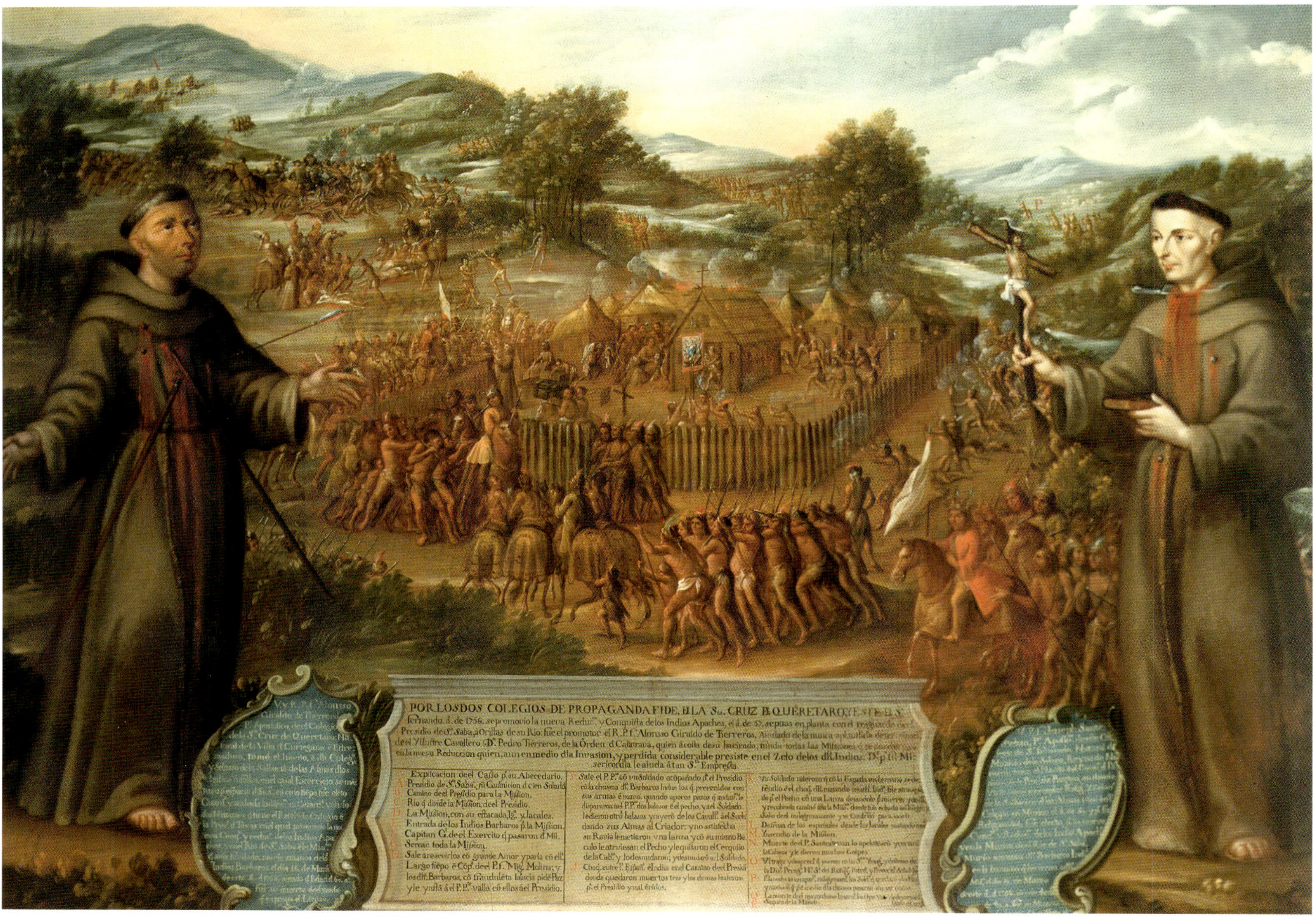

PLATE 5. Artist: unknown, *The Destruction of Mission San Sabá in the Province of Texas and the Martyrdom of the Fathers Alonso Giraldo de Terreros, Joseph Santiesteban*, ca. 1763. Oil. Courtesy of New Phoenix Sunrise Corporation, Phoenix, Arizona.

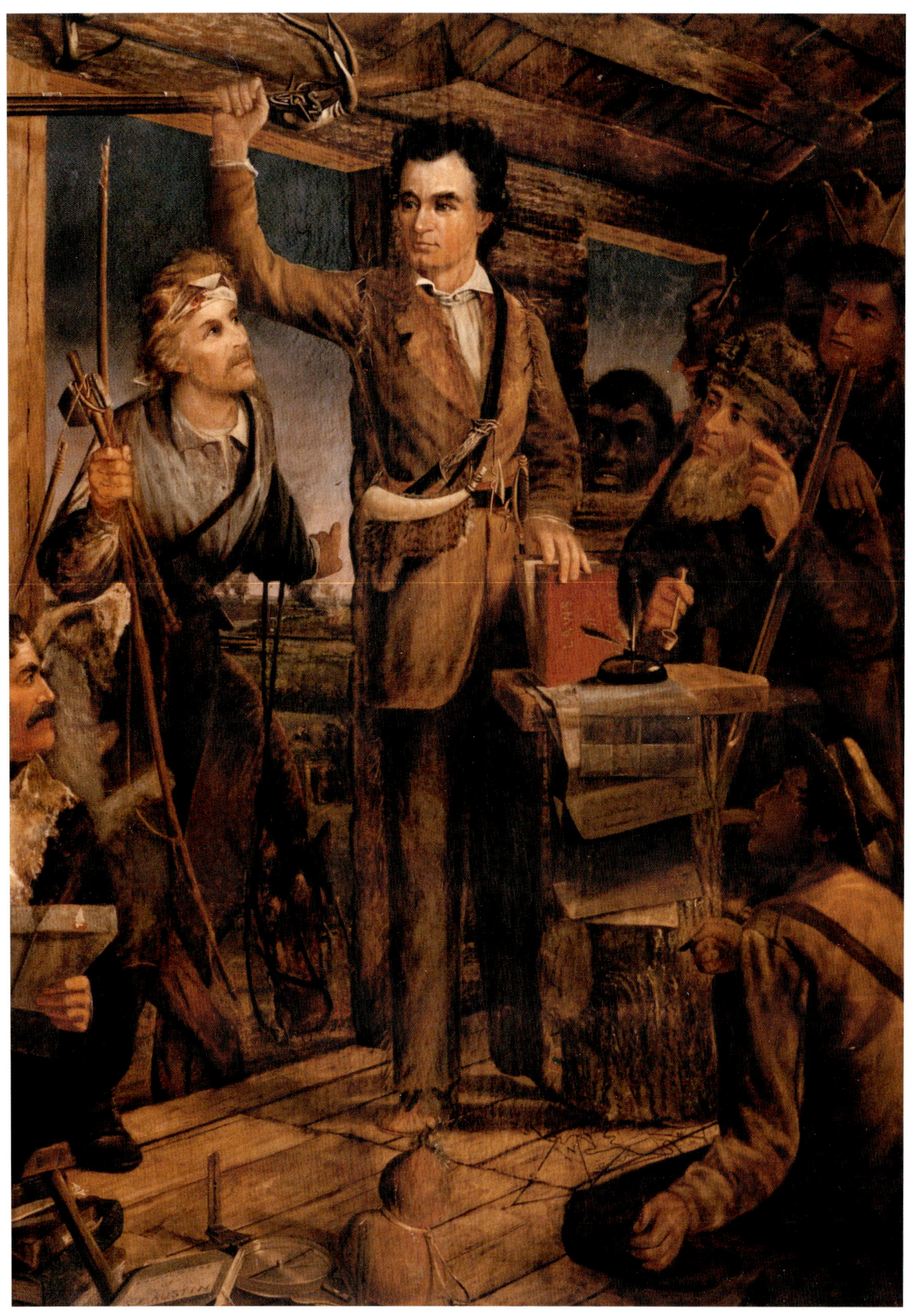

PLATE 6. Henry Arthur McArdle, *The Settlement of Austin's Colony* or *The Log Cabin*, 1875. Oil. Archives Division-Texas State Library. Acc. no. 1989/227-1.

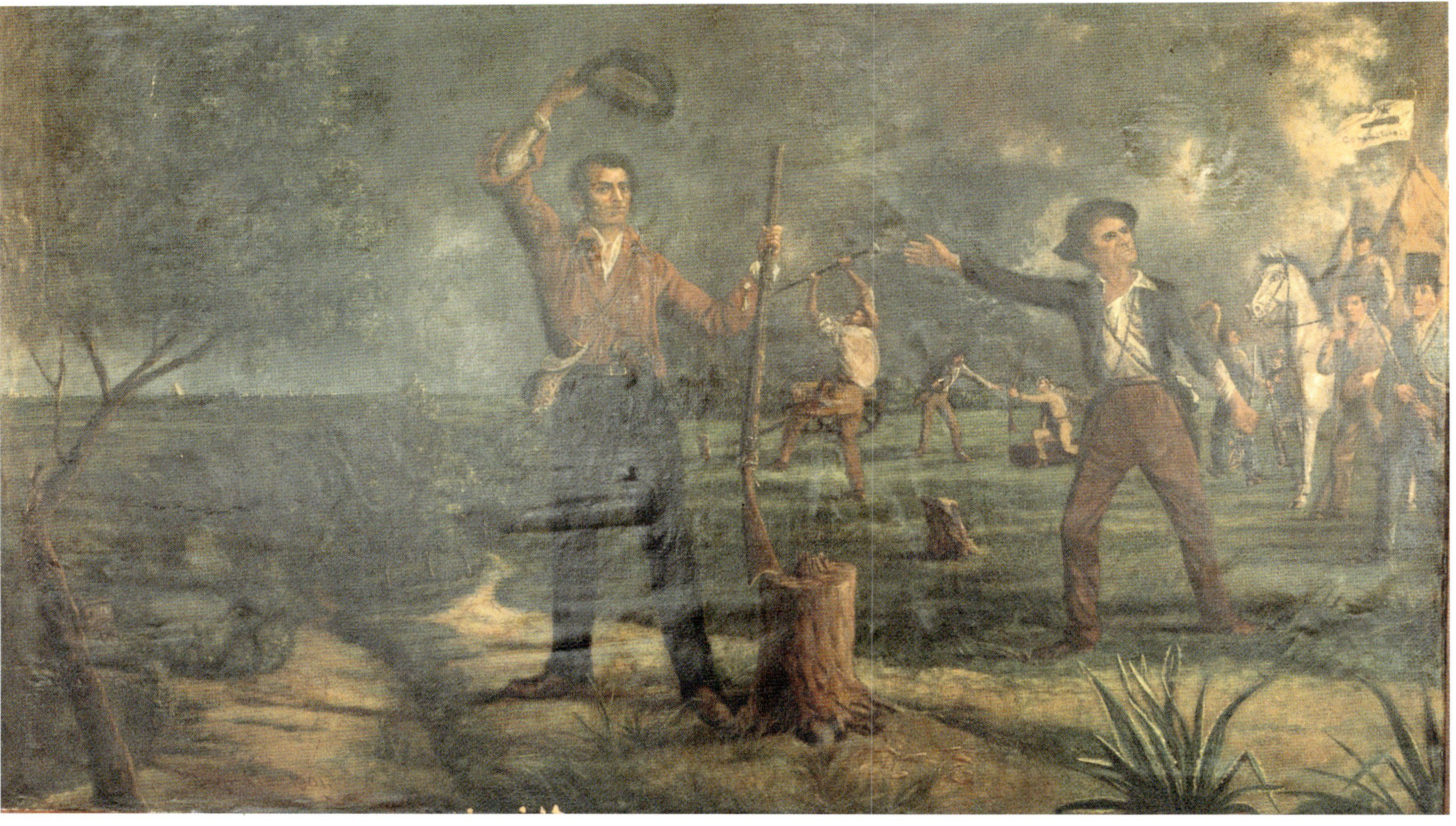

PLATE 7. Henry Arthur McArdle, *Ben Milam Calling for Volunteers,* 1901. Oil. The Alamo, Daughters of the Republic of Texas.

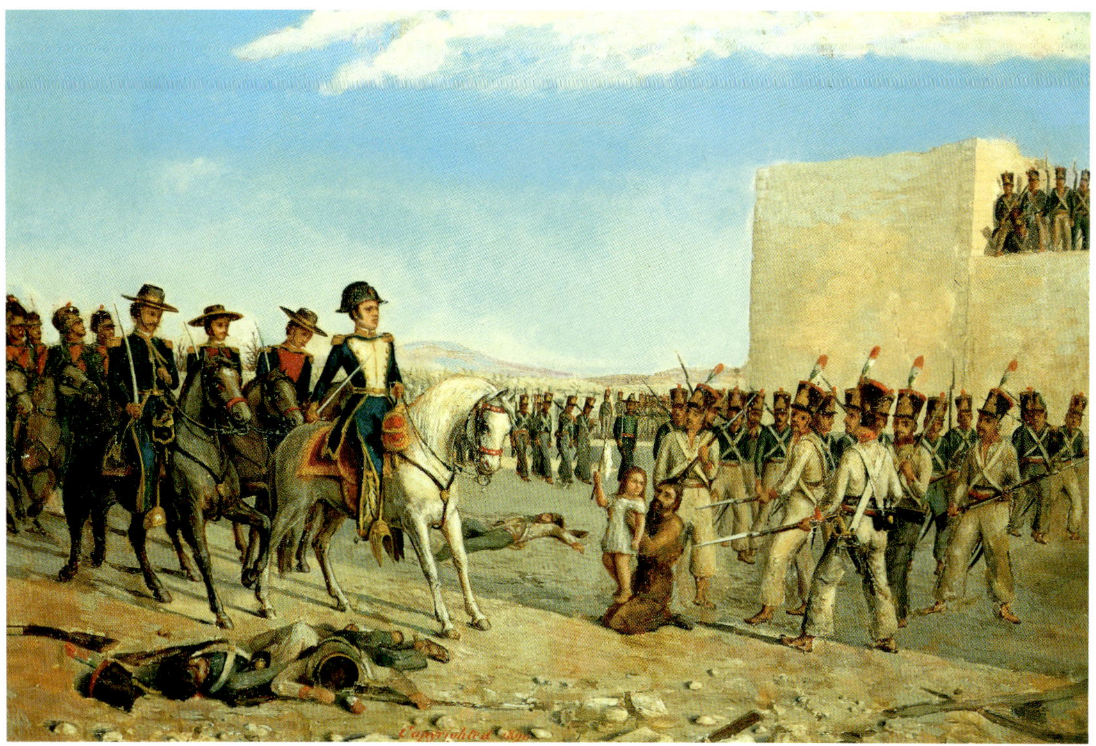

PLATE 8. Theodore Gentilz, *Death of Dickinson*, 1896. Oil.
Daughters of the Republic of Texas Library at the Alamo,
San Antonio, Texas.

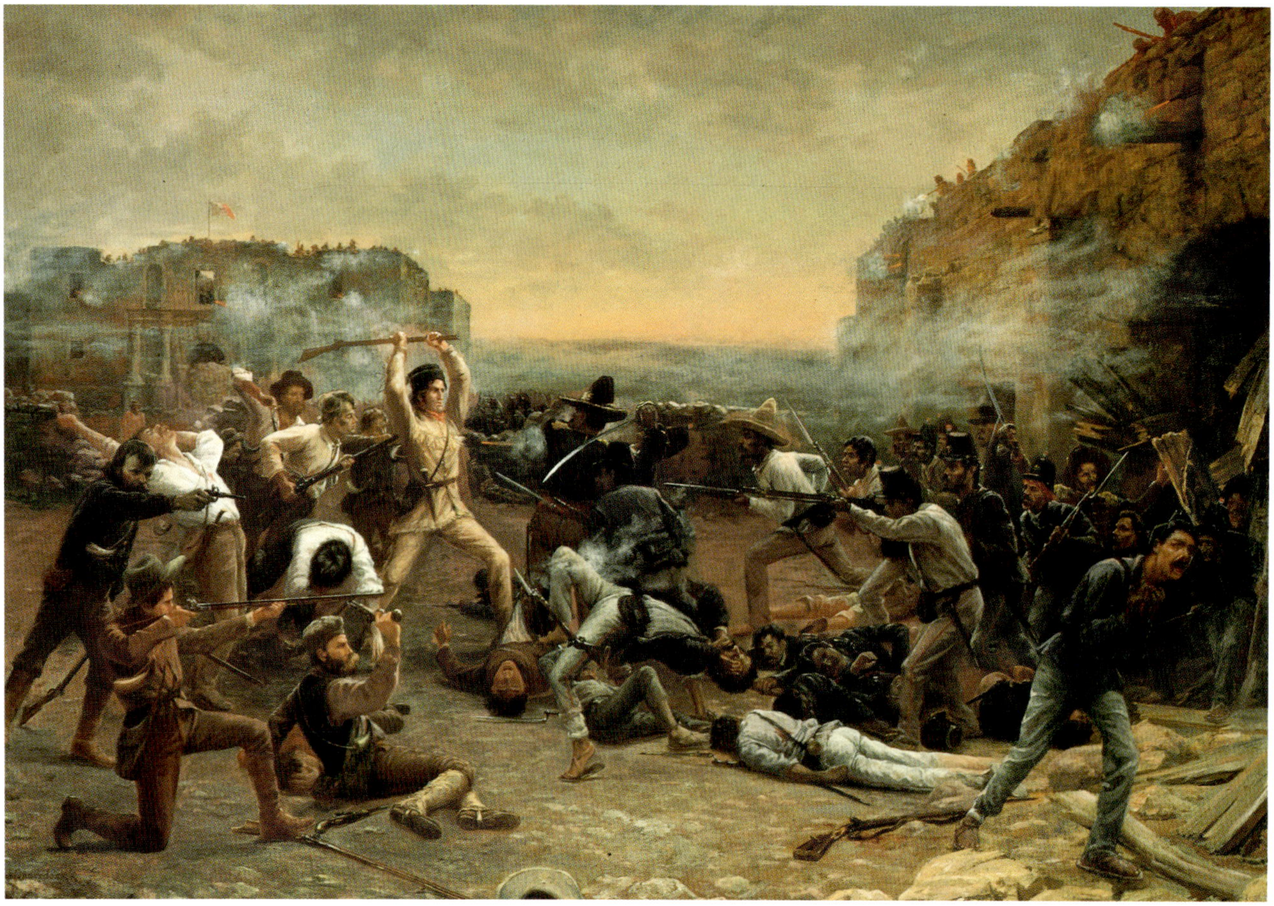

PLATE 9. Robert Jenkins Onderdonk, *The Fall of the Alamo* or
Crockett's Last Stand, 1903. Oil. Friends of the Governor's
Mansion, Austin, Texas.

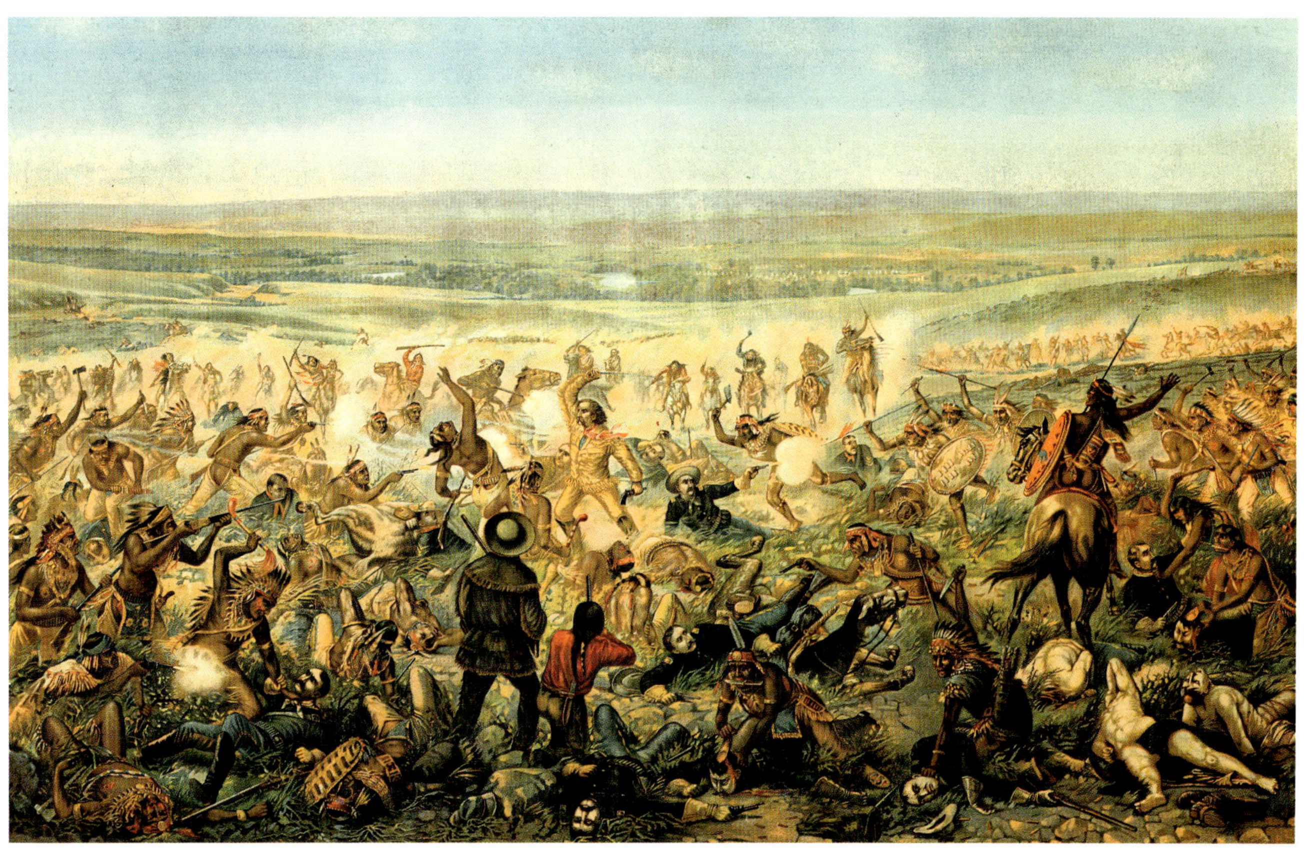

PLATE 10. Drawn on stone by Otto Becker, *Custer's Last Fight,* 1896.
Chromolithograph, after Cassilly Adams, *Custer's Last Fight,* 1895.
Amon Carter Museum, Fort Worth, Texas. Acc. no. 1964.194.

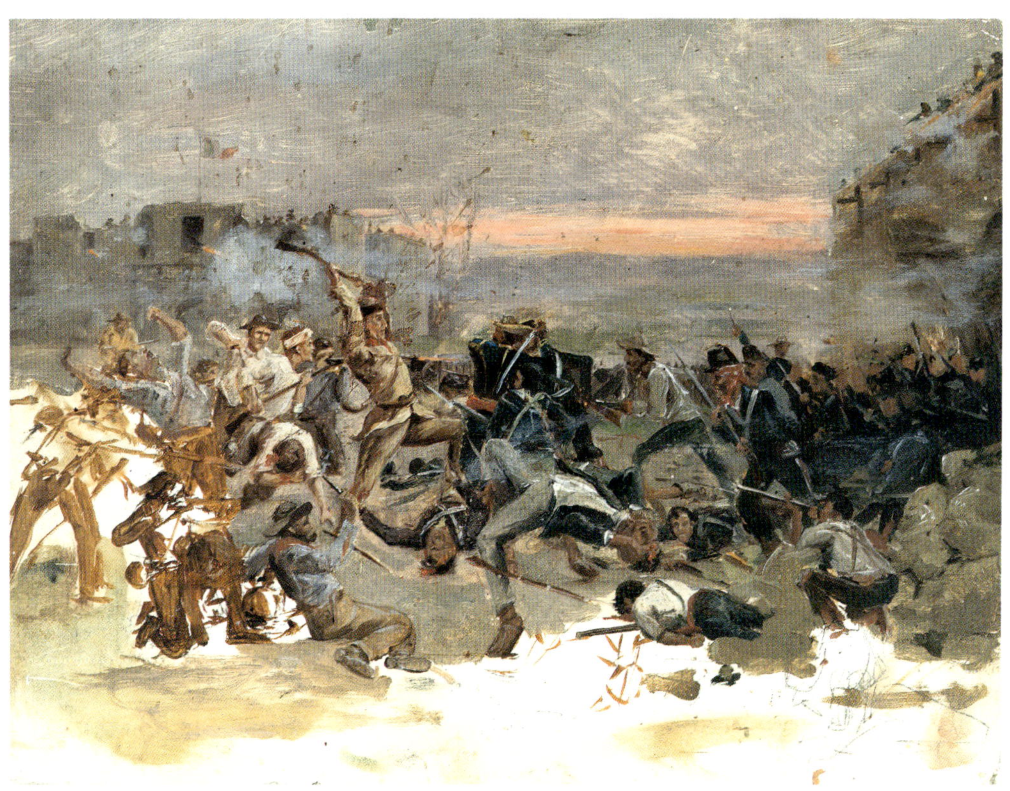

PLATE 11. Robert Jenkins Onderdonk, *Death of Crockett,*
sketch for *The Fall of the Alamo,* 1901. Oil, pencil on paper board.
Dallas Museum of Art, gift of Eleanor Onderdonk. Photograph
by Tom Jenkins. Acc. no. 1960.185.

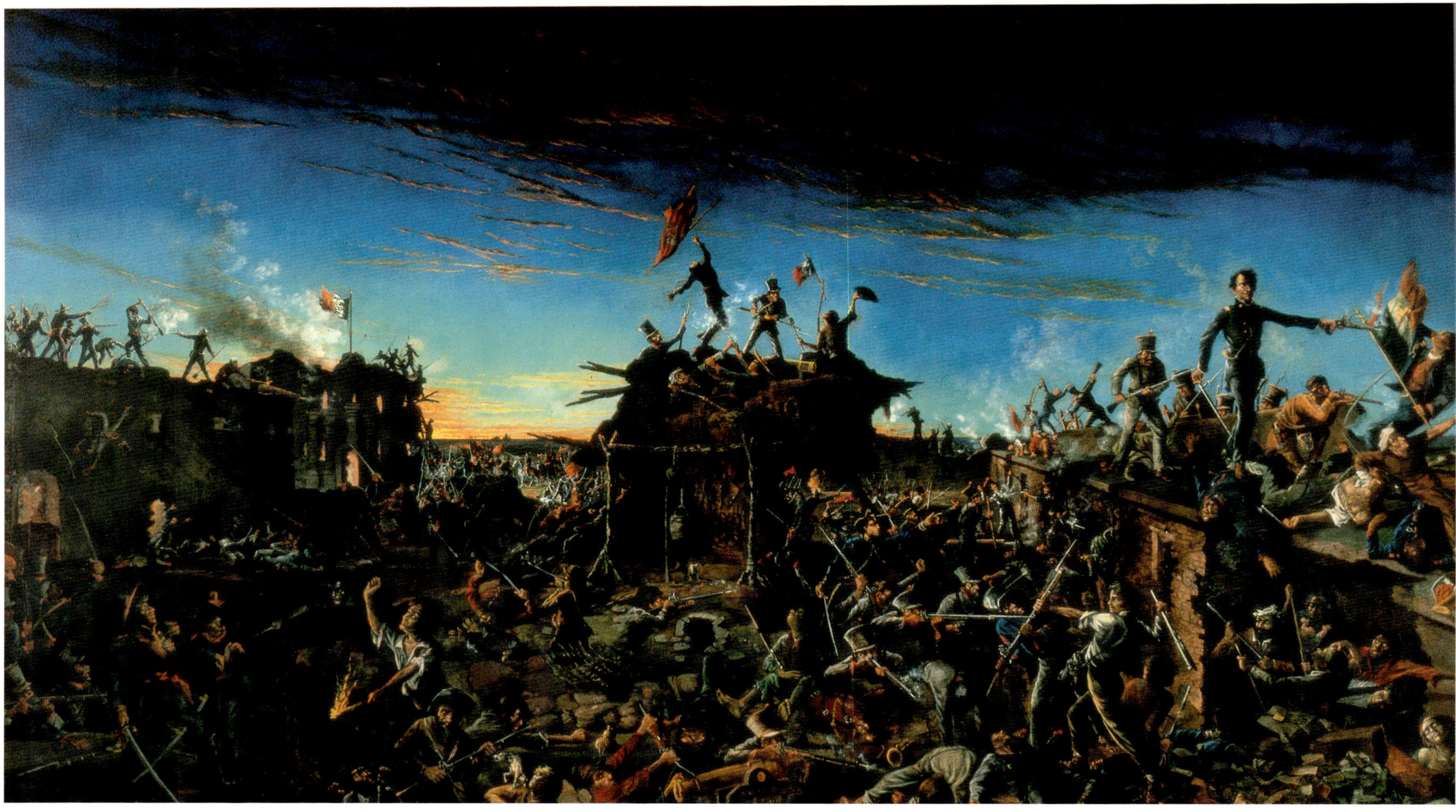

PLATE 12. Henry Arthur McArdle, *Dawn at the Alamo,* 1905. Oil. Archives Division-Texas State Library. Photograph by Eric Beggs. Acc. no. 1990/39-2.

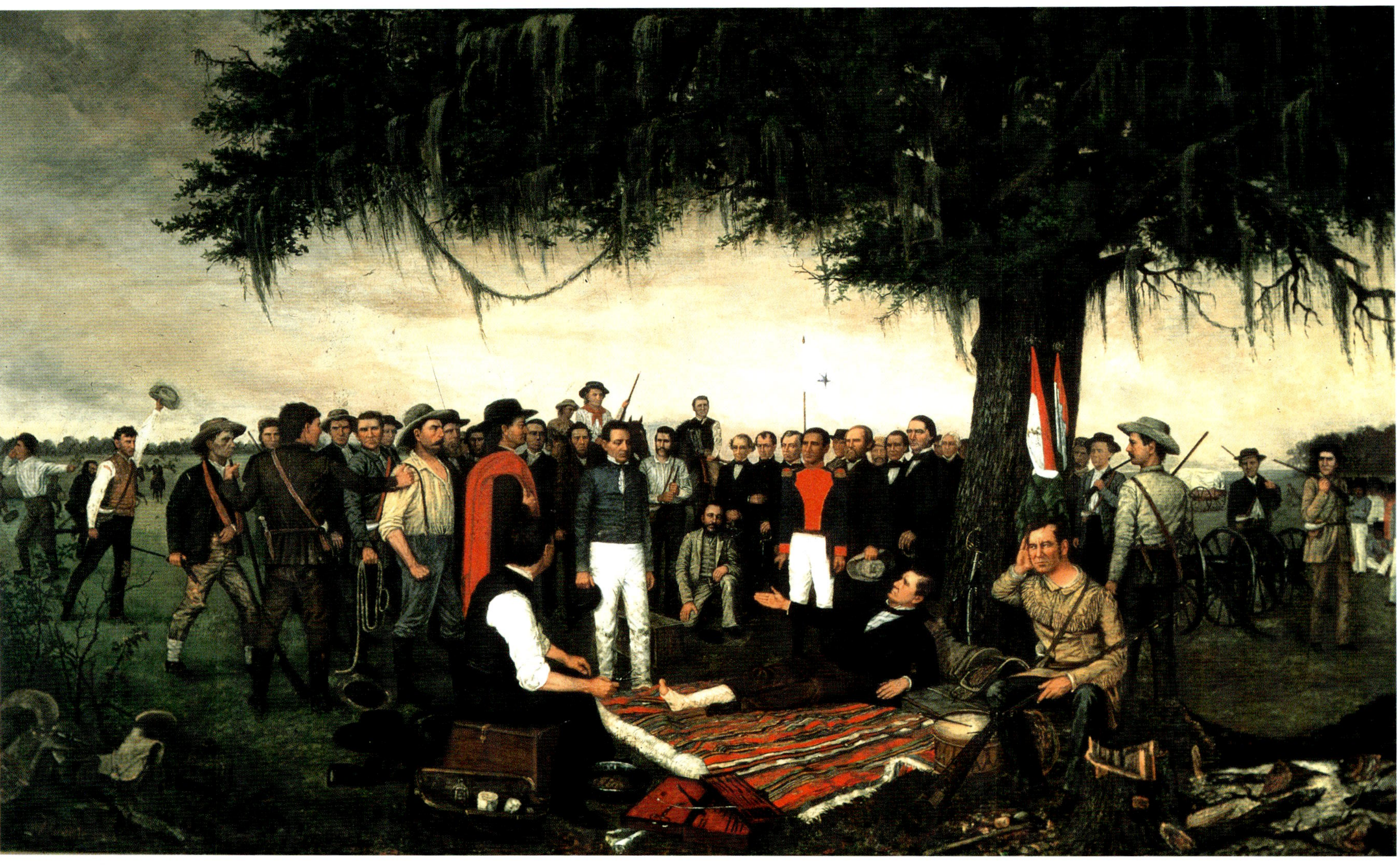

PLATE 13. William Henry Huddle, *The Surrender of Santa Anna*, 1886. Oil. Archives Division-Texas State Library. Photograph by Eric Beggs. Acc. no. 1990/18-1.

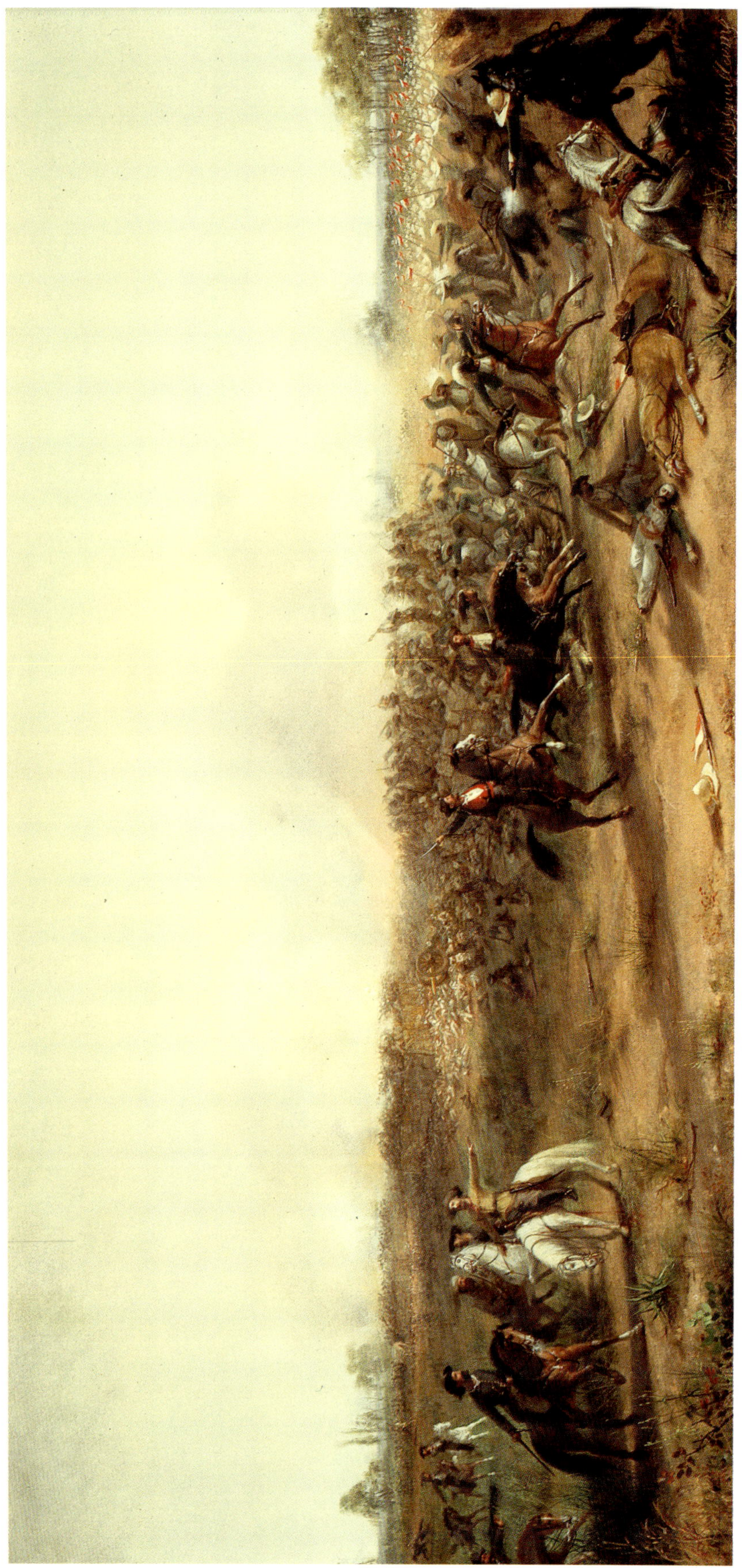

PLATE 14. L. M. D. Guillaume, *The Battle of San Jacinto*, 1892. Oil. Courtesy of The R. W. Norton Art Gallery, Shreveport, Louisiana.

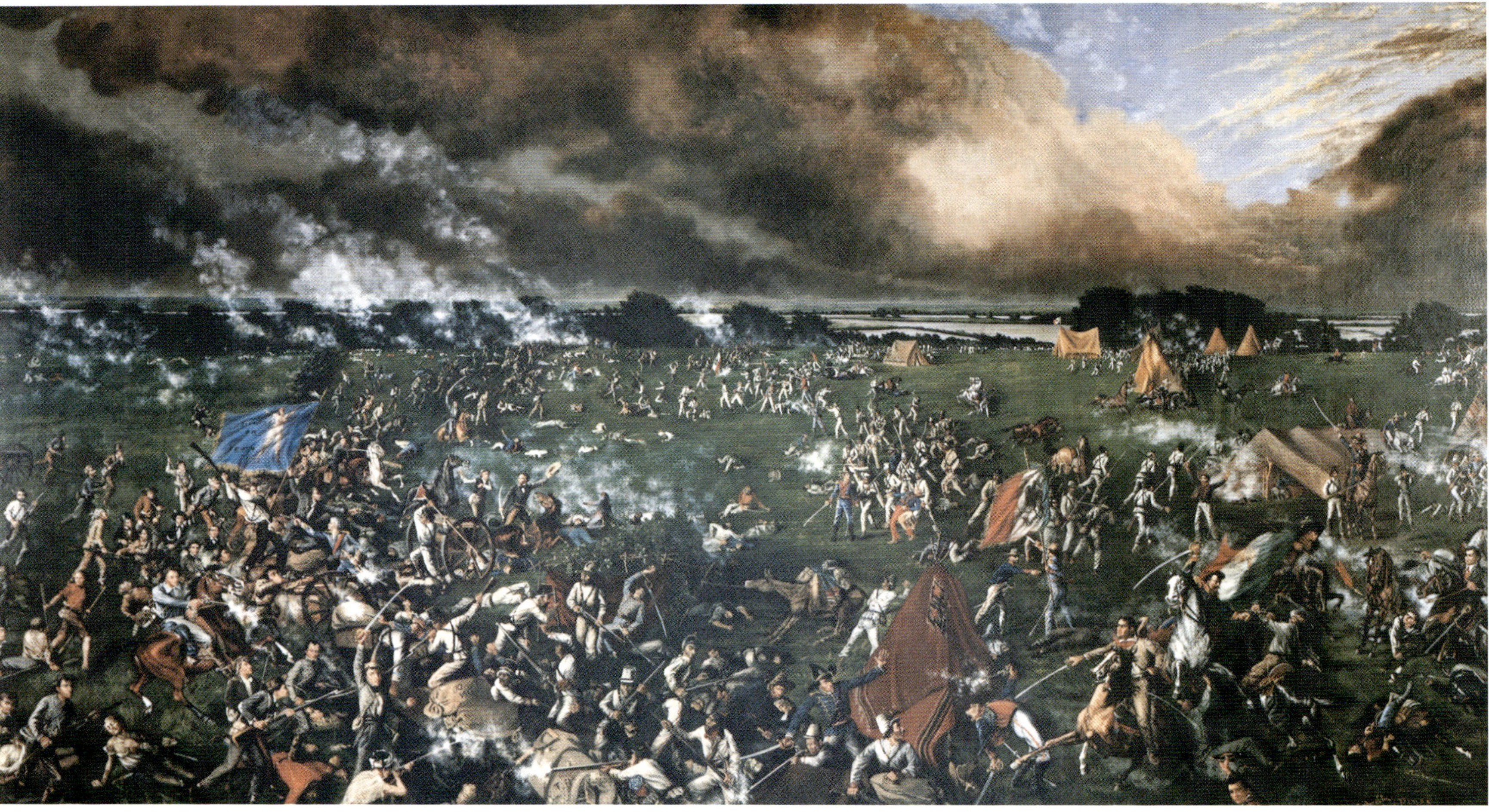

PLATE 15. Henry Arthur McArdle, *The Battle of San Jacinto,* 1895. Oil. Archives Division-Texas State Library. Photograph by Eric Beggs. Acc. no. 1990/39-1.

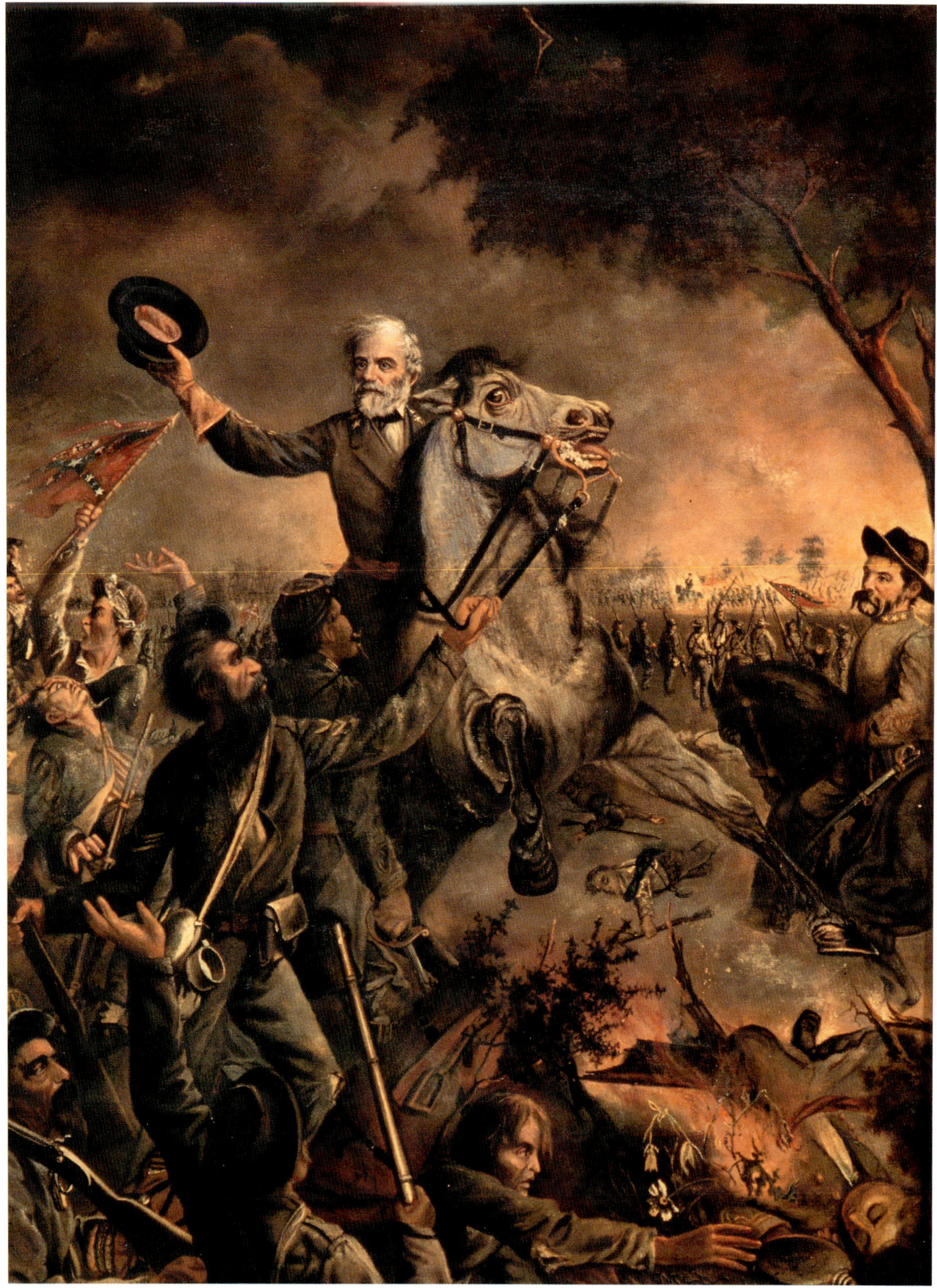

PLATE 16. Henry Arthur McArdle, *Lee at the Wilderness*, 1885.
Oil. Private collection.

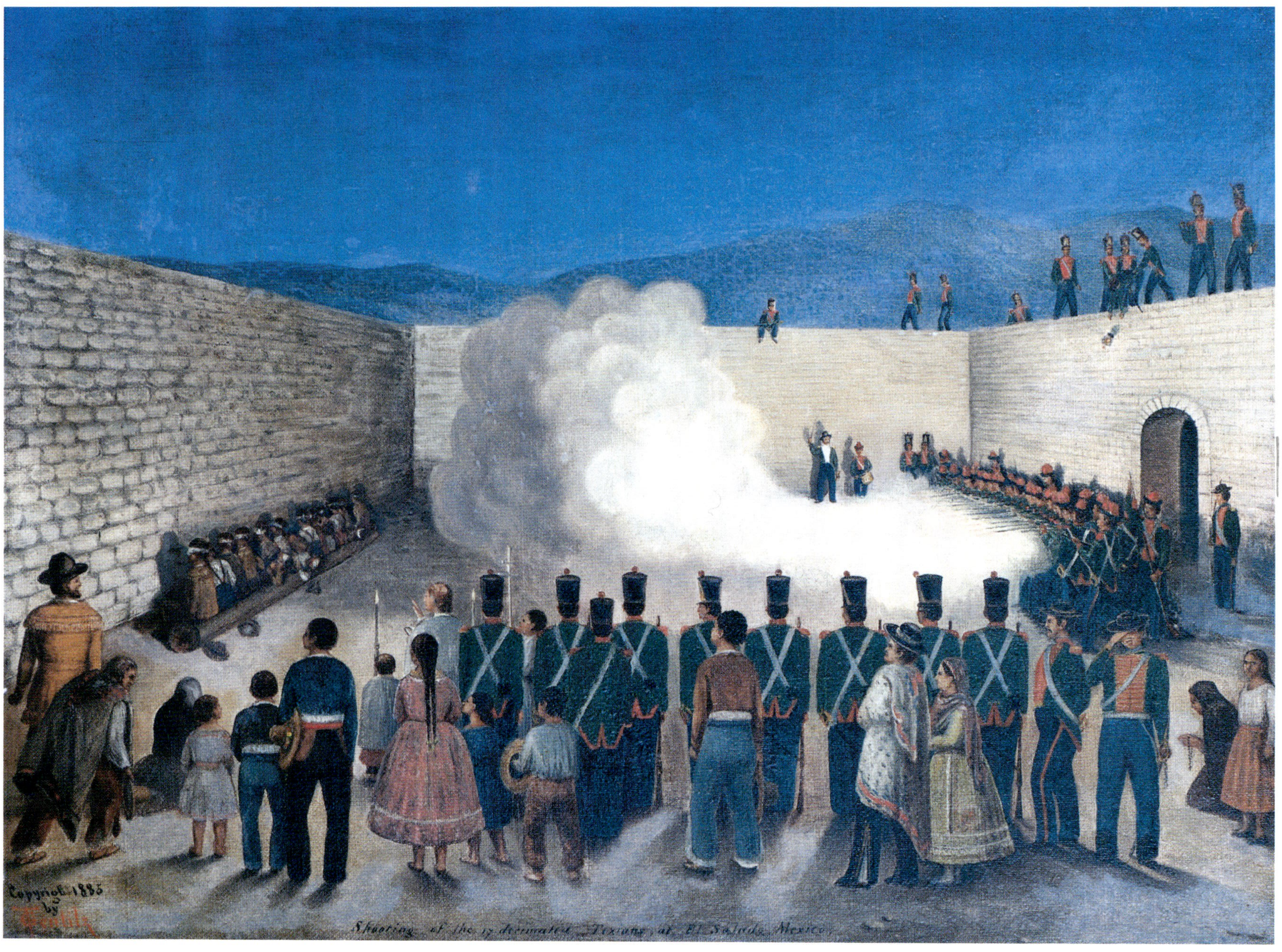

PLATE 17. Theodore Gentilz, *Shooting of the 17 Decimated Texians at El Salado, Mexico,* 1885. Oil. Collection of Mr. and Mrs. Larry Sheerin, San Antonio, Texas.

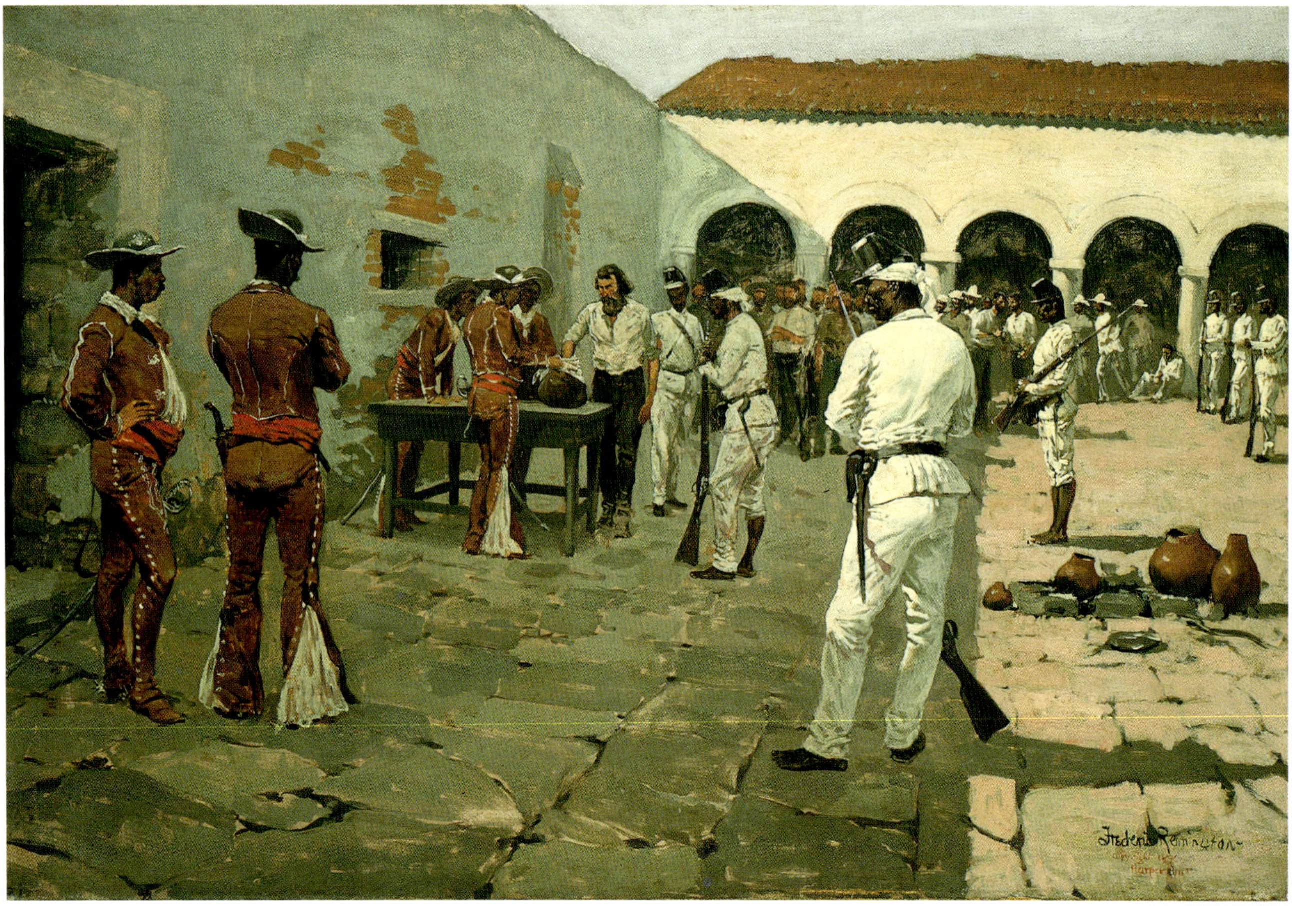

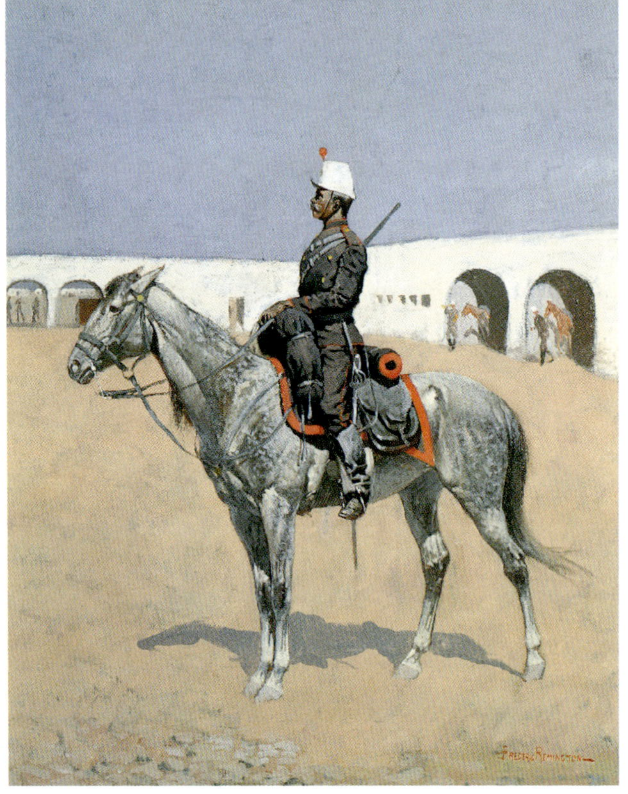

PLATE 18. Frederic Remington, *The Mier Expedition: Drawing of the Black Bean,* 1896. Oil on canvas. The Museum of Fine Arts, Houston, Texas. The Hogg Brothers Collection, gift of Miss Ima Hogg. Acc. no. 43.14.

PLATE 19. Frederic Remington, *Cavalryman of the Line, Mexico,* 1889. Oil on canvas. Amon Carter Museum, Fort Worth, Texas. Acc. no. 1961.238.

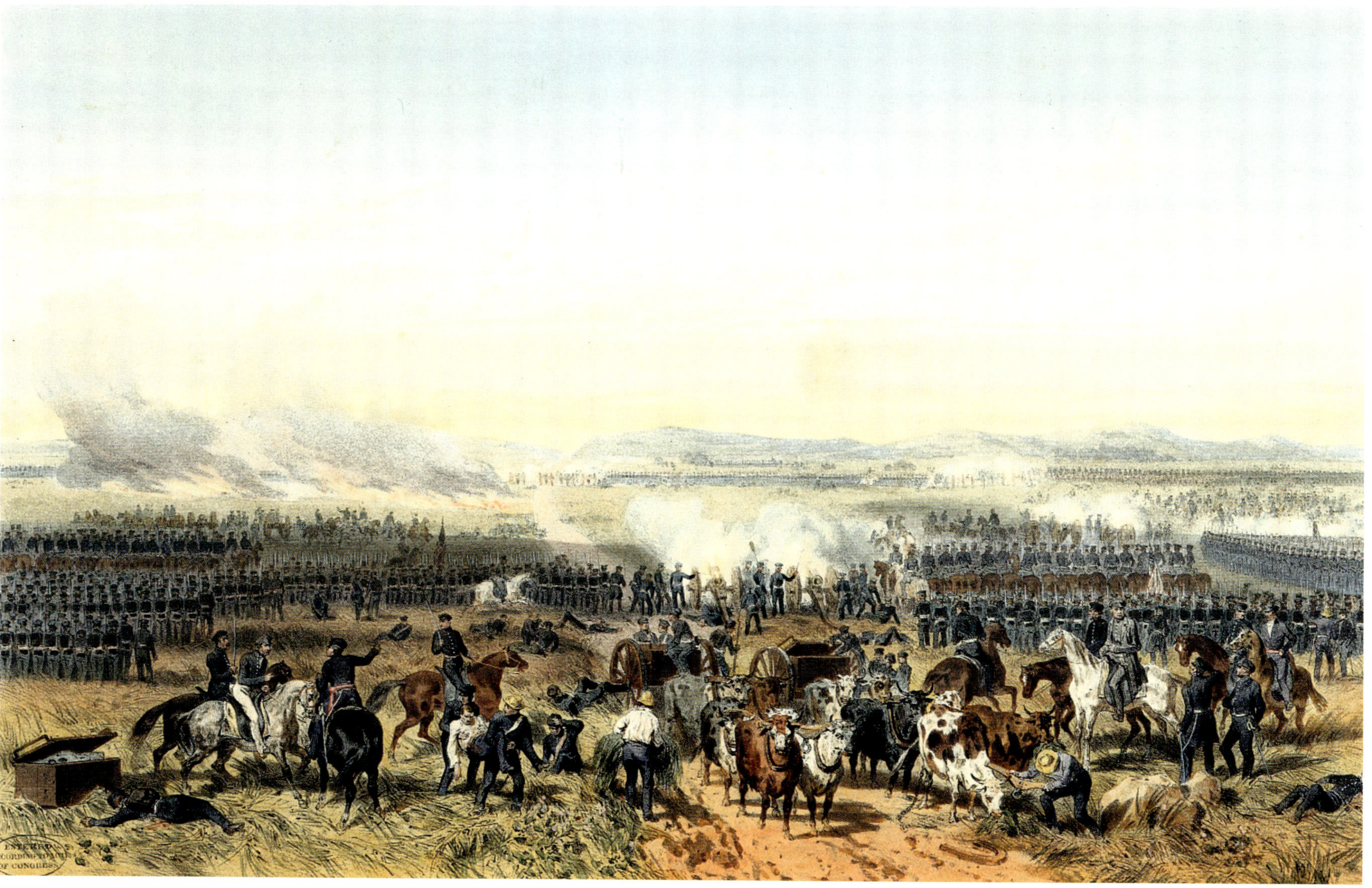

PLATE 20. Carl Nebel, *Battle of Palo Alto*, 1851. Toned lithograph (hand-colored). Amon Carter Museum, Fort Worth, Texas. Acc. no. 1972.186.1.

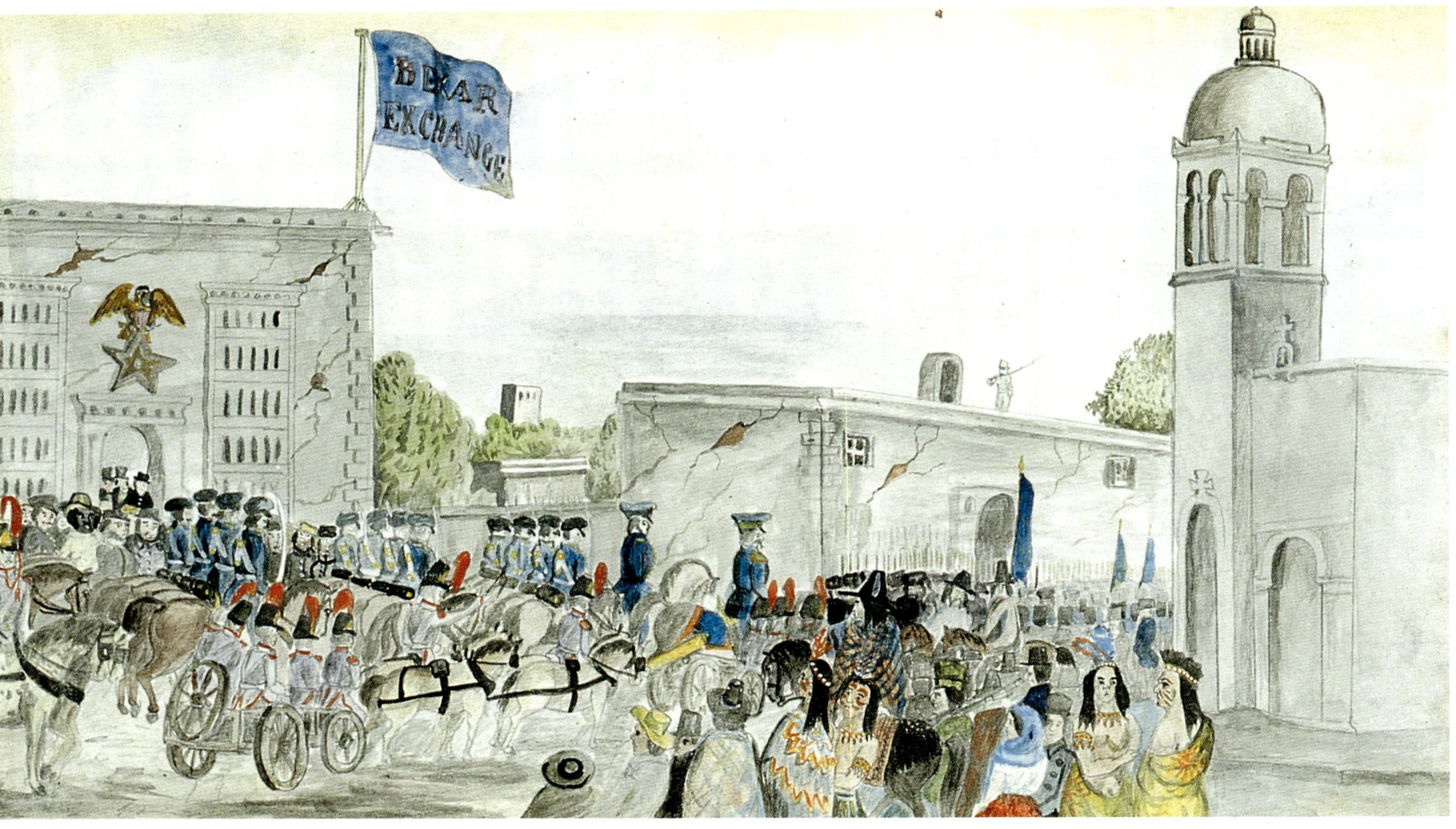

PLATE 21. Samuel Chamberlain, *Main Plaza, San Antonio,* n.d. Watercolor. The San Jacinto Museum of History, La Porte, Texas.

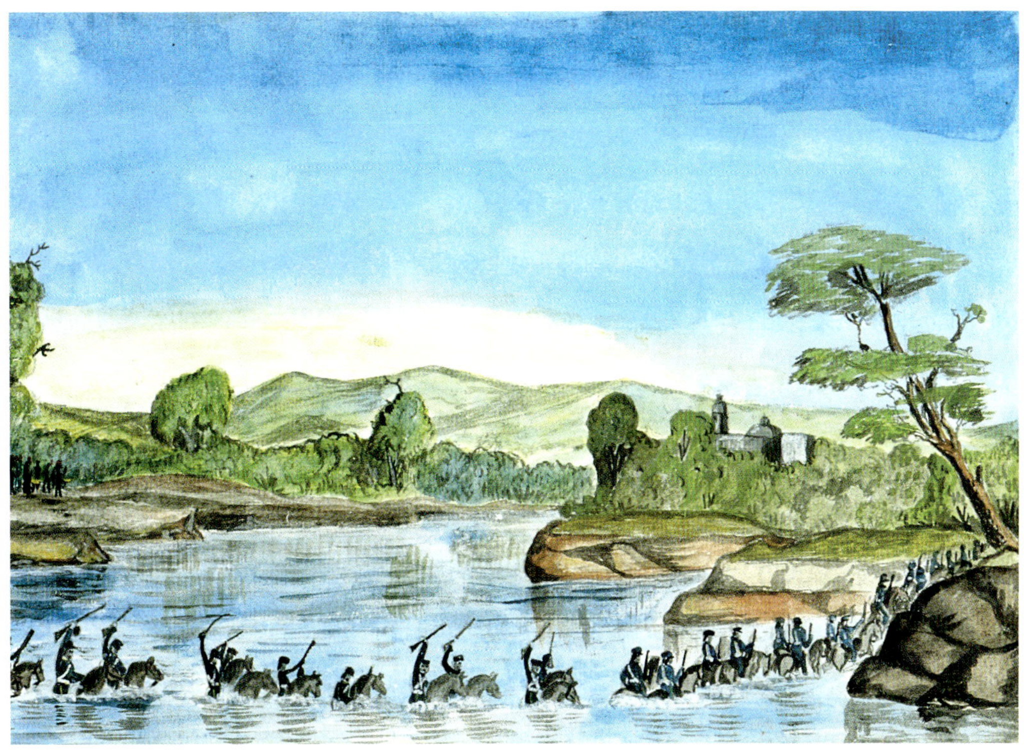

PLATE 22. Samuel Chamberlain, *Gen. Wool's Army Goes into Mexico*, n.d. Watercolor. The San Jacinto Museum of History, La Porte, Texas.

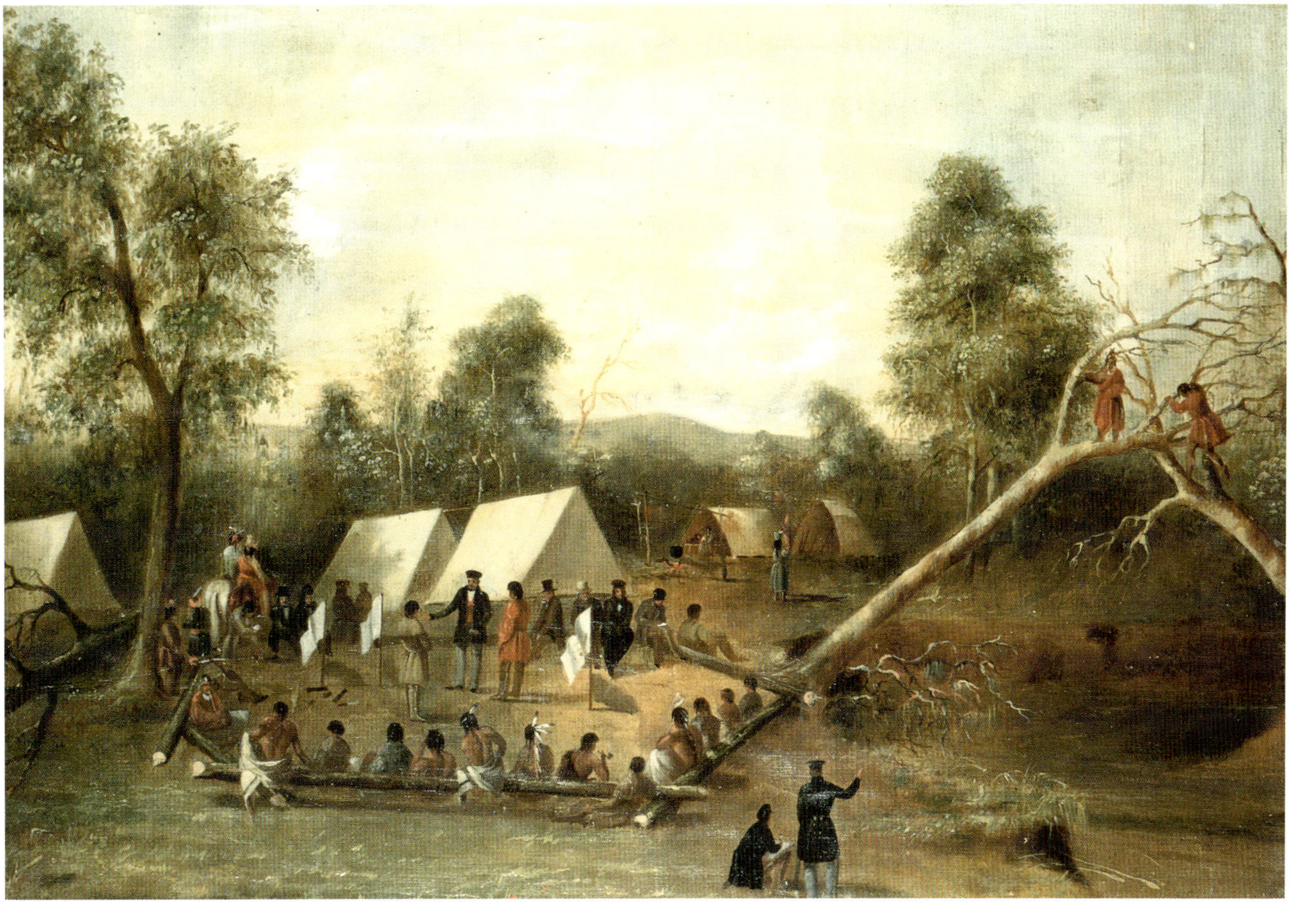

PLATE 23. John Mix Stanley, *Tehuacana Creek Indian Council*, 1843. Oil. Courtesy of Susan and Pierce Butler, Nashville, Tennessee.

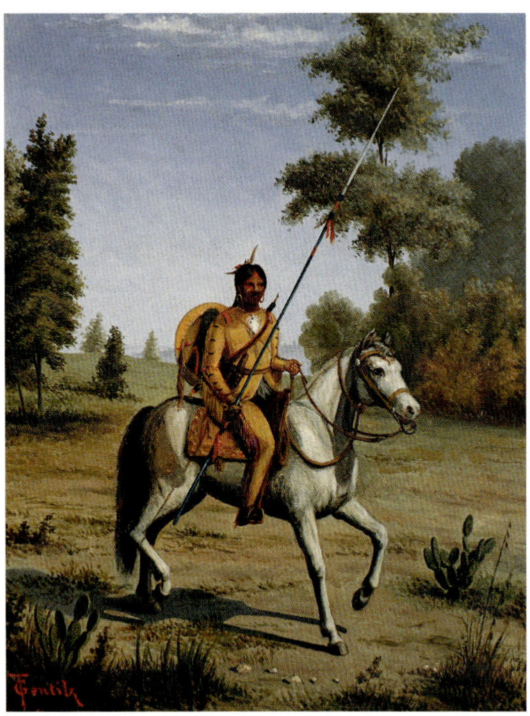

PLATE 24. Theodore Gentilz, *Comanche Chief,* n.d. Oil on canvas. Courtesy of the San Antonio Museum Association, San Antonio, Texas. No. 37-6790-271 P(2).

PLATE 25. Theodore Gentilz, *Comanches on the Warpath,* 1896. Oil on canvas. Courtesy of the San Antonio Museum Association, San Antonio, Texas. No. 37-6790-271 P(3).

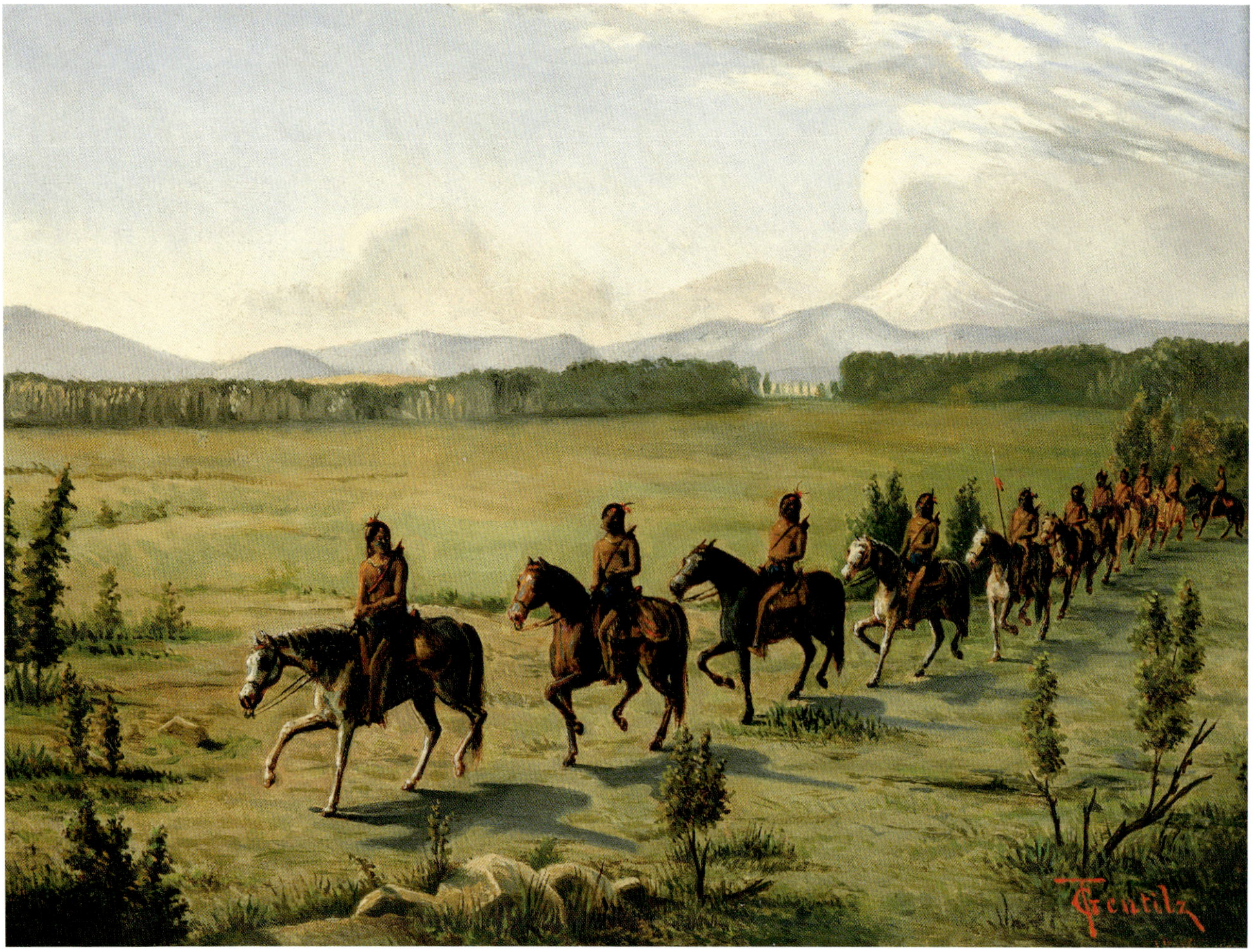

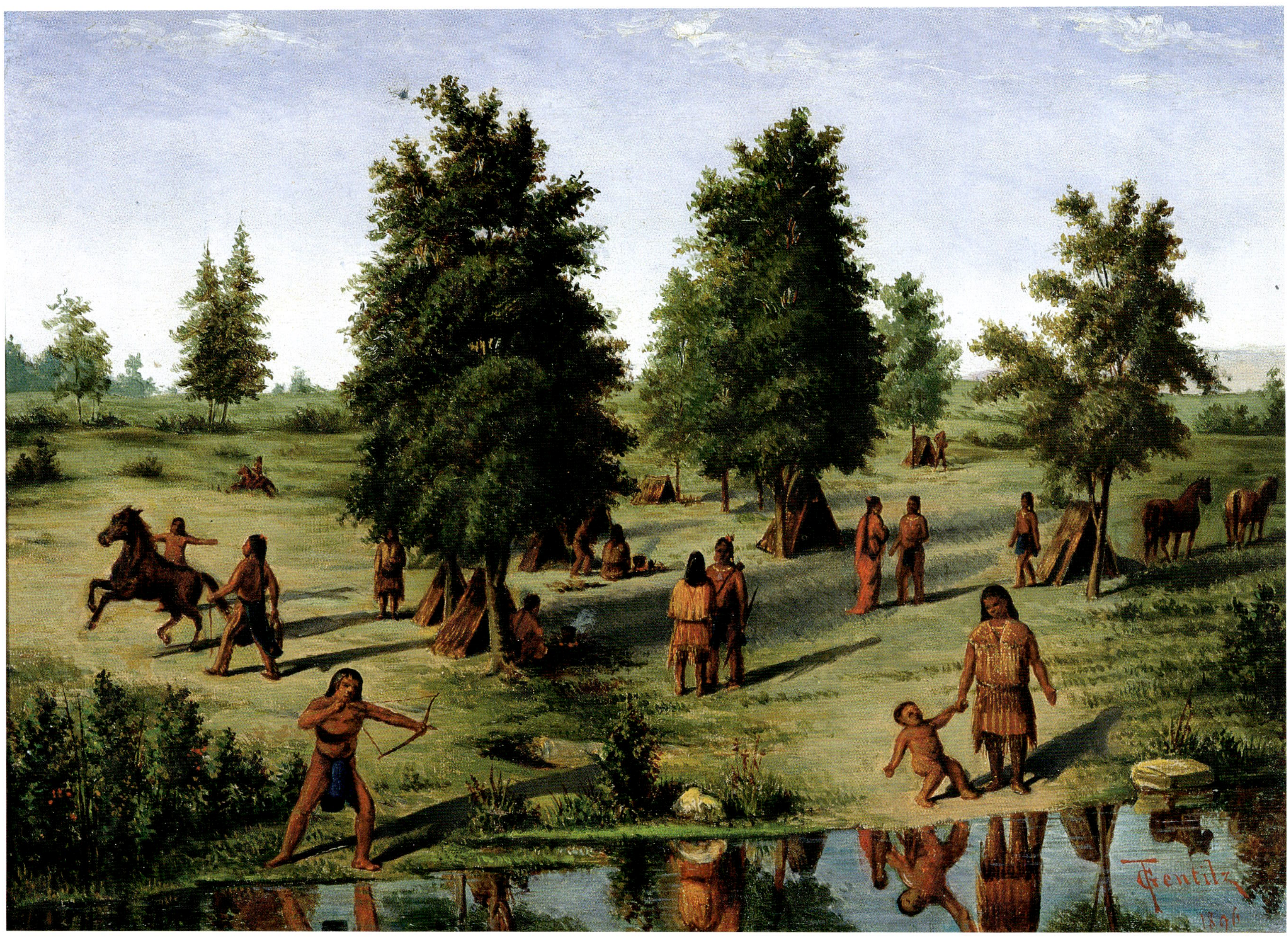

PLATE 26. Theodore Gentilz, *Camp of the Lipans*, 1896. Oil on canvas. Courtesy of the San Antonio Museum Association, San Antonio, Texas. No. 37-6790-271 P(1).

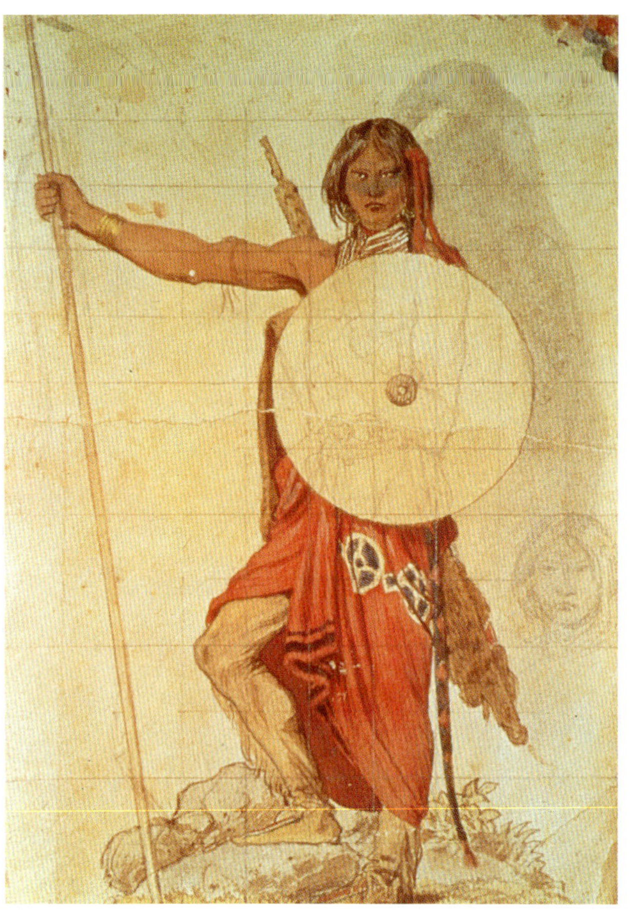

PLATE 27. Friedrich Richard Petri, *Plains Indian with Shield,* n.d. Watercolor. Courtesy of the William Hill Land & Cattle Company; photograph from the Texas Memorial Museum, Austin, Texas.

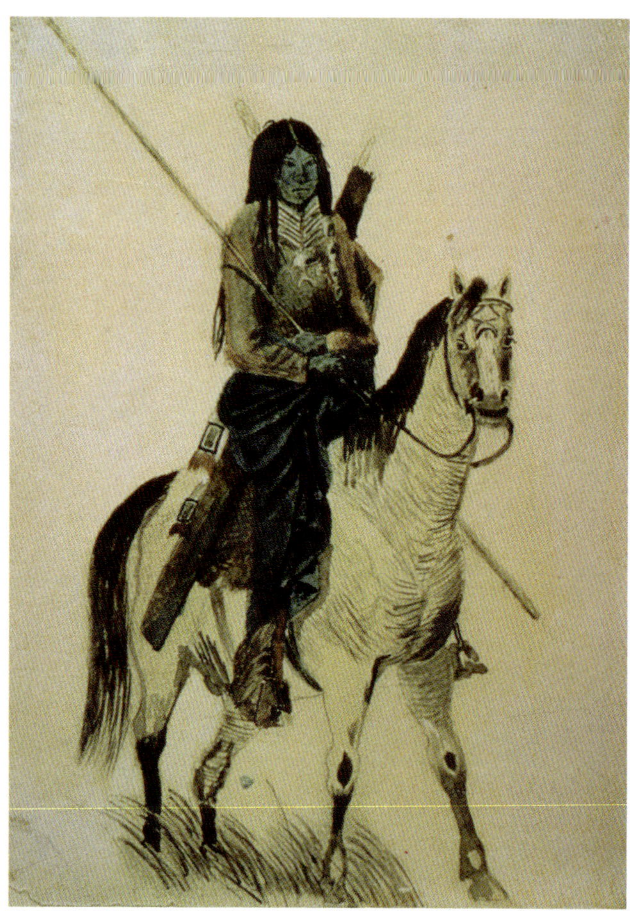

PLATE 28. Friedrich Richard Petri, *Plains Indian Warrior in Blue,* n.d. Watercolor. Courtesy of the Texas Memorial Museum, Austin, Texas. TMM no. 2197-1.

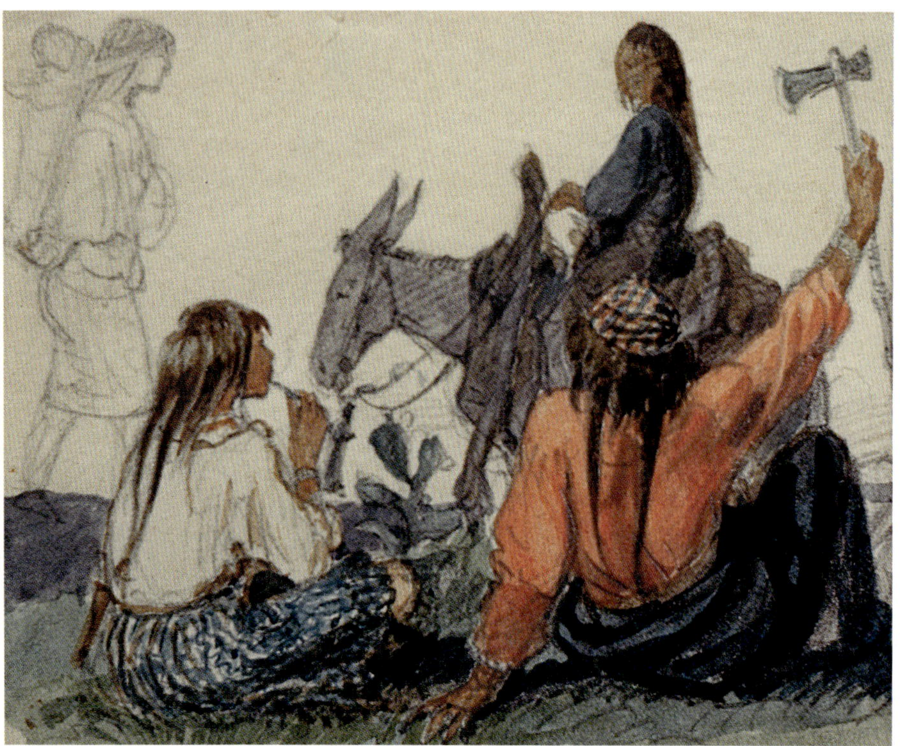

PLATE 29. Friedrich Richard Petri, *Indian Woman on Saddled Mule,* n.d. Watercolor. Courtesy of Dr. and Mrs. H. E. von Rosenberg; photograph from the Texas Memorial Museum, Austin, Texas.

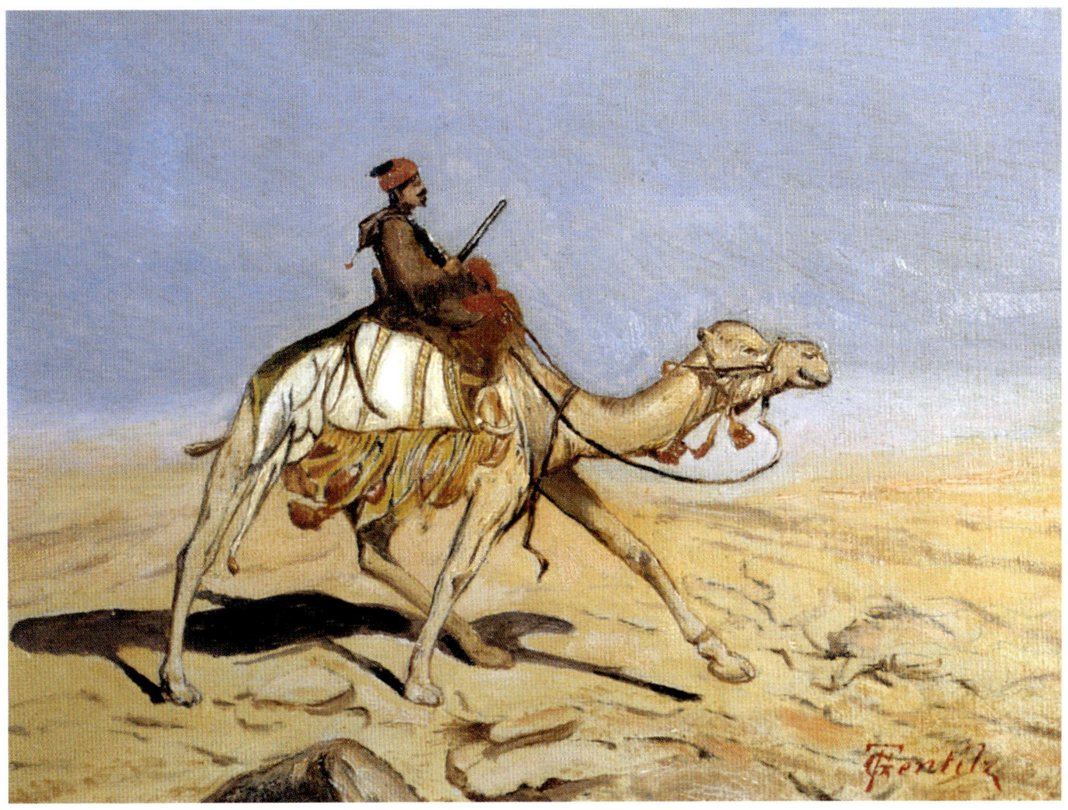

PLATE 30. Theodore Gentilz, *Camel and Rider,* 1856–1857. Oil.
Collection of Mrs. Monte Tomerlin, San Antonio, Texas.
Photograph by Mark Edward Smith, Austin, Texas.

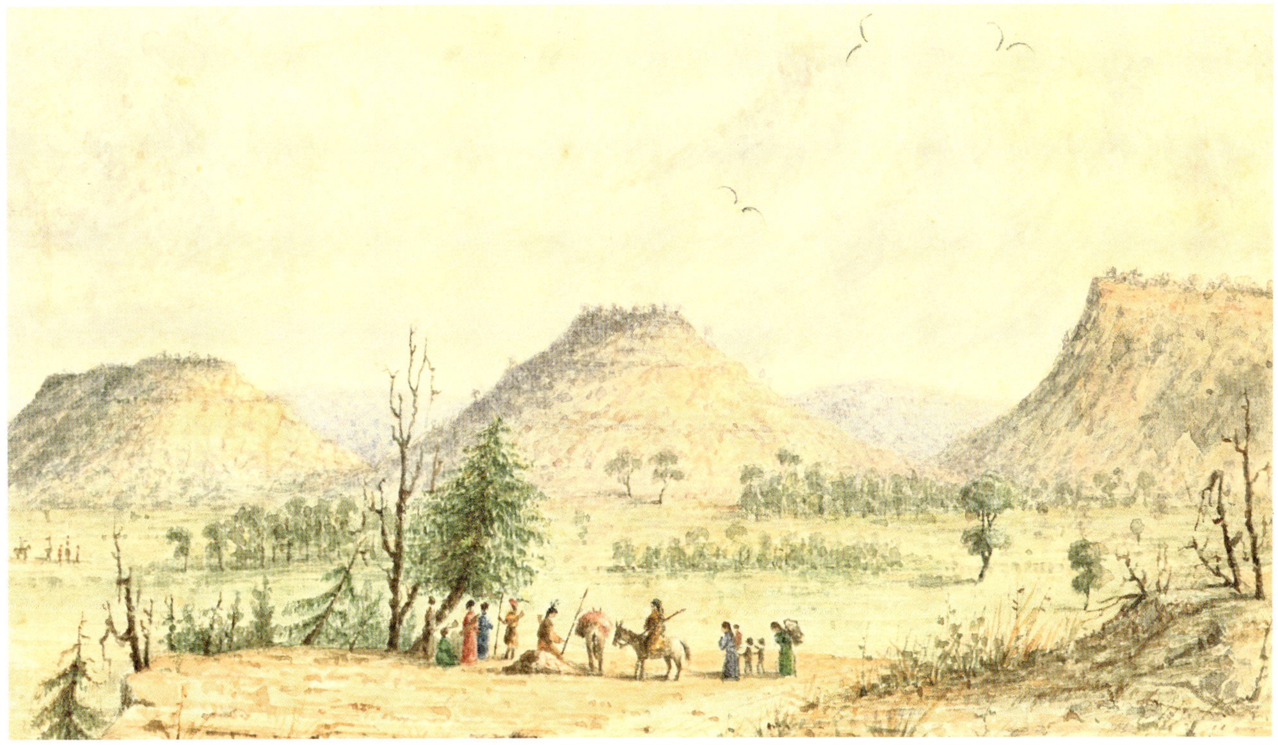

PLATE 31. Arthur Tracy Lee, *View Near Fort Croghan,* ca. 1850.
Watercolor. Department of Rare Books and Special Collections,
University of Rochester Library.

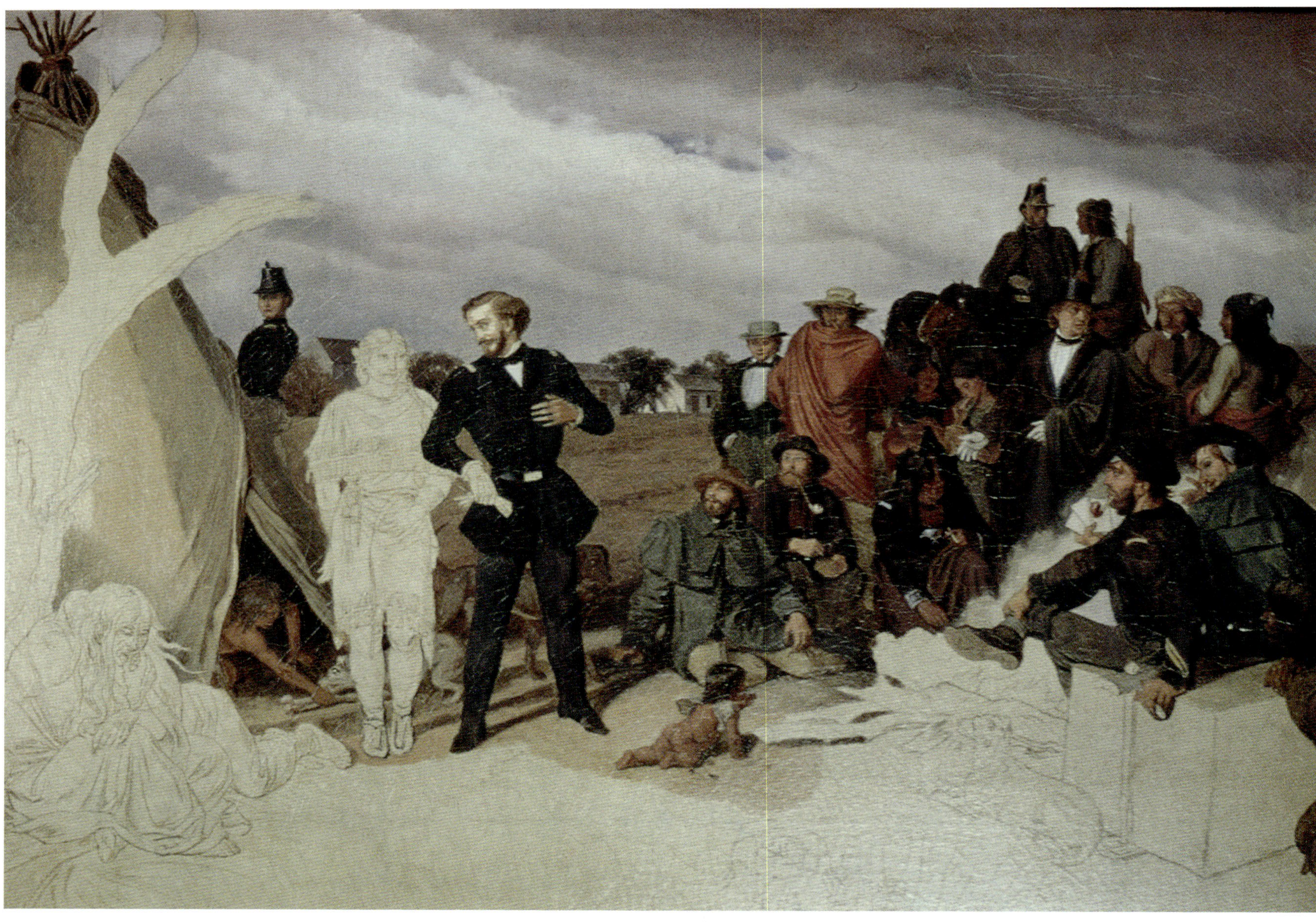

PLATE 32. Friedrich Richard Petri, *Fort Martin Scott*, ca. 1853. Oil on canvas. Courtesy of the Texas Memorial Museum, Austin, Texas. TMM no. 2225.

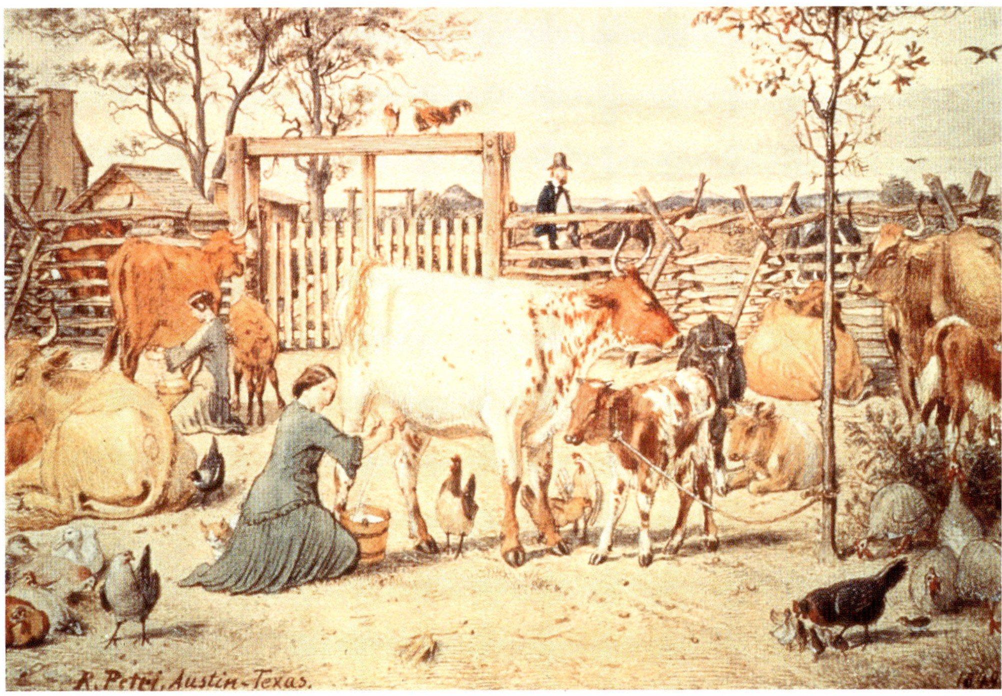

PLATE 33. Friedrich Richard Petri, *The Pioneer Cowpen*, ca. 1853.
Watercolor. Russell Fish III; photograph from the Texas
Memorial Museum, Austin, Texas.

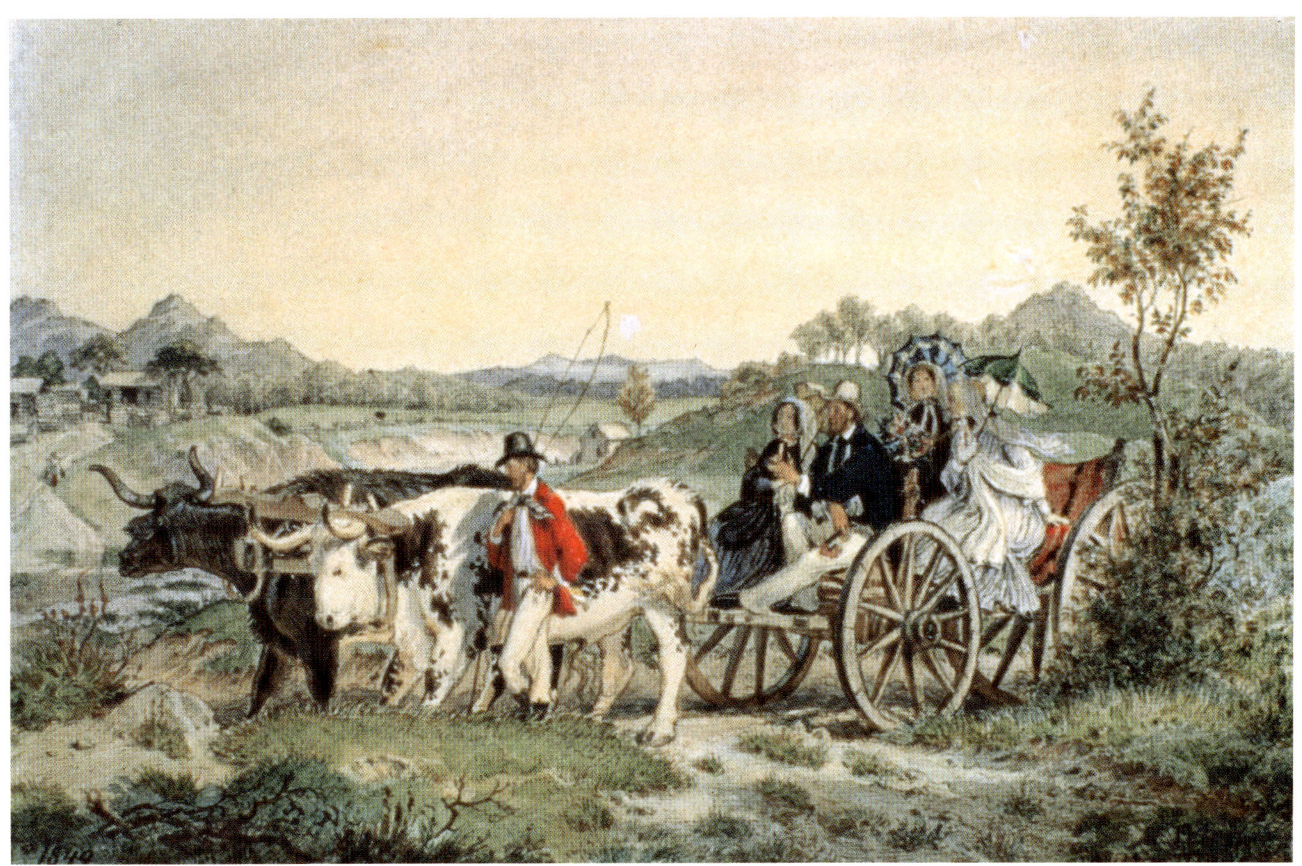

PLATE 34. Friedrich Richard Petri, *Going Visiting*, ca. 1853.
Watercolor. Russell Fish III; photograph from the Texas
Memorial Museum, Austin, Texas.

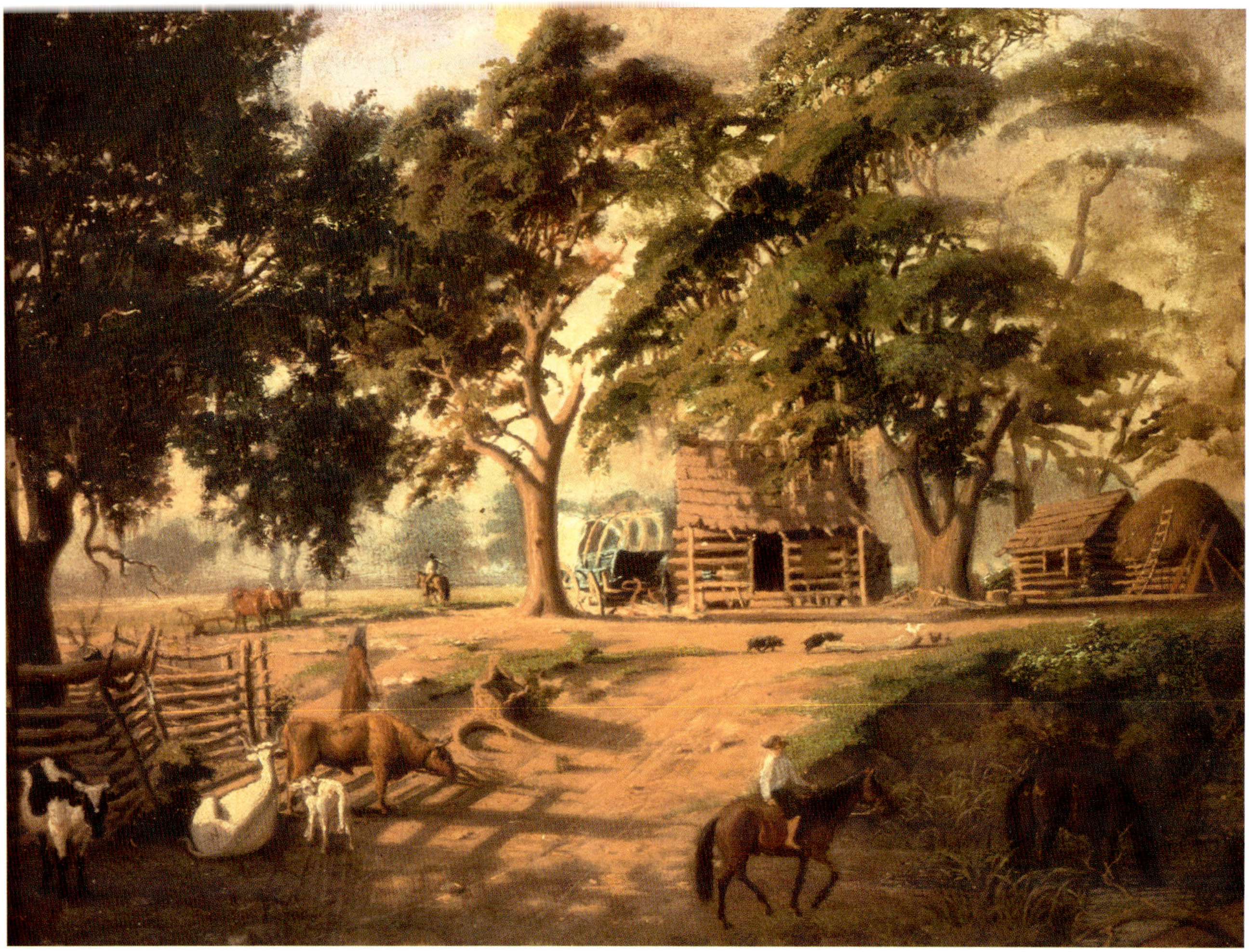

PLATE 35. Carl G. von Iwonski, *Log Cabin, New Braunfels,* ca. 1853. Oil. Daughters of the Republic of Texas Library at the Alamo, San Antonio, Texas.

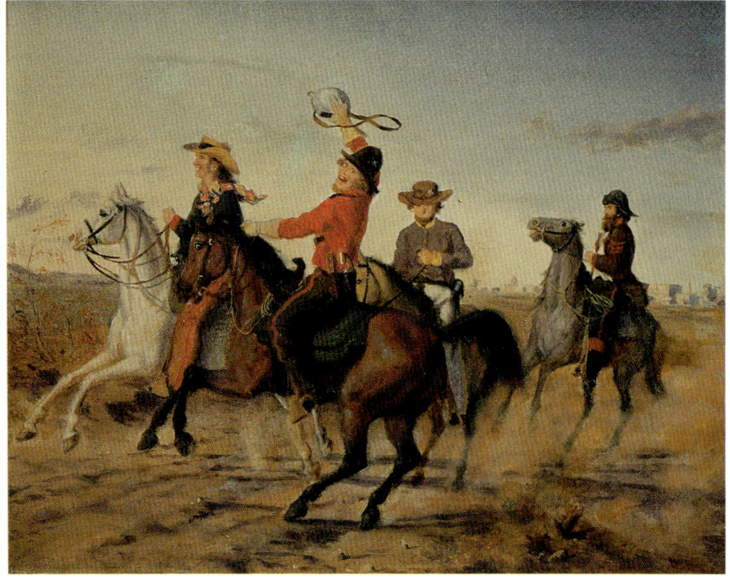

PLATE 36. Carl G. von Iwonski, *The Terry Rangers* or *Sam Maverick and the Terry Rangers,* ca. 1862. Oil on canvas. Courtesy of the San Antonio Museum Association, San Antonio, Texas. No. 31-4801 G.

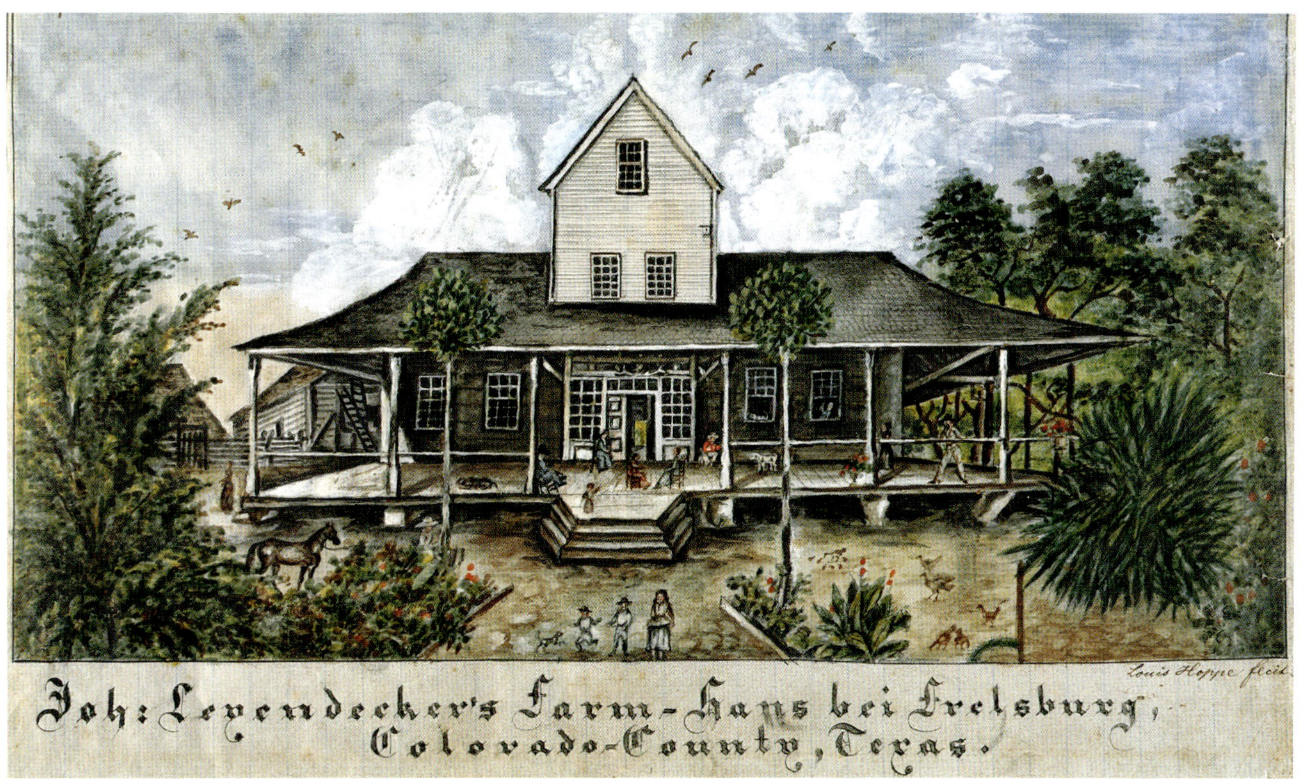

PLATE 37. Louis Hoppe, *Joh[ann] Leyendecker's Farm-Haus bei Frelsburg, Colorado County, Texas,* ca. 1863. Opaque watercolor on lined note paper. Courtesy of the San Antonio Museum Association, San Antonio, Texas. No. 76-163G(1).

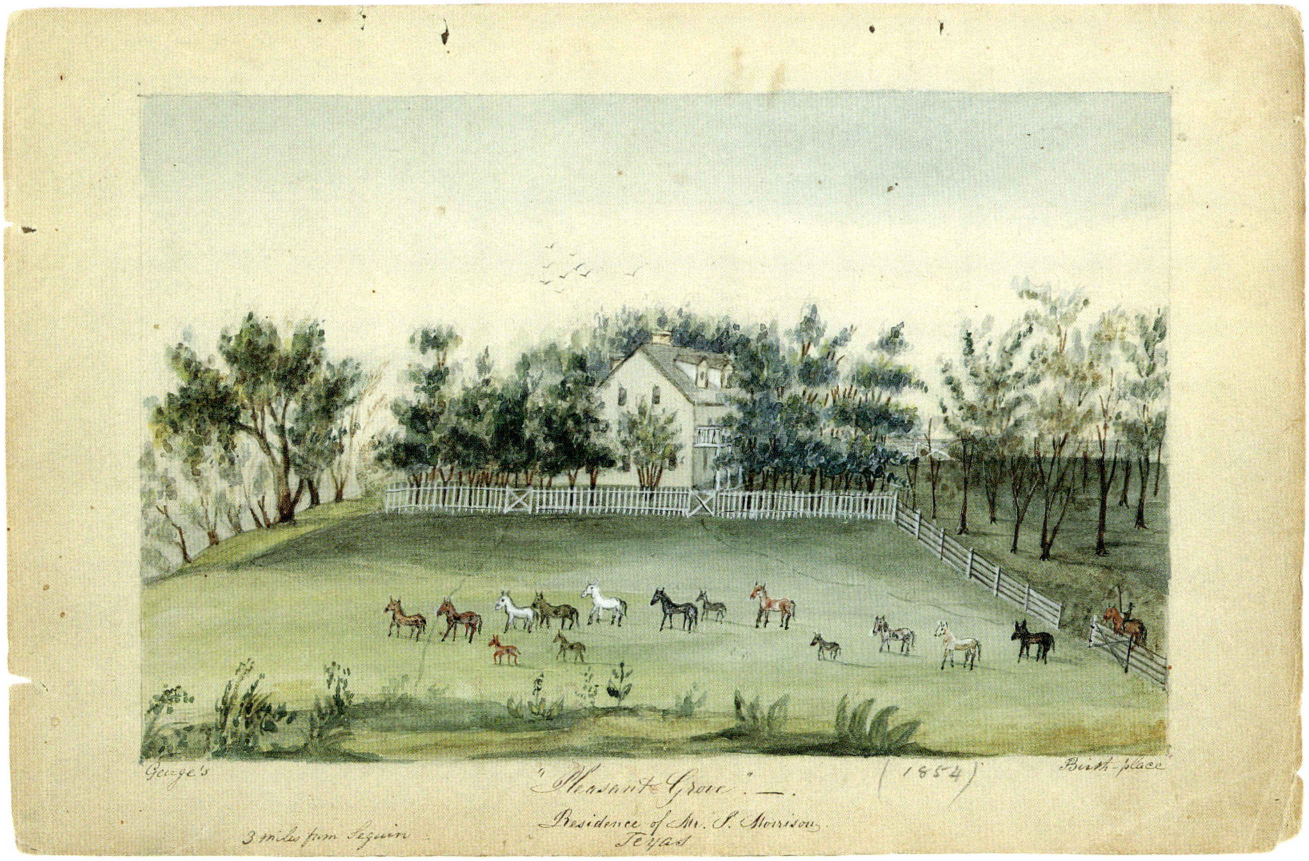

PLATE 38. Sarah Hardinge, *"Pleasant Grove." Residence of Mr. J. Morrison,* 1853–1854. Watercolor, gouache, and graphite on paper. Amon Carter Museum, Fort Worth, Texas. Gift of Mrs. Natalie K. Shastid. Acc. no. 1984.3.9.

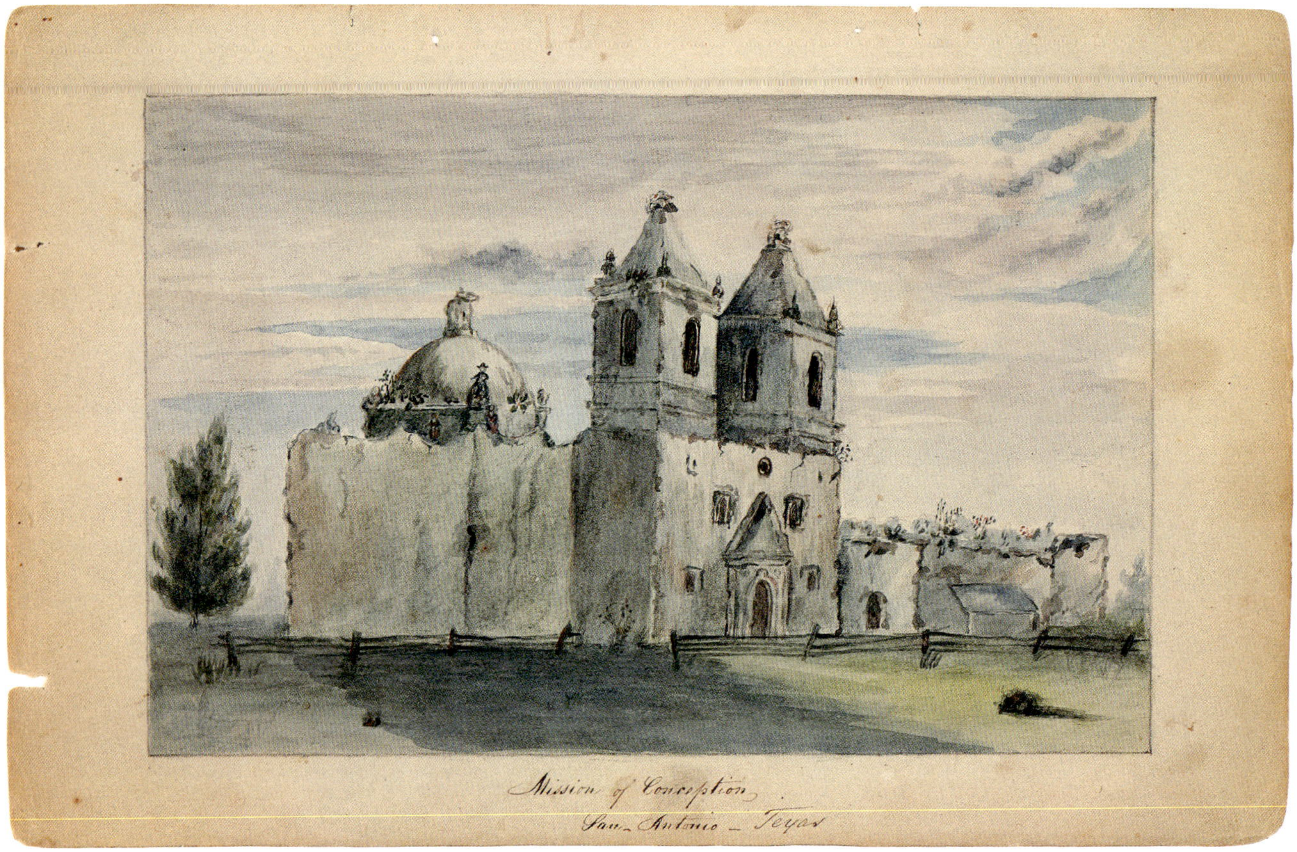

PLATE 39. Sarah Hardinge, *Mission of Conception, San Antonio, Texas,* 1852–1853. Watercolor, gouache, and graphite on paper. Gift of Mrs. Natalie K. Shastid. Amon Carter Museum, Fort Worth, Texas. Acc. no. 1984.3.5.

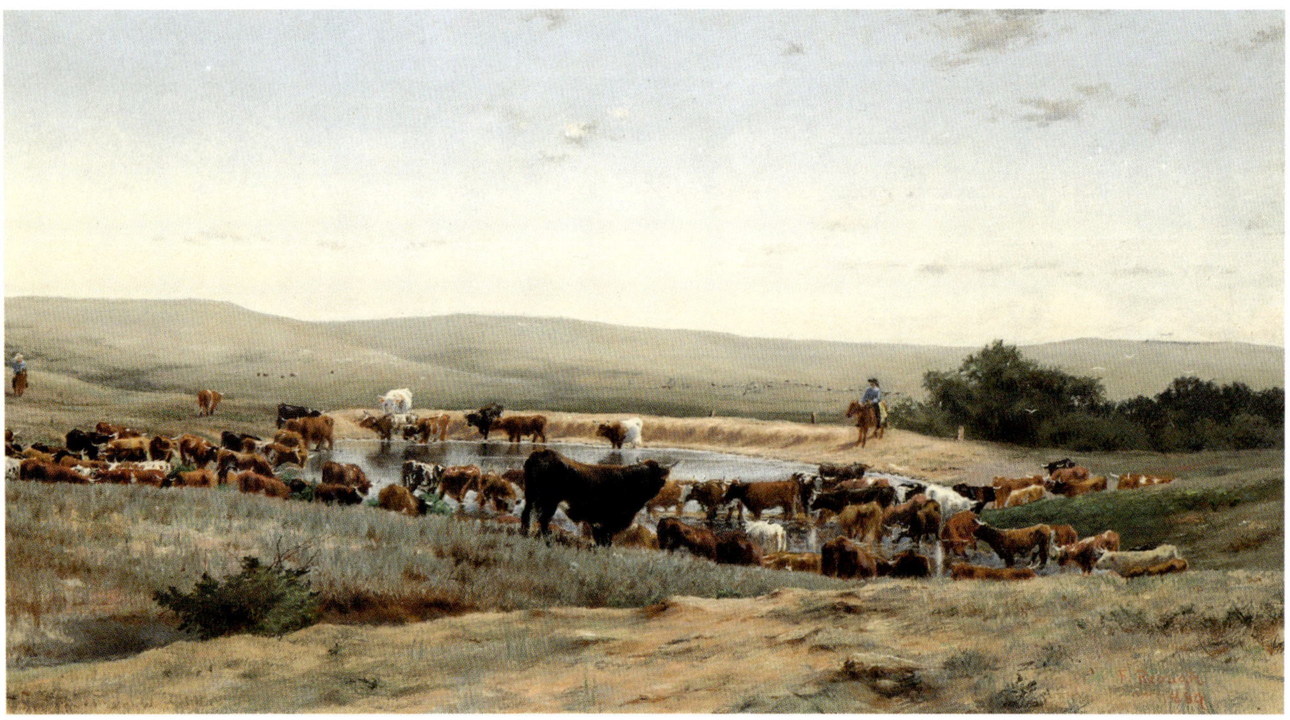

PLATE 40. Frank Reaugh, *Watering the Herd,* 1889. Pastel on paper mounted on canvas. Panhandle-Plains Historical Museum, Canyon, Texas. From the Frank Reaugh Estate. Acc. no. 1865/894.

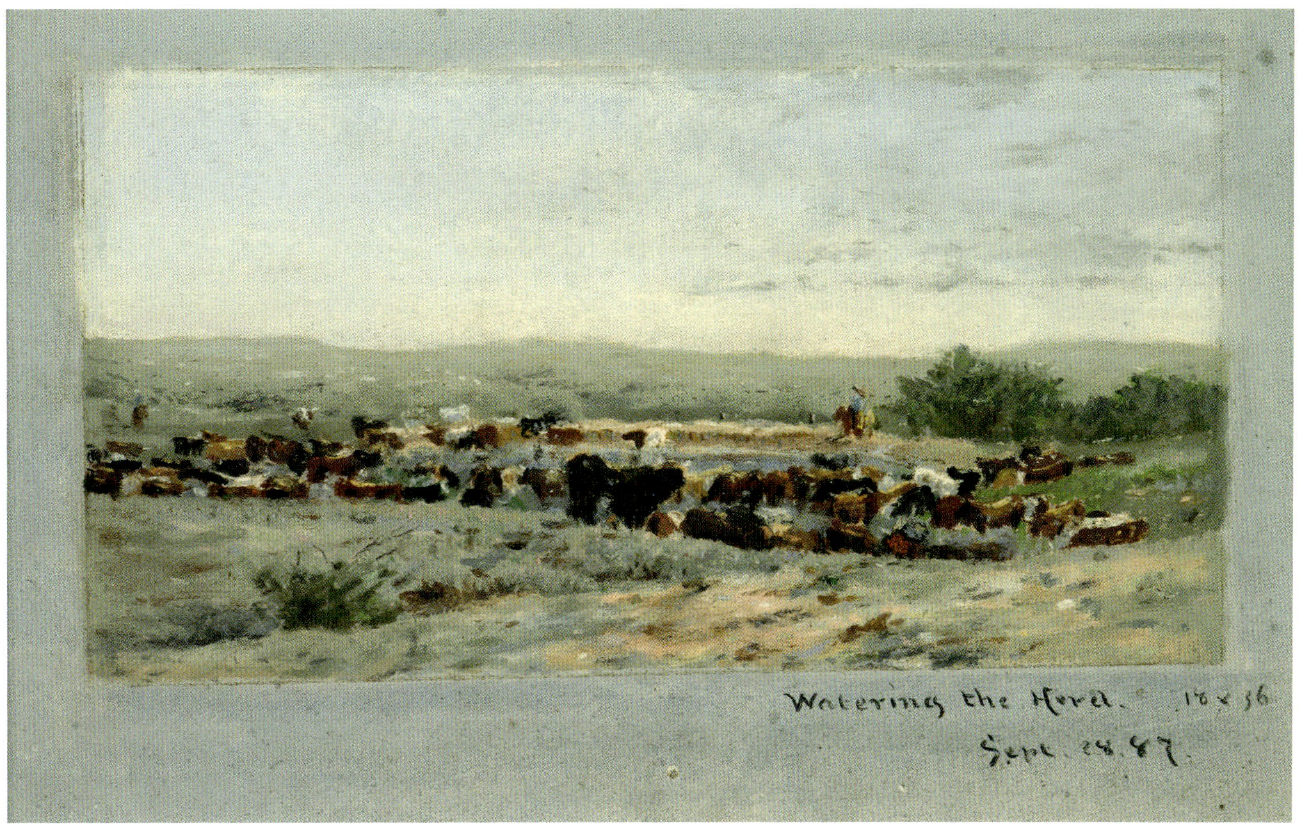

PLATE 41. Frank Reaugh, *Watering the Herd*, 1887. Pastel.
Harry Ransom Humanities Research Center Art Collection,
The University of Texas at Austin. No. 74.69.179.

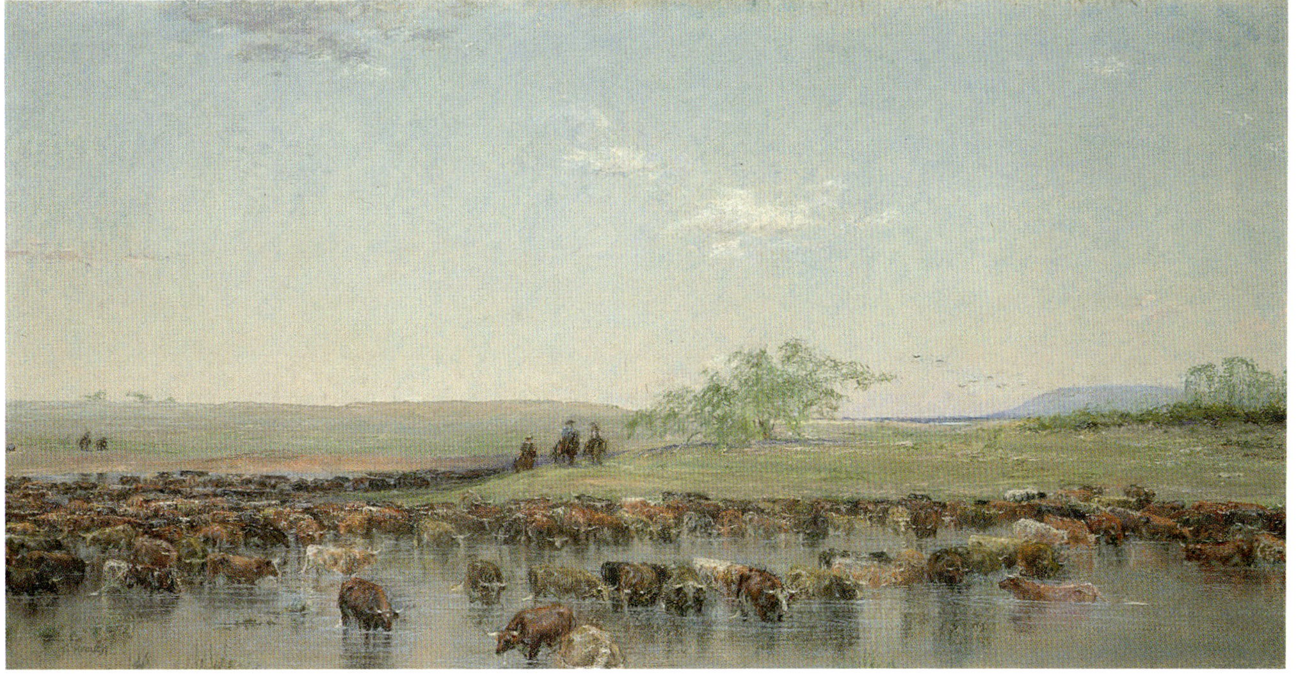

PLATE 42. Frank Reaugh, *Watering the Herd*, 1932. Pastel.
Harry Ransom Humanities Research Center Art Collection,
The University of Texas at Austin. No. 74.69.152.

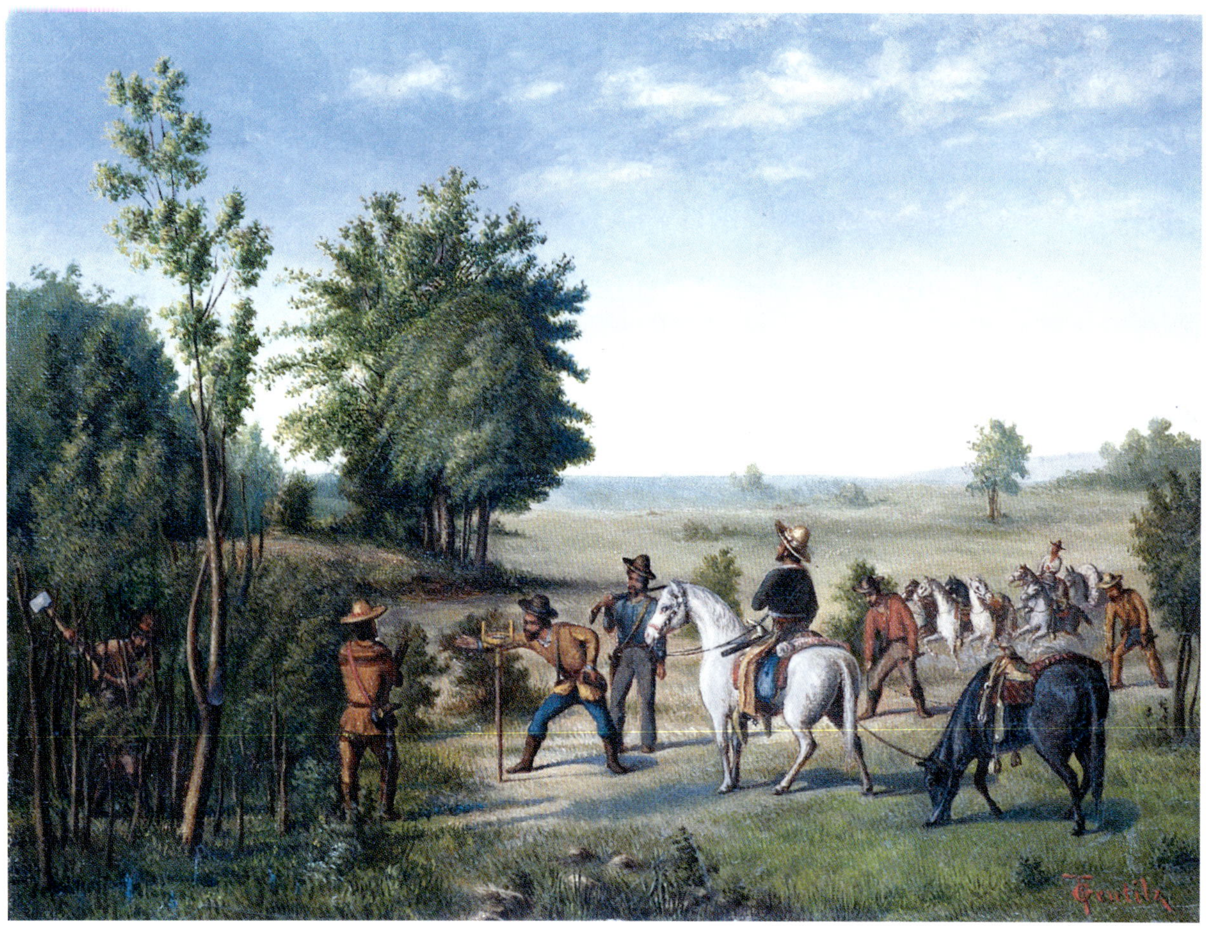

PLATE 43. Theodore Gentilz, *Surveying in Texas before Annexation to the U.S.* or *Stick Stock,* 1845. Oil. Mr. and Mrs. Larry Sheerin, San Antonio, Texas.

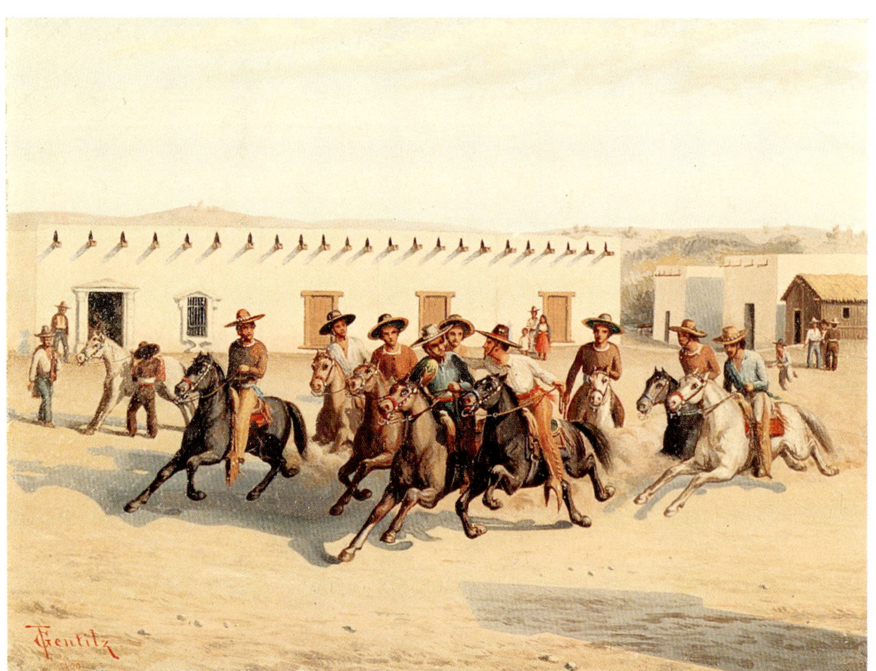

PLATE 44. Theodore Gentilz, *Corrida de la Sandía [The Watermelon Race],* 1890. Oil. Daughters of the Republic of Texas Library at the Alamo, San Antonio, Texas.

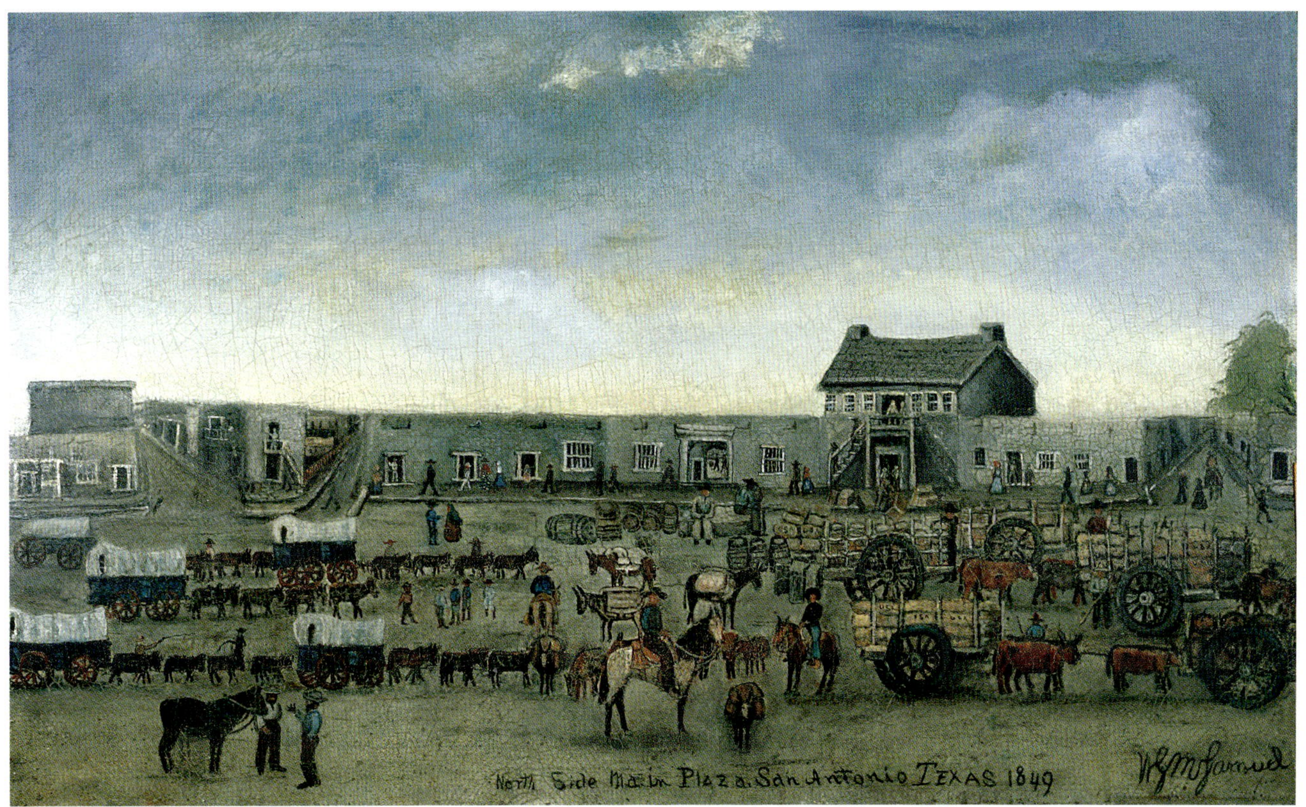

PLATE 45. W. G. M. Samuel, *North Side, Main Plaza,*
San Antonio, Texas, 1849. Oil on canvas, mounted on panel.
Courtesy of the San Antonio Museum Association, San Antonio,
Texas. No. 72-27 LE(4).

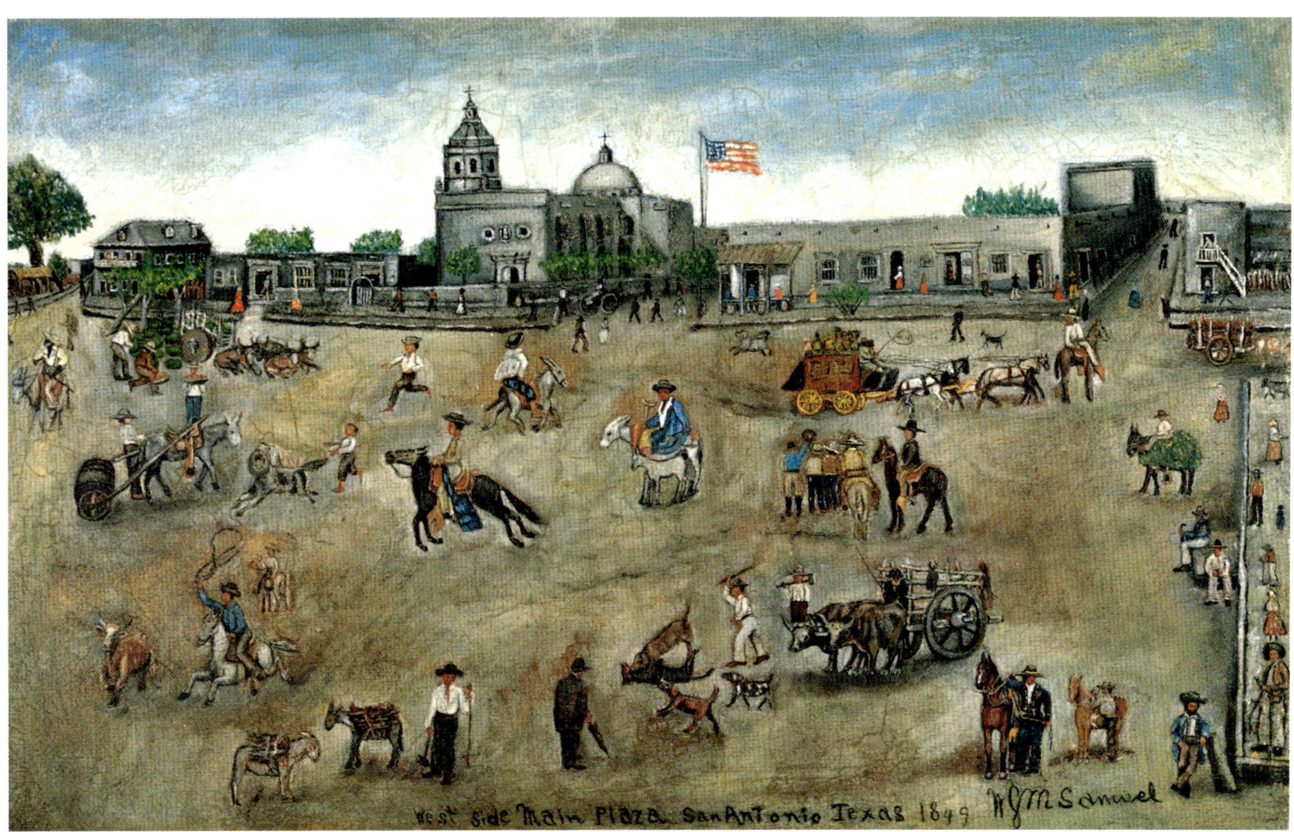

PLATE 46. W. G. M. Samuel, *West Side, Main Plaza,*
San Antonio, Texas, 1849. Oil on canvas, mounted on panel.
Courtesy of the San Antonio Museum Association, San Antonio,
Texas. No. 72-27 LE(3).

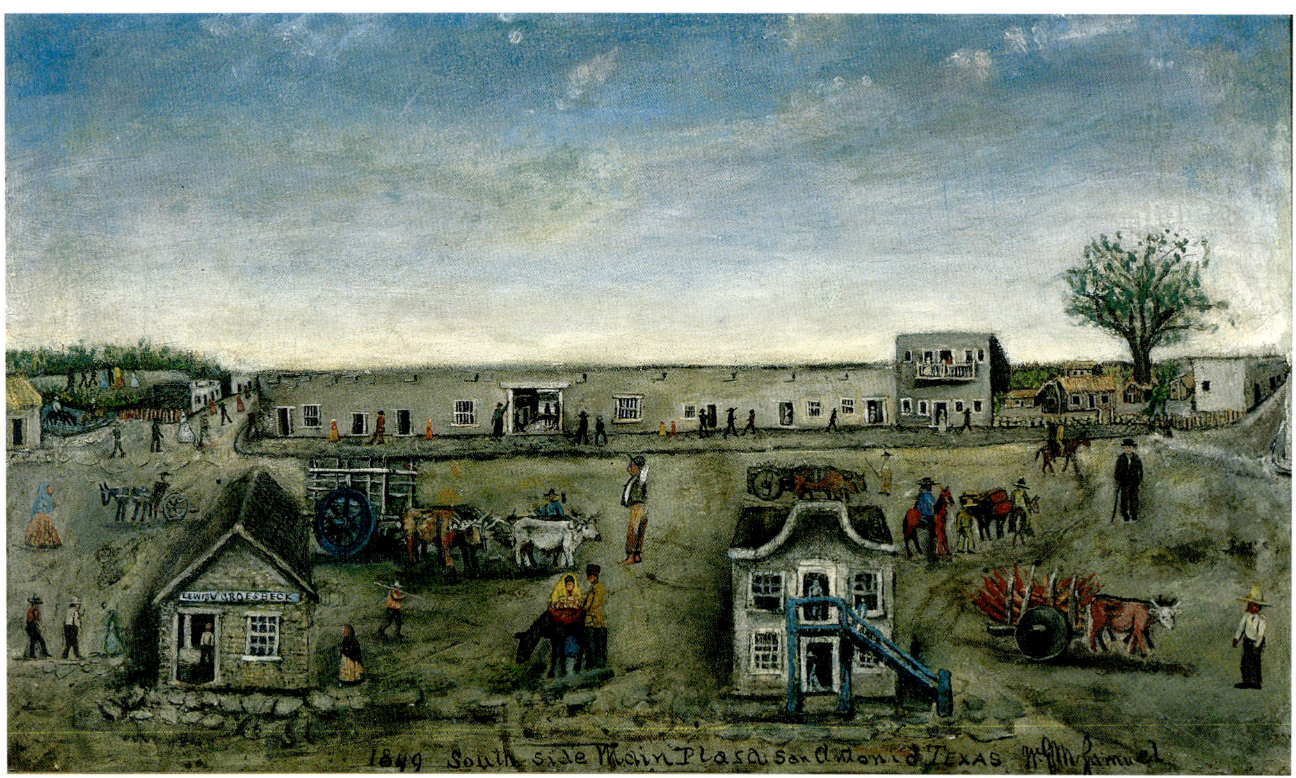

PLATE 47. W. G. M. Samuel, *South Side, Main Plaza,*
San Antonio, Texas, 1849. Oil on canvas, mounted on panel.
Courtesy of the San Antonio Museum Association, San Antonio,
Texas. No. 72-27 LE(2).

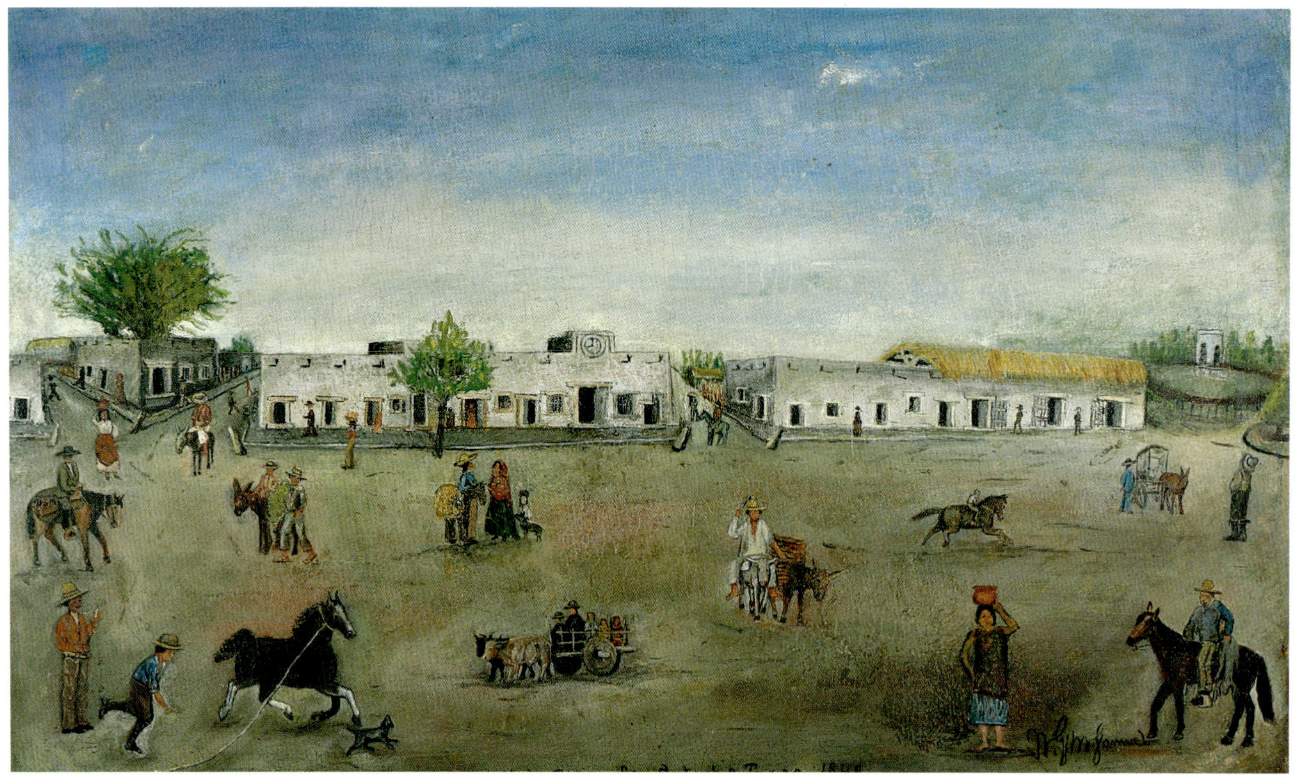

PLATE 48. W. G. M. Samuel, *East Side, Main Plaza,*
San Antonio, Texas, 1849. Oil on canvas, mounted on panel.
Courtesy of the San Antonio Museum Association, San Antonio,
Texas. No. 72-27 LE(1).

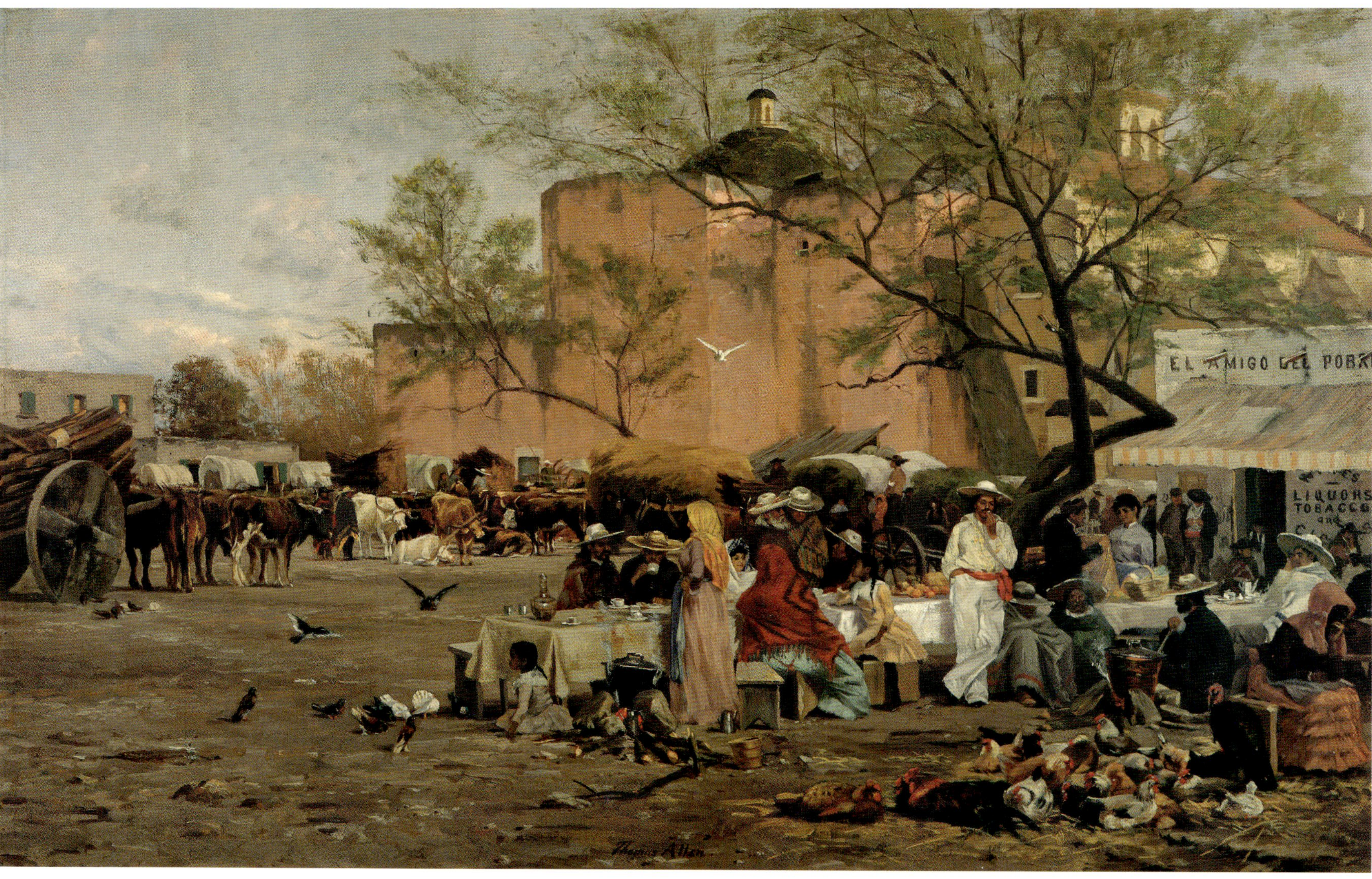

PLATE 49. Thomas Allen, *Market Plaza, San Antonio*, 1878–1879. Oil on canvas, mounted on panel. Courtesy of the San Antonio Museum Association, San Antonio, Texas. No. 36-6518-193 P.

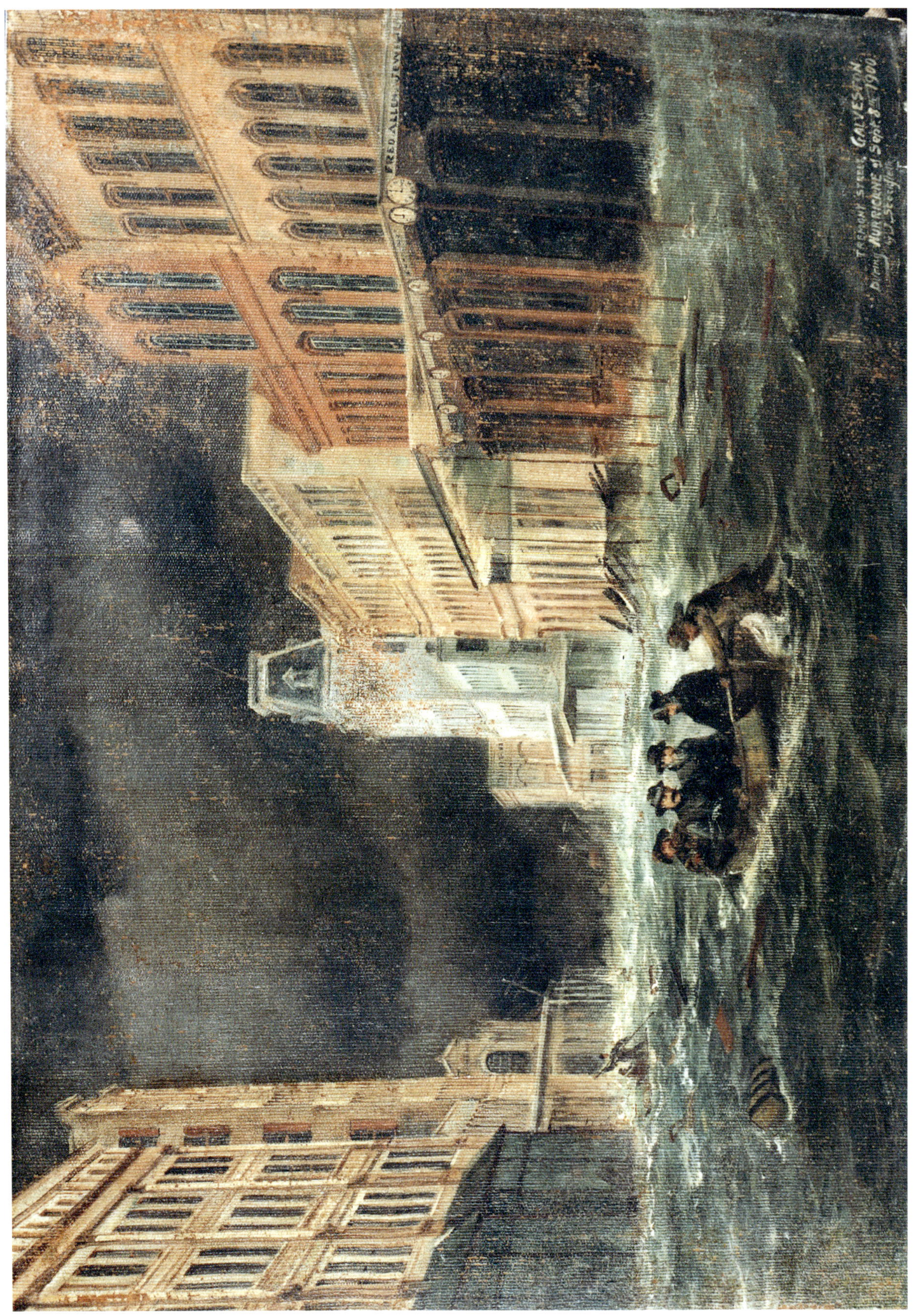

PLATE 50. Julius Stockfleth, *Tremont Street, Galveston, During Hurricane September 8, 1900*, 1900. Oil. Courtesy of Mr. and Mrs. William Simpson, Galveston, Texas.

Painting Texas History to 1900

CHAPTER ONE

Populating That Immense Territory

ARTISTS' VISUAL narratives of the history of Texas before it gained independence from Mexico reflected the realities of life in a sparsely populated, mysterious, and often dangerous land that, by the mid-1700s, had become a focal point of a "clash of imperial energies."[1] Renderings of the earliest Texas historical scenes fall into three categories: firsthand, experiential accounts by American Indians; European perspectives, largely thirdhand and found in a variety of media, especially maps; and, finally, historical paintings in the European/American tradition.

Although the earliest artistic narrations of Texas historical scenes are many centuries old, they have not come under intensive scrutiny until the past fifty years. In August 1933, Forrest Kirkland, an amateur paleontologist, pursuing a suggestion by his father, sought out what had been described to him as some "mysterious paintings" left by Indians near San Angelo, Texas.[2] Kirkland, a Dallas commercial artist, immediately fell to copying these murals painted on rock (Fig. 1). This side trip set Kirkland on an all-consuming mission that lasted more than a decade and took him to far-flung corners of Texas. Kirkland's efforts broke his health, leading to his death at the age of fifty, but they sparked popular interest in these earliest paintings of Texas history.[3]

Since the time of Christ and continuing into the nineteenth century, Indians throughout the desert and plateau Southwest had engaged in some form of rock art, either paintings applied with brushes and crayons (pictographs) or carvings (petroglyphs) on the walls of caves, or "shelters." America's Apache, Navajo, and Puebloan tribes painted for practical reasons, as did the painters of Europe's Franco-Cantabrian region and Africa's Bushmen. Some pictographs pointed the way to water and game animals, others depicted daily life and spiritual experiences, while still others simply entertained the artists and their audiences.[4] This chapter will not attempt to comprehensively survey all of the many examples of Indian rock paintings but will examine briefly a few of their characteristics that are of interest in the context of paintings as narratives of Texas history.

Even though Paint Rock was the first site that Kirkland visited, he spent most of his time and energy in copying pictographs near the confluence of the Pecos and Rio Grande rivers. Dating from as early as A.D. 600, these pictographs exemplify the style known as "Lower Pecos River" and are characterized by the artists' use of numerous colors in many combinations, including red, orange, yellow, black, and white, made from substances such as carbon, clay, and ocher. These artists were members of a Paleo-Indian culture composed of groups with small, dispersed populations who lived as gatherers and hunters and, occasionally, as fishermen. A bison kill site at the confluence of Devil's River and the Rio Grande and several pictographs depicting herds of deer indicate that these animals served as a source of food and tools of bone and antler for native peoples of the Lower Pecos River (Fig. 2).[5]

But the central and most interesting element of these pictographs is the recurrence of dark, purplish-red, hooded figures. These anthropomorphic beings have been variously interpreted as representing dancers, mythical beings, or ordinary men. However, the most widely

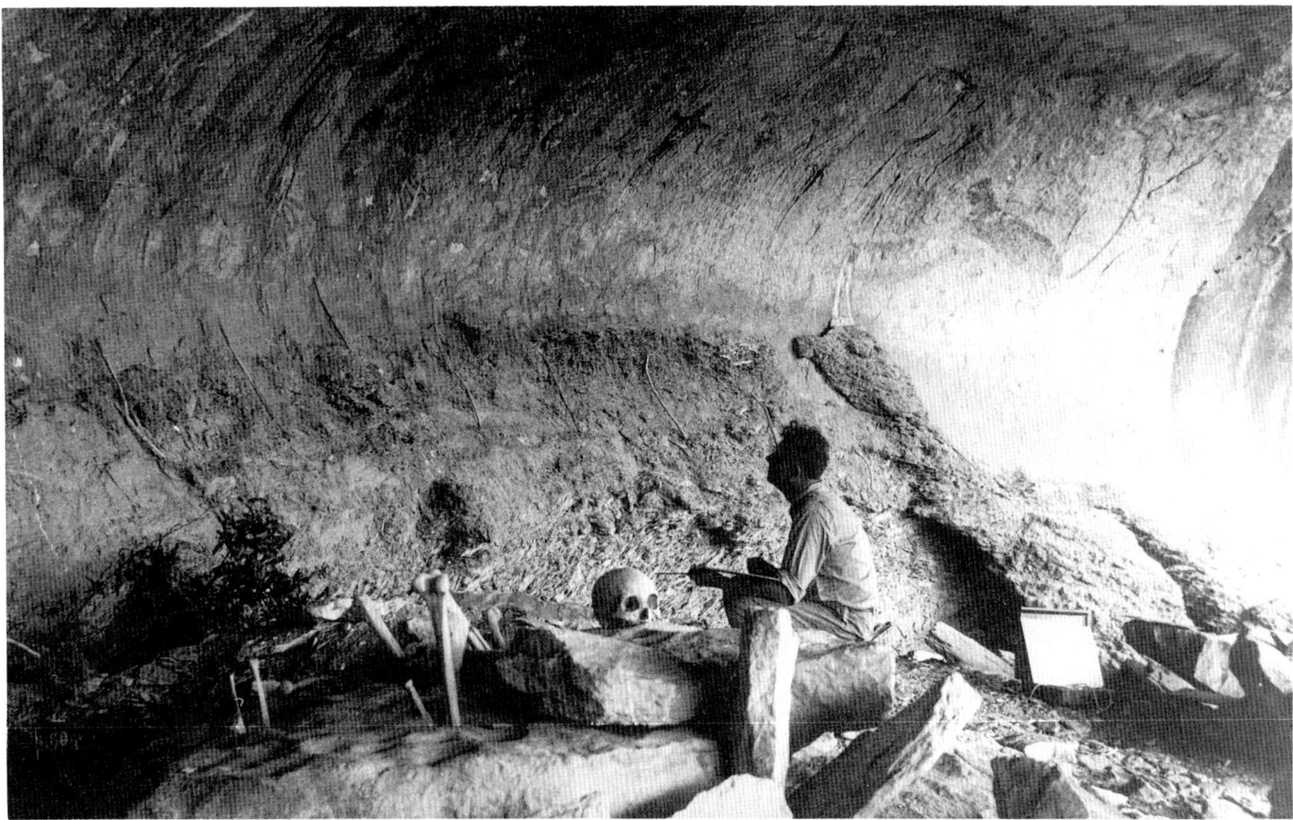

FIGURE 1. Forrest Kirkland in Panther Cave, Lower Pecos River, n.d. Jerry Bywaters Collection on Art of the Southwest, Hamon Arts Library, Southern Methodist University, Dallas, Texas.

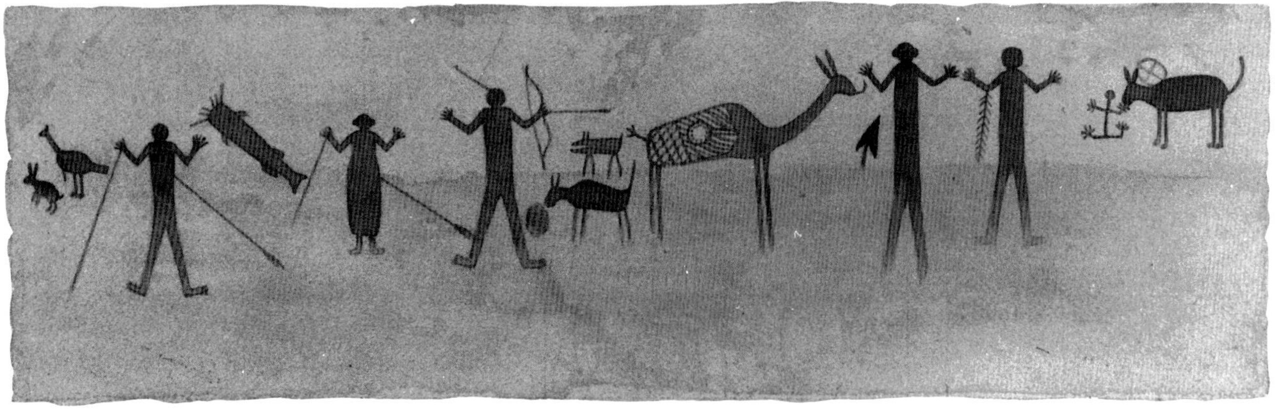

FIGURE 2. *Deer and Hunters,* Painted Rock Shelter, Lower Pecos River, n.d. Indian pictograph, watercolor copy by Forrest Kirkland. Courtesy of the Texas Memorial Museum, Austin, Texas. TMM no. 2261-47.

accepted interpretation is that they are depictions of sha-mans, tribal members who were believed to have had some kind of supernatural abilities or powers. They are rendered in a variety of types, and usually are denoted by a horned headdress, feathered sash, and a rotund or winged body. In several pictographs, these figures hold darts and prickly-pear pouches, accoutrements of their religious functions (Fig. 3). The exact meaning of the shaman may well have varied among the various tribes and included that of a god of the chase, a costumed deity, or a kind of "medicine man." The depiction of these fig-ures evolved over centuries, and some Indian bands may have intended their pictographs to denote any one or a combination of these elements.[6]

Whatever their exact meaning within a given tribe, these pictographs make clear that shamans were con-cerned with such matters of tribal life as healing, hunt-ing, warfare, and weather conditions. Several pictographs portray shamans in conjunction with animals, especially deer and cougars (Pl. 1). Quite possibly, shamanistic so-cieties executed pictographs during or immediately after group rituals that occurred at seasonal intervals. These rituals often included ingestion of the hallucinogenic mescal bean, and some shamans depicted the resulting visions in pictographic form. Experiences of exception-ally potent visions at certain caves caused the societies to regard these locations as possessing extraordinary powers

and to congregate there repeatedly, as demonstrated by walls with several layers of overpainted pictographs.[7]

Another notable feature of many pictographs is the incorporation of evidence of contact with Europeans, such as paintings of horses and Christian symbols, ele-ments that can aid in dating the paintings. At Hueco Tanks, an important watering spot near El Paso, Mesca-lero Apaches left a pictograph from the nineteenth cen-tury that depicts the figure of a man in a yellow coat, black pants, and polka-dotted vest or shirt (Pl. 2). At Meyers Springs, in the Lower Pecos area, the enormous size and painstaking execution of one large pictograph portraying a "white" world point to the fact that it car-ried great social importance for its artist (Fig. 4). This pictograph includes two church towers, possibly an at-tempt by the artist to draw on the perceived supernatural powers of the crosses atop the church; the hand-holding dancers in the pictograph are engaged in a ritual related to either the Christian religion or that of an Indian tribe. Near Big Bend, in Rattlesnake Canyon, another picto-graph portrays the death of a missionary (Fig. 5), and an adjoining cave painting includes the representation of a church with three crosses and the figure of a bearded man smoking a pipe (Fig. 6).[8]

A slight possibility exists that the Rattlesnake Canyon pictographs may have resulted from the Indians' contact with Mission Santa Cruz de San Sabá, approximately two

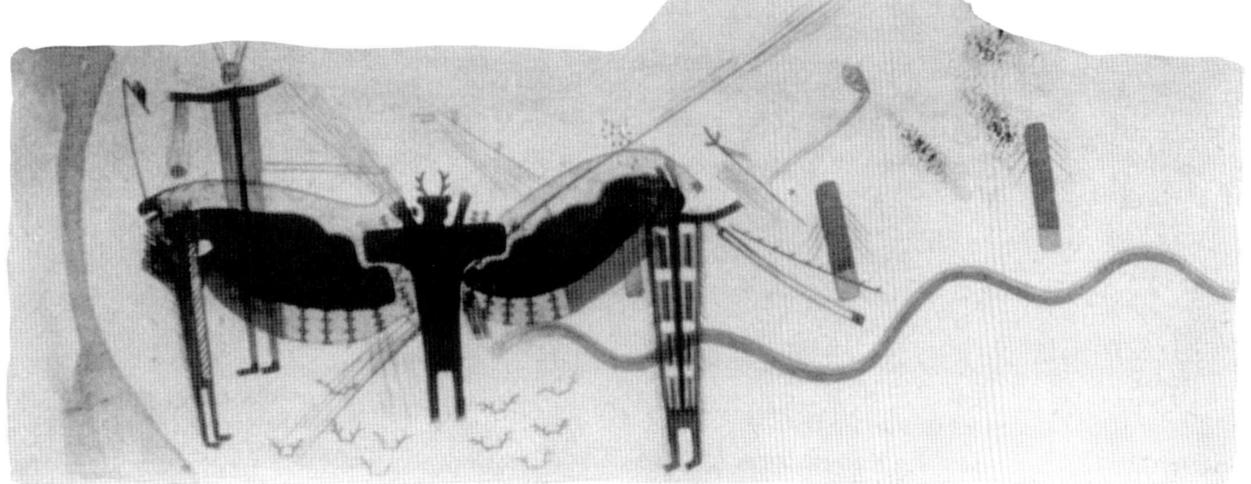

FIGURE 3. *Shamans,* Seminole Canyon, Fate Bell Shelter, Lower Pecos River, n.d. Indian pictograph, watercolor copy by Forrest Kirkland. Courtesy of the Texas Memorial Museum, Austin, Texas. TMM no. 2261-12.

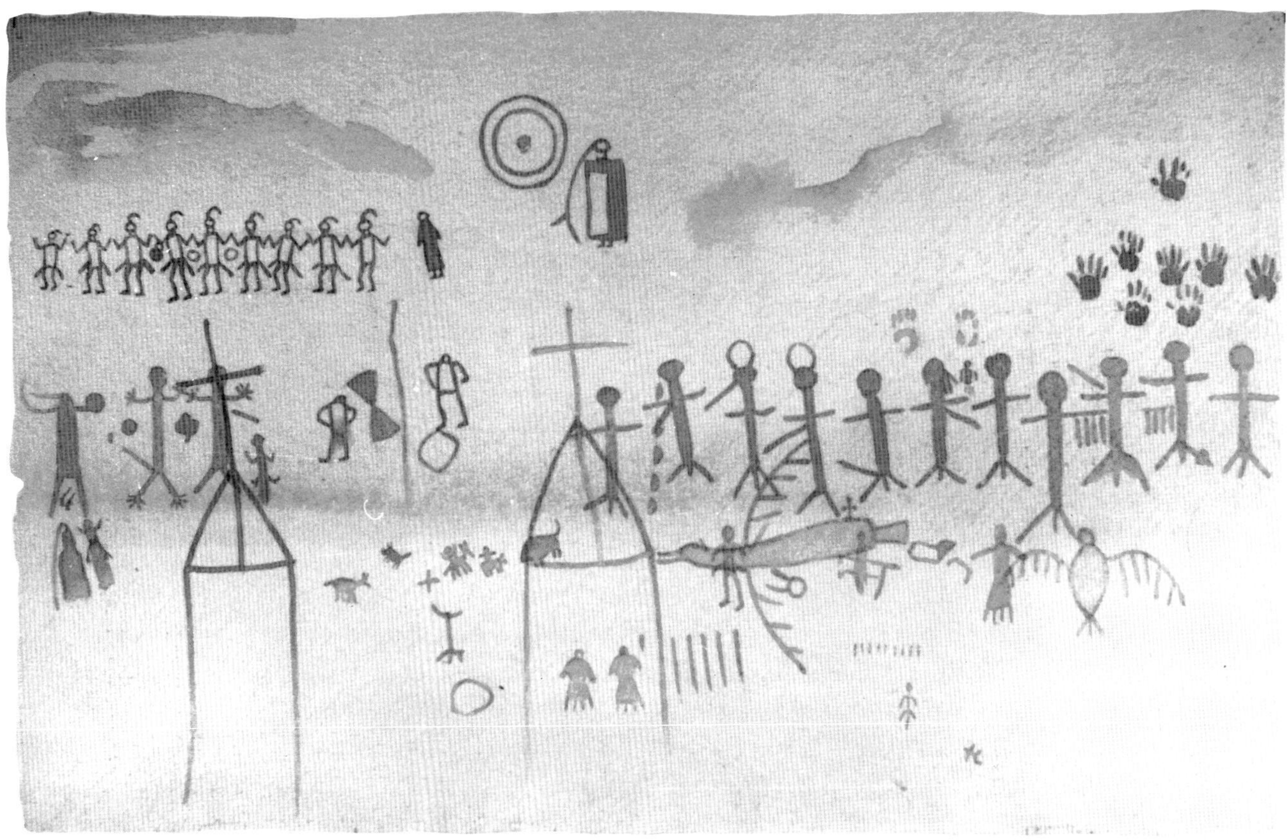

FIGURE 4. *Church and Dancers,* Meyers Springs, n.d. Indian
pictograph, watercolor copy by Forrest Kirkland. Courtesy of the
Texas Memorial Museum, Austin, Texas. TMM no. 2261-72.

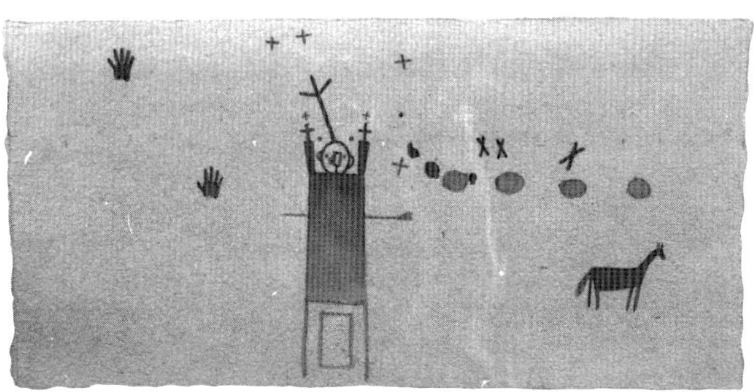

FIGURE 5. *Death of a Missionary,* Rattlesnake Canyon, near
Big Bend, n.d. Indian pictograph, watercolor copy by Forrest
Kirkland. Courtesy of the Texas Memorial Museum, Austin,
Texas. TMM no. 2261-3.

hundred miles to the northeast; the history of this mission is discussed below in connection with the painting
that depicted its destruction by Comanche Indians. During the eighteenth century, raiding parties of Apaches,
Comanches, and Tonkawas rested at Paint Rock while on
forays to Spanish *ranchos* to the south, and evidence of
their contact with Europeans is especially prominent on
its surfaces. Although isolated geographically from the
sites of most of the other Texas pictographs, these images
are some of the most intriguing evidences of this contact
and include representations of flaglike emblems, a tally of
some kind (Fig. 7), and a target (Fig. 8). Paintings in red
of the figure of a devil and of a church with two towers
topped by crosses reflect the familiarity of some of these
Indians with Christianity. The painting of this church is
partially covered by a black smudge, and one scholar believes that the pictograph may depict the burning of the
San Sabá mission (Fig. 9).[9] After this attack, the Comanches began leaving their own artistic records at Paint
Rock as one way of declaring their control of the site.[10]

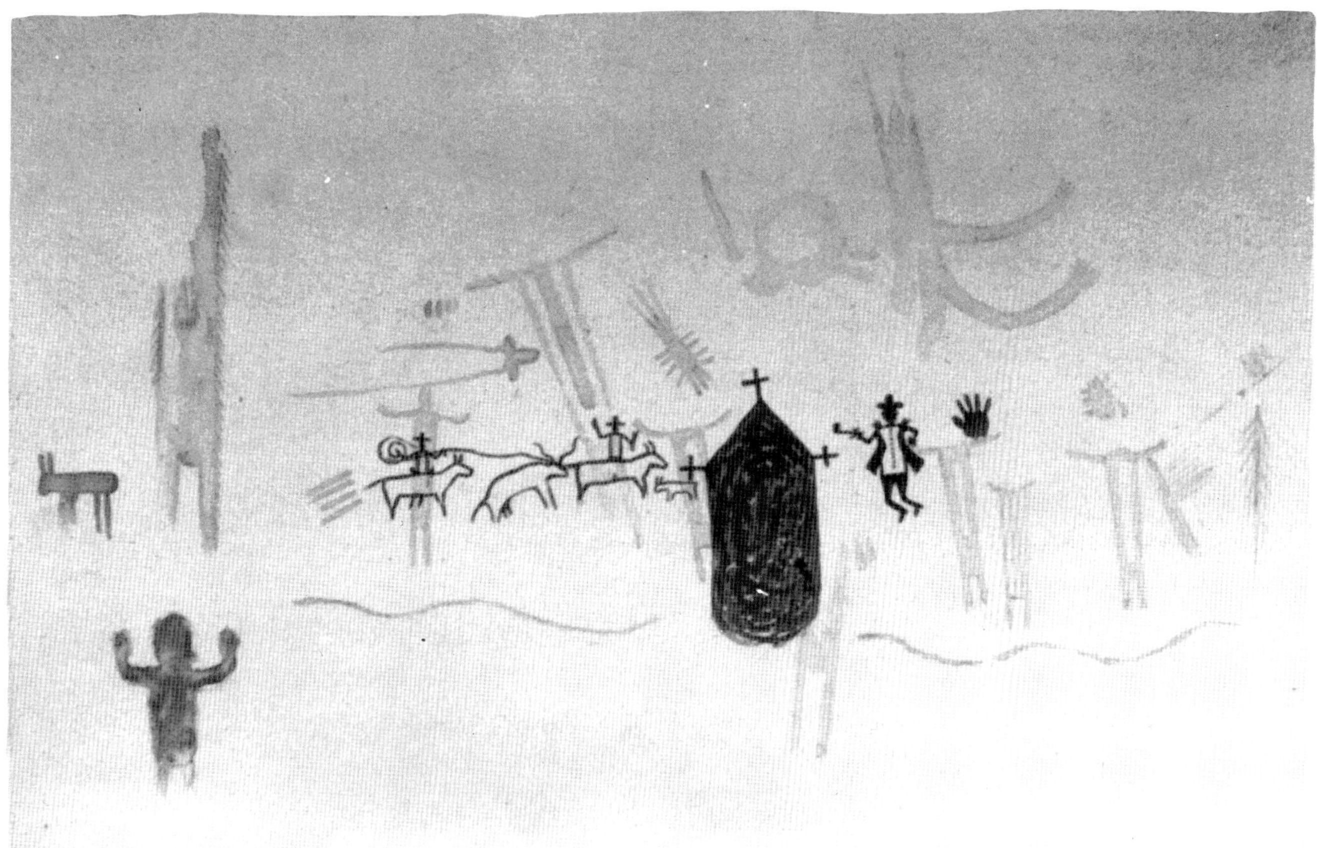

FIGURE 6. *Church and European with Pipe,* Pressa Canyon,
Lower Pecos River, n.d. Indian pictograph, watercolor copy by
Forrest Kirkland. Courtesy of the Texas Memorial Museum,
Austin, Texas. TMM no. 2261-63.

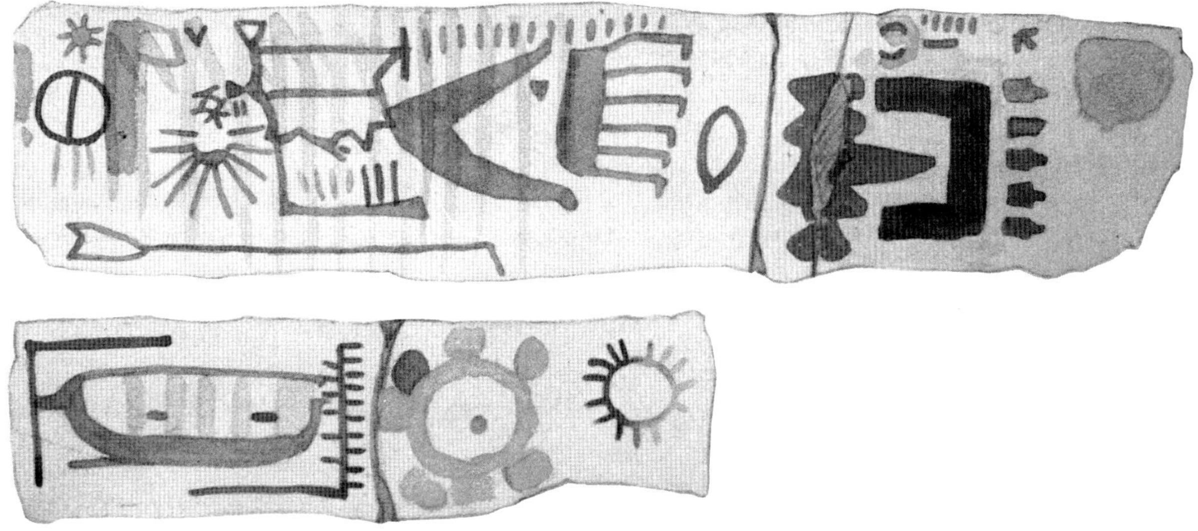

FIGURE 7. *Tally Symbols,* Paint Rock, n.d. Indian pictograph,
watercolor copy by Forrest Kirkland. Courtesy of the Texas
Memorial Museum, Austin, Texas. TMM no. 2261-107.

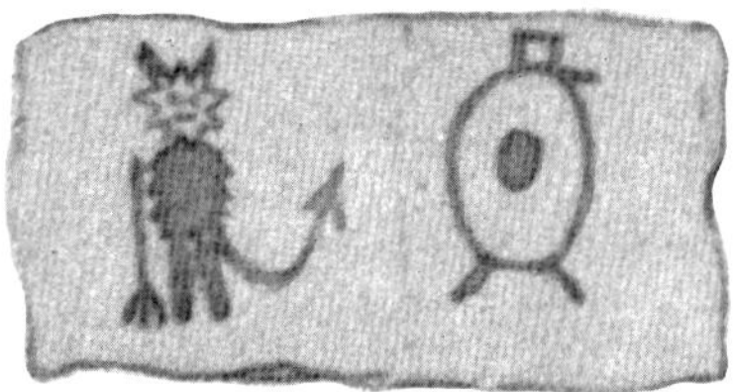

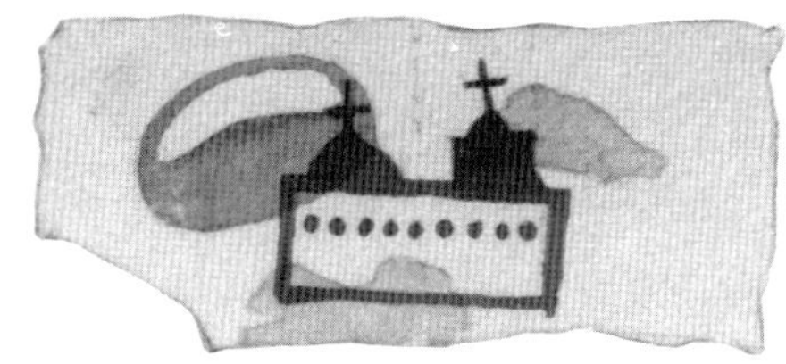

FIGURE 8. *Devil and Target,* Paint Rock, n.d. Indian pictograph, watercolor copy by Forrest Kirkland. Courtesy of the Texas Memorial Museum, Austin, Texas. TMM no. 2261-106.

FIGURE 9. *Church with Two Crosses,* Paint Rock, n.d. Indian pictograph, watercolor copy by Forrest Kirkland. Courtesy of the Texas Memorial Museum, Austin, Texas. TMM no. 2261-103.

Even though these visual records left by the earliest inhabitants of Texas would seem to have little in common with subsequent paintings of Texas historical scenes by white artists, they do bear a few key resemblances. Pictographs emphasized the importance of narrative and, consequently, the priority of realistic depiction of either the artists' experiences or of recountings of events handed down through an oral tradition. In addition, these paintings were infused with the artists' cultural and/or religious perceptions of the world, as evidenced by the prominence of the shaman in many pictographs and hostile depictions of Europeans in others. Another common thread running through the work of European and Indian artists was the portrayal of the other's culture as exotic and difficult to comprehend.

One of the perceptions of the New World that suffused many written and pictorial accounts by the Europeans who encountered these and other Indian tribes in the first half of the sixteenth century was the belief that a new Garden of Eden had been discovered. In travel accounts and reports back to the centers of government of the colonizing nations, explorers and early colonizers attempted to demystify North and South America by describing the continents' flora, fauna, and climatic conditions. These writings functioned as the basis for the earliest pictorial renderings of the newly discovered lands. Artists and writers strived to present ostensibly factual information about America, but their works are equally notable for what they reveal about their creators' own preconceptions and how they wanted to sway their audiences to agree with these notions.[11]

The accounts left by individuals who traveled in the Southwest during the sixteenth century are frequently unclear as to whether they entered the confines of the present state of Texas. However, even allowing for equation during this time of "Texas" and "Southwest," very few visual images from the time can be linked to the region. Perhaps the most striking is Jan Mostaert's (ca. 1472– ca. 1556) *An Episode of the Conquest of America* or *A West*

Indian Scene (ca. 1540–1550; Pl. 3), one of the earliest European paintings depicting the Americas. At this time, "West Indies" referred to the entire New World, the extent of which was unknown. A pastoral landscape, complete with peacefully grazing domesticated cattle and sheep, dominates the canvas, reflecting the preoccupation with nature that characterized the work of Mostaert, one of the leading Dutch painters of his day. But this tranquility is shattered by invading Spanish soldiers entering the scene in the lower right corner of the canvas and Indians who resemble Graeco-Roman warriors rushing in panic to confront them.[12]

Mostaert may have intended the painting to function as an allegory of Spanish occupation of the Low Countries, which only ended after protracted fighting that began in 1568. But he also incorporated a few elements indicating that he had at least minimal familiarity with explorers' accounts of the New World. The most striking of these features is the depiction of a cagelike dwelling atop the cliff that dominates the landscape. In the 1530s, both the shipwrecked Alvar Núñez Cabeza de Vaca and the explorer Fray Marcos de Niza had returned to Mexico with stories of the cliff-dwelling Pueblo tribes of the Southwest. The earliest reports of Francisco Vásquez de Coronado's expedition mentioned specifically these tribes' use of ladders as well as the practice of their chiefs and elder tribal members occasionally shouting instructions from huts atop the cliffs. Living in the Spanish-occupied Netherlands during the ensuing decade, Mostaert may well have heard these tales in corrupted and/or embellished form.[13]

Part of the charm that this New Eden held for Europeans was not only the perceived innocence of its inhabitants but also the exotic novelty of much of its flora and fauna. Early on, a quintessentially Texas creature, the armadillo, came to represent this exotica. The first mention of the armadillo appeared in reports written by Spanish explorer Fernández de Enciso in 1518; a decade later, it was portrayed as a small piglike creature on a privately

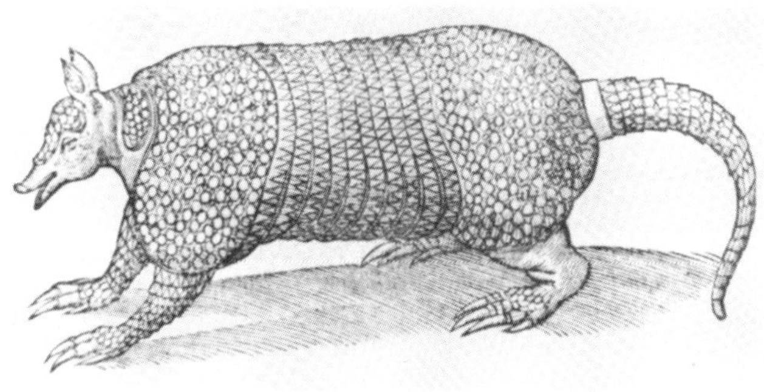

FIGURE 10. N. Monardes, *An Armadillo*, 1605. Woodcut. From *Auctarium ad Exoticorum Libros;* photograph from *The New Golden Land* by Hugh Honour. Photograph by King Douglas, Dallas, Texas.

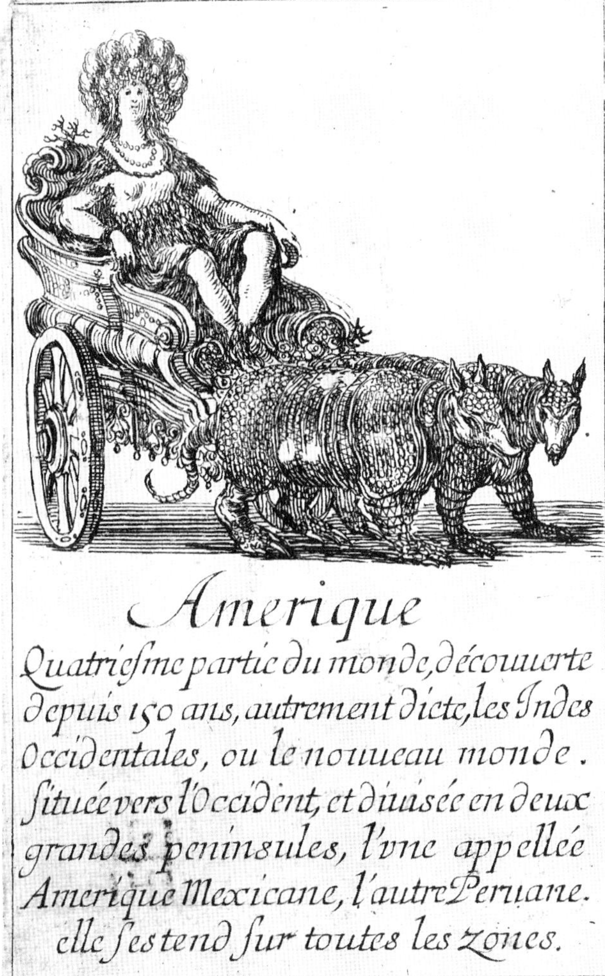

FIGURE 11. Stefano della Bella, *America*, 1644. Etching. All rights reserved, The Metropolitan Museum of Art, New York, NY. Gift of the Estate of James Hazen Hyde, 1959. Acc. no. 59.654.19(28).

published Spanish map. In 1540, one of the most detailed (and amusing) early descriptions of the armadillo appeared in Englishman Roger Barlow's *Brief Summe of Geographie*: "Ther is a kynde of small beastes no bigger than a pigges of a moneth olde, and the fete the hede and the eares be like a horse, and his bodie and his head is all covered saving his eres with a shell moche like the shell of a tortuga, but it is the very proportion of an armed horse for this shell hangeth downe by his sides and afore his brest moving as it were hanged by gynowes hinges, or moche like the lappes of a complete harneis. It is an admiration to behold it. Hit fedeth like a horse and his taile is like a pigges taile, saving it is straight."[14]

By the seventeenth century, stuffed specimens of the armadillo made for more anatomically accurate renderings, as evidenced by a woodcut in 1605 in N. Monardes' book, *Auctarium ad Exoticorum Libros* (Fig. 10). But, at approximately the same time, the creature still inspired the sensational: in 1594, festival architecture celebrating the arrival of Austria's Archduke Ernst in Antwerp incorporated the image of an armadillo as a representation of America—being ridden sidesaddle by a young woman. A half-century later, in 1644, playing cards used to teach history and geography to the future King Louis XIV of France depicted two armadillos in harness pulling a woman of regal appearance in a chariot (Fig. 11).[15]

As demonstrated by the armadillo image on the 1529 Spanish map, Europeans also expressed their artistic conceptions of Texas and the New World in the field of cartography; in some respects, mapmaking functioned as a branch of the fine arts during the sixteenth, seventeenth, and eighteenth centuries. At this time, maps were produced by the process of copper engraving, in which lines were cut into the metal, which was then inked. After the ink was wiped from the smooth portions, the inked grooves and seams were then transferred to paper in a high-pressure press. Although this was an expensive process, it produced a more graceful image than did woodcuts. Too, copper plates lasted many years and could be reused and adapted to changed cartographic data by simply filling in old grooves or cutting new ones.[16]

Maps wedded art to the study of science and history and frequently carried the only evidence of a historical fact or phenomenon; a sampling of maps drawn between the late sixteenth and early eighteenth centuries demonstrates how knowledge and perceptions of Texas developed during these years. One of the earliest maps to include the American Southwest, *Americae Sive Novi Orbis, Nova Descriptio,* or *America the New World, Newly Described* (1570; Fig. 12), illustrates just how little accurate information concerning the region was available to cartographers at this time. This was one of fifty-three maps published by map collector and entrepreneur Abraham Ortelius under the title *Theatrum Orbis Terrarum* (*Theater of the World*), for which accomplished craftsman Frans Hogenberg engraved virtually all of the plates. Often cited as the first modern atlas, this series illustrated the culmination of the scientific community's recognition of the inadequacy of the Ptolemaic conception and depiction of the globe that had held sway for centuries. However, it furnished little information concerning the region later known as Texas, save for the coastal outline and a few place names gleaned from the scant information available from Spanish exploration up to that time. On *Americae Sive Novi Orbis, Nova Descriptio*, "Hispania Nova" embraces Texas, and the Rio Grande is designated "R. Palmar" ("River of Palms").[17]

During the next century, further exploration and colonization brought the New World increasingly into the European commercial sphere, and cartography reflected this growing familiarity. In 1656, Nicolas Sanson d'Abbeville demonstrated how knowledge about North America in general and Texas in particular had increased since Ortelius's time in *Le Nouveau Mexique et La Floride* (Fig. 13). Appointed as royal geographer to King Louis VIII in 1640, Sanson had been instrumental in establishing a new approach to cartography in Paris in the 1630s. He and his associates produced maps that were more scientifically accurate and less decorative than were those of the Dutch. For instance, French cartographers left blank

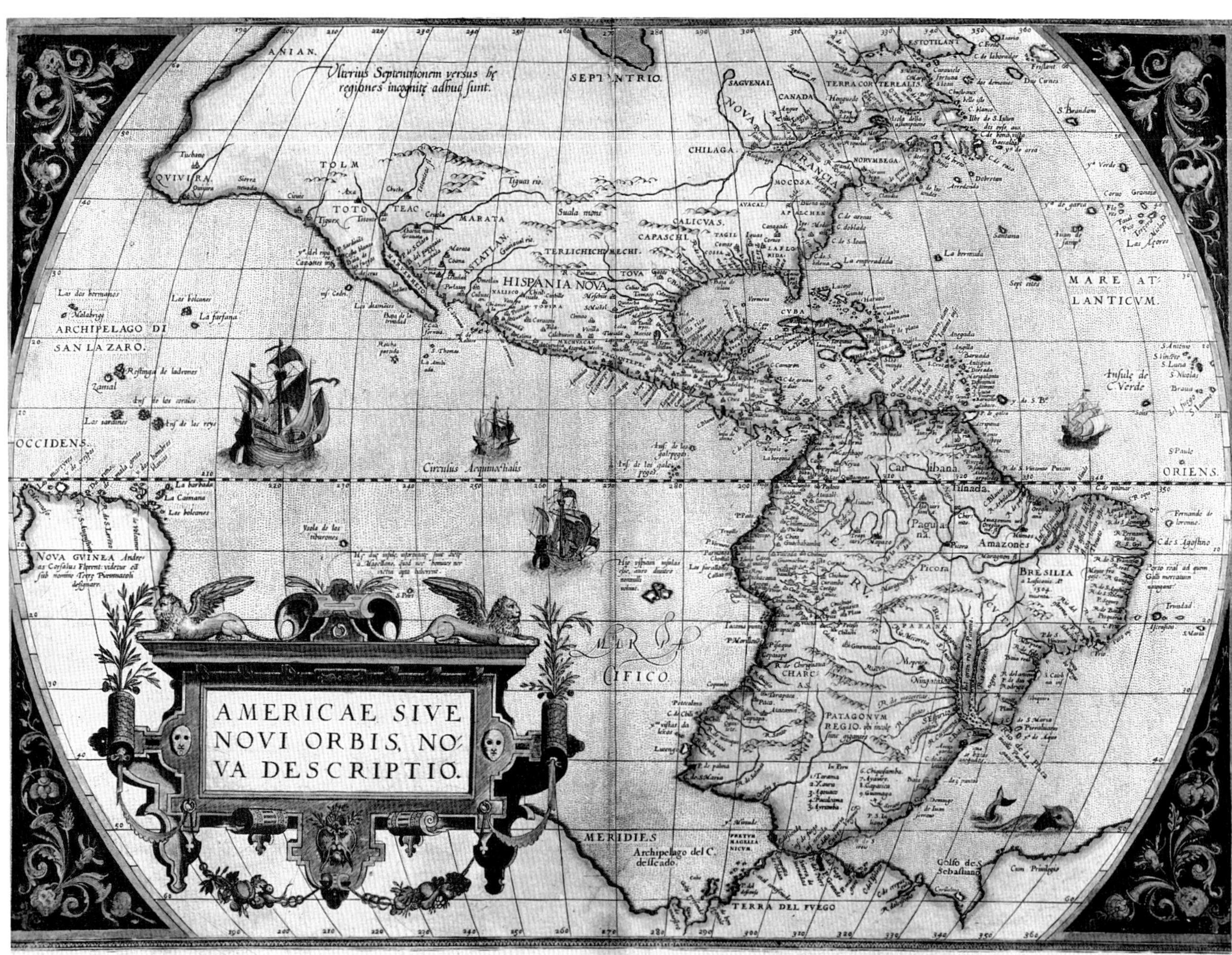

FIGURE 12. Abraham Ortelius, *Americae Sive Novi Orbis, Nova Descriptio*, 1570. Engraved by Frans Hogenberg. The San Jacinto Museum of History Association, Houston, Texas.

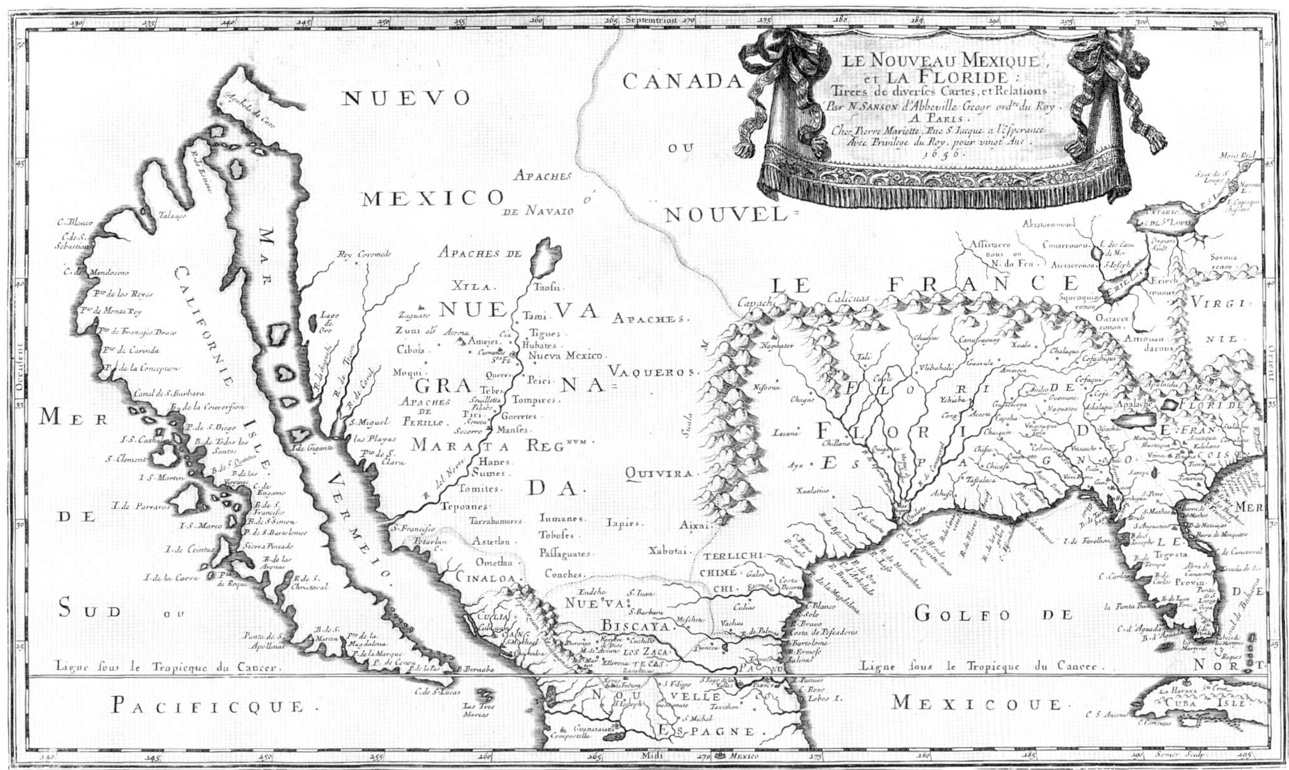

FIGURE 13. Nicolas Sanson d'Abbeville, *Le Nouveau Mexique et La Floride*, 1656. Hand-colored engraving. Courtesy of Paul C. Ragsdale, New Braunfels, Texas. Photograph from the Ragsdale Collection, Amon Carter Museum, Fort Worth, Texas.

those regions about which they were ignorant, while their Dutch counterparts filled in these areas with ships, sea monsters, or other forms of decoration. Accordingly, *Le Nouveau Mexique et La Floride* provides a fairly accurate indication of the extent of European knowledge of the Southwest in the mid-seventeenth century.[18]

This first atlas map that included significant information on Texas compiled a number of place names and knowledge of landforms that the French had been able to assemble from earlier maps and from tales of various explorers. It continued to designate the Rio Grande as the "River of Palms" and gave the location of many Indian tribes, notably the Apaches, but it also perpetuated misapprehensions that had developed during the preceding century of exploration. It labeled a region in central Texas as "Quivira," the name of the location of the mythical golden Seven Cities of Cíbola that had drawn Coronado's expedition onto the Great Plains between 1540 and 1542. Compounding the confusion, Sanson included a reference to "Cíbola," which he located somewhere in the

present state of Nevada. South of "Apaches," "Vaqueros," now translated as "cowboys," probably designated Indians who hunted buffalo, since Spanish explorers referred to buffalo as "vacas" ("cows"), rather than indicating any intent to juxtapose cowboys and Indians.

Sanson's work also indicated that Texas was becoming something more than an exotic spot on Europeans' maps and was no longer being perceived simply as a source of highly unusual flora and fauna. It pointed up the increasing interest on the part of France in the southern regions of North America that would bring that nation into conflict with Spain, especially in the wake of explorations of the Mississippi River by René Robert Cavelier, Sieur de la Salle. In 1683, commissioned by King Louis XIV of France to found a settlement on the Gulf, La Salle established the beginnings of a small settlement, Fort St. Louis, near the mouth of the Brazos on what is today the Texas coast. After waiting nearly two years for resupply and reinforcements, La Salle and a few men set out to get help. On the trek, La Salle was murdered, and only two members of his party survived. In the meantime, the Spanish governor of Coahuila, Alonso de León, led an armed contingent in search of the French fort, which they found as a burned-out and deserted ruin.[19]

In 1705, French royal geographer Nicolas de Fer departed from Sanson's scientific approach and highlighted imperial rivalries for Texas in his map entitled *Les Costes aux Environs de la Riviere de Misisipi* (Pl. 4). Instead of the entire continent, de Fer focused on that part of it that had been the stage for France's most recent competition with Spain, the Gulf Coast. But this map lacked the encyclopedic information that had characterized Sanson's work and functioned better as a piece of propaganda than as a guide to geographical information. In one sense, de Fer made a substantive break with his predecessors: rather than striving to convey information comprehensively, he overtly favored an ideological viewpoint over an objective approach, reflecting a tension common to many subsequent artistic depictions of Texas history.[20]

Instead of incorporating information from other explorers and attempting to exhibit the total amount of cartographic knowledge of the region, de Fer's map drew most of its information from La Salle's observations. De Fer clearly, if imprecisely, depicted the site of Fort St. Louis on Matagorda Bay, the route of La Salle's last journey, and the route taken by de León's search party. In addition, he located and named the various Indian tribes and villages visited by La Salle; one notation on the map refers to the diversity of tribal languages. But ethnographic and geographic information is overshadowed by two prominent illustrations, spread across the upper portion of the map, one depicting the murder of La Salle and the other depicting the death of another expedition member, possibly La Salle's murderer. These scenes flank a central cartouche bearing the title "Discoveries of Monsieur de la Salle in 1683 and Reconnaissances by Monsieur le Chevallier." By emphasizing the explorer's accomplishments and sacrifice, the map becomes a cartographic icon devoted primarily to lionizing La Salle.

Despite France's failure to establish a permanent settlement at Fort St. Louis, La Salle's probings convinced Spanish colonial authorities that their hold on Texas was in danger, and they began to cast about for ways to consolidate possession of the area. In the early 1680s, Spain had already established missions near El Paso; in 1690, fear of the French led to the establishment of missions San Francisco de los Tejas and Santísimo Nombre de María in East Texas. However, both of these were abandoned three years later. But, in 1714, after French entrepreneur Louis Jouchereau de St. Denis made his way across Texas in order to establish trade relations with the Spaniards, Viceroy Duque de Linares ordered the establishment of new outposts in East Texas. In order to supply these East Texas missions, Mission San Antonio de Valero and Presidio San Antonio de Béjar were established in 1718. Over the next four decades, Spanish authorities established missions and presidios along a crescent extending from Los Adaes in present-day Louisiana to the southern tip of Texas.[21]

The destruction of one of these missions, Santa Cruz de San Sabá, served as the subject of the earliest known Texas historical narrative painting by a professional artist. At daybreak on 16 March 1758, approximately two thousand Comanche, Bidai, Tejas, and Tonkawa warriors materialized outside the walls of the mission, which was located near the present site of the town of Menard. Angered by Spanish attempts to find favor with the Apaches, the traditional enemies of these tribes, the Comanches and their allies swarmed over the mission grounds, killed six of the inhabitants, including two of the mission's three priests, left the rest for dead, and burned the mission buildings to the ground. The attackers also killed two members of a troop of soldiers who had ridden out from Presidio San Luis de las Amarillas, three miles away, to protect the mission.[22]

The only priest who survived the attack, Father Miguel de Molina, returned to Colegio de San Fernando, a Franciscan seminary in Mexico City, to recover from his wounds, and his story of the Comanche terror soon became well known. His idealism had never run as deeply as had that of his fellow priests, and he spoke freely of the attackers' "cruel and bloody way of life" and their intentions to "deceive the trustful."[23] The details of the massacre sent shock waves of horror through the capital city of New Spain. In particular, the violent death of one of the mission's priests, Father Alonso Giraldo de Terreros, a member of one of the city's most prominent families, emphasized the reality of one side of life on the northern frontier from which Mexico's upper classes wished to be insulated. The attack sparked similar reactions in Spain, inspiring one Franciscan monk, Father Miguel de Arroyo, to compose a lengthy poem praising the valor of the priests who were killed.[24]

Despite this reaction or, perhaps, because of it, Father Terreros's cousin, Pedro Romero de Terreros, commissioned a huge (83″ × 115″) painting that would express both the horror and significance of the event. Pedro Terreros had amassed a fortune from silver-mining ventures and had been the primary financial supporter of Mission Santa Cruz de San Sabá. He was determined to commission a work that would immortalize his cousin's martyrdom as well as visually narrate the massacre, as indicated by the painting's complete title, *The Destruction of Mission San Sabá in the Province of Texas and the Martyrdom of the Fathers Alonso Giraldo de Terreros, Joseph Santiesteban* (ca. 1763; Pl. 5). Speculations concerning the identity of the painter employed by Terreros have ranged from indefiniteness to dogmatic certainty, but he likely worked in the studio of Don Miguel Cabrera, the dominant painter of mid-eighteenth-century Mexico. A great deal of evidence suggests but does not prove conclusively that one of Cabrera's artists, José de Páez, executed the painting.[25]

In *Destruction of Mission San Sabá*, the placement of the figures of the two slain priests makes their deaths the window through which the viewer interprets the painting on both an actual and an ideological level, emphasizing that these deaths invested the massacre with the element of heroic sacrifice. At the foot of each of these large figures is a shield bearing a biographical sketch of the priest, who is depicted in the manner in which he died, complete with weapons and blood in appropriate places. In addition to biographical information, the shields commend the priests' character and sacrifice, mentioning Father Terreros's selfless "motive of a new conquest in the reservation for the Apache Indians" and that Father Santiesteban "because of his righteousness was elected to the new conquest and reservation for the Apache Indians. . . . he was killed at the hands of barbarous Indians."[26]

The shields bracket a scroll that briefly summarizes the purpose of the mission's founding and praises its major financial supporter, "the illustrious Knight don Pedro Therreros of the order of Calatrava."[27] In the fashion of painters of other historical tableaus, the artist has placed an alphabetized key to the eighteen events depicted in the painting in the lower half of the scroll. These vignettes are illustrated by three hundred separate figures, and each incident is marked by a large red letter.[28] The easiest way to comprehend the unfolding of the attack and the painting's explanation of it is to arrange the quoted text of the scroll in the order that the selected events occurred and supplement this text with other accounts.

The first incident of the assault, which was not included in the painting, involved a mission guard, Juan Leal, who was set upon by three Indians while cutting wood on the banks of the river. They led him and the wife of one of the soldiers, whom they had captured and stripped of her clothing, back to the stockade walls of the mission. Heavily armed, the Indians claimed to be interested only in killing Apaches and not Spaniards. However, Leal later asserted that many of the Indians wore elements of French uniforms and commented that this was the Spaniards' first confrontation with Indians using firearms, which they probably had obtained from French traders.[29]

Inside the mission, the first warning was a "furious outburst of yells and war cries . . . outside the gates of the enclosure," followed by the alarm of the sentry ("E: The Entrance of the Barbarous Indians into the Mission").[30] Because the tribes allied with the Comanches had previously been on friendly terms with the Spaniards, they were able to persuade Corporal Ascencio Cadena of their friendly intentions, and he acquiesced by allowing them to enter the compound ("G: [The Indians] Surrounding the Mission"). Soon, some three hundred Indians had made their way inside the gates, led by a Comanche chief in a red jacket reminiscent of those worn by French soldiers (Lower right corner-"F: The Captain General of the Army [of the Indians] advancing at the head of one thousand men").[31]

Fathers Molina and Terreros had an extended parlay with the leaders of the band, who expressed a desire to enter the presidio in order to acquire horses ("H: [Father Terreros] goes out to greet them with great love and speaks with them a long time in the company of Father Miguel Molina; and those barbarians, with fraud and deceit, requested peace and asked the Father President to accompany them to the Presidio"). Father Terreros wrote what was essentially a safe conduct pass to that effect, which he gave to a Tejas chief who rode away on a "borrowed" horse. At the outset of this conference, the priests had ordered gifts distributed to the Indians; by its conclusion, the padres were chatting with the leaders while trying to ignore the ransacking of the mission property going on all around them ("R: Plundering of the Mission").[32]

The Tejas chief soon returned in a rage, claiming that soldiers had killed three of his men before giving his party a chance to enter the presidio. Father Terreros and a soldier, Joseph García, mounted their horses to accompany the Indians back to the presidio but were shot out of their saddles almost immediately (Center left-"I: The Father President left with a soldier for the Presidio accompanied by a gang of barbarous Indians, who halted them with weapons in hand, when they had gone only a few paces. They shot the Father President twice in the chest and fired several other rounds at the soldier, knocking both from their horses, and sending their souls to the Creator. And not having satisfied their bloodlust, they impaled him [Father Terreros] with a spear, and with his own walking stick pierced his chest. They scalped him and stripped him, and they stripped the soldier").[33]

In the ensuing combat, two more Spaniards were killed but the remaining nine, most of them wounded, managed to gain the safety of Father Terreros's quarters and lock themselves inside. Possibly because they were not socially prominent individuals, the artist did not depict the deaths of these two mission inhabitants. Instead of pursuing the survivors, the Indians set fire to the stockade and continued to pillage the warehouse, kill the mission cattle (and its cats), and destroy the religious icons (Center–"M: Burning of the Mission" and "O: The outrages and desecrations that were performed upon the holy images and the destruction of the divine banner of Nuestra Señora de Refugio, the patroness and protector of the Mission"). The Spanish were able to pick off a number of Indians from their refuge, but fire drove these survivors of the assault into a building by the church and then into the church itself ("L: The defense of the Spaniards from the huts, in which many [Indians] were killed"), where Father Santiesteban had been killed at the beginning of the attack. He had remained in the chapel to pray after ending Mass in the wake of the Indians' appearance and Father Molina's warning ("N: The death of Father Santiesteban. They beat him and then cut off his head and kicked it about").[34]

However, all of the action did not occur inside the mission walls. As the main body of Indians surged into the grounds, a smaller band encountered an eight-man scouting party under the command of Sergeant Joseph Antonio Flores on the road to the presidio, some two miles south of the mission. The Indians killed two of Flores's men and sent the rest fleeing toward the presidio ("J: Fight between the Spaniards and Indians on the road to the Presidio where they [the Spaniards] left three dead, and the rest flee to the Presidio badly wounded"). The figure of three Spanish dead stems from Sergeant Flores's erroneous statement that three of his men were shot off of their horses in this attack.[35]

Actually, one of these three men, Joseph Vásquez, was lanced while trying to escape on his horse through the underbrush, stripped, and left for dead. He continued crawling through the brush and had reached the mission when two Indians spied him and threw him into one of the several fires on the grounds. Somehow, Vásquez rolled clear of the flames, suffering only a burned hand, and staggered to the relative safety of Father Terreros's room (Upper center–"K: A valiant soldier who, with sword in hand, defended himself in said battle, killing many Indians. He was pierced through the chest with a spear, left for dead and stripped; recovering, he walked to the Mission, where he was thrown on the fire; he escaped from it miraculously and was confessed before dying").[36] The artist's key is clearly a bit of artistic license meant to enhance the pathos of the scene, since the story of this ordeal came from Vásquez himself a few days afterwards as he was recovering, not dying, from his wounds.[37]

That night, all of the Spaniards except for the mission's chief steward, Juan Antonio Gutiérrez, were able to escape the mission under cover of darkness ("P: During the night the remaining soldiers escaped miraculously, and the women and children passed through the rabble unseen"). The unfortunate Gutiérrez, incapacitated by a severe thigh wound, was killed and his body mutilated the next day ("Q: "Death of the Majordomo. While he was still alive they gouged out his eyes and then skinned his entire body").[38]

The Destruction of Mission San Sabá was the only painting executed in Mexico in the mid-1700s that attempted to document a contemporary historical event; the few other works of art that visually depict scenes from this period in the nation's history are in the category of "historical views." Just as most American painters of the time took their artistic cues from Great Britain and, to a lesser extent, continental Europe, so colonial Mexican painters followed primarily European artistic precedents. And these precedents dictated that "history painting" referred to classical and Biblical themes. If an artist wished to portray contemporary historical figures, he dressed them in classical garb and treated the incident in which they were involved as an allegory. Traditionally, American art historians have pointed to Benjamin West's *The Death of General Wolfe* as the painting that started a "revolution" in historical painting toward realism in the portrayal of contemporary historical events (1770; Fig. 14). Although *The Destruction of Mission San Sabá* did not have a similar effect on American painting, it was painted at approximately the same time and, therefore, has an equally valid claim to the distinction of being one of the first historical paintings to portray its participants in contemporary dress.[39]

In assessing the significance of *The Destruction of Mission San Sabá*, Texas historian A. C. Greene has commented that the painting includes details omitted by subsequent historical accounts and praises the work's "role in preserving facts in the face of generations of fancy."[40] But *The Destruction of Mission San Sabá* is important primarily as an artifact, as the earliest known painting of a

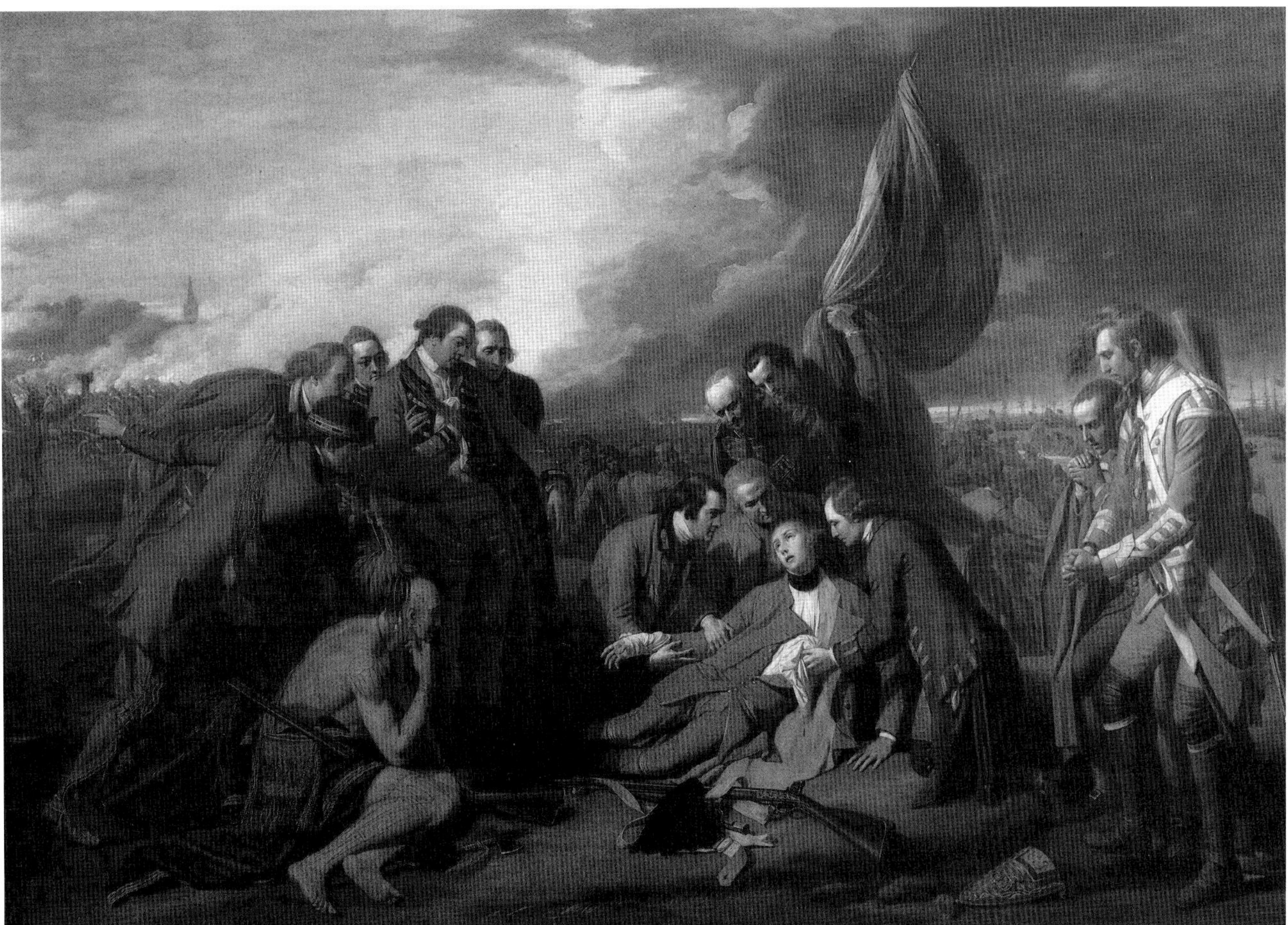

FIGURE 14. Benjamin West, *The Death of General Wolfe*, 1770.
Oil on canvas. National Gallery of Canada, Ottawa.
Acc. no. 1921/8007.

Texas historical scene by a professional artist. This significance should not be confused with whether the contents
of the work function as a historically reliable account of
the attack. Comparison with Father Molina's deposition
indicates that the painter did include many of the events
mentioned by the priest, although the wording of the
alphabetized key is not a literal transcription of his account. But the artist also omitted some events, such as
Juan Leal's experience, while embellishing others.

Taking note of Father Molina's eye-witness account,
Greene has termed *The Destruction of Mission San Sabá* "a
letter from the battlefield."[41] Certainly, the painting has
much to commend it as a piece of visual, documentary
evidence of the battle, especially since it was executed
shortly after the massacre, and a survivor may have advised the artist. However, as in the case of any "letter,"
this one has a point of view. While the painting *may* serve
as something of a visual documentary of the massacre, it
was intended primarily to be a work of hagiography,

with history being a secondary, although admittedly important, consideration. This is evidenced by the prominence of the depictions of Fathers Santiesteban and Terreros and the attention devoted to their lives. Indeed,
the canvas was soon famous in Spain as well as Mexico
and served beautifully as a piece of "contemporary propaganda and . . . current morality."[42] The painting seems
to have been celebrated at the time primarily for its ideological overtones rather than for its aesthetic or documentary qualities. It carried the message that Fathers
Santiesteban and Terreros had been martyred not only in
the service of God by barbaric heathens but also in the
service of Spain, since their murderers allegedly had been
in league with Spain's foremost imperial rival, France.

The San Sabá massacre did more than shock the sensibilities of colonial Mexico. The attack on the mission
proved to be a crucial incident in New Spain's process of
trying to subdue its northern frontier, as this first armed
clash with Comanches led to events that profoundly

altered the entire Spanish philosophy of settlement in Texas. Seventeen months after the massacre, Colonel Ortiz Parrilla led a punitive expedition against the tribes responsible for the destruction of the mission. The Spaniards and their Indian allies met the Comanches and members of other northern tribes on the Red River at a Wichita (Taovaya) village, near a place that came to be known, ironically, as "Spanish Fort." Led by the Wichitas, the Indians charged out from behind protective barricades and fought Ortiz Parrilla's troops to a draw. The Spaniards retreated to San Sabá, then made their way to San Antonio; this northernmost penetration of the Southwest by a Spanish military force directed against Indian enemies proved to be a failure.[43]

A decade later, King Charles III sent his inspector general, the Marqués de Rubí, on a fact-finding tour of the northern frontier of New Spain. Rubí was charged with assessing the situation on the frontier and with formulating policies in light of what he discovered. In 1772, the king promulgated virtually all of Rubí's suggestions in the "New Regulation of the Presidios."[44] This directive resulted in Spain's reorganization of its northern frontier, which ratified the 1768 abandonment of Mission San Sabá and Presidio de San Luis Amarillas. *The Destruction of Mission San Sabá* dramatized the event that, more than any other single incident, crystallized the changes that had been wrought by the northern tribes' acquisition of French firearms and Spanish horses over the previous half-century.

Although the Rubí report prompted Spain to withdraw most of its missions from Texas, settlements planted by the Spaniards remained, as did much of the administrative apparatus of the Spanish Empire. During the next two decades, another group of interlopers frustrated Spanish officials in their attempts to secure the Texas border even more than had French infiltration. By 1790, a few American citizens, such as horse-hunter and trader Philip Nolan, had begun to filter into Texas. Killed in an 1801 battle with Spanish soldiers, Nolan was a harbinger of the surge of United States interest in the lands across its southwestern border that would be ignited by the Louisiana Purchase in 1803. Within a few years after the Purchase, many more Americans had passed through Texas. Some were part of an official expedition of exploration led by U.S. Army Major Stephen H. Long in 1819–1820; others served in armed, civilian-supported campaigns seeking to end Spanish control of Texas, such as those led by filibusters James Magee in 1812–1813 and James Long in 1820. Magee's "Green Flag Rebellion" and the Long Expedition became intertwined with the larger revolt of Mexico against Spanish rule that began in 1810 and culminated in Mexican independence on 27 September 1821.[45]

A few months before Mexico won its independence, Spain mounted a final attempt to promote settlement of its northeastern province. On 1 March 1821, the Spanish Minister for Overseas Affairs stressed that "the populating of Texas required the most urgent circumspection as well as the greatest prudence in the matter of the distribution of the land of that immense territory."[46] Hoping that such a population would furnish a buffer between hostile Indian tribes and the *ranchos* of northern Mexico, Spanish authorities already had awarded an entrepreneur from Missouri, Moses Austin, the title of "empresario," which entailed the power to issue grants of thousands of acres of land but also the accompanying responsibility to recruit a minimum of three hundred families to accept these grants. Although the agreement acknowledged that grantees would come from the United States, these individuals had to fulfill several conditions, including proof that they were of "good character" and renunciation of American citizenship and Protestantism in favor of Spanish citizenship and Roman Catholicism, before they could receive grants of up to four thousand acres per family.[47]

On 10 June 1821, Moses Austin died before he could assume these obligations, which were then taken on by his son, Stephen Fuller Austin. Even though the younger Austin had to deal with government officials of a newly independent Mexico, he found them to be as eager to build up the population of Texas as had been their Spanish predecessors. A report by Mexico's Committee on Foreign Relations, formed just three days after independence was declared, rhapsodized that Texas was "so fertile, of such benign climate, and so rich in metals and natural resources" that it could easily be mistaken for "Paradise."[48] Over the next nine years, in order to draw settlers to this New Eden, the Mexican government awarded twenty-five empresario grants. Although all of these empresarios did not fill their recruitment quotas, they played a crucial role in bringing Anglo-American settlers into Texas during the 1820s. Within his colony, an empresario acted as a combination of immigration officer, chief surveyor and registrar of land titles, organizer of the colony's militia, and final arbiter of disputes between colonists.

In 1874, Major Moses Austin Bryan, Stephen F. Austin's nephew, suggested to painter Henry McArdle that the artist immortalize Austin's role in the settlement of Texas. This suggestion meshed well with research on

Texas historical subjects begun a few years earlier by McArdle, who hoped to procure state patronage. He envisioned *The Settlement of Austin's Colony* (1875; Pl. 6), also known as *The Log Cabin*, as the first of a series of works in "which I hope to illustrate to posterity the grand achievements of the heroes and statesmen of the Texas Revolution."[49] In 1888, after Major Bryan was unable to fulfill his verbal commitment to pay for the finished canvas, McArdle unsuccessfully lobbied a committee appointed by the state legislature for a portion of a ten-thousand-dollar appropriation designated for paintings for the new Capitol. But the committee, consisting of Governor Lawrence Sullivan Ross, Secretary of State Y. M. Moore, and Commissioner of Insurance, Statistics, and History L. L. Foster, directed that these funds go to one of McArdle's professional rivals, William Henry Huddle. However, the legislature did allow McArdle to hang *The Settlement of Austin's Colony* in the Capitol until it was purchased by Texas art collector and popular historian James DeShields in 1901; the legislature bought the canvas from DeShields in 1928.[50]

In *The Settlement of Austin's Colony*, McArdle depicted a moment in 1824 when Stephen F. Austin, "Empresario, General, Judge, and 'Father of the Colony,' issuing land titles and surrounded by his aid[e]s, is arrested in his work by the hasty entrance of a scout (a new comer which is readable by his excited manner and store clothes)." Warning of approaching "Carauchua" (Karankawa) Indians, the unnamed scout, his headband stained with blood, points upriver to burning cabins in the distance that are visible through the window and door.[51] Although the title of the painting does not link it to a particular event, McArdle's brief explanation indicates that he had in mind Austin's campaign against the Karankawas in the late summer of 1824. During the previous year, settlers in the Austin Colony had had recurring hostilities with this fierce and occasionally cannibalistic tribe. They interspersed frequent requests to Mexican authorities for protection from the Karankawas with expressions of determination to "give them a good drubbing" and to "sweep away every . . . Karrankowa [*sic*] Indian from the face of the earth"; in the autumn of 1823, even the usually moderate Austin regarded war with the tribe as "inevitable."[52] Following the 1824 campaign, which destroyed approximately half the tribe, and a failed peace treaty, a lasting treaty between the colonists and the Karankawas was signed in 1827. Ironically, diseases from white colonists that devastated the tribe soon reduced its few remaining members to a condition of almost total dependence on their former adversaries.[53]

Instead of depicting any of the colonists' battles with the Karankawas, McArdle chose to assemble a collection of portraits of a few notable figures in the colony while attempting to adhere to an ideal of historical symbolism. For McArdle, Indian wars gave an occasion to celebrate courage by intrepid Anglo settlers in the face of danger. He was especially concerned to present Austin as a capable leader in either peace or war: the empresario, whose sword represents his authority, reaches for a musket over the doorway with his right hand. In his left hand, the volume entitled *Laws of Mexico* indicates Austin's role as lawgiver and arbiter of disputes, although the lawbook's English title definitely constitutes a bit of artistic license by McArdle. Two of the colony's most important figures are relegated to the margin of the scene: Land Commissioner Baron de Bastrop, who was instrumental in enabling Moses Austin to obtain the empresario grant, and Samuel M. Williams, secretary of the colony and an early advocate of Texas independence from Mexico, look on from the extreme left and right, respectively. Seated in front of Williams, Ran Foster, the colony's chief scout, gazes pensively at Austin as the empresario's cook, Simon, stares through the open window behind Foster's right shoulder. At Austin's feet, Horatio Chriesman, surveyor for the colony, glances up from his task of diagraming a tract of land. Some observers noted McArdle's attention to historical detail as evidenced by his inclusion of Chriesman's compass and water gourd, which the surveyor customarily carried on expeditions, in the immediate foreground.[54]

Despite sporadic conflicts with Indian tribes, the Austin Colony prospered, and other American settlers, motivated by Mexico's offer of plentiful land at extremely low prices, flocked to the region that one of them termed "a lazy man's paradise."[55] Still other American citizens circumvented the legalities of the Mexican land distribution and settlement system. By 1821, approximately eighty families of Anglo-Americans had settled around the trading centers of Jonesborough and Pecan Point on the Red River in the northeastern corner of Texas. Far removed from any effective jurisdiction of the Spanish and, later, the Mexican government, these intruders were closely linked by commerce, communication, and family ties to states such as Kentucky, Missouri, and Tennessee. By the end of the 1820s, a total of twenty thousand Anglos lived legally and illegally in the Mexican administrative departments of Brazoria and Nacogdoches in central and eastern Texas and already had molded a culture that strongly resembled that of the southern frontier regions of the United States.[56]

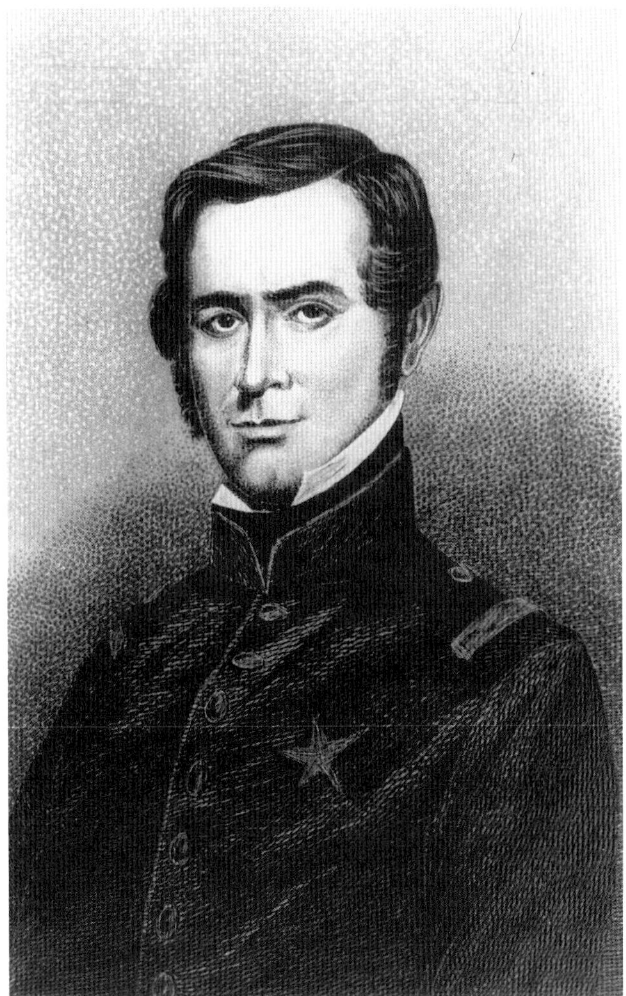

FIGURE 15. Ben Milam, n.d. Archives Division-Texas State Library. Acc. no. 1979/181-4.

Many Mexican authorities noted these influences with an anxiety that had been mounting since the introduction of the empresario system. Before Mexican independence, some Spanish officials had voiced reservations about the decision to issue empresario grants to United States citizens, and, during the 1820s, several measures were introduced in the Mexican Congress to establish an "Anglo-free" zone in Texas of up to 450 miles wide. In 1829, the Barradas Expedition's attempt to retake Mexico for Spain heightened the already aroused sensitivities of Mexican officials toward any threat to the nation's sovereignty. In the same year, General Manuel Mier y Terán, commander of an expedition that had just completed a survey of the U.S.–Mexican boundary in accordance with provisions of the 1819 Adams-Onís Treaty, warned of the impending "catastrophe of Texas."[57]

These fears culminated in the Decree of 6 April 1830, which, among its other provisions, forbade further immigration from the United States. Austin and other empresarios were able to skirt this regulation, which was not stringently enforced, but the decree angered a great many colonists. A year later, a Mexican propaganda campaign designed to prompt Mexican citizens to settle in Texas included newspaper articles portraying the region in glowing terms. Accompanying advertisements played on the earlier image of "exotic Texas," such as that found in one notice that trumpeted the "extraordinary effect that [Texas] bear oil possesses in beautifying the hair."[58] But these efforts resulted in meager settlement, and, in June 1832, government officials were further frustrated when disputes over collection of customs duties escalated into armed confrontations between small groups of firebrand Anglo-Texans and Mexican soldiers stationed at the ports of Anahuac and Velasco. The incident at Anahuac resulted only in the jailing and subsequent release of the Anglo-Texan leaders, Patrick Jack and William Barret Travis. However, the Velasco confrontation proved to be more serious, as the insurgents forced the garrison's commanding officer, General Domingo de Ugartechea, to evacuate his troops. Austin and other moderate Anglo leaders condemned these "troublemakers," but relations with Mexican authorities had been permanently strained.[59]

Confrontational Anglo-Texans had been emboldened by a revolt in Mexico led by professed liberal Antonio López de Santa Anna that overthrew the Anastasio Bustamente government during the summer of 1832. The following October, Texan colonists convened for a week in San Felipe, the center of Anglo-American settlement, and passed resolutions requesting Santa Anna to lift immigration and customs regulations and grant separate statehood to Texas. These resolutions made frequent reference to the Mexican Constitution of 1824, which had contained language that encouraged Anglo- and Hispanic-Texans alike in their desire for separation from the state of Coahuila and statehood for Texas. Although Mexican authorities declared this 1832 gathering illegal, the colonists soon scheduled another for the next spring, which met in April 1833, also in San Felipe. This second convention adopted all of the resolutions of the previous autumn and took the even bolder, unauthorized step of drafting a constitution for a separate state of Texas within the Mexican federation. The delegates commissioned a reluctant Stephen F. Austin to travel to Mexico City to present the colonists' proposals to Santa Anna, who had assumed the presidency.

After cooling his heels for several months in the capital without being granted an audience by the Mexican leader, Austin imprudently suggested in a letter to the San Antonio *ayuntamiento* (municipal government) that Texas form a state government without approval of the national authorities. While Austin was returning to Texas, after Santa Anna had rejected his proposal of separate statehood, Mexican authorities' discovery of this letter resulted in the Texan leader's arrest in January 1834.[60] During Austin's ensuing eighteen-month imprisonment, Santa Anna declared publicly that "I shall send four to six thousand men to Texas to punish those turbulent, insolent North Americans . . . if they resist in the least, all their property will be confiscated and I shall convert Texas into a desert."[61] In September 1835, after Austin's release and return to Texas, his pronouncement that "war is our only resource" swept away the last significant Texas opposition to armed resistance.[62]

In October 1835, an armed band of Anglo-Texans forced the strategic withdrawal of a Mexican force at Gonzales in a dispute over ownership of a cannon that had been lent to the community by Mexican authorities as protection against Indian attack. In the weeks following this success, Austin led an army of colonists and American volunteers toward San Antonio, where General Martín Perfecto de Cós was entrenched with 700 Mexican regulars. Austin's undisciplined force fluctuated between 300 and 600 men as its members periodically visited their homes on the march from Gonzales. By the end of October, the Texans had surrounded San Antonio and had begun a siege that soon degenerated into a stalemate. The Mexican army had insufficient firepower to drive off the besiegers, but many Texan leaders, including Austin and former Tennessee governor Sam Houston, felt their own forces to be inadequate for an assault on the Mexican position.[63]

On 18 November, Austin was informed that the Texans' provisional government had appointed him as one of three commissioners to travel to the United States in order to raise support for the Texan cause. He attempted to disband his army, but 400 men voted to continue the siege and elected Edward C. Burleson as their commanding officer. On 3 December, following Burleson's hesitance to order an assault, two leaders of the army's more aggressive faction, Ben Milam and Frank Johnson, futilely attempted to change their commander's mind. After this conference, Milam disgustedly emerged from Burleson's tent and shouted, "Who will go with old Ben Milam into San Antonio?" Some 240 men, many of them

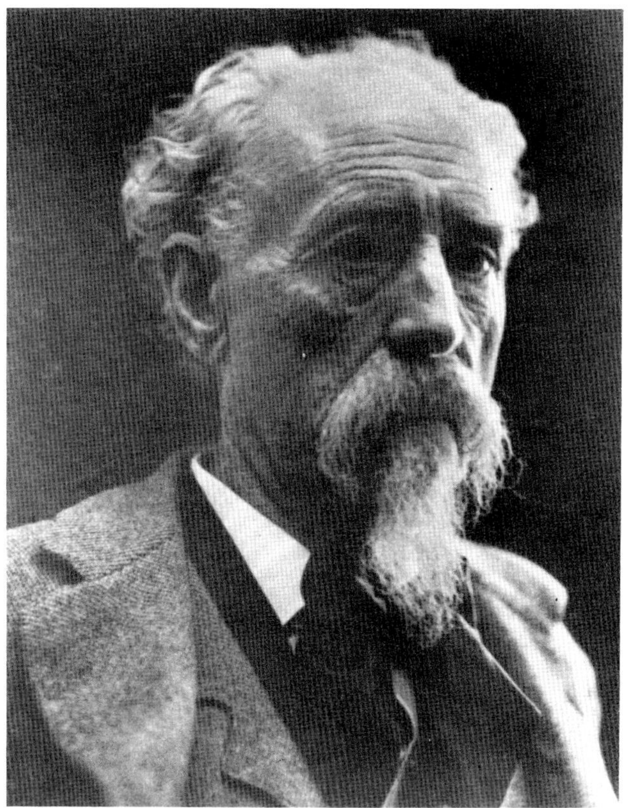

FIGURE 16. Henry Arthur McArdle, n.d. Archives Division-Texas State Library. Acc. no. 1979/181-8.

members of the volunteer New Orleans Greys, shouted their approval. On the dawn of 5 December, Milam led the Texan assault on the fortified city. After five days of house-to-house fighting, in which Milam was killed by a sniper's bullet, General Cós surrendered.[64]

Henry McArdle attempted to capture the drama of Milam's challenge in *Ben Milam Calling for Volunteers* (1901; Pl. 7). In many respects, this work resembles *The Settlement of Austin's Colony*, even though a quarter-century separates the execution of the two paintings. Each canvas focuses on a heroic individual and emphasizes portraiture rather than action in narrating a dramatic incident. In focusing on these vignettes, McArdle treated the scenes as static collections of portraits. His more effective paintings, such as *Dawn at the Alamo* (1905) and *The Battle of San Jacinto* (1895), emphasized action and were composed on a far larger scale; these works are discussed in Chapters 2 and 3, respectively.

In executing *Ben Milam*, McArdle strived to offset his artistic deficiencies with extensive research and the same attention to detail that had marked *The Settlement of Austin's Colony*. His research, conducted in late 1900 and during 1901, consisted primarily of correspondence with J. R. Milam, son of the fallen Texas hero. These letters were accompanied by photographic reproductions of portraits of Milam and contained J. R. Milam's observations on aspects of his father's physical appearance, such as his "dark, piercing eyes."[65] In depicting his subject's facial features, McArdle relied on a photograph taken of a portrait of Milam in his American uniform from the War of 1812 (n.d.; Fig. 15). Milam's pose, standing erect and right arm bent at the elbow, resembles strongly that of the figure of Austin in *The Settlement of Austin's Colony*.

McArdle drew other elements of *Ben Milam* from the account of Texas Revolution veteran Creed Taylor, which Taylor had dictated to James DeShields shortly before the veteran's death. DeShields later edited these recollections and published them as *Tall Men with Long Rifles* in 1935. The genesis of DeShields's relationship with Taylor is as clouded as McArdle's motivation for undertaking the Milam painting. But DeShields evidently possessed this manuscript by 1900, when McArdle began researching the events of the battle of San Antonio while working with DeShields on other projects. McArdle followed closely Taylor's description of Milam's brief speech: the Texan leader is "waving his old slouch hat above his head," and the narrow path behind the tree stump in the foreground may result from Taylor's recollection that Milam "drew a line on the ground with the stock of his rifle."[66] The artist also included the flag carried by the victorious Texans from Gonzales, bearing the crude drawing of a cannon above the legend, "Come and Take It," which Taylor had also mentioned.[67] The composition of *Ben Milam* reflects the close working relationship between DeShields and McArdle, in which patron and artist freely exchanged ideas and research material (Fig. 16).

Despite the loss of Milam, a charismatic leader, the battle for San Antonio represented a resounding success for the Texas insurgents. As part of the conditions of his surrender, General Cós pledged never again to take up arms against the Texas settlers. But the entire 1835 campaign's series of victories by a hastily assembled volunteer army over professional soldiers bred overconfidence and a false sense of security in the Texans. As Cós and his troops marched toward the Rio Grande, many members of the victorious army believed that they had seen the last of armed struggle against Mexico.

CHAPTER TWO

Let Us Band Together as Brothers

THE OPTIMISTIC BELIEF of many of the Texan insurgents that the 1835 battle for San Antonio marked the end of fighting against the Mexican army proved to be a strategic miscalculation, as Santa Anna led approximately six thousand troops into Texas in February 1836. At the same time, he sent another force of twelve hundred men under General José Urrea sweeping northeastward from Matamoros across the coastal plains. Within a week after entering Texas, Santa Anna's soldiers were clattering into San Antonio, exhausted from a forced march over dry, rugged terrain. Instead of striking initially at the heart of the insurgency, the Anglo-American settlements in the eastern regions of Texas, the Mexican leader had decided to attack fewer than two hundred Texans who had fortified Mission San Antonio de Valero, better known as "the Alamo," which their forces had captured the previous December.[1]

The Alamo's defenders typified the population of the United States southwestern frontier in the 1830s. A motley collection of Tejanos, Americans from all parts of the United States, and citizens of several European nations, each of them had been drawn to Texas and the Alamo by a wide variety of circumstances. Nineteenth-century painters would give special prominence to three of their number: James Bowie, David Crockett, and William Barret Travis. Bowie, a highly successful frontier entrepreneur, had profited from slave trading and marriage to the daughter of a wealthy Mexican landowner, while also earning a reputation as a skillful and ferocious fighter. Crockett was the most famous Alamo defender and had

arrived in Texas only a few weeks before Santa Anna's army. Disgusted after losing his seat in the United States Congress as a representative from Tennessee, he hoped to make a fortune by speculating in Texas lands. William Travis was less open about his reasons for emigrating to Texas from his native Alabama. Rumored to have fled his home under suspicion of murder, Travis had quickly risen to a leadership role in the circles of Texan extremists agitating for independence from Mexico soon after he arrived in Texas in 1831.[2]

Santa Anna's motives for halting his advance to reduce this Texas outpost were questioned by his contemporaries as well as by later historians. Simply bypassing San Antonio and leaving the garrison intact would not have threatened the Mexican army's war-making capabilities, such as communication or supply lines. Furthermore, Santa Anna, the self-styled "Napoleon of the West," violated key principles of the French leader's strategy by laying siege to the Alamo, a fortified position in a militarily insignificant area of Texas. But the Texan defenders also overestimated the Alamo's importance, even after the garrison's commander, Colonel J. C. Neill, was ordered by Texan commander-in-chief Sam Houston to destroy the Alamo and withdraw from San Antonio in January 1836. As did Santa Anna, Neill's successors, Bowie and Travis, attributed a misplaced strategic importance to San Antonio that prodded them to defend the Alamo. Their belief that the mission grounds could be adequately fortified contradicted the opinion of their chief engineer, Green B. Jameson. Jameson was proven to be correct:

following a two-week siege, Santa Anna's troops overwhelmed the Alamo garrison in a frontal assault, though they suffered a casualty rate of 25 percent. The great irony of the Alamo's subsequent symbolism is that the battle was brought on by the decision of the attacking army's leader to besiege a strategically inconsequential position manned by a garrison in defiance of orders by its government's commander-in-chief.[3]

Immediately following the Texan war for independence, the battle for the Alamo caught the fancy of the American popular imagination. Despite this national fascination, Texans were curiously apathetic concerning any attempt at preservation of the site of the war's most widely known battle. San Antonio residents gave little thought to such efforts, preferring instead to do a brisk trade in relics fashioned from rubble of the Alamo buildings. In the early 1840s, after encouragement from Captain Reuben Potter, a veteran of the Texas Revolution and one of its first historians, two of the city's artisans did sculpt a monument to the Alamo defenders out of crushed pieces of the mission's masonry. In 1858, after this sculpture had been displayed in several Texas towns, the Texas state legislature purchased it and placed it in the Capitol vestibule; only fragments survived an 1881 fire that destroyed the building.[4]

When nineteenth-century artists did begin to treat the Alamo as a subject, their initial works concentrated on the site itself rather than on the events of the siege and battle. Even though these works played an important part in the development of the Alamo as an icon and symbol, they are architectural studies and/or landscape scenes rather than examples of historical narrative painting. This chapter mentions them only insofar as they relate to those paintings dealing with the events of the battle and focuses instead on four nineteenth-century artists who executed works concerning various aspects of the massacre: Louis Eyth, Theodore Gentilz, Henry McArdle, and Robert Onderdonk.

Unlike *The Destruction of Mission San Sabá*, Alamo battle paintings were not executed until at least four decades following the event that they depicted. This time lag meant that these works expressed the culmination of public reaction to accounts of the battle and served as ideological and emotional filters for subsequent depictions in other visual media. While each Alamo artist ascribed varying functions and aspirations to his painting(s), all of them resembled the artist of *The Destruction of Mission San Sabá* in their efforts to achieve the twin goals of documentation and hagiography. An un-

derstanding of these painters' intentions to create visual historical documents as well as patriotic symbols entails scrutinizing their use of written and oral historical sources, of advisors, the role of patronage, audience expectations, and the varying emphases on each of these factors in the work of each artist. Prior to examining individually these questions of artistic creation and intent, a brief survey of the Alamo's evolution as a popular culture symbol will serve to place the battle paintings within a context of remembrance.

By the 1870s, the Civil War and Reconstruction had effected a fundamental change in the Texas historical consciousness, as Texans found their war for independence to be the ideal touchstone for easing the pain of recent defeat. On the eve of the Civil War, Reuben Potter had offered a harbinger of this interest with publication of a pamphlet that served as a reference point for remembrance of the Battle of the Alamo for the remainder of the century.[5] In the postwar years, the 1873 founding of the Texas Veterans Association reflected a grassroots effort to utilize memories of the Revolution for patriotic ends. The next year, soon after the first post-Reconstruction Texas government took office, former soldiers from both sides of the "late unpleasantness" formed San Antonio's Alamo Rifles militia company, adopting a patriotic name that could unify both groups of veterans.[6]

The centennial celebration of the United States in Philadelphia also heightened interest in Texas history in less martial and occasionally unexpected ways. San Antonio businessmen who visited the festivities drew inspiration from the flood of 1876 souvenirs and began utilizing reproductions of the visual image of the Alamo for similar purposes. Other parties also undertook unprecedented attempts to memorialize the Alamo site, such as in 1877, when a few Texas newspapers suggested its purchase by the state of Texas. This suggestion was fulfilled in part three years later when the state bought the chapel, the building most often referred to as "the Alamo."[7]

Despite these gestures, the site was still largely neglected; visitors were "surprised and indignant at the condition in which they found the shrine of Texas liberty," bemoaning its use as "a grocery warehouse . . . a strange, very strange mingling of fame and sourkraut [*sic*]."[8] Ironically, this physical deterioration of the site coincided with increased artistic interpretation of the battle in novels, plays, and poems. Instead of dealing with mundane problems of the Alamo's physical maintenance, Texans had turned their attention to its "historic and symbolic landscapes."[9]

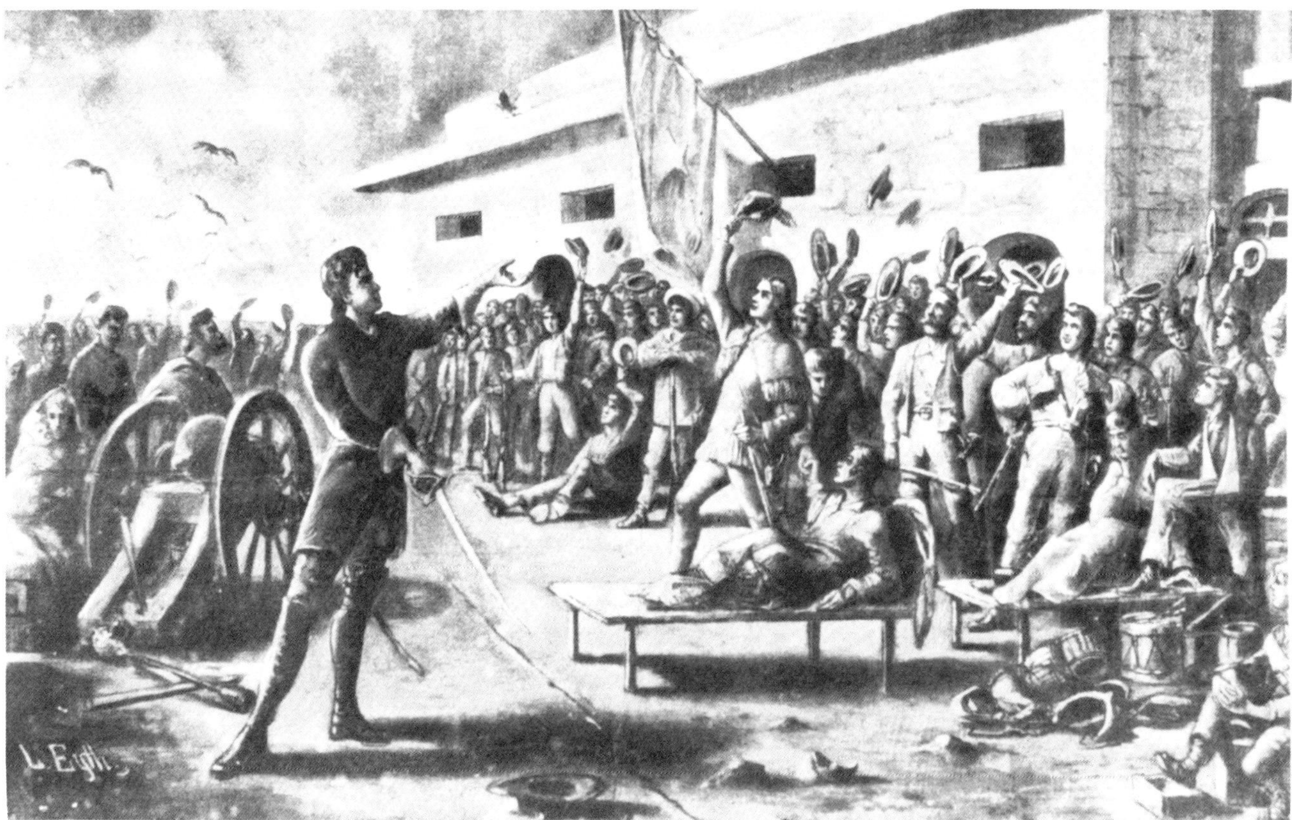

FIGURE 17. Louis Eyth, *The Speech of Travis to His Men at the Alamo,* ca. 1878. Medium unknown. Unlocated; photograph from Pauline Pinckney, *Painting in Texas;* courtesy of the University of Texas Press. Photograph by King Douglas, Dallas, Texas.

The earliest known paintings of the battle appeared during these years of renewed interest in the symbolic value of the Alamo. Unfortunately, only photographic reproductions exist of Galveston portraitist Louis Eyth's (1838–ca. 1889) *The Speech of Travis to His Men at the Alamo* (ca. 1878; Fig. 17) and *Death of Bowie: A Command from the Mexicans that He Be Killed* (ca. 1878; Fig. 18). Eyth left no collection of papers and is one of the most mysterious figures in the cultural history of Texas. Although his only professional training was as a daguerreotypist, he was able to earn a commission from the Texas state government to copy a portrait of Stephen F. Austin for the Capitol in 1873. This appointment brought him to the attention of James DeShields, who then commissioned Eyth to illustrate several of his books. The whereabouts of Eyth's Alamo paintings are unknown; they may have been destroyed in a 1918 fire in DeShields's home in the Oak Cliff section of Dallas, along with several works by Henry McArdle that also are unlocated.[10]

Despite the scarcity of facts regarding Eyth and many of his works, he obviously based *Speech of Travis* on a story by W. P. Zuber of Nacogdoches that appeared in the 1873 *Texas Almanac*. Zuber maintained that, a few days after the Alamo fell, a haggard, middle-aged man, carrying a blood-stained bundle of clothing, had appeared at his family's door. The decrepit figure claimed to be Moses Rose, a veteran of the Napoleonic wars who had slipped over the wall of the Alamo the night before Santa Anna's army stormed the fortress. According to Zuber, Rose related that Alamo commander William Travis, after receiving definite word that his men would receive no reinforcements, assembled the garrison and appealed, "Let us band together as brothers and vow to die together."[11] Following his speech, Travis drew a line in the dirt with his sword between himself and his men, giving them the option to "escape with dignity" or to cross over the line and, as Jim Bowie, the garrison's former co-commander, had written in one appeal for aid, "die in these ditches."[12]

As Texas folklorist J. Frank Dobie noted over sixty

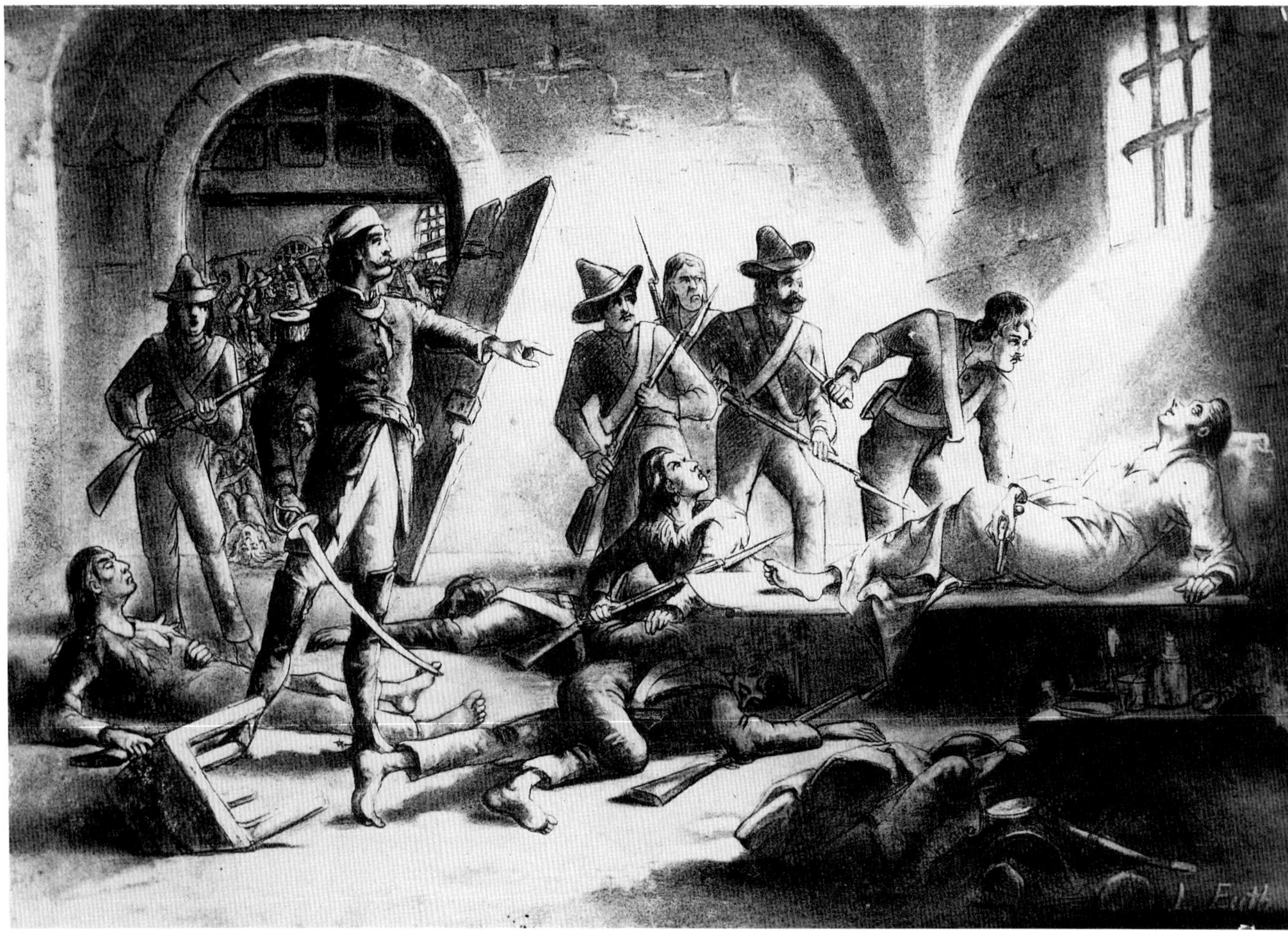

FIGURE 18. Louis Eyth, *Death of Bowie: A Command from the Mexicans that He Be Killed,* ca. 1878. Medium unknown. Unlocated; photograph from the Daughters of the Republic of Texas Library at the Alamo, San Antonio, Texas.

years later, Zuber's story "was something new, dramatic and vital to inflame the imagination of the Texas people, a people who . . . cherish the Alamo as they cherish no other spot either in Texas or in the world beyond." [13] Zuber acknowledged freely that the speech was the result of a composite of gleanings from his own slight acquaintance with Travis, Travis's speeches and writings, and, even, ideas from Zuber's mother. Nevertheless, the tale was popularized as fact almost immediately by such authors as Sidney Lanier and began to appear in Texas history textbooks during the 1880s. One of the Alamo's survivors, Susannah Dickinson, wife of the garrison's artillery commander, Captain Almeron Dickinson, confirmed belatedly that Travis had made a speech to his men in which he presented them with the option of fleeing the fortress. Perhaps, if Travis indeed did address the garrison in this fashion, he had in mind Ben Milam's words to the Texan forces before their successful storming of San Antonio. If, on the other hand, Zuber chronicled a fictional incident, he may well have drawn inspiration from accounts of Milam's challenge. While scholars have debated the veracity of Travis's speech as well as whether a "Moses Rose" ever escaped from the Alamo, the image of 183 men willingly choosing death over surrender furnished subsequent generations of mythmakers with a dramatic hinge for the entire saga of the Alamo. The incident served the function of transforming a motley assortment of frontiersmen into "true Texans" and, more importantly, heroes and has remained as the "most cherished moment of the Alamo myth [that] captures [the] democratic spirit." [14]

A surviving pencil sketch for *Speech of Travis* indicates

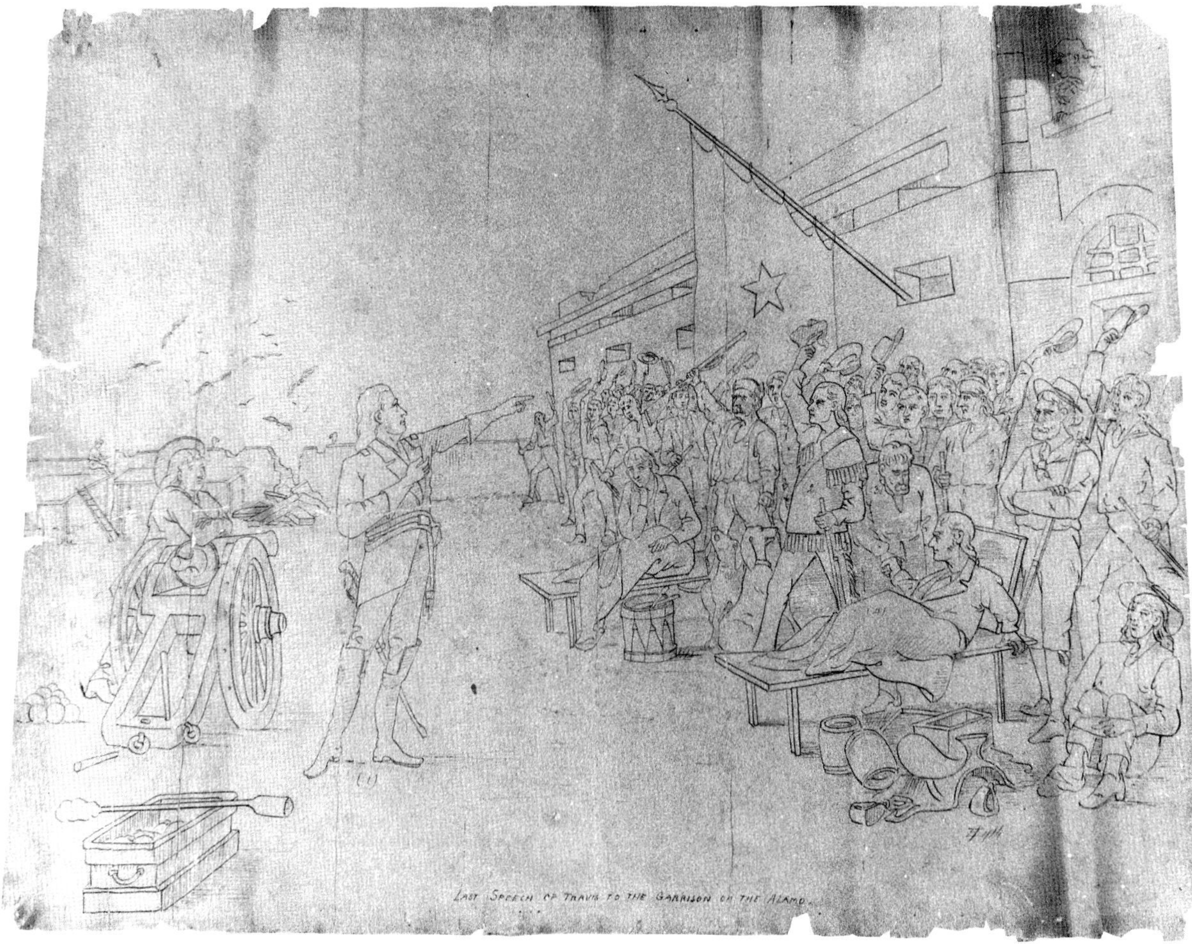

FIGURE 19. Louis Eyth, *Last Speech of Travis to the Garrison of the Alamo*, sketch for *The Speech of Travis to His Men at the Alamo*, n.d. Pencil. James T. DeShields Collection, San Antonio, Texas. Photograph by Mark Edward Smith, Austin, Texas.

that Eyth altered his conception of this scene very little before its completion (ca. 1878; Fig. 19). In both the sketch and the finished version, the response of Travis's listeners at first seems incongruous with the solemn content of his speech until the viewer recognizes that the attention of Travis and his men is directed toward the flag in the right center portion of the scene. This element of Eyth's work is also controversial, for a great deal of confusion has surrounded the question of the design of any flag that the defenders may have flown. Recent scholarship has determined that only the azure flag of a volunteer unit, the New Orleans Greys, was displayed above the fortress. Due to the fragmentary information concerning Eyth, it is difficult to ascertain precisely what information he utilized for his rendering of this flag, but sorting out various nineteenth-century accounts sheds

light on his method of composition. In 1860, Reuben Potter originated the notion that the Alamo garrison displayed a version of the Mexican national flag that substituted "1824" for the eagle and serpent in the banner's center in order to denote allegiance to the principles of the Constitution of 1824. Though widely accepted for many years thereafter, this account evidently played little or no role in Eyth's composition. Other versions of the story of the siege stated that the defenders flew the two-starred state flag of Coahuila-Texas, and Eyth might have garbled this information in painting a banner with a single star. But Eyth also may have employed a variation of the post-1836 Texas flag in an effort to convey the idea that the defenders believed themselves to be fighting for the creation of a separate nation.[15]

An 1836 volume, *Col. Crockett's Exploits*, lends the

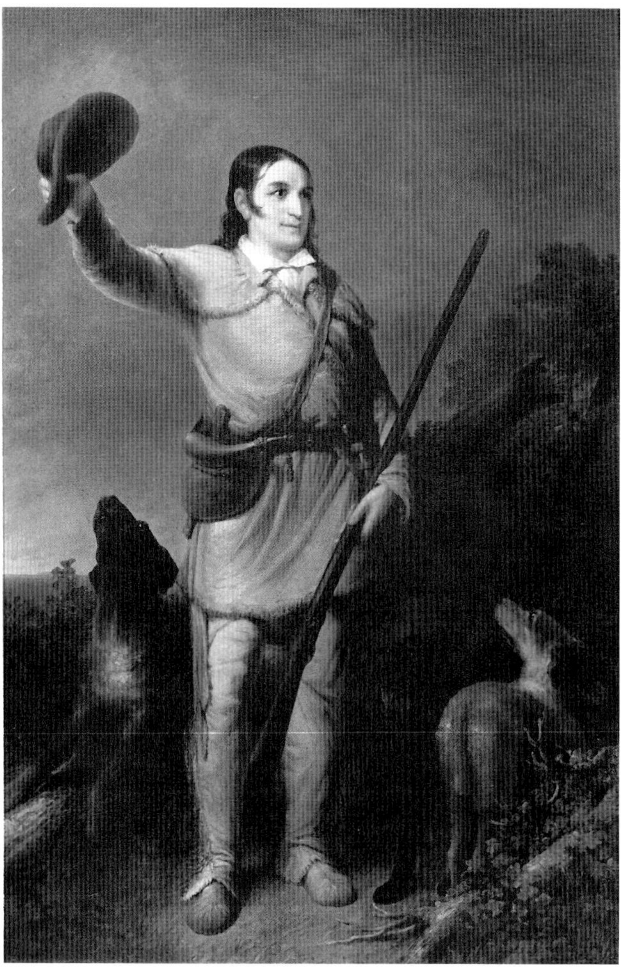

FIGURE 20. John Gadsby Chapman, *David Crockett*, n.d. Oil. Harry Ransom Humanities Research Center Art Collection, The University of Texas at Austin. Acc. no. 65.349.

strongest clue as to the source of Eyth's inspiration for *Speech of Travis*. Maintaining the fanciful but common and persistent notion that Davy Crockett survived the battle, the writer paraphrases a wildly inaccurate "memorandum" allegedly left by Crockett declaring that the defenders "unfurled an immense flag of thirteen stripes, red and white, alternately, on a blue ground with a large white star, of five points, in the centre, and between the points the letters TEXAS . . . three cheers went up and drum and trumpets hurled back their challenge to the foe."[16] Although this flag differs from Eyth's and the writer makes no mention of Travis's speech, the artist has combined this tale with Zuber's story to convey the impression that these men are looking triumphantly beyond their deaths to a vision of a nation that will esteem their deaths as sacrifices essential to its birth.

The possibility of Eyth's familiarity with this account is reinforced by Crockett's prominence in the scene. Directly beneath the flag, he hails Travis's words as his fellow defenders toss their hats into the air. Eyth's Crockett bears a strong resemblance to John Gadsby Chapman's portrait of the Tennessean that hung in the Texas Capitol until it burned in 1881; fortunately, a smaller version of this painting survives (n.d.; Fig. 20). Eyth clearly patterned his portrayal of Crockett after this work, even though one of Eyth's contemporaries, Texas humorist and newspaperman Alexander E. Sweet, had claimed that Chapman's Crockett resembled "the effeminate youth of the present day who sucks at the end of a [candy] cane."[17] As in *Speech of Travis*, Crockett is flourishing a hat in his right hand in this portrait. But Eyth has substituted the "peculiar cap" that Susannah Dickinson noticed at the side of Crockett's corpse after the battle.[18] Mrs. Dickinson was the only source for many details of the battle, especially those dealing with Mexican brutality, and her recollections served as an important, but sometimes inadequate, nineteenth-century source of Anglo-Texan versions of the events at the Alamo.[19] Eyth depicts the frontiersman in a half profile, as opposed to Chapman's full-faced view, but his artistic debt to Chapman is evident in the details of Crockett's buckskin costume and, even, his sideburns.

A few of the individuals in the scene do not join in this celebration of approaching self-sacrifice. The figure of Jim Bowie, bedridden with pneumonia since early in the siege, lends the most somber note. Eyth's work conforms to another celebrated aspect of the Zuber story, as Bowie is able only to half-rise on his cot and grip the hand of one of his fellows to request that he be carried across the line in order to declare his solidarity with the garrison. Behind Bowie, a soldier stares pensively at the ground, chin resting in his hand. Could Eyth have meant this figure to represent Moses Rose, weighing his decision? Directly across from him, at the extreme left, Eyth has included Mrs. Dickinson and her child, huddled to the left of a cannon.

In contrast to the generally triumphant *Speech of Travis*, Eyth's *Death of Bowie* depicts the moment when Mexican soldiers broke into the sickroom of the Alamo's former co-commander in the low barracks, east of the main gate. Eyth's painting follows the most widely accepted version of Bowie's death as four soldiers, bayonets fixed, hesitate at his bedside and gaze intently upon his prone form in an uncertainty that may arise either from compassion or from a belief that Bowie is already dead.

A dandified, saber-wielding Mexican officer overrules the infantrymen's hesitation as he commands them to execute their wounded prey. The Mexican soldiers have only a slightly less genteel appearance than does their commander, and the entire atmosphere is one of curiously stiff restraint. The two dead soldiers lying nearby reflect the toll that Bowie took of the enemy before his death, but the facial expressions of two dying Texans on the floor lend a touch of unintentional comic relief.[20]

This heroic version of Bowie's death was generally accepted because it originated with Susannah Dickinson, the best-known Alamo survivor, and it also conformed to Texans' patriotic expectations, unlike Mexican reports that had characterized Bowie as cowering in bed. These stories did not affect Bowie's public image, since he had already solidly established his credentials as a "man's man" by 1836, notably through the invention and skillful use of the oversized knife that bore his name. Assuming, probably correctly, that such allegations of cowardice were misinterpretations of Bowie's death or outright fabrications, Anglo-Texans instead adopted an attitude of "if the defenders of Texas fought from their very death beds, how could they be defeated?"[21]

As early as 1852, Bowie's death was being idealized when a relative claimed falsely that "Bowie's enemies honored him" by burying his body separately from those of the other defenders.[22] A more widely known element of the story of Bowie's death dwelled on the brutality of the soldiers who killed their disabled enemy. This kernel of truth was nourished by such fictional, sensationalistic accounts as that of one "Apolinario Saldigna," who allegedly served as a fifer in the Mexican army band. "Saldigna" charged that, as Santa Anna toured the mission grounds after the battle, he "enjoyed this scene of human butchery."[23] He went on to say that, following a lengthy search, four soldiers brought out a bedridden man, who was identified as Bowie. After Bowie defied a captain by claiming that the Texans had been fighting for the Mexican Constitution in the face of Santa Anna's usurpation of powers, the officer had his soldiers cut out Bowie's tongue and throw their prisoner alive onto the pyre of the bodies of his dead comrades, which was then set ablaze.[24]

Eyth's depiction of Bowie's death conveys this message of martyrdom, although its details correspond more closely to Mrs. Dickinson's account. His rendering of Bowie's physical features reflects late nineteenth-century misconceptions concerning Bowie's physical appearance; Eyth and other Texas artists had access to few, if any,

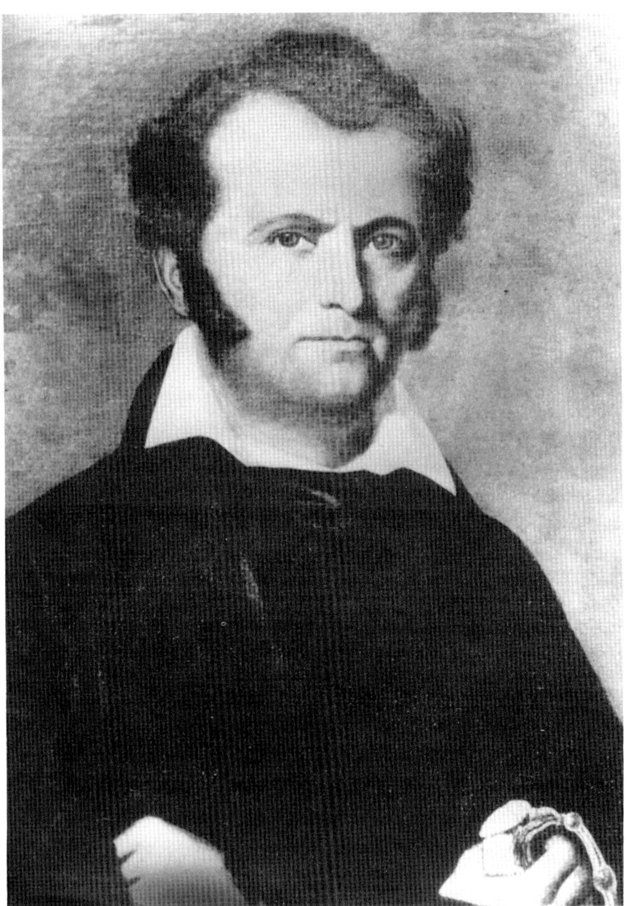

FIGURE 21. Book illustration after George P. A. Healy, *James Bowie*, ca. 1831–1834. Photograph from Archives Division-Texas State Library.

accurate visual portrayals of him. This figure of Bowie, drawn from the same study as Eyth used for *Speech of Travis*, possibly was derived from a portrait by Boston painter George P. A. Healy that had been reproduced as a book illustration (ca. 1831–1834; Fig. 21). But Eyth idealized Bowie by giving him the appearance of an early church martyr in a medieval woodcut rather than that of a knife-fighting frontier entrepreneur, an effect heightened by sunlight streaming strategically through a window grate.[25]

The next Alamo battle scene to appear was completely opposite in style and intent from Eyth's two vignettes. Theodore Gentilz's (1819–1906) restrained and understated *Fall of the Alamo* (1885; Fig. 22) reflects the artist's education at L'Ecole Imperiale de Mathematiques et de Dessin in his native Paris. Gentilz (1864; Fig. 23) emigrated to Texas in 1844 to serve as artist and chief engineer for French colonizer Henri Castro but quickly de-

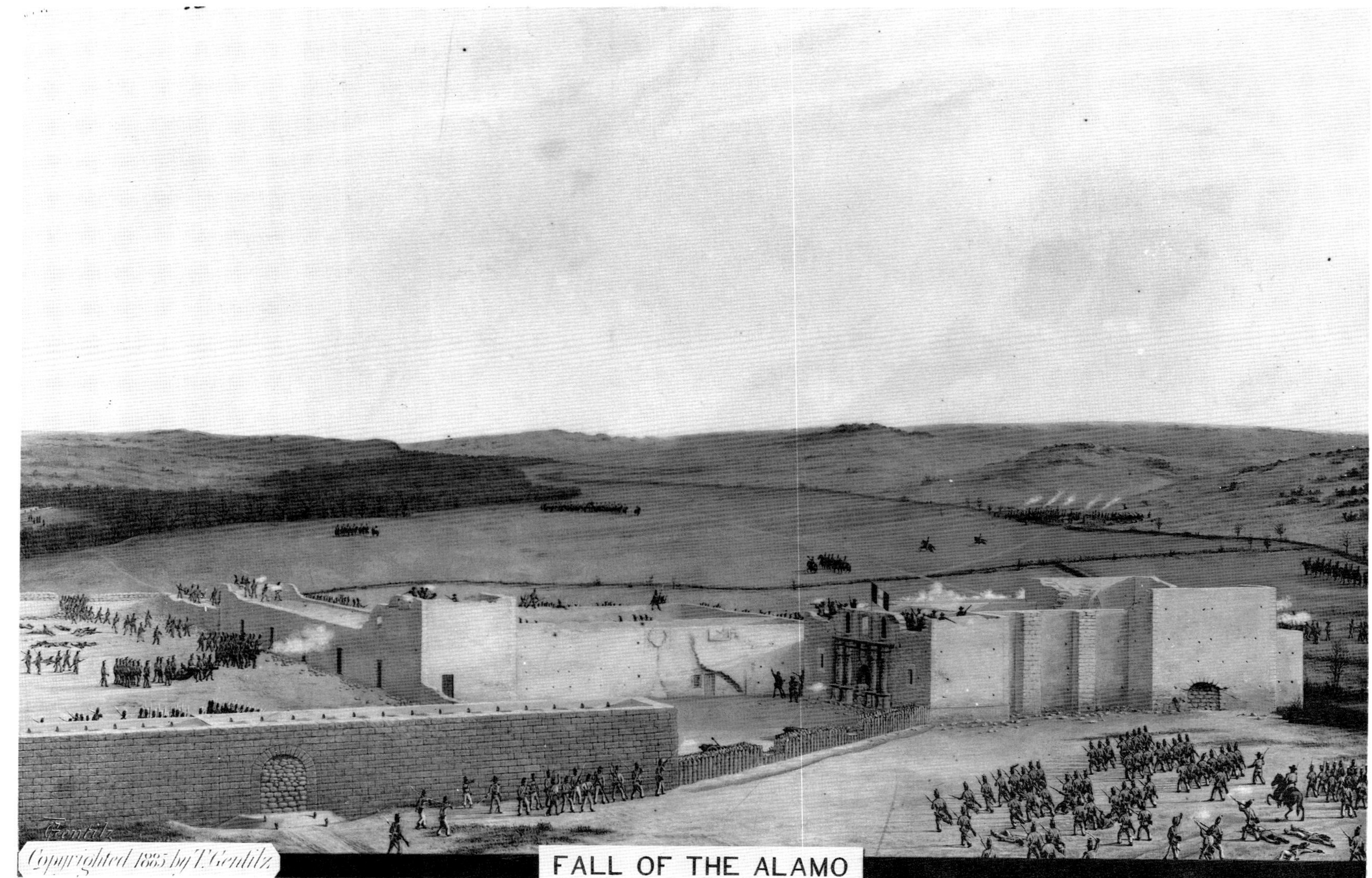

FIGURE 22. Theodore Gentilz, *Fall of the Alamo,* 1885. Painting destroyed; photograph from the Daughters of the Republic of Texas Library at the Alamo, San Antonio, Texas.

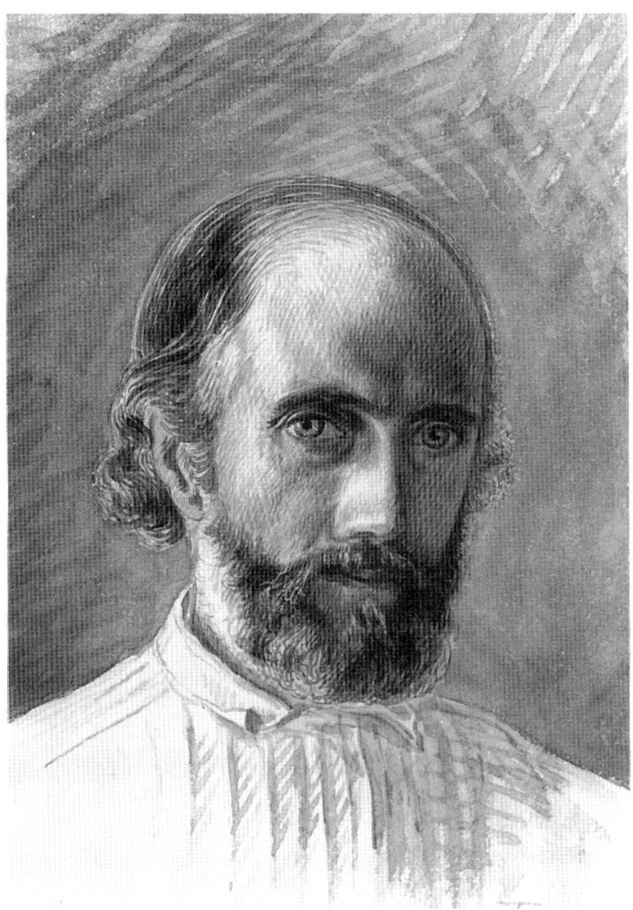

FIGURE 23. Theodore Gentilz, *Self-portrait*, 1864. Watercolor on cream paper. Courtesy of the San Antonio Museum Association, San Antonio, Texas. No. 45.87 487.P (14).

veloped an interest in the history and architecture of the San Antonio missions. Within a year of his arrival, he began sketching these structures and interviewing San Antonians in order to obtain details of the siege of the Alamo. But Gentilz evidently did not complete *Fall of the Alamo* until four decades later, when he copyrighted the painting in 1885, a year before its publication as an illustration for the text of Hiram H. McLane's play celebrating the Texas semicentennial, *The Capture of the Alamo*.[26]

Gentilz's version contrasts strikingly with other paintings of the battle. He views it with a technical, dispassionate eye and does not concern himself with presenting heroes or villains. Instead, Gentilz was intent on producing an accurate reconstruction of the scene, and his preliminary sketches reflect painstaking effort in measuring the Alamo grounds and committing these measurements to scale drawings (n.d.; Fig. 24). He also identified the noncombatants and made lists of the armies' officers as

well as descriptions of their uniforms, weapons, and flags. Gentilz's sketches of the battle and its participants depict figures in battlefield poses of marching, kneeling, and dying and of military accoutrements (n.d.; Fig. 25). His mathematical training also prompted Gentilz to make scale drawings of fortifications and of deployments of troops and artillery as well as perspective studies of the position of the sun throughout the day at the same time of year as the siege. But a surprising inaccuracy in Gentilz's *Fall of the Alamo* is the inclusion of the arched gable with which the U.S. Army capped the Alamo parapet between 1850 and 1852. The painting's action occurs as Mexican troops are attempting to breach the long barracks and the outer fortifications of the northern palisade. Instead of the hand-to-hand, detailed fighting of other Alamo battle paintings, Gentilz offers a bird's-eye view of finely executed troop maneuvers, complete with figures having the appearance of toy soldiers.[27]

A decade later, Gentilz took an approach resembling more closely that of Eyth's vignettes in *Death of Dickinson* (1896; Pl. 8) by focusing on the fate of Captain Almeron Dickinson. The atmosphere of *Death of Dickinson* recalls that of Eyth's *Death of Bowie* as grim-faced Mexican soldiers await orders to execute their prisoners. However, Gentilz produced a more skillfully executed canvas than did Eyth. His studies and preliminary sketches of knives, bridle bits, and the dead bodies of soldiers and horses reflect detailed research similar to that employed in composing *Fall of the Alamo* (n.d.; Fig. 26). Especially interesting is a sketch of the scene—replete with Gentilz's lines of perspective—that illustrates how he handled the painting as a mathematical construction, placing the figure of Dickinson within a triangle formed by the horsemen and buildings and conveying the effect of the figures' shadows continuing beyond the edge of the canvas (n.d.; Fig. 27).[28]

Gentilz's depiction of the captain pleading for his life by holding aloft his young daughter, who clutches a white flag, runs counter to most accounts of Dickinson's death, including that given by Susannah Dickinson. She recalled that, as the third assault breached the walls, she had lifted up her daughter to Captain Dickinson for one final embrace shortly before he died with the other members of the garrison. She always denied any account of her husband's death that ran counter to her belief that he died at his post defending the cannon on the rear wall of the chapel.[29]

Choosing to disagree with this generally accepted version of Dickinson's death, Gentilz drew his idea for the

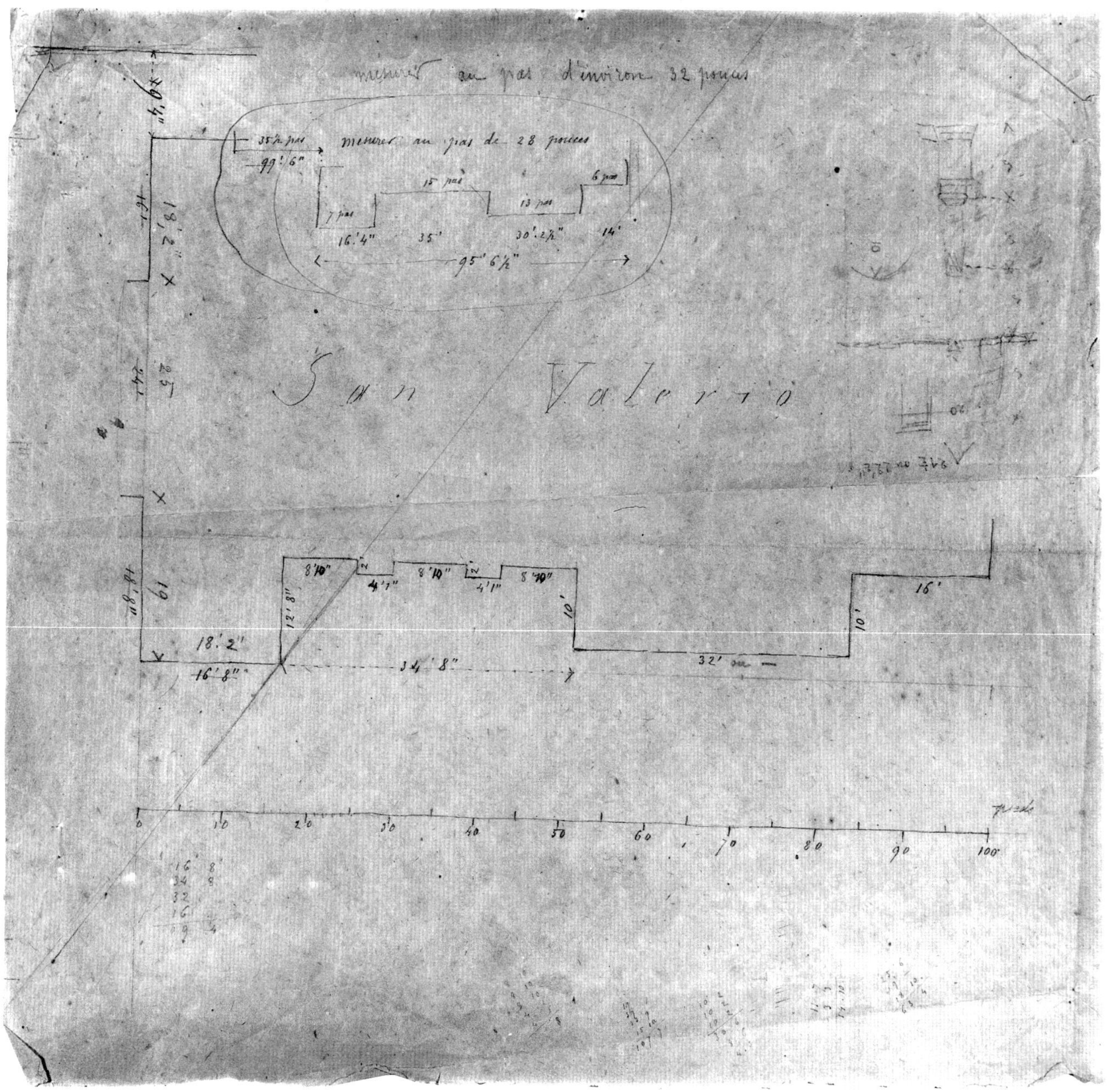

FIGURE 24. Theodore Gentilz, sketch for *Fall of the Alamo*, n.d. Pencil. Daughters of the Republic of Texas Library at the Alamo, San Antonio, Texas.

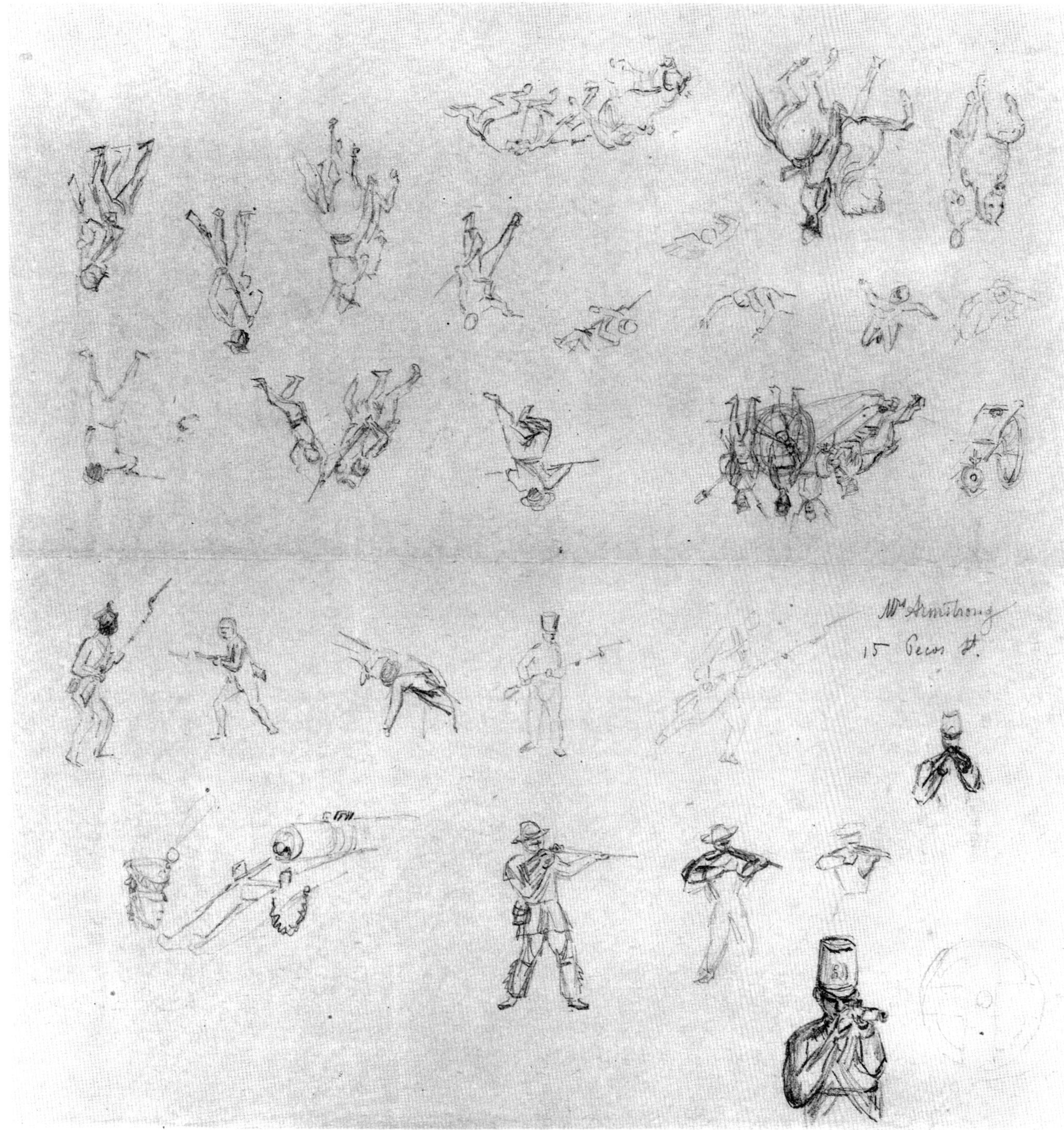

FIGURE 25. Theodore Gentilz, sketch for *Fall of the Alamo,*
n.d. Pencil. Daughters of the Republic of Texas Library at the
Alamo, San Antonio, Texas.

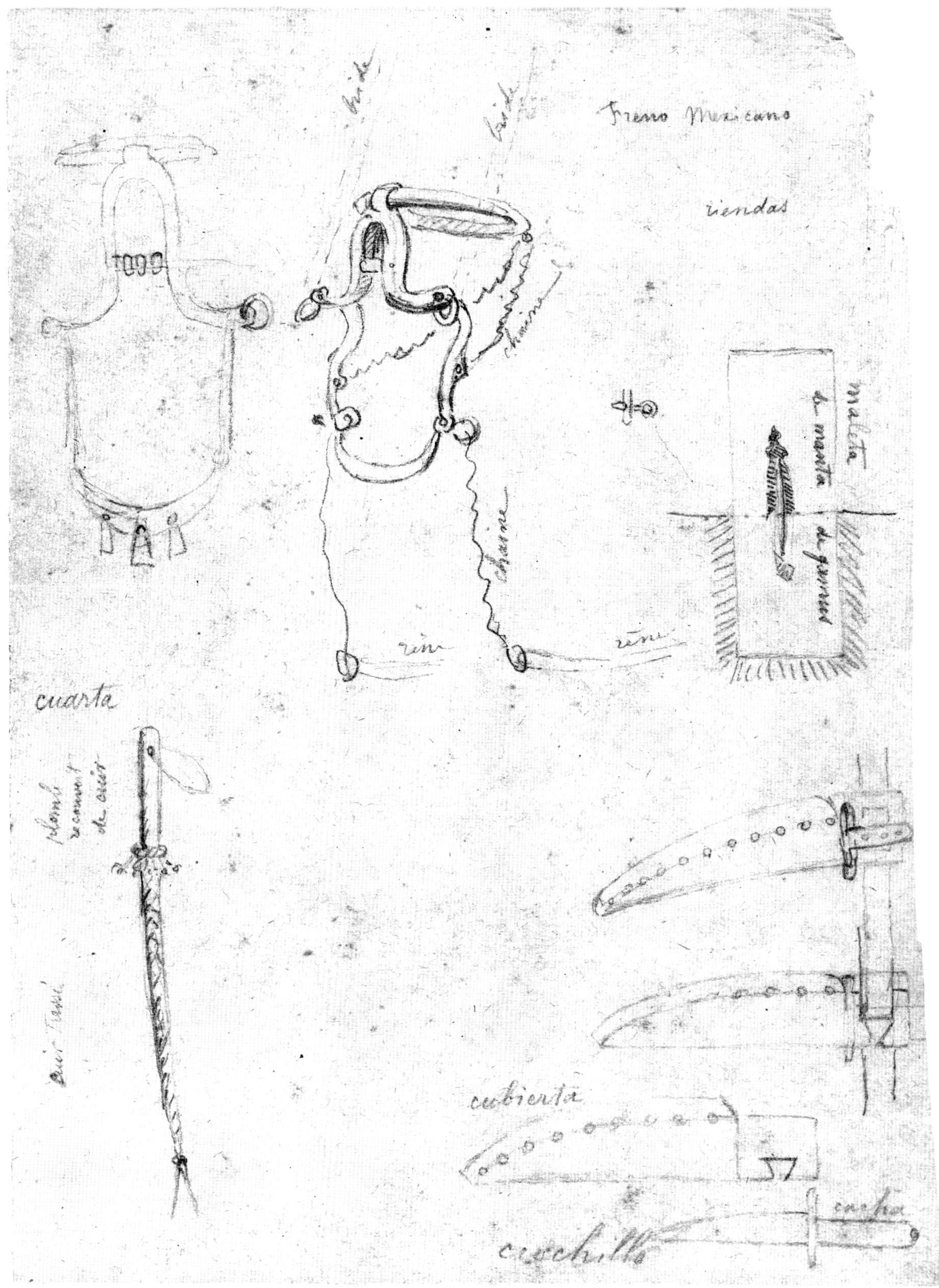

FIGURE 26. Theodore Gentilz, sketch for *Death of Dickinson*, n.d. Pencil. Daughters of the Republic of Texas Library at the Alamo, San Antonio, Texas.

FIGURE 27. (*Opposite page*). Theodore Gentilz, sketch for *Death of Dickinson*, n.d. Pencil. Daughters of the Republic of Texas Library at the Alamo, San Antonio, Texas.

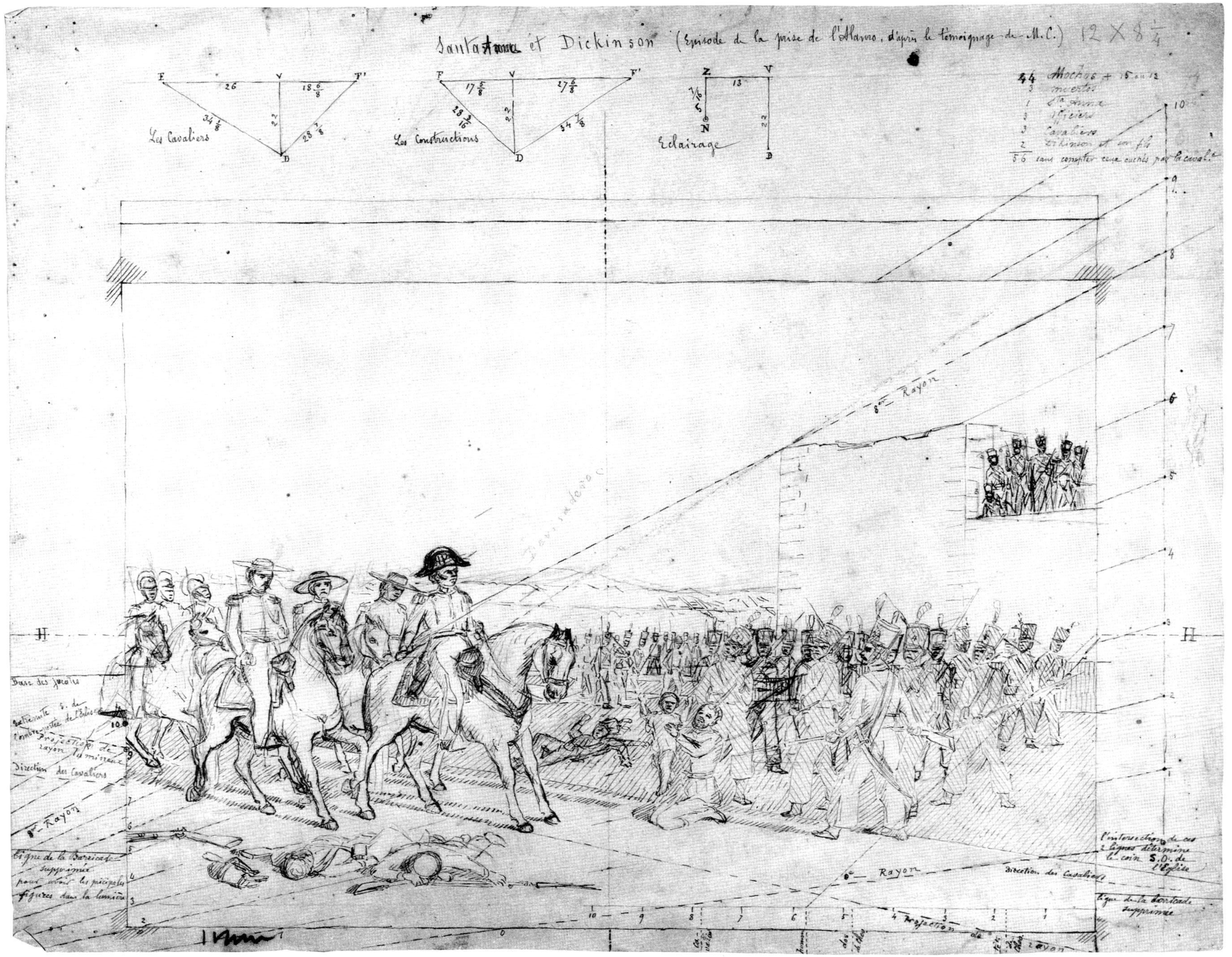
Santa Anna et Dickinson (Episode de la prise de l'Alamo, d'après le témoignage de M.C.) 12 × 8 ¼
Les Cavaliers
Les Constructions
Eclairage
Rayon
8e Rayon
Direction des Cavaliers
Projection du rayon lumineux
Barre des jacales
l'intersection de ces 2 lignes détermine le coin S.O. de l'Eglise
ligne de la barricade supprimée
ligne de la barricade supprimée pour avoir les principales figures dans la lumière
Projection
H
H

painting from the recollections of Antonio Cruz Arrocha, a resident of San Antonio at the time of the siege. Arrocha maintained that, following the battle, Dickinson appeared from a hiding place carrying his child, who held a white flag, and knelt before Santa Anna as the Mexican commander approached the chapel. Showing no mercy, Santa Anna ordered his hesitant infantrymen to bayonet the pair, which they did. In 1860, Reuben Potter published a more widely known variation of the story, which recounted that, as Dickinson leaped from a window in the east end of the church with his child on his back, both were cut down by Mexican bullets.[30]

Since Gentilz lived in San Antonio less than a decade after 1836, he had first-hand access to more eyewitness sources of the siege and battle than did later artists. By the time he arrived in the city, guided tours of the Alamo, complete with historical observations, had become a thriving sideline enterprise for San Antonio residents. English journalist William Bollaert recalled that one tour guide, pointing out places where the Alamo heroes had died, recounted "the brutalities of Santa Anna and his followers."[31] But Gentilz did worry that the information gleaned from his own interviewees was unreliable; as he admitted, "witnesses altered the facts" and had "a tendency to arrange things according to their own view[s]."[32] Still, the artist made the assumption that "if the same fact is recounted in the same manner by a number of witnesses, it must be considered as true."[33]

But Gentilz did not specify what constituted a "number of witnesses"; quite conceivably, word got around the town of San Antonio that a professionally trained European artist was hunting up Alamo stories among the residents, who prepared their accounts accordingly. The few historians familiar with *Death of Dickinson* have questioned its veracity while praising the dispassionate "accuracy" of *Fall of the Alamo*. However, Gentilz's use of Arrocha's story, which belies the cool technicality of *Fall of the Alamo*, as the subject of a painting is in keeping with the artist's sentiments regarding the battle. Gentilz clearly regarded the Alamo in conventional nineteenth-century Texan fashion, as indicated in his brief summary of its history in the margin of one of his sketches, which repeated Texans' frequent equation of the Alamo battle with the massacre of King Leonidas's Spartan army in 480 B.C. This notation declared that "Travis, Bowie, Crockett, and their noble companion martyrs defied Santana [*sic*] and the Mexican army and enacted the tragedy which gives the Alamo the name of the 'Thermopylae of America.'"[34]

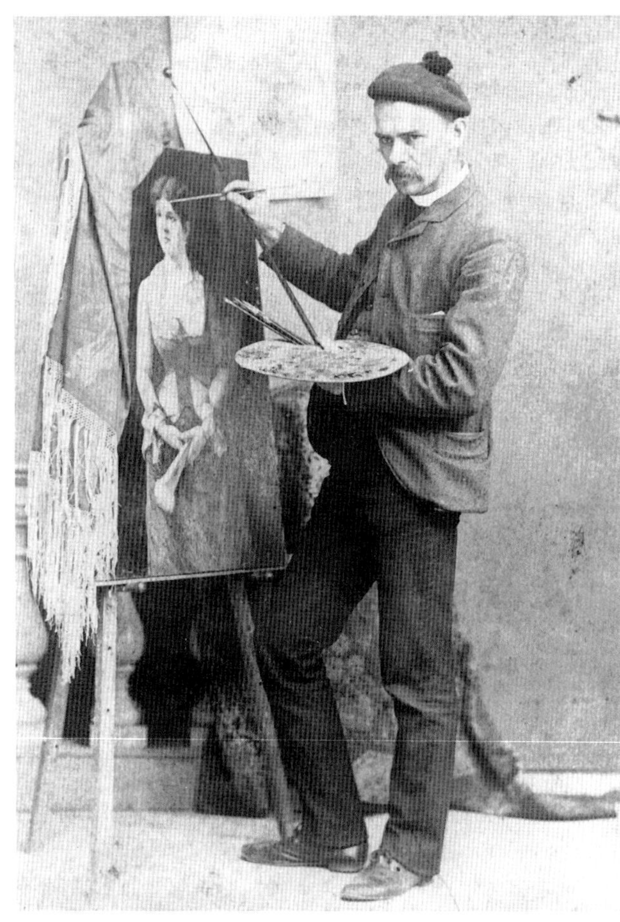

FIGURE 28. Robert Jenkins Onderdonk in his studio, ca. 1883. Gould-Onderdonk Papers.

The year after *Death of Dickinson* appeared, the first ceremonies to commemorate the anniversary of the battle of the Alamo were held in Alamo Plaza on 6 March 1897. During the 1890s, increased interest in the Alamo had made the site a popular tourist destination and a profitable subject for exploitation by manufacturers of inexpensive souvenirs. This interest was the culmination of improvements of Alamo Plaza, beginning in 1878 with the completion of a street car line to the area that sparked a marked increase in retail activity around the plaza during the 1880s. This heightened public attention also was evident in an increasingly heated debate concerning proper care of the Alamo, a dispute that culminated in a 1905 act by the Texas legislature turning this responsibility over to the Daughters of the Republic of Texas. During the last years of this "Second Battle of the Alamo," two artists' fascination with the events of the massacre resulted in completion of two of the best-known Alamo battle paintings.[35]

The first of these canvases, Robert Jenkins Onderdonk's *The Fall of the Alamo* (1903; Pl. 9), also known as *Crockett's Last Stand*, provided a dramatic counterpoint to the work of an artist noted for more serene paintings. James DeShields commissioned Onderdonk (Fig. 28) to execute this work, one of his few historical paintings, in what proved to be the first of several transactions between the two men. In commissioning the work, DeShields also may have urged Onderdonk to create a scene similar in flavor to Otto Becker's popular 1896 lithograph, *Custer's Last Fight* (Pl. 10), whose Custer figure resembles the composition of Onderdonk's Crockett.[36]

Onderdonk's research for his portrayal of Crockett centered on resolving two questions: the frontiersman's physical appearance and, of equal importance, the manner and exact location of his death. In a 1903 letter to DeShields, Onderdonk derided a recently published Crockett portrait as "a popular version" inferior to his own proposed conception and claimed that his own painting would dispel "fairy tales," which he did not go on to specify.[37] But Onderdonk himself consulted at least one "popular version," a postcard reproduction of a watercolor portrait of the Tennessee hunter by Anthony Lewis DeRose. This portrait was painted in 1834, at the height of Crockett's nationwide popularity as an exotic representative of the West that spawned the first of the Davy Crockett almanacs. Onderdonk also enlisted Frank M. Edwards, another San Antonio artist, to pose as the model for the Crockett figure in Onderdonk's studio. Although Onderdonk finally borrowed only DeRose's profile view of Crockett for his own use, critics praised *The Fall of the Alamo* for its portrayal of the "tall, straight figure of that American pioneer . . . [his] face taken from a portrait."[38]

Conflicting and sketchy reports of Crockett's role in the siege and final assault made resolution of the second of Onderdonk's research problems more difficult. In the first few days of the siege, Travis had reported that "'Hon. David Crockett was seen at all points, animating the men to do their duty during a bombardment.'"[39] Most accounts agree that Crockett and his Tennesseans defended the weakest point of the Alamo fortifications at the southwest corner of the main compound, the approximate point where Onderdonk stationed him in his painting.[40] But there has been less harmony concerning when and how Crockett met his death on the morning of 6 March 1836.

In concluding that "Crockett was not killed in the Alamo but defending the gateway of the building in the first assault," Onderdonk apparently relied on a published interview with an elderly San Antonio woman, Andrea Castañon Ramírez Villanueva, who claimed the status of a survivor of the Alamo battle.[41] This woman was better known as "Madam Candelaria," and the truthfulness of her account has been the subject of considerable controversy throughout the twentieth century. While Onderdonk was faithful to her recollection of where Crockett fell, he disagreed with Madam Candelaria's contention that Crockett was one of the first defenders to die, shot down while deliberately walking, unarmed, from the chapel toward the Alamo walls.[42]

At the time that Onderdonk executed *The Fall of the Alamo*, most Texans believed that Crockett had gone down fighting. One of the first uses of this version of Crockett's death as a patriotic device was by one of the frontiersman's acquaintances in an attempt to console the Crockett family a few weeks after the Alamo fell: "I cannot restrain my American smile at the recollection of the fact that he died as a United States soldier should die, covered with his slain enemy, and, even in death presenting to them in his clenched hands, the weapons of their destruction."[43] Seventy years later, Onderdonk gave his audience a visual rendering of this story, and one reviewer voiced his approval that Onderdonk had painted a canvas in which "Davy and Old Betsy . . . marched out into the open court where they could meet the swarthy foes and deal death to as many as possible."[44]

But this version, related by Mrs. Dickinson and Travis's servant, Joe, conflicted with some of the first reports of the battle that had reached the United States. These recorded that Crockett and a few other defenders had surrendered and were summarily executed by Santa Anna. This account was also accepted and, despite their discrepancies, both versions existed side by side for many years. Intense controversy concerning their mutual contradiction did not flare up until the late twentieth century, although embellished versions did surface prior to this time, including "eyewitness" accounts of Crockett working in Mexican silver mines. Another fanciful variation of the "surrender" story stated that General Cós interceded fruitlessly for Crockett with Santa Anna. When the Mexican leader refused to grant clemency, the enraged frontiersman allegedly attempted to stab him immediately before he himself was bayoneted. Texans spread this tale, as they had that of Bowie's defiance, to emphasize Texan valor as well as enemy brutality, declaring that it is "what Santa Anna would have done if it were true."[45]

In 1901, after completing a study sketch for the painting, which at that time he titled *Death of Crockett* (1901; Pl. 11), Onderdonk wrote DeShields of his determination that the finished work convey a sense of "battle murder and sudden death" and of his intention "in painting a picture of this kind to make it intensely interesting and realistic; everything must be painted from nature."[46] Certainly, Onderdonk was able to draw upon an array of resources and knowledge gained from varied and extensive training to fulfill these goals. After studying at New York City's prestigious National Academy of Design, he had helped to found the Art Students' League, where he received instruction from noted painters James Carroll Beckwith, William Merritt Chase, and Walter Shirlaw. These teachers emphasized life studies of the human form; Shirlaw's work especially was noted for its lifelike figures. With these lessons in mind, Onderdonk involved his entire family in the composition of *The Fall of the Alamo*. He photographed his sons and their friends clad in uniforms and carrying weapons from the 1830s, posed in various stages of fighting and dying. Onderdonk worked from these photographs in his studio, just as Gentilz had worked from sketches of similar details for his two Alamo paintings.[47]

All of Onderdonk's efforts paid off, winning praise for the finished work as being "strongly realistic . . . every figure stands out with striking individuality and trueness to nature . . . every feature, every detail, has been carefully studied and worked out."[48] During display of the canvas by the Dallas Art Association in 1904, one reviewer praised the artist for including "the blood recurrent of life . . . as it oozes and trickles upon the stone floor of the Alamo" in a work that "reaches sublime heights."[49]

These opinions indicate that contemporary audiences found no contradiction between Onderdonk's painstaking attempts at accuracy and his more subjective intent of glorification. Even though Onderdonk claimed that he did not wish to cast the Alamo's defenders as larger-than-life heroes, he had explained to DeShields that "the grouping and lines are all made with reference to showing the overwhelming rush of the Mexicans and the determined stand of the few Americans."[50] Critics and audiences went further, praising the painting as "a soul inspiring scene" suffused with the "savage glory of battle."[51] One newspaper solicited a critique of the work by an anonymous "brother artist" who praised Onderdonk for utilizing the "soft light of dawn . . . idealizing the whole and showing the spirit of the true battle painter who can depict battle without a great horrible exhibition of slaughter, wounds and bloodshed."[52] Indeed, the de-

fenders' clothes seem a bit too clean to have endured a two-week siege and, in fact, the garrison appears at least to be holding its own against the Mexican onslaught. Although turn-of-the-century Texas viewers' expectations meshed with Onderdonk's goals of realism, many of them ultimately placed a higher value on the overriding sentiment of a work that would impress on the viewer's mind that as "the heroes died . . . the sun of Texas liberty arose to shine with renewed and undying splendor."[53]

These same expectations and aesthetic standards surfaced two years later in response to Henry McArdle's *Dawn at the Alamo* (1905; Pl. 12), which attempted to capture the entire sweep of the hand-to-hand combat during the climactic moments of the battle. Not content to portray selected incidents in the fashion of Eyth, Gentilz, and Onderdonk, McArdle strived to present an accurate portrayal of the Mexican victory while also conveying a sense of the carnage and confusion of the final assault. He researched the events of the climax of the siege for almost three decades before he was satisfied with his conception of the scene.

McArdle completed an initial version of *Dawn at the Alamo* in 1875, intending it to follow *The Settlement of Austin's Colony* in his proposed series of paintings depicting Texas heroes (Fig. 29). He corresponded with several individuals whom he regarded as experts on the battle, including Reuben Potter and Santa Anna. The former Mexican leader, writing shortly before his death, justified his actions at the Alamo to McArdle on the grounds of the "obstinacy" of the "insulting" Travis and his men and by his own fear of Sam Houston's imminent arrival with a "respectable" amount of troops. McArdle later responded to this explanation by noting "glorious 'obstinacy,' glorious heroism!"[54]

For his part, Reuben Potter (ca. 1886; Fig. 30) feared that the artist might somehow convert the scene into a Texan victory and inundated McArdle with information concerning Alamo fortifications and the uniforms and weapons of both armies, stressing the importance of adherence to these details. Potter played a critical and heretofore overlooked role in shaping McArdle's conception of *Dawn at the Alamo*, assuming duties resembling those of historical consultants and technical advisors employed by twentieth-century film directors. McArdle first consulted Potter in July 1874, and the two men kept up a brisk correspondence for the next six months concerning the composition of the painting. Potter had been obsessed with properly commemorating the fall of the Alamo for three decades; in Henry McArdle, he found a kindred spirit as well as an artist who would finally

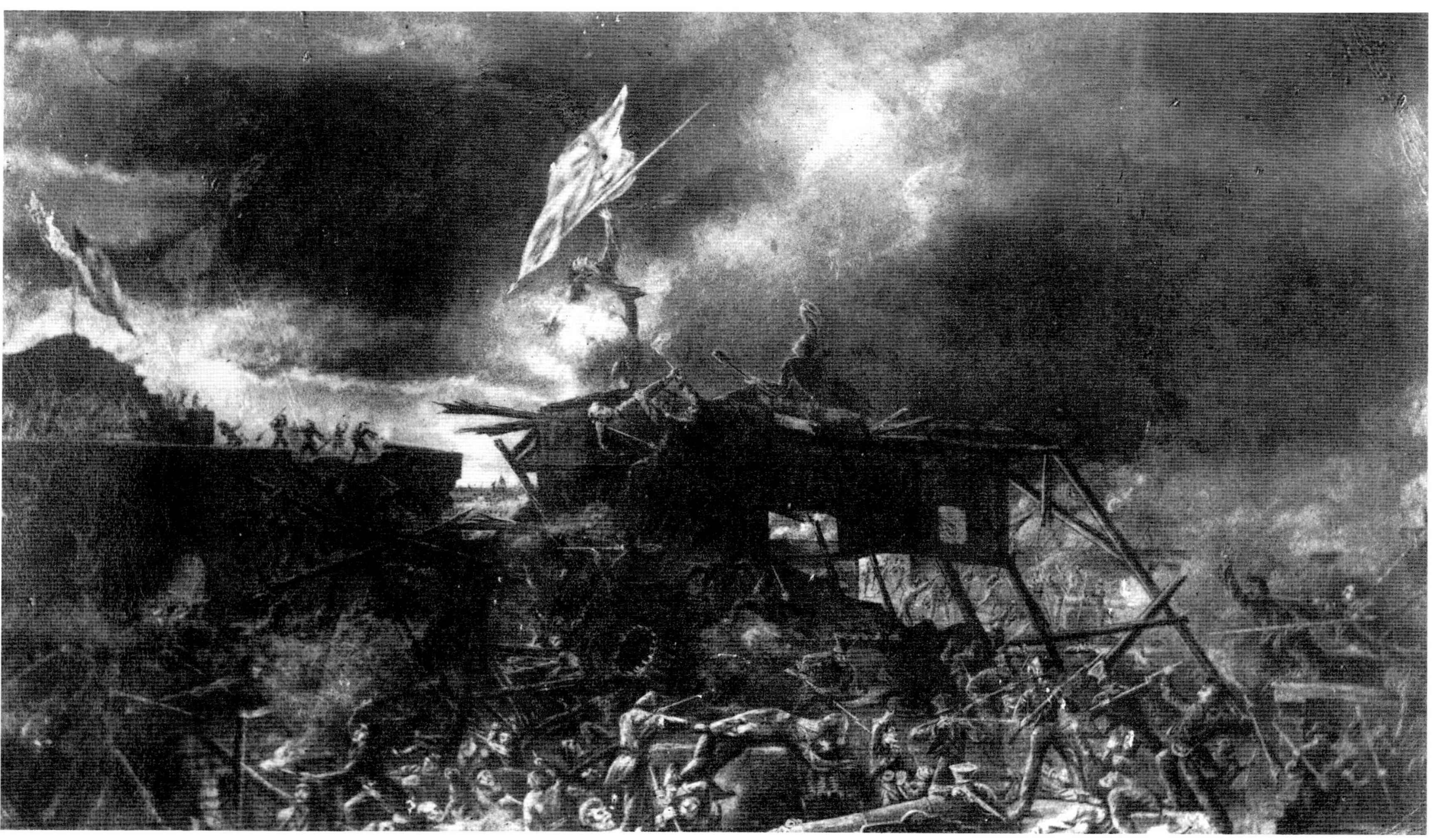

FIGURE 29. Henry Arthur McArdle, *Dawn at the Alamo*, 1875. Painting destroyed; photograph from Archives Division-Texas State Library. Acc. no. 1979/181-18.

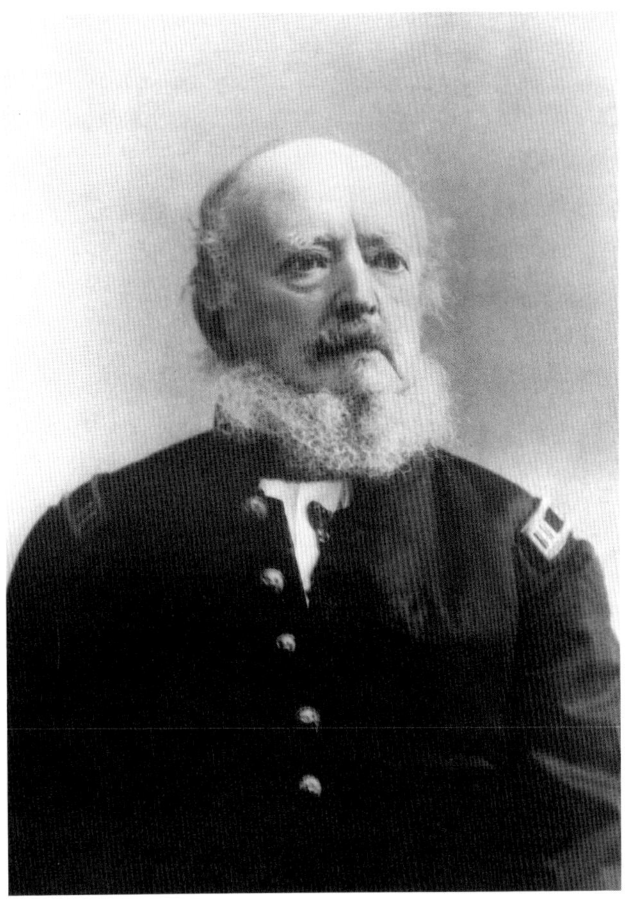

FIGURE 30. Reuben Potter, ca. 1886. Archives Division-Texas State Library. Acc. no. 1979/181-9.

handle the subject in the fashion that Potter believed appropriate. He fueled McArdle's initial interest in Texas history and, despite occasional disputes between the two men, Potter succeeded in having many of his own perceptions of the massacre incorporated into *Dawn at the Alamo*.[55]

In his first letter to McArdle, Potter went beyond mere "nuts-and-bolts" and suggested an overall philosophical approach: "I am aware that historical events, when represented by painting, must be idealized for artistic effect."[56] He then went on to deliver his opinions on the valor of the Mexican soldiers, parallels of the Alamo with Thermopylae, and the proper placement of figures in the painting. After seeing an initial study for *Dawn at the Alamo*, Potter also urged, albeit unsuccessfully, that McArdle omit the well-known but inaccurate gable from the chapel roof in order to furnish a more pleasing point of view and that the artist title the work "The Prophetic Dawn at the Alamo." But Potter's insistence soon turned

to grudging acquiescence on some points, such as McArdle's intention to portray the battle with an air of victory for the defenders. And, although Potter chided McArdle for "render[ing] the picture more historical than was my suggestion," he conceded the effectiveness of its conception.[57]

McArdle's artistic intent reflected a general attempt by Texans to seek classical parallels in the experiences of their state's history. The artist was well acquainted with classical literature and informed the president of Baylor University as early as 1871 of his desire to learn Greek and Latin.[58] Reuben Potter's advice reinforced these inclinations, as he acknowledged "idealization" to be acceptable and opined that "this battle has special advantages for this purpose."[59] Potter specifically pointed out, using the language of a theatrical production, the potential symbolism of the Texans' flag for patriotism and moral uplift, and he termed McArdle's use of the morning star as reminiscent of the "'Lone Star of Texas' . . . a noble allegorical conception embodied in the aspect of Nature."[60] He even justified McArdle's omission of the fighting within the chapel by drawing a parallel with "a famous painting of antiquity" depicting Agamemnon's sacrifice of his daughter and declared that "in every grand picture something ought to be left to the imagination."[61]

In addition to offering advice, Potter agreed to McArdle's request that he write "puff pieces" for newspapers that would extol the painting in order to promote its purchase by the Texas state legislature. In November 1874, after seeing McArdle's "preliminary sketch and explanatory description," Potter enthused that the projected work would serve as an "atonement" for past neglect of the Alamo as an artistic subject.[62] He called upon the state legislature to appropriate funds immediately as an advance payment toward purchase of the finished version of the work. Potter also sought to legitimize McArdle's efforts by evaluating his artistic talents favorably on an international scale, praising "the same art which in Shakespeare gives force to the historical drama . . . [McArdle] can hardly be excelled in the poetic ideality of his profession."[63]

Within a few months after the painting went on public display, McArdle enlisted the aid of another prominent veteran of the Texas Revolution, Colonel Frank W. Johnson, in his efforts to obtain a legislative appropriation. Johnson appealed to "patriotism and gratitude" and challenged the public to begin a grass-roots campaign to purchase the canvas.[64] But these appeals fell on deaf ears of Texans struggling with the severe economic and political difficulties engendered by the Civil War and Reconstruction. McArdle finally loaned *Dawn at the Alamo* to the state, and it was on exhibit in the Capitol when destroyed by the 1881 fire; this 1875 image now exists only in the form of a photographic reproduction.[65]

Over the next three decades, McArdle became obsessed with incorporating changes into a revised rendering of the battle scene, which he hoped would improve his chances of selling it to the state. He sought out opinions on aesthetics to supplement Potter's historical observations and mailed sketches or photographic reproductions of the 1875 painting to his former art instructor in Baltimore, David A. Woodward. Woodward encouraged his erstwhile student by praising the placement of the figures and the "grand and truthful conception" of the work.[66] And, as he had done with his other advisors, Johnson and Potter, McArdle sought to enlist Woodward's aid in marketing the painting. Woodward, an advocate of large canvases, believed that Texas had missed an ideal opportunity to purchase this "picture of suitable size for their State House."[67]

Although McArdle did exhaustive research and solicited numerous opinions, his strongest motivation to complete the canvas may have come indirectly from Robert Onderdonk. By 1901, Onderdonk undoubtedly was familiar with the 1875 *Dawn at the Alamo* and, possibly, with McArdle's quarter-century of revisions and had set out to paint a more believable and less garish picture of the battle. Certainly, his correspondence with DeShields (e.g., his letter entitled "THE ALAMO: The Story of a Great Painting") hints at Onderdonk's belief in his ability to execute the definitive Alamo battle painting in order to curry favor with the two artists' common patron.[68] Whether or not the two artists regarded themselves as competitors, McArdle's revised *Dawn at the Alamo* appeared two years after Onderdonk's work.

McArdle's finished canvas, bearing the same title and painted on a more grandiose scale than the 1875 *Dawn at the Alamo*, drew even more approval than had its predecessor. One reviewer, evidently dissatisfied with Onderdonk's *Fall of the Alamo*, praised McArdle's painting as "the first adequate pictorial representation of that ever-memorable struggle."[69] The additional three decades of research had supplied McArdle with information and opinions that combined to make the second *Dawn at the Alamo* different in several respects from the earlier version. The artist also incorporated ideas that he previously had neglected; one of Potter's 1874 suggestions, that the viewer should feel as if he were looking into a volcano, describes the atmosphere of the later canvas more accurately than that of the first *Dawn at the Alamo*.[70]

While Potter definitely influenced the atmosphere of the painting, McArdle also relied on photographs and other artists' renderings in his depiction of architectural elements and other design features of the scene. In one undated photograph, marked "spectator's viewpoint," the Alamo Saloon abuts the chapel in an architectural juxtaposition that no doubt horrified McArdle. The artist explained that this viewpoint situated the viewer on the west pavement of Alamo Plaza, south of Houston Street, facing southeast. McArdle's papers also include photographic reproductions of Gentilz's *Fall of the Alamo* and a reproduction of John Beckmann's lithograph, *"Alamo" 1845* (Fig. 31). In reconstructing the mission grounds, McArdle also combined features from Green Jameson's 1836 plan of fortifications, an 1855 plat of the Alamo area by François Giraud, and Potter's plan of the grounds, published in 1878 (Fig. 32).[71]

A towering cannon platform in the center of the main plaza, one of the most prominent features of both versions of *Dawn at the Alamo*, was of McArdle's own invention and furnished a stage for the struggle for the red Mexican flag of "no quarter." Although an 1836 fortifications manual had called for a cannon platform by a garrison occupying the same strategic position as did that of the Alamo, such a structure did not appear in any of the Alamo plans consulted by the artist. The 1875 version of *Dawn at the Alamo* depicted the platform as the remnant of a wooden stockade's corner blockhouse, supported by timbers about to be consumed by the fire that envelops the wall on the right. A Texan defender and Mexican soldier fall from the platform as they struggle for a pistol. The photograph of the painting is too dark for a viewer to determine which figure actually shoots the solitary Mexican standard-bearer, who falls backward, the flag plummeting downward as a wounded Texan cannoneer triumphantly waves his cap. In composing this vignette, McArdle may have drawn on accounts of the death of Lieutenant José María Torres, who was killed while attempting to plant the Mexican national flag at the Alamo.[72]

Thirty years later, McArdle had elaborated significantly on this scene, quite possibly with encouragement from David Woodward. In addition to the original grouping, a Mexican soldier ascends the left side of the platform. This structure now appears as an earthwork fortification of equal or greater height than the chapel and the west wall ramparts, its size is completely at odds with these other architectural features of the painting, and it is

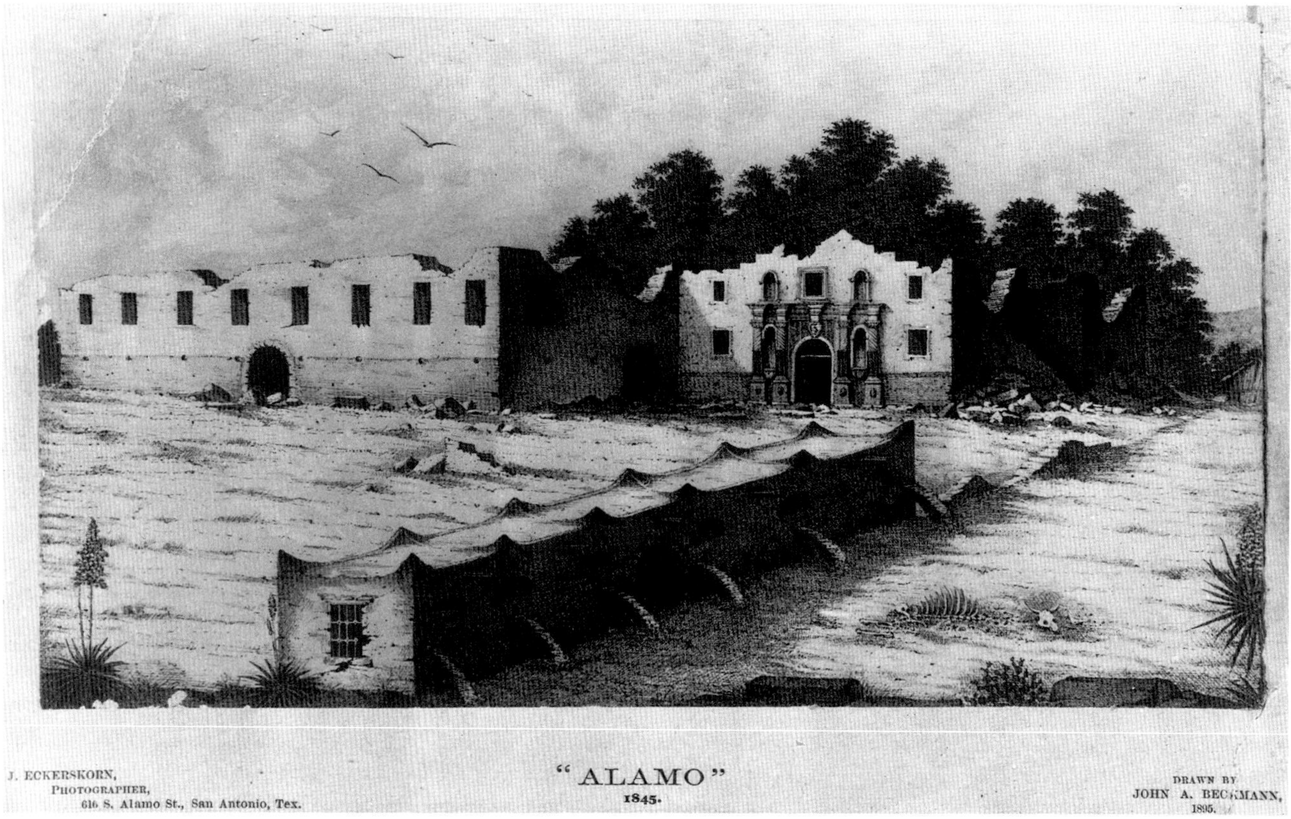

FIGURE 31. John Beckmann, *"Alamo" 1845*, 1895. Archives
Division-Texas State Library. Acc. no. 1979/181-23.

outside the confines of the chapel, opposite the front of
the church. Directly across from the ascending soldier,
one of his fellow infantrymen prepares to bayonet the
cannoneer. McArdle evidently had completed some of
these changes in the original design by 1889, when he
solicited advice from Woodward, who praised the "beau-
tiful pyramidal form of the topmost group of figures."[73]
The artist had great sympathy for Susannah Dickinson,
regarding her as a heroine, and may have included the
figure of the artilleryman in order to memorialize her
husband. In giving greater prominence to the banners of
both armies than he did in the earlier painting, McArdle
observed that the "flag of Mexican liberty" flutters sym-
bolically between the cannoneer and his assailant, "about
to go down on the last spot where it ever waved."[74]

While the cannon platform was still at the center of
the 1905 *Dawn at the Alamo*, it now shared architectural
billing with the west wall ramparts to the right and the
Alamo chapel to the left. In the 1875 canvas, save for inclusion of the gable, McArdle had followed Potter's description of the appearance of the chapel. By the 1890s,

the chapel's heightened importance as a Texas symbol undoubtedly influenced McArdle to feature it more prominently, its windows aglow with fire and the first rays of
dawn. Too, Potter had died in 1890, freeing McArdle to
indulge his penchant for artistic license without fear of
criticism from that source. Despite having taken such liberties with the Alamo's architectural features, McArdle
was praised for having gathered "information at first
hand from contemporary sources, and built up again the
ancient monastic fortress that once filled the greater part
of what is now Alamo Plaza."[75]

In the 1875 painting, architectural elements and atmospheric effects had threatened to overshadow the human
features of most of the Alamo's combatants. Following
Potter's suggestions, McArdle revised the scene to enhance the symbolism of the battle in his visual characterizations of many of these individuals. But his depiction
of all of the Mexican troops as wearing regulation uniforms, complete with shakos, is less accurate than Onderdonk's portrayal of them clad in peasant cotton as well as
in more conventional military uniforms. Furthermore, in

contrast to Onderdonk's combatants, McArdle's fighting men are frozen, postured figures. As Onderdonk had done, McArdle enlisted his own son, Ruskin, as a model, sometimes rousing the boy from sleep in the dead of night in order to be able to capture a particular inspiration in a sketch. But McArdle proved to be less adept than Onderdonk in handling the human figure and in portraiture.[76]

The 1905 *Dawn at the Alamo* approximated conceptions by other artists, such as Eyth and Onderdonk, of the respective characters of the opposing armies. The Mexican soldiers' facial expressions enhance an image of plasticene, psychotic murderers, while the Alamo's defenders wear expressions of either determination or peaceful martyrdom. The face of the dead Texan soldier at the lower right corner resembles that of a classical Greek sculpture, as does the visage of Major Robert Evans, who is attempting to ignite the fort's powder magazine with a flaming torch. McArdle took pains to include Evans in both paintings, and Potter praised the artist for employing the torch's "lurid glare . . . in a way so natural and historical, the light so needful for the effective character of the scene."[77]

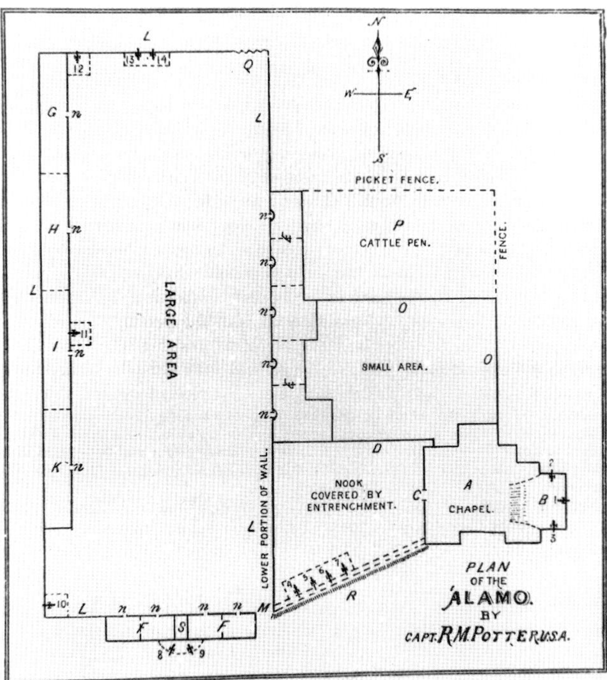

FIGURE 32. Reuben Potter, *Plan of the Alamo Grounds*, ca. 1860–1878. Published in *Magazine of American History*; photograph from DeGolyer Library, Southern Methodist University, Dallas, Texas.

In his second letter to McArdle, Potter mentioned Evans in a passage that the artist marked "note this especially": "Evans's torch was a bright thought . . . [it] lights up two noble personifications . . . the ghostlike Bowie and the intended Samson of that temple, who bears the torch."[78] This light was especially crucial because it was illuminating the figure of one of the Alamo's "Big Three," Jim Bowie. McArdle was determined to include Bowie, Crockett, and Travis in the painting, even if it meant taking what Potter endorsed as "a license as poetical as it is allowable."[79] In the lower left corner, directly above Evans's torch, a deathlike Bowie, roused from his "couch of anguish [by] the roar of battle," thrusts one of the knives bearing his name at two terrified Mexican soldiers, who believe that he is a ghost. McArdle readily acknowledged this distortion in his notes but attempted to rationalize it by noting that Bowie had perished only "after he added a few to the host of the slain."[80]

Directly across from Bowie and Evans, in the lower right corner of the canvas, McArdle's Crockett conforms to the "last stand" mode, "dealing death to all within his reach."[81] McArdle had opted not to follow Potter's suggestion to depict Crockett as restraining a pregnant Susannah Dickinson from rushing into the fray in an attempt to save her husband. But McArdle did alter his 1875 composition, in which Crockett, clad in a full suit of buckskin and coonskin cap, grasped the bayonet of one of the soldiers. In both paintings, Crockett is cast as a defender of the helpless, swinging "Old Betsy" to ward off Mexicans from a small group consisting of Travis's servant, wounded Texans, and Susannah Dickinson and her baby. Woodward praised McArdle's figure placement in the painting's lower right corner, noting that "Crockett with the connecting figures makes a splendid composition of itself."[82]

McArdle also depicted Crockett as fighting directly below William Travis; in reality, the two men defended widely separated points of the mission grounds. McArdle went against the grain of popular preoccupation with Crockett, as exemplified by Onderdonk's work, and intended from the beginning to make Travis the primary hero of *Dawn at the Alamo*; notations in the artist's copy of Potter's article, "The Fall of the Alamo," indicate his admiration for the Alamo's commander. Also, even though Travis was one of the first defenders killed, McArdle depicted him as surviving until near the end of the battle. This visual lionization of Travis, begun within two years after Zuber's publication of the Moses Rose account of the drawing of the line, constituted the first reaction by an artist against a persistent image of Travis as a displaced aristocrat who may have committed suicide during the Mexican attack. In several reviews of the 1875 canvas, he is the only member of the garrison mentioned by name, identified as the defender in a "death grapple" with an enemy soldier. This depiction of Travis's death corresponded at least faintly with the account of his servant, who stated that the final act of the Alamo commander, mortally wounded in the forehead, was to run his sword through a Mexican general.[83]

After Potter complained that Travis did not have sufficient prominence in the 1875 canvas, McArdle decided to exaggerate the physical size of the Alamo commander and make his figure dominate the right side of the second *Dawn at the Alamo*. In this version, standing atop the sprawling body of a Mexican soldier, Travis appears taller, but his larger-than-life figure is woefully out of proportion to the others in the painting, and his head also appears to be too large for his body. McArdle also used a grotesquely oversized human figure as a symbolic device elsewhere in *Dawn at the Alamo*, employing Potter's idea for the combatants atop the chapel to serve "as outward signs of inward throes" of the unseen hand-to-hand combat raging within its walls.[84] In depicting Travis's facial features, McArdle evidently relied on a photograph of Martin D. McHenry of Shelbyville, Kentucky, believed by many Texans to have resembled the Alamo commander. In response to another suggestion from Potter, McArdle portrayed Travis's death in a wholly fictitious way, as a Mexican infantryman bayonets him in the back, personifying the theme of Mexican brutality common to other renderings of the battle by nineteenth-century painters. Despite these problems, James DeShields pointed out the only remotely accurate aspect of this portion of the painting, noting that "Travis, the hero of the massacre, [was] placed where he actually fell."[85]

In light of McArdle's goals for the painting, Travis was the natural hero. Travis's stirring requests for aid heightened the image of the Alamo defenders as representatives of the traditions and ideals of American democracy. His taste for the literature of romantic adventure and history, coupled with his dislike of "Spaniards" and hatred of "Tories [and] submission men," made him the ideal personification of McArdle's portrayal of the forces of democracy against a "barbarous foe of alien tongue and race."[86] While Onderdonk wanted to portray Crockett in a heroic light, he was still depicted as first among equals in an egalitarian garrison. In order to enhance Travis's

status, McArdle set him apart from the rest of the Alamo's volunteer defenders by erroneously clothing him in a military uniform.[87]

McArdle composed *Dawn at the Alamo* as a vehicle to inspire patriotism, in part by playing up perceived virtues of the defenders and emphasizing the diabolical characteristics of the Mexicans. Of course, Eyth, Onderdonk, and, to a lesser extent, Gentilz, also had cast the combatants as personifications of certain virtues and vices. McArdle joined these other painters in portraying the Alamo as a part of the American "patriotic landscape," its defenders transformed into "cultural heroes whose courage and willing sacrifice . . . provide archetypal models of devotion to the principles of the nation."[88]

In addition to ideological statements, Alamo battle paintings were intended to serve as historical documents, ostensibly as reliable as any written historical narrative. Any assessment of these works, especially those of McArdle and Onderdonk, must take details of this aspect of the artists' intent into account. Indeed, the title page of the *Dawn at the Alamo* scrapbook alleges its importance as a "substantiation of the historical accuracy and truth of the paintings." Due to the extensive research left by McArdle, *Dawn at the Alamo* looms as the most striking example of this dual artistic intent. McArdle saw no contradiction between proclaiming his painting as "accurate" and taking liberties with several of its important components, such as Bowie's death. Just as Thomas Moran rearranged the topography of the Grand Canyon of the Yellowstone in order to foster the contemplation of sublime Nature by his viewers, so McArdle tinkered with elements of the Alamo's fall to evoke a sense of verisimilitude and a patriotic response.

Late nineteenth-century viewers, in an age that paid increasing homage to a "scientific method" stressing theories built on factual evidence, demanded that an artist "do his homework" by assembling a foundation of factual detail as the underpinning for any historical painting intended to elicit an emotional response. In spite of the particular emphasis of an individual artist—Gentilz's "information," Onderdonk's "mythology," and McArdle's "vision"—each of them regarded himself as the creator of an "accurate" historical document.[89] Texan audiences deemed detailed realism as even more essential to the hagiography of the victims of the massacre at the Alamo than did Mexican and Spanish viewers of *The Destruction of Mission San Sabá*. These expectations cropped up repeatedly in assessments of the battle paintings. For example, Onderdonk debated whether the distant position of the flag in *The Fall of the Alamo* merited its inclusion, but at least one reviewer noted the presence of "the old Federal flag of 1824."[90] James DeShields proclaimed that *Dawn at the Alamo* "show[ed] a truthful reproduction of the grim old fortress under siege and at the fatal hour. The scene is awe-inspiring and realistic."[91] Gentilz, the artist with access to the largest number of potential witnesses, perhaps realized that the battle itself was a historical minefield and depicted events, real or imagined, that occurred before and after the hand-to-hand combat on the morning that the Alamo fell.

This merging of the goals of factual accuracy and idealization of the battle for purposes of spiritual reverence expressed ascendant attitudes of the late nineteenth century. Artists' veneration of the Alamo, partaking of meta-physical awe and reverence as well as the desire for accurate historical and physical reconstruction of the battle and its site, foreshadowed that of Alamo buffs of the twentieth century. In 1901, during the dispute concerning ownership of the Alamo site, Clara Driscoll, who had furnished financial aid to the Daughters of the Republic of Texas in their attempts to preserve the Alamo, had asserted that "all the unsightly obstructions that hide [the chapel] away should be torn down and the space utilized for a park."[92] No art critic could have summed up more succinctly the sentiment of idealization that finally suffused perceptions of the Alamo and of the paintings depicting the events that earned the mission its enduring fame.

CHAPTER THREE

Freedom's Light

WITHIN A WEEK after the Mexican victory at the Alamo, accounts of the massacre had reached the rest of the Texan military forces and were being carried through the Anglo settlements in eastern Texas. On 27 March, 350 Texans at the garrison of Goliad who had surrendered to General José Urrea were executed on Santa Anna's orders. These two massacres left the Texans with one remaining army, a disorganized group of approximately 800 effective volunteers under the command of General Sam Houston. After receiving news of the Goliad massacre, Houston ordered a retreat toward the Texas–United States boundary at the Sabine River. Most of the province's Anglo population fled eastward along with Houston's undisciplined army in what became known as the "Runaway Scrape."[1]

While pursuing Houston, Santa Anna made the mistake of dividing his command, reducing the number of his own force to 1,300 men. When the two armies finally took up positions on the banks of the San Jacinto River, near the present site of the city of Houston, Santa Anna further handicapped himself by paying little attention to his army's defensive position. Such carelessness had characterized his handling of the entire campaign and played directly into the hands of the outnumbered and outgunned Texan frontier irregulars. During the afternoon of 21 April, Houston's army, primarily an infantry force supported by only two cannons and a troop of 60 cavalrymen, audaciously launched a frontal assault on the Mexican position that completely routed Santa Anna's soldiers in a matter of minutes. The Mexican leader was captured on the following day and, within a few weeks, signed two

treaties renouncing his nation's territorial claims north of the Rio Grande.[2]

The Battle of San Jacinto had greater military significance and resulted in more profound political repercussions than did the siege and fall of the Alamo. But the Alamo, infused with an atmosphere of ultimate sacrifice and martyrdom, traditionally has occupied a more central position in Texan historical consciousness than has the rapid victory of Houston's army. This may be due in part to the fact that, at San Jacinto, the Texas army slaughtered vengefully a great many Mexican soldiers who were fleeing from the battlefield. Too, Houston's tactics for success at San Jacinto, though markedly more successful militarily than the Texan defense of the Alamo, depended on deception and stealth and provided less material for heroic legends. The Alamo's primacy in the collective Texas memory was established during the upsurge of interest in Texas history after the Civil War by influential figures such as Reuben Potter, who declared that the Alamo, not San Jacinto, had marked the birth of the Republic of Texas.[3]

Nineteenth-century painters reflected this bias by executing only three works concerning San Jacinto. The earliest of these paintings, William Henry Huddle's (1847–1892; Fig. 33) *The Surrender of Santa Anna* (1886; Pl. 13) depicted the battle's aftermath rather than the actual fighting. In Huddle's painting, Houston takes center stage, his wounded ankle being dressed by Surgeon General Dr. Alexander H. Ewing. Deaf Smith, chief scout of the Texas army, occupies a place of honor beside Houston and strains to listen as the fallen leader beckons to Santa Anna to be seated on an ammunition box. Smith had commanded a small band of Texans that had destroyed Vince's Bridge, the Mexican army's lone escape route, before the battle. Beside the trunk of the tree that came to be known as the "Treaty Oak," Mirabeau B. Lamar, commander of the Texan cavalry and a future president of the Republic of Texas, watches the proceedings from beside Thomas J. Rusk, Houston's confidant and secretary of war of the provisional Texas government. Other prominent figures, such as Edward Burleson, Ben McCulloch, and Santa Anna's aide, Colonel Juan Almonte, also are clustered with this group. On Santa Anna's right, a few Texans futilely anticipate an order from Houston to administer retributive justice at the end of a rope. They finally were dissuaded from executing Santa Anna by Houston's argument that the Mexican leader could be useful as a political bargaining chip with the government of Mexico.[4]

In attempting to narrate this pivotal moment in Texas history, Huddle incorporated portraiture and landscape as well as still life, evidenced by the details of Dr. Ewing's medical kit. In preparation for executing the landscape portion of the painting, Huddle traveled to the San Jacinto battlefield and sketched the "Treaty Oak," to which he later devoted a separate canvas. However, Huddle had executed few landscapes at this point in his career, and he may have been assisted in this aspect of the painting by Hermann Lungkwitz, a German immigrant who had been painting the Texas landscape for a quarter-century and who shared a studio with Huddle in Austin during the 1880s. On their frequent sketching trips together into the Texas Hill Country, Huddle painted far fewer landscapes than did his German colleague, who would have been able to render valuable assistance in the execution of *The Surrender of Santa Anna*.[5]

Although one art historian has praised the "kinetic energy" of *The Surrender of Santa Anna*, Huddle failed to convey what must have been a tension-charged atmosphere during this meeting.[6] Huddle's method of composition resembled that employed by George Caleb Bingham, albeit with less lively results. Huddle relied on daguerreotypes, photographs, and his personal acquaintance with the individuals in the scene in his efforts to portray accurately the facial features of these portrait subjects.[7]

Huddle's professional background as a portraitist and his motivation for and timing of the execution of the painting explain its composition and slightly static atmosphere. A Civil War veteran, Huddle set out upon a well-defined career path after leaving his family's gun-

smithing business in Paris, Texas, in 1870. His first art teacher was his cousin, Flavius Fisher, who later became a well-known portrait painter in Washington, D.C. But Huddle's career did not blossom until after he moved to Austin in 1876, following two years of study at the National Academy of Design and the Art Students' League in New York City. In the Texas capital, Huddle rapidly carved out a professional niche by painting portraits of Texas political and military figures, beginning work on his "Gallery of the Governors," a series of portraits of Texas chief executives.[8]

During the mid-1880s, portrait fees enabled Huddle to finance further study at Munich's Bavarian Royal Academy, a decision that may well have been encouraged by his studio partner, Hermann Lungkwitz. Information concerning this period in Huddle's life is fragmentary but indicates that he arrived in Munich in October of 1884 and departed in late March 1885. Immersion in urban European culture may have given him an education equal to anything that he learned in the classroom.

Certainly, Huddle's letters to his fiancée and to Lungkwitz reflect his wonderment at the exotic nature of the Bavarian capital. Huddle's initial reaction to Munich is found in a letter he wrote to Nannie Carver, his future wife, that reads as a corroborative source for Mark Twain's *Innocents Abroad*:

> *My dear friend: . . . It is now about one month since I left Austin and not one word have I heard from anyone and all Together I feel as if I had 'got left' . . . I don't know how to go about telling you about this town, and country— everything is so different from home—art, beer, and music is everywhere, picture galleries by the mile—statues of the great in war, statesmanship, art, and literature stand everywhere there is room for one. The King lives at this place— he is not in town now (I guess he will call on me when he returns) and Dukes and Princes and such Cattle all thick as Colonels.*[9]

But Huddle later hinted at disillusionment with his pursuit of additional training, observing wistfully shortly before he left Munich, "I have studied hard and don't regret the try, but . . . all my time has been occupied painting heads—only one day on each head and often scraping it out and painting it in the same canvas next day."[10]

Huddle returned from Germany as Texas was preparing to celebrate its fiftieth anniversary of independence from Mexico. As Theodore Gentilz had done with *Fall of the Alamo*, Huddle decided to capitalize on the state's historical consciousness by rendering the first painting of Santa Anna's surrender. However, unlike Gentilz, he had not researched his subject over four decades and thus was not able to include the same degree of accurate detail. For example, Huddle portrayed Santa Anna as wearing the jacket of a Mexican enlisted man instead of the plainer civilian clothing in which the general actually had attempted to disguise himself. Too, one eyewitness acount of Santa Anna's interview with Houston maintained that it occurred within the Texan commander's tent, which Houston had roped off to keep away five hundred curious and vengeful Texans.[11]

But such details were less central to Huddle's goals than were the thirty-four portraits in *The Surrender of Santa Anna*. These included many subjects whom Huddle had painted previously and knew well and that enable this canvas to be interpreted as an example of "vanity art" as well as a historical document or an iconographic artifact. Several of these individuals, or members of their families, had gained positions of influence in Texas, and Huddle may have thought that their appearance in such a significant painting would enhance the possibilities of its purchase by the state. Since most written accounts of the surrender mentioned only the relative positions of Houston, Santa Anna, and a few other notables, Huddle had some latitude in how he populated the canvas. For instance, he felt free to omit Lorenzo de Zavala, who acted as an interpreter for the conversation between Houston and Santa Anna. Also, after he completed the painting, Huddle added the likeness of at least one individual he had omitted, Houston's interpreter, Moses Austin Bryan, kneeling between Santa Anna and Colonel Almonte. The artist was instructed to include Bryan by the state legislature, a stipulation included in the appropriations bill for the state's purchase of the canvas. Omission of an individual of such importance indicates the problems caused by Huddle's relatively rapid researching and execution of the painting. In light of this handicap and the scarcity of detailed, written accounts of the incident, the artist's inclusion of other figures in the scene warrants further study.[12]

Huddle hoped that a favorable reception of this painting by the general public would prompt a legislative appropriation for its purchase as well as for his "Gallery of the Governors." However, the artist did not rely solely on public opinion to persuade state officials. In 1888, State Senator H. D. McDonald, representing Huddle's hometown of Paris, introduced legislation to purchase the "Gallery of the Governors" for ten thousand dollars. Soon involved in the controversy concerning McArdle's attempt to win state patronage, McDonald interceded

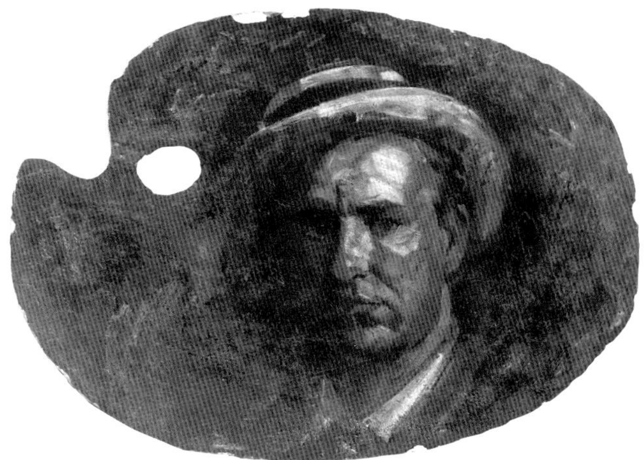

FIGURE 33. William Henry Huddle, *Self-portrait on Palette*, n.d. Estate of Marguerite Huddle Slaughter, Austin, Texas. Photograph by Mark Edward Smith, Austin, Texas.

successfully with Governor L. S. Ross to ensure that the money would be used to purchase Huddle's works. During this period, Huddle also enlisted the aid of powerful friends in American art circles. He finally received seven thousand dollars for twenty portraits and one thousand dollars for a portrait of Thomas J. Rusk in addition to the funds for *The Surrender of Santa Anna*.[13]

Huddle's political instincts and influential acquaintances proved to be an ideal combination in his quest to become the de facto official Texas painter. He and his wife, Nannie, were able to move easily in the same circles as the state's policymakers, the personable couple's shared interest in art giving them an image as mildly exotic. Huddle's stint in a European art academy reinforced official Texans' belief in his superiority as a painter. Despite his successes, though, Huddle's career carries a tinge of frustration, evidenced most strongly in his Munich letters. Portraiture, which seemed initially to be his surest route to artistic success, had become a chore for him. But, reliant on income from this source, Huddle could not afford to forsake it and, ultimately, was trapped by portrait painting. After escaping the Royal Academy's daily drudgery of "painting heads," his first significant work was an attempt at historical narrative painting. But *The Surrender of Santa Anna* became an elaborate exercise in portraiture, though it won the legislature's official approval and soon became a Texas history icon. While Huddle was certainly the favorite artist of many powerful Texans of his day, he was limited finally by his training and the expectations of the same official audience that gave him immediate success. Huddle died of a stroke at age forty-five, before he could fully extend his artistic vision to historical narrative painting.

The earliest painting of the San Jacinto battle itself was executed by an artist who had been unwilling or unable to research his subject thoroughly. L. M. D. Guillaume's (1816–1892) lack of familiarity with details of the battle is evident in his depiction of the Texan victory as having been predominantly a cavalry engagement in *The Battle of San Jacinto* (1892; Pl. 14). Although Mirabeau Lamar's cavalry force did play an important role in the battle, most of the Texan army was on foot, and few of the Mexican soldiers had time to mount and sustain combat on horseback. In addition to this misperception of the battle's essential character, Guillaume's version of San Jacinto is a strange mixture of massed action, swirling smoke, and several immobile, unrecognizable figures. His rendering of Sam Houston resembles a dapper French cavalry officer, complete with goatee, rather than the Texans' commander-in-chief, who presented a more disheveled appearance on the day of the battle. Too, the buckskin-clad figure apparently directing troops and mounted on an exhausted horse to Houston's left appears to be posing for a sculptor.[14]

Guillaume, a native of Nantes, France, had never been in Texas, and his motivations for painting this scene remain unclear. He executed *San Jacinto* at the end of his career, the last several years of which were spent working under the patronage of wealthy businessman and art patron W. W. Corcoran of Washington, D.C. Corcoran and Guillaume strongly supported the Southern cause in the Civil War, and after the war Corcoran dispensed patronage to artists who shared these sympathies.[15] But other aspects of their relationship are obscure, including the question of whether Corcoran commissioned *San Jacinto* or Guillaume undertook it on his own initiative.

Corcoran may have acquired an interest in San Jacinto during the 1840s and 1850s, through his dealings in heavily discounted Republic of Texas commercial paper. These maneuverings were part of an attempt to reap profits from schemes connected with financing of the $10 million debt that Texas had run up during its years as an independent nation between 1836 and 1845. In the 1850s, two of San Jacinto's most prominent veterans, Sam Houston and Thomas J. Rusk, served as Texas senators in Washington and voted with Corcoran's interests on every piece of legislation affecting this issue that came before the U.S. Congress. Guillaume perhaps undertook the painting as a belated token of gratitude to these figures after Corcoran's death in 1888.[16]

Guillaume's career paralleled that of William Huddle in several respects. In addition to ties to Virginia, both men were personable and cultivated an influential clientele; Guillaume had been persuaded to move to the United States in 1852 by the American ambassador to France, William Cabel Rives. In Richmond and Washington, D.C., he built a reputation as a competent copyist of portraits by eighteenth-century artists as well as becoming known as a portraitist in his own right. Guillaume further resembled Huddle in his "great man" approach to historical portraiture. *Allegorical Figure of the French Republic*, Guillaume's first painting executed for public exhibition, was displayed at the 1837 Paris Salon and had a historical subject. Following the Civil War, Guillaume painted numerous equestrian portraits of Confederate officers in battlefield settings, a style that he employed in *San Jacinto*. As did Huddle, he endeavored to use this experience in historical portraiture as a base for historical narrative painting. Although painted in a far more realistic style than was *San Jacinto*, Guillaume's *The Surrender of General Lee to General Grant, April 9, 1865* (ca. 1875; Fig. 34) also distorted elements of its historical subject, even though Guillaume had witnessed the event.[17]

The atmosphere of *San Jacinto* resembles that of the battle paintings of Guillaume's mentor, the popular French history painter Paul Delaroche (1797–1867), who was noted for his "polished, appealingly sentimental" depictions of historical scenes.[18] Delaroche's many cavalry scenes undoubtedly influenced Guillaume to feature cavalry combat prominently in his portrayal of the Texan victory. As did Delaroche, Guillaume utilized light for dramatic effect, exemplified by the shaft of sunlight knifing through the clouds behind Houston and illuminating a Mexican artillery piece surrounded by the corpses of its defenders. Unfortunately, Guillaume also combined inferior elements of Delaroche's works. The stiff, frozen figures in the foreground of *San Jacinto* resemble the sculptured frieze effect of Delaroche's *The Taking of the Trocadero* (1827–1828). The middle distance and background of Guillaume's painting, especially the clashing infantrymen atop the barricades, reflect Delaroche's opposite extreme of chaotic, swirling action, found in *Charlemagne Crossing the Alps* (1847), which Delaroche's biographer described aptly as a "writhing mass of interlocked horse and humanity."[19]

Despite these flaws, Delaroche was praised for reconciling the genres of battle and portrait painting, fulfilling critics' expectations that painters also serve as historians. Unlike later painters, who feared critics' labeling of their work as "illustration," Delaroche regarded historical narrative painting as a high calling. Most of his canvases took as their subject the theme of unlawful usurpation of rightful rule, earning Delaroche the designation of "court painter to all decapitated sovereigns."[20] Ironically, Guillaume turned his former teacher's favorite theme on its head by depicting in *San Jacinto* the overthrow of an absolute ruler by democratic usurpers.

Although Guillaume enjoyed great popularity in the nation's capital and in Virginia, his rendering of the Battle of San Jacinto received scant attention. Consequently, Henry McArdle's *The Battle of San Jacinto* (1895; Pl. 15) was the only nineteenth-century painting depicting the actual events of the battle to receive wide exposure, and it merits extended discussion. In the fashion of *Dawn at the Alamo*, McArdle endeavored to depict the totality of the battle, hoping to place San Jacinto alongside the Alamo in terms of heroic proportion and significance. McArdle employed similar research methods and compositional techniques in executing both paintings. For example, he was careful to include any individual whose likeness he had been able to reconstruct through either personal acquaintance or photographs. More importantly, both paintings are executed in the painstaking style of "picto-maps," reflecting McArdle's award-winning student career at the Maryland Institute for the Promotion of the Mechanic Arts.[21] Narration of these events, including accurate depiction of uniforms and accoutrements, contributed to McArdle's overall purpose of bringing his viewers to an awareness and appreciation of the "grand sweep" of each battle as the sum total of specific vignettes involving readily identifiable individuals.

San Jacinto, set in an open battlefield rather than an enclosed fort, furnished McArdle with an even better opportunity than did *Dawn at the Alamo* to display the skills that he had honed as a Civil War topographical artist. McArdle initially intended to pattern the painting after one of several renderings of the Mexican War's Battle of Chapultepec, but *San Jacinto* owes more to his first attempt at battle painting, *Lee at the Wilderness* (ca. 1872; Fig. 35). McArdle regarded this tribute to Robert E. Lee as one of his finest works and remained inconsolable for the remainder of his life after its destruction in the 1881 Capitol fire. An examination of this painting aids in gaining an understanding of the artist's aesthetic approach, intent, use of compositional elements, research methods, and of the audience expectations that recurred two decades later in *San Jacinto*.[22]

McArdle began work on *Lee at the Wilderness* soon after moving to Independence, Texas, in 1867. He had

served under Lee and may have been present at the Battle of the Wilderness. This incident had become famous for the action of a few members of Hood's Brigade in restraining Lee from leading their charge on a Union position at a critical point in the battle, the Texans shouting "Lee to the rear" until their commander-in-chief relented in his determination. McArdle's papers include no mention of written accounts of the incident, and he likely combined these rudimentary oral histories with his own knowledge of the battle.[23] In preparation for this painting, McArdle researched details of Civil War flags, weapons, uniforms, and troop placements. In the fashion of his consultations with Potter on *Dawn at the Alamo*, he contacted individuals having extensive knowledge concerning these subjects, such as former Confederate General Pierre G. T. Beauregard. In addition to utilizing photographs to supplement his personal knowledge of the facial features of Texas veterans of the battle, McArdle employed some of these men as studio models in executing preliminary sketches of the scene.[24]

Lee at the Wilderness anticipates *The Battle of San Jacinto* in several respects. In visually narrating both events, McArdle employed fire, smoke, and climatic elements to impart a dramatic, near-mystical atmosphere to a critical historical moment. Lee and the men of Hood's Brigade seem to materialize from billowing, roseate clouds and columns of smoke. Years later, McArdle explained similar aspects of *San Jacinto* and their intended effects. McArdle was careful to situate the viewer on an elevation facing northeastward across the battlefield, looking away from the setting sun. He hoped that the shadows of sunset would "add to the dramatic effect of the death-grapple"

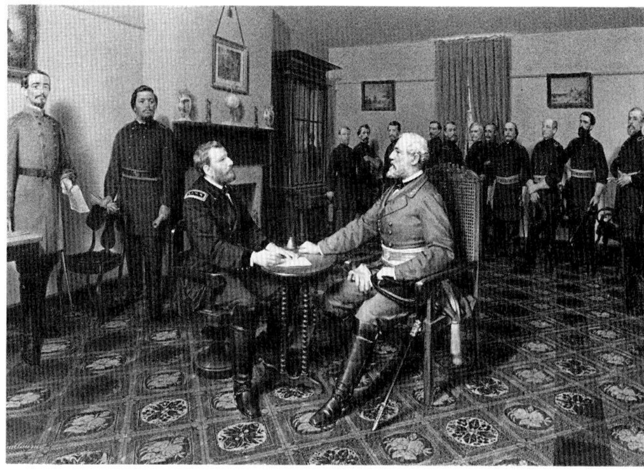

FIGURE 34. L. M. D. Guillaume, *The Surrender of General Lee to General Grant, April 9, 1865*, ca. 1875. Oil. National Park Service, U.S. Department of the Interior. Photograph by Richard Frear.

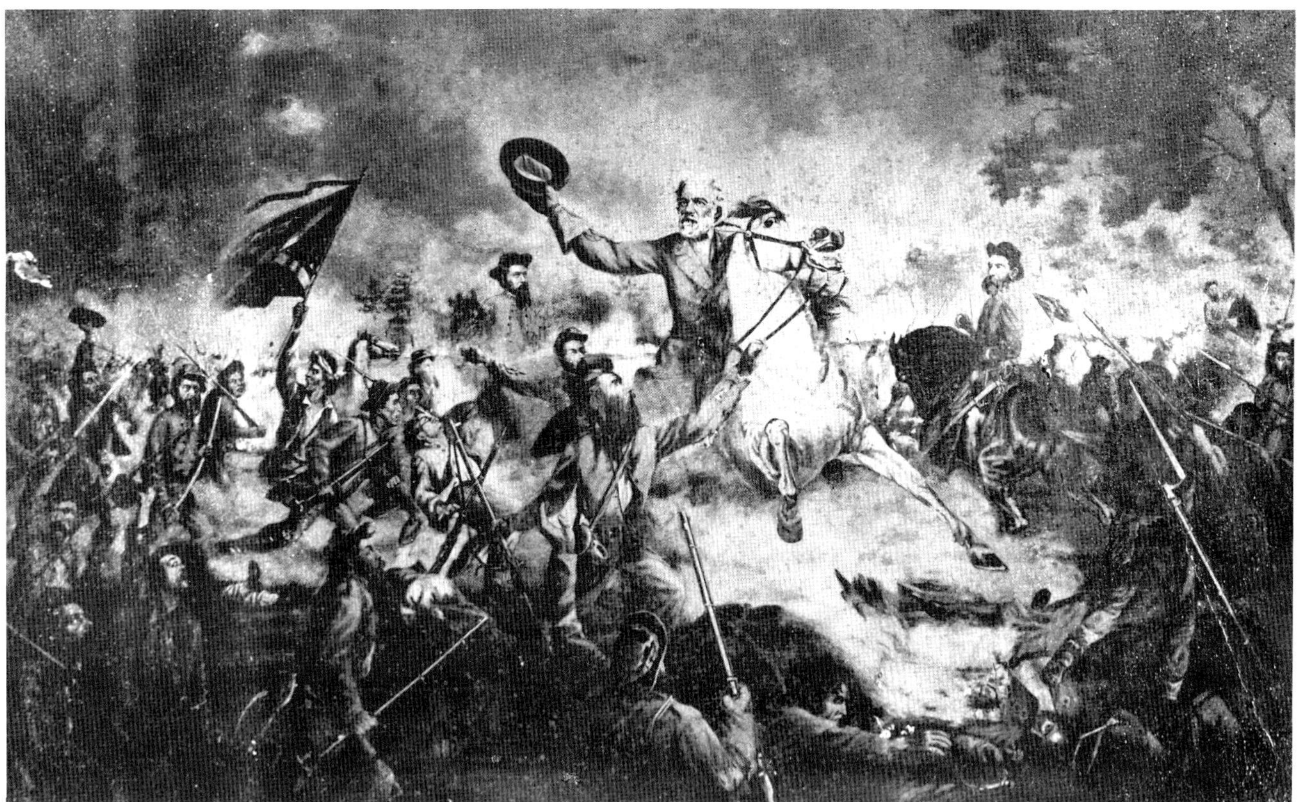

FIGURE 35. Henry Arthur McArdle, *Lee at the Wilderness*,
ca. 1872. Painting destroyed; photograph from the Archives
Division-Texas State Library. Acc. no. 1989/78-1.

and convey "intense and graphic power . . . softened
by poetic fervour."[25] In the final section of his description of the painting, entitled "Freedom's Light: Triumph
of Texas' Independence (The aspect of the Heavens),"
McArdle elaborated on his manipulation of clouds and
sunlight, a manipulation anticipated in *Lee at the Wilderness*: "Dark, inauspicious, and threatening clouds which
overspread the heavens are suggestive of the suffering,
danger, and death under which Texas had struggled . . .
last rays of the setting sun break through the gloom, typical of the light and freedom and victory which is to be
the result of the Texian victory at San Jacinto."[26]

Lee at the Wilderness and *San Jacinto* have another
common characteristic: McArdle repainted each painting for two of his patrons. Although circumstances surrounding execution of both of these repainted canvases
are unclear, McArdle's chronic need for money seems to
have motivated him in each case. Four years after *Lee at
the Wilderness* was destroyed in the 1881 Capitol fire, the
artist painted a smaller version, cropping the left and
right extremes of the original scene (1885; Pl. 16). This
work was in payment for a debt of four hundred dollars

that McArdle owed to a pioneer Texas physician who had
furnished him with painting supplies so that the artist
could repaint the works destroyed in the fire; the canvas
is still owned by the physician's descendants. And, in
1901, DeShields had paid McArdle four hundred dollars
for a slightly scaled-down (5′ × 7′) version of *San Jacinto*, which is unlocated.[27]

Lee at the Wilderness served as an important way station in the development of McArdle's "picto-map" style
that became more prominent in *Dawn at the Alamo* and
San Jacinto, which are filled with a greater number of action portraits grouped as self-contained vignettes. As in
the later battle paintings, several of the figures in *Lee at
the Wilderness* have distorted proportion and perspective.
In the right foreground, a wounded Confederate soldier
reaches for a canteen beside the head of a dead comrade
who lies in a patch of burning grass. The size and placement of these two figures do not harmonize with those
in the rest of the painting but appear to be included primarily for melodramatic effect, as were several figures of
dying Texans in *Dawn at the Alamo*. In a typical public
reaction to *Lee at the Wilderness*, one reviewer noted that

the "unity" of this "breathing canvas" caused the viewer to take in the scene in its entirety rather than concentrate on any single aspect of it.[28]

While such acclaim delighted McArdle, he was most concerned with the reaction of one particular group, the Hood's Texas Brigade Association. During June 1873, this organization of the unit's veterans gathered for a reunion in Austin, where McArdle was exhibiting *Lee at the Wilderness*. The painting had already garnered considerable praise, and, during the reunion, Austin's Avenue Hotel and Hillyer's Gallery were selling individual photographic copies of the work for two dollars. McArdle hoped to sell *Lee at the Wilderness* to the association, but its members were unable to raise sufficient funds. During the next few years, the artist continued to exhibit it and others of his historical paintings, occasionally in conjunction with other veterans' reunions. During the 1875 Texas State Fair in Houston, former Confederate President Jefferson Davis wept openly while viewing the canvas. In an attempt to sell *Lee at the Wilderness* to the state of Texas, McArdle placed it in the State Capitol, where it burned within a few years.[29]

Despite their similarities, *Lee at the Wilderness* was a less ambitious undertaking than *San Jacinto*. The two works are comparable in size, but instead of a sprawl of detailed vignettes of equal importance, *Lee at the Wilderness* has a central focus so that McArdle highlights the heroism of the Confederate commander and the devotion of his men. Comparison of McArdle's portrayal of Lee with his treatment of Texas commander-in-chief Sam Houston in *San Jacinto* emphasizes this difference. In contrast to McArdle's casting Lee as a "godlike" figure, Sam Houston appears as one of a number of soldiers in *San Jacinto*.[30] This "everyman" portrayal was in keeping with an image of Houston as a Jacksonian "man of the people" that was projected by his political allies, who related tales of Houston loaning money to his troops and helping them to push artillery and wagons out of the mud.[31] But controversy dogged Houston throughout his life in Texas. Despite its success, his strategy in the weeks leading up to San Jacinto was the subject of considerable debate for several years; also, his strong personality had a polarizing effect on Texas politics throughout the 1840s and 1850s.

Houston was not unanimously beloved in Texas, and his enemies accused him of being an arrogant, self-serving politician who had profited politically from an inflated war record. This controversy gave rise to false charges that the Texan army's commander had dodged the area of heaviest combat and fiercest fighting. In response,

veteran William Taylor, who claimed to have witnessed Houston conducting himself with consummate bravery, urged McArdle to clear Houston's name by depicting him in an egalitarian yet heroic light. McArdle followed Taylor's suggestion, accurately depicting Houston as attempting to continue to lead the Texan charge after having had his horse shot from under him and his right ankle shattered by a musket ball. In the center left portion of the canvas, beside a Mexican battery, the Texan commander waves his white planter's hat as he prepares to lead his men afoot against a small band of riflemen forming behind Mexican General Manuel Fernández Castrillón. In a vignette reminiscent of the central portion of *Lee at the Wilderness*, Houston's unarmed aide, disregarding his own safety, leads a horse to his commander.[32]

This depiction of Houston in a heroic manner contrasted sharply with McArdle's treatment of the cowardice of Santa Anna, who personified San Jacinto veteran Walter Lane's description of the majority of the Mexican troops as "running like turkeys" from the battlefield.[33] In the painting's upper right portion, the Mexican leader, mounted on a black horse and wearing a white sombrero, flees the battlefield. A brown mule, trailing a rope from his neck, races behind him while a black mule kicks his hind legs into the air before the fleeing "Napoleon of the West." McArdle explained that he had included this prosaic vignette to demonstrate that "even [Santa Anna's] mules have lost respect for him."[34]

But McArdle's depictions of Mexican combatants included a number of portrayals of valor as well as venality. Reuben Potter, while terming San Jacinto one of the most important battles of history, also described it as one "in which the effective valor was all on one side, and the slaughter, wrought mainly in pursuit, was almost wholly on the other."[35] Hints of this ambivalence concerning stereotypes of the opposing armies had appeared in Potter's earliest advice for *Dawn at the Alamo*, such as his assertion that the "bravest attacks" on the morning of 6 March demonstrated the valor of the Mexican soldiers.[36] Potter elaborated on this theme in writings on San Jacinto. He lauded the initial composure of many of the Mexican troops and went on to note that they had plundered the countryside far less than had the Texans during the preceding six weeks. Potter's designation of Captain Juan Seguin's small force of Tejanos as "the only contingent of native Texans" and requests of McArdle by other prominent Texans to emphasize this detachment's heroism precluded any attempt by the artist to depict all ethnic Mexicans as inferior to Anglos.[37]

Although McArdle began extensive research on the

painting after Potter's death, he followed closely his late advisor's account. *San Jacinto* presented ethnic Mexicans on both sides in a fashion that went beyond a simple light-skinned/dark-skinned, good/evil mentality, and the artist described several Mexican combatants as "brave," "chivalrous," and "gallant."[38] McArdle also received several suggestions concerning composition of the many action portraits from David Woodward, who advised his former student to render the combatants in proper "heroic proportion."[39] In his written explanation of *San Jacinto*, McArdle declared that, despite its mass of detail, the painting's "unity has never been lost sight of."[40] This unifying element is the bravery shown by soldiers of both sides in the many discrete and simultaneous vignettes, such as Antonio Trevino and Henry Karnes engaged in mounted combat for possession of a Mexican flag (see lower right corner) and General Castrillón's attempt to rally a semblance of resistance (see center right portion). Many Texans were especially sympathetic toward Castrillón, whom they regarded as an elderly, noble warrior who was murdered by bloodthirsty Texas soldiers even after their commanding officers ordered them not to fire on the Mexican general.[41]

In order to legitimize the use of these subjective elements in his quest for "pictorial history," McArdle pursued the same aesthetic of accuracy as he did in *Dawn at the Alamo*. In executing *San Jacinto*, McArdle contended that he "aimed at natural action and historic truth."[42] As did Huddle, McArdle journeyed to the battlefield but, due to the wider scope of his subject, conducted far more detailed research. This required several excursions and included measuring and photographing all areas of the battlefield, siting the positions of individual units, and drawing up diagrams and models of the battle. The intricate accuracy of McArdle's detailed preliminary studies prompted Woodward to encourage the artist to alter selected features of the battlefield in order to achieve more dramatic visual effects.[43]

In addition to researching the topographical and tactical elements of the battle, McArdle attempted to collect or inspect examples of weapons and uniforms that might have been used at San Jacinto. In tracking down this data, he consulted published reports of the battle by Sam Houston and Mexican Army Colonel Pedro Delgado. He again sought out General Beauregard as well as U.S. Army General O. O. Howard for details regarding the flags, military fortifications, uniforms, and weaponry of both armies. But these efforts of the indefatigable McArdle frequently elicited little more than encouragement from these two well-known figures. However, the artist realized that such correspondence could impress state legislators with his thoroughness and result in endorsements of his work by recognized military authorities. Ultimately, though, McArdle's most fruitful sources of detailed information proved to be San Jacinto veterans, many of them relatively unknown, and their families.[44]

McArdle's relationships with these individuals shaped many aspects of *San Jacinto*. A key motivation for his timing of the painting, which meant interrupting revision of *Dawn at the Alamo*, was the opportunity to interview and correspond with veterans and their families and to execute the canvas in their lifetimes. McArdle made full use of contacts with veterans that he had gained while working on *Lee at the Wilderness* and the original *Dawn at the Alamo*. These veterans rewarded the artist with official endorsements of the truthfulness of the painting, which he attempted to turn to his advantage in efforts to find a buyer for the canvas.[45]

The large number of survivors of the battle ensured that McArdle would be bombarded with many more opinions than he could incorporate in his finished canvas. In referring to his use of several diagrams of the battlefield, McArdle admitted that the painting was "not a slavish transcript of the model—though the strongest (?) realism is preserved."[46] His use of a question mark raises an interesting point: was the artist simply not sure whether he was using the most appropriate word, or was he defending the accuracy of the painting? He points out that the work was "too intricate in detail for an entirely satisfactory description."[47] Again, does this express a desire not to bore the reader, or was McArdle searching for a way to avoid criticism from dissenting San Jacinto veterans who might find fault with his artistic conception of the battle?

McArdle's fear is understandable in light of historical controversies concerning the battle, especially those dealing with the commanders of the two opposing armies. Questions about Houston's conduct paled in comparison to the debate over which Texans should have been credited with having captured Santa Anna. McArdle avoided this dispute, but his depiction of Santa Anna as fleeing on horseback was challenged by Houston's defender, William Taylor. Another veteran, J. M. Hill, who furnished the artist with a great deal of information, also pointed out McArdle's artistic liberty in portraying the battle as occurring near sunset. McArdle was especially sensitive to such criticism because many veterans had subscribed funds for completion of the painting, which was repeatedly delayed.[48]

In addition to the advancing age of the San Jacinto

veterans, the Texas legislature's 1888 purchase of Huddle's *The Surrender of Santa Anna* seems to have prodded McArdle into beginning work on *San Jacinto*, just as Onderdonk might have sped completion of *Dawn at the Alamo*. With very few exceptions, McArdle began gathering research material shortly after the completion of Huddle's painting in 1886, and this research activity increased markedly after 1888. He disdained Huddle's work, although the men had studied together at the National Academy and the Art Students' League. McArdle regarded Huddle as an unworthy competitor, and especially resented his rival's successful marketing tactics with the state legislature. McArdle complained to General Beauregard that, even though he had rendered many items more accurately than had Huddle, state officials would offer "inevitable advance criticism" of McArdle's "truthful representation," since they already had purchased the "so-called *Surrender of Santa Anna* (a misnomer as you know)."[49]

In 1901, hopeful that the legislature would appropriate money for the purchase of this and others of his paintings, McArdle received permission to hang *San Jacinto* in the Senate chamber. He had already been discouraged by David Woodward from attempting to sell the painting on the East Coast, despite his former teacher's praise of the work as "successful and elaborate."[50] In 1905, McArdle placed *Dawn at the Alamo* in the Senate chamber with similar hopes of purchase by the state, a sale that had not materialized by his death in 1908. The artist's family then embarked on a long struggle to persuade the legislature to purchase both canvases, which continued to be displayed in the Capitol. In 1927, the Fortieth Legislature finally appropriated a total of $25,000 for the purchase of both paintings and a trunk full of notes, letters, and sketches amassed during McArdle's research. Valuing each canvas at $12,500, lawmakers appropriated $10,000 for fiscal 1927–1928 and $15,000 for fiscal 1928–1929. State officials had originally offered the family a total of $10,000 when negotiations had commenced soon after McArdle's death. Nevertheless, the state did get a bargain: by 1927, the family had set a "rock-bottom" price of $30,000, since the two works had been appraised at $25,000 each. This hard bargaining by the legislature stirred up a public outcry against what was perceived as shoddy treatment of the artist's family. In recalling the negotiations many years later, McArdle's son observed that "some of those senators didn't know as much as a chicken about art. One senator . . . said you could get photographs that big a lot cheaper."[51]

McArdle's difficulty in selling his paintings to the state seems puzzling in light of their widespread public approval. In the late 1880s, the legislature had readily appropriated $10,000 for Huddle's works, portraits that demonstrated a more limited artistic vision than did McArdle's battle paintings. The two artists' canvases now hang in the same building and, coincidentally, complement each other. But this harmony belies the fact that McArdle and Huddle executed their paintings at different times, for different reasons, and with different goals. A thorough analysis of the respective meanings and messages of these works must deal with such issues as well as how each painter's personality, artistic emphasis, and the expectations of art by dispensers of state patronage contributed to rapid success for one artist and a protracted, futile struggle for official recognition by the other.

Both Huddle and McArdle were regarded as colorful personalities but in quite different ways. Huddle's profession simply added an exotic tang to his image in his circle of Austin friends. A well-liked "man about town," he fit easily into the relatively (for frontier Texas) sophisticated atmosphere of Austin, as evidenced by the frequent, good-natured jibes directed at him by local newspaper columnist Alexander Sweet.[52] By contrast, McArdle seems to have had a much smaller circle of friends. Moreover, his eccentricity had a slightly bizarre quality and permeated all aspects of his life. While Huddle was readily absorbed into a circle of bankers, businessmen, landowners, and politicians, McArdle perennially had the air of the stereotypical, preoccupied university professor who was teaching in order to finance, however meagerly, pursuit of his artistic goals and ideals.

These two artists' choice and execution of subjects highlighted their sharp personality differences. Huddle began painting portraits of prominent Texans within a few months after his arrival in Austin. He may well have been encouraged to move to the state capital for this very purpose by Flavius Fisher, his successful portraitist cousin in Washington, D.C. Initially content to be considered as Texas's foremost portrait painter, Huddle executed a large number of canvases and built up a sizable clientele. Income from portraiture enabled him also to engage in still-life painting, which may have been his first love but was not as lucrative. For McArdle, portraiture was secondary, a necessary evil that assisted in the financing of his ambitious artistic plans. McArdle was an ideologue and visionary; in direct contrast to Huddle, he set out to fulfill personal aesthetic goals, assuming that public acclaim would guarantee purchase of his canvases.

But McArdle miscalculated, failing to take into account that approval by the general public would not translate automatically into official acceptance by a government bureaucracy. Living away from Austin, without "friends at court," McArdle was powerless to protest when the state purchasing board classed his paintings as "a number of character not contemplated to be purchased under the law" and refused to purchase any of his works during his lifetime.[53] Huddle, on the other hand, realized early in his career that, in order to become the official painter of Texas, he had to strive primarily to please the decision-makers and hope that he could receive a modicum of the general public's praise in the bargain.

Nearly a century after Huddle and McArdle began painting Texas subjects, novelist/historian Wallace Stegner characterized writing concerning the American West as "literature almost without a Present."[54] In rejecting McArdle's blood-stained visions of Texas history and enshrining Huddle's formal, well-scrubbed procession of somber faces, Texas state officials attempted to present an orderly, sanitized art almost devoid of a Past. The "character" of paintings considered desirable by these officials was indicated by their appropriation for Huddle's "Gallery of the Governors." Huddle's paintings conveyed an image of staid respectability for a state that, only within the previous decade, had been connected to the rest of the United States by rail and had subdued Indian raids on its southwestern frontier. At the height of America's Gilded Age, Texas legislators opted for dignified serenity instead of McArdle's scenes of violence. State officials paid homage to martial exploits but dollars for images confirming Texas's integration into the American mainstream. While the general public had a visceral attraction to McArdle's turgid scenes of death, its elected representatives chose to suppress this aspect of the state's past in an attempt to cast a homogenous veneer of respectability over late nineteenth-century Texas.

CHAPTER FOUR

Men with the Bark On

CONFLICT BETWEEN Texas and Mexico did not cease with Santa Anna's surrender at San Jacinto. Mexico refused diplomatic recognition of the Republic of Texas, and the new nation's nine-year existence was punctuated by armed conflict between the two countries. These hostilities became interwoven with tensions between Indian tribes and Texas settlers, which continued after United States annexation of Texas and the Mexican War had resolved the military and political aspects of Texas-Mexico relations. Nineteenth-century painters found abundant subject material in the violent incidents that occurred on the battleground that was the Texas frontier during the quarter-century between the Texas Revolution and the Civil War.

In the summer of 1841, Texas President Mirabeau B. Lamar heightened tensions with Mexico by commissioning 321 men to undertake a trek across Texas to Santa Fe. Lamar suggested that this overland expedition to New Mexico would afford the twin benefits of investigating the potential of that region's mines and an "opportunity for chastising the Comanches."[1] Actually, he regarded the Santa Fe Expedition as the first step in his dream of building a Western empire stretching to the Pacific. But the members of this ill-conceived and poorly prepared venture underwent severe hardships during their journey. Upon arriving in Santa Fe, the expedition's survivors were arrested by the Mexican Army, marched across the deserts of northern Mexico, and imprisoned until April 1842.[2]

A few weeks before these Texans were released from prison, Mexico, again governed by Santa Anna, retaliated for the Santa Fe Expedition by sending troops into Texas that occupied San Antonio for a few days before returning to Mexico. The following September, General Adrian Woll led another Mexican force triumphantly into the city. Although it also withdrew peacefully, this force was attacked during its return march and suffered the loss of one hundred men. Woll's troops crossed back over the Rio Grande only a few days before Sam Houston, who had been elected president of Texas in the autumn of 1841, sent General Alexander Somervell to Laredo as a prelude to organizing a counterinvasion of Mexico. But Somervell only was able to assemble a force in San Antonio consisting primarily of frontier adventurers out for personal gain. In Laredo, this proposed orderly military invasion degenerated rapidly into a free-for-all when many of the Texans sacked the border town on 9 December 1842. An angry General Somervell confiscated their plunder and turned it over to the town's *alcalde* before disavowing the mission and withdrawing with two hundred men.[3]

Three hundred Texans, including Samuel H. Walker and W. W. "Big Foot" Wallace, both of whom soon gained fame in the Mexican War, refused to follow Somervell's orders and crossed into Mexico, striking out downstream along the Rio Grande. After a brief clash with Mexican troops at the remote settlement of Mier, they surrendered and were marched across the northern Mexican desert to prison at Salado, one hundred miles west of Saltillo. Following a short-lived escape by the Texans into the surrounding wasteland and their subsequent recapture, Santa Anna ordered that the entire group be executed. However, the American and British ambassadors in Mexico City persuaded him to execute only one-tenth of the prisoners' number. To accomplish this execution-by-decimation, the Mexican commander, Colonel Domingo Huerta, ordered each prisoner, blindfolded, to draw from a pitcher containing 159 white and 17 black beans. Those drawing black beans were shot on 25 March 1843. The survivors, though treated harshly in prison, were freed in September 1844.[4]

The returning prisoners' story sparked an immediate and widespread outcry in Texas against the executions. Despite this popular outrage, only two nineteenth-century painters depicted the incident. The first of these works, Theodore Gentilz's *Shooting of the 17 Decimated Texians at El Salado, Mexico* (1885; Pl. 17 and Fig. 36) apparently resulted from the same desire to capitalize on the semicentennial of Texas independence that had prompted the artist to paint *Fall of the Alamo*. Composed in much the same fashion as *Death of Dickinson*, it is marked by a somewhat naive overall concept but great attention to detail. Gentilz patterned the work after an engraving by one of the prisoners, Charles McLaughlin, that had been reproduced in 1845 as an illustration for a first-person narrative of the ordeal by another prisoner, Thomas J. Green. In fact, Gentilz simply transferred many of the elements of this illustration to his own canvas. Unlike *Fall of the Alamo*, *Shooting of the 17 Decimated Texians* did not grow out of the artist's decades-long fascination with the subject, and his papers do not indicate that Gentilz undertook the same type of meticulous research as he did for his Alamo paintings. Furthermore, Gentilz varied only slightly the title of McLaughlin's work, *Shooting of the Decimated Texians at Solado* (Fig. 37).[5]

McLaughlin had followed closely Green's written account of the execution. Both men drew their information from the condemned men's interpreter, who had remained in the courtyard until all of the Texans had died. The rest of the prisoners, including Green and McLaughlin, were detained on the other side of one of the courtyard walls, terrified by the sound of shots and the groans of their comrades. The composition of McLaughlin's work, with its faceless, stiff figures assembled within a walled courtyard drawn with mathematical precision, played to Gentilz's artistic strengths. Gentilz's painting also combined certain elements of *Fall of the Alamo* and *Death of Dickinson*. As does *Fall of the Alamo*, it focuses on no one of the stiff figures but is technically well drafted and portrays, as does *Death of Dickinson*, a tragic and heroic scene. Gentilz's painting retains virtually all of the details that McLaughlin gleaned from the interpreter's account. For example, almost unnoticeably, in the upper right portion of the painting a soldier faints as the fatal shots are fired, and his comrades prevent him from tumbling over the wall. His falling blue shako contrasts against the tawny adobe wall as a clue to the viewer to look to the source of this action.[6]

But Gentilz added his own touches to the scene. These apparently minor alterations of McLaughlin's work mitigate the horror of the event or at least lend an air of humanity to the Mexicans. In the lower right corner, instead of McLaughlin's men and women engaged in conversation and peddling trinkets, Gentilz substituted a grimacing soldier turning his back on the carnage and the figure of a kneeling Mexican woman reciting her rosary. In the lower left, Gentilz removed completely the street vendor who occupied the space in the book illustration. Most obviously, Gentilz followed Green's account more closely by positioning the executed men with their backs to the firing squad. Also, Gentilz portrayed all of the civilians, and one of the soldiers standing at attention, with their eyes riveted on the doomed Texans. By contrast, the viewer sees only the backs of McLaughlin's soldiers in the immediate foreground. McLaughlin's spectators appear nonchalant as the firing squad methodically reloads, pouring fire into its victims.

These discrepancies may be explained in part by the fact that Gentilz and McLaughlin were depicting different moments of the execution. Green recalled that the firing continued for "ten to twelve minutes," with one Texan, Henry Whaling, taking fifteen bullets before dying.[7] McLaughlin conveys the sense of this continous action, especially in his rendering of three soldiers pausing almost casually as their victims topple from their log bench. Gentilz instead chose to depict the firing of the first volley of shots as the doomed men are still seated in an orderly row. His painting gives no hint that the execution was anything other than quick, clean, and, under the circumstances, as humane as possible.

But Gentilz's alteration of the McLaughlin illustration also illustrates the background and cultural affinities of the two men. Green, in the preface to his memoir, aired his views forthrightly, declaring that the volume understated Mexico's "vices . . . and general degradation."[8] He went on to glorify the Mier Expedition's motives and roundly condemned President Houston for his official disavowal of its exploits. Green's account of the execu-

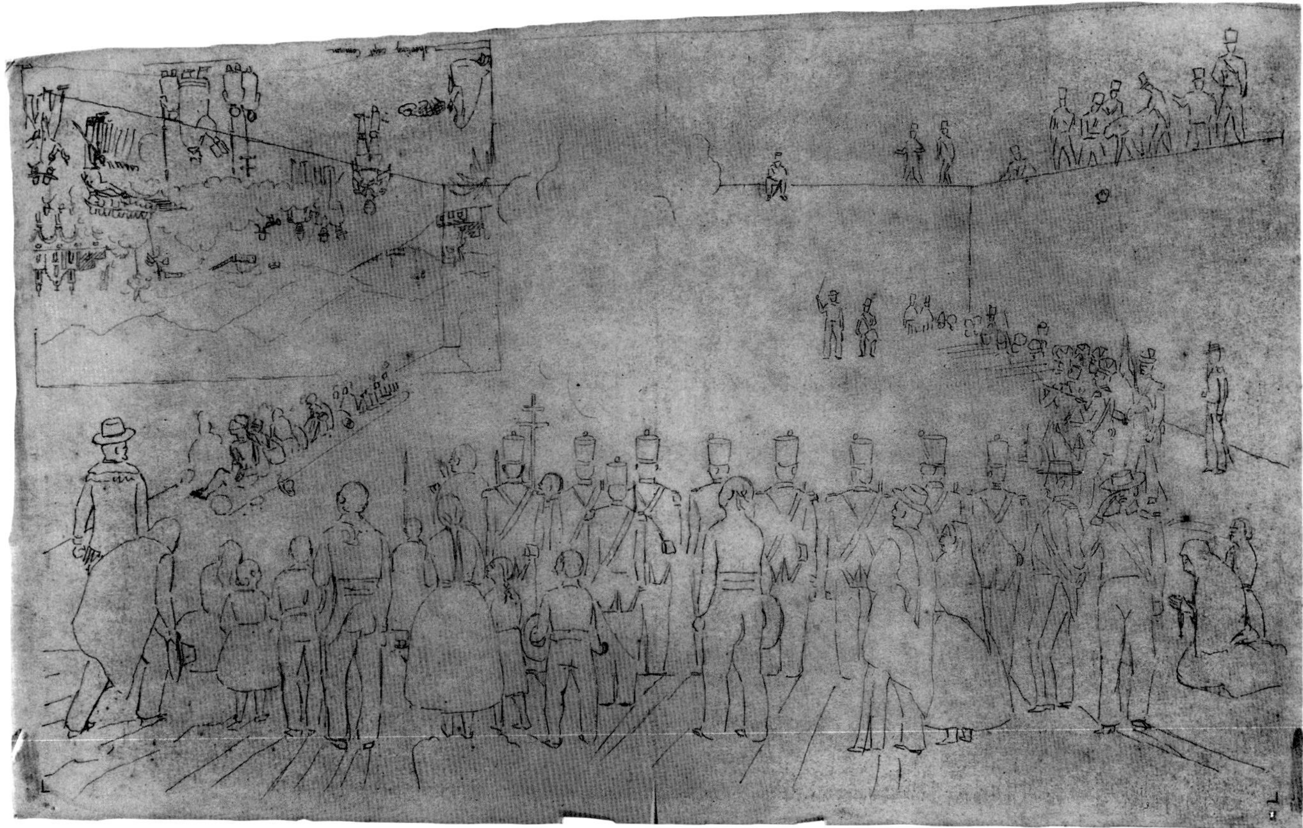

FIGURE 36. Theodore Gentilz, sketch for *Shooting of the 17
Decimated Texians at El Salado, Mexico*, 1885. Daughters of the
Republic of Texas Library at the Alamo, San Antonio, Texas.

tions quoted heroic last words of the doomed Texans and
emphasized Mexican cruelty.[9] Unlike Green, Gentilz had
lived among San Antonio's Mexican population for forty
years and devoted most of his artistic energies to sympathetic portrayals of its culture and folkways. While
the French artist certainly believed in celebrating Texan
heroism, his treatment of the execution of the Mier prisoners indicates that he also was concerned with presenting at least some Mexicans as human beings capable of
compassion.

In addition to this work, Gentilz considered painting
another scene from the unfortunate Mier Expedition but
only progressed as far as execution of a study sketch. Entitled *Shooting Capt. Cameron* (n.d.; Fig. 38), this sketch
appears in the upper left corner of the study sketch for
Shooting of the 17 Decimated Texians. During their march
to imprisonment, Ewen Cameron had orchestrated the
escape of the Mier prisoners that resulted in Santa Anna's
order for their execution. Green exalted Cameron as the
leader of the escape effort in which "the Texians gave

the world another evidence of their superiority over the
Mexicans."[10]

For Anglo-Texans steeped in the Romanticism of
James Fenimore Cooper and Sir Walter Scott, Ewen
Cameron proved to be the ideal tragic hero of the Mier
Expedition. Admired as "manly," "dignified," and possessed of a "quiet coolness," he had led the repulse of a
group of Mexican soldiers at Mier by ordering the Texans
to throw rocks instead of taking time to reload their
weapons.[11] Even though Cameron had drawn a white
bean at Salado, Santa Anna ordered his execution shortly
before the surviving prisoners were marched into Mexico
City. Gentilz's sketch followed closely McLaughlin's illustration of the execution as narrated by Green (1845;
Fig. 39). When led before his firing squad, Cameron disdained the offer of a priest to hear his confession and of
a blindfold. Both Gentilz and McLaughlin captured the
next moment when the Scotsman threw open his shirt
and commanded the Mexican soldiers to fire.[12]

A decade after Gentilz appealed to Texans' sense of

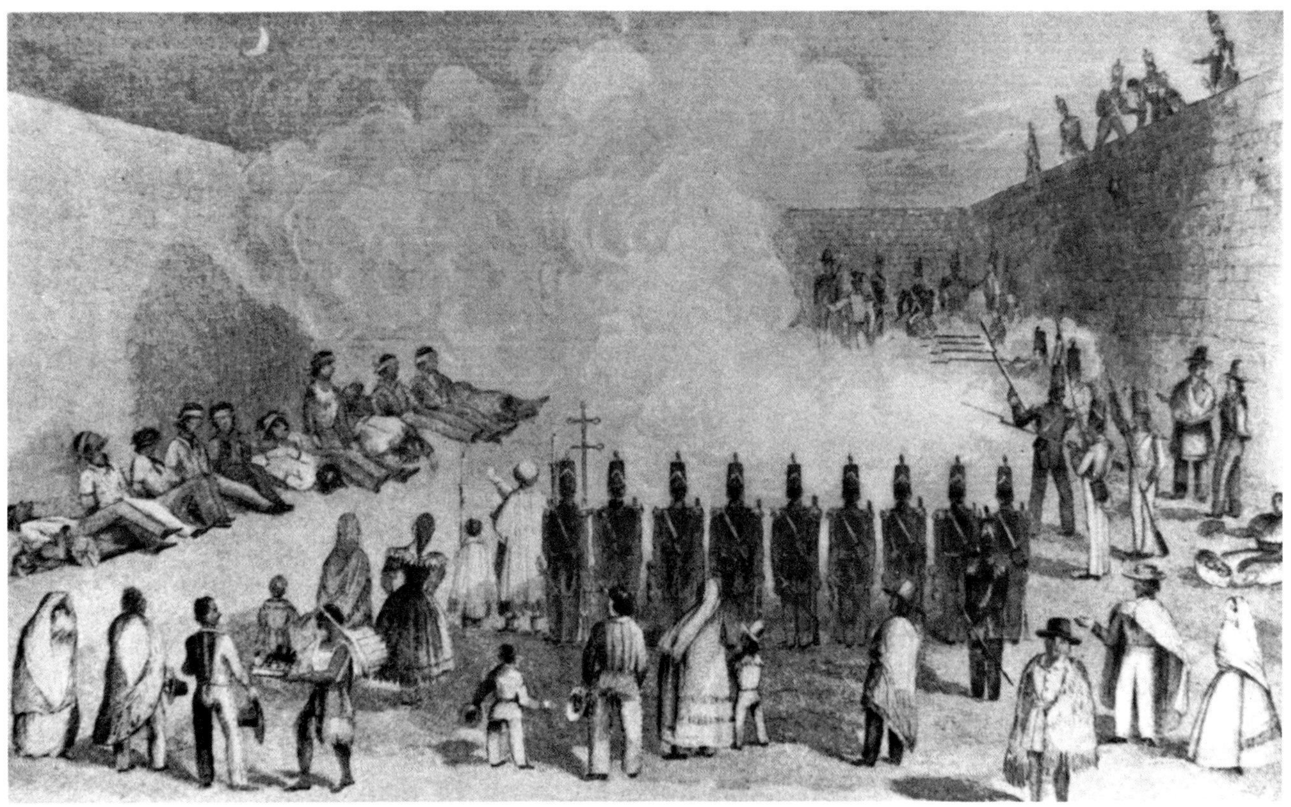

FIGURE 37. Charles McLaughlin, *Shooting of the Decimated Texians at Solado*, 1845. Engraving. From Thomas J. Green, *Journal of the Texian Expedition Against Mier*. Photograph by King Douglas, Dallas, Texas.

pathos and outrage concerning the execution of the most unfortunate members of the Mier Expedition, New Yorker Frederic Remington (1861–1909) painted the moments that decided their fate. In 1888, the artist had had an unpleasant sojourn in Texas, complaining of the heat, mosquitoes, and food and finally writing to his wife, "I fully agree with Phil Sheridan, if I owned Texas and Hell, I would rent Texas and live in Hell."[13] But, as America's interest in the state increased during the 1890s, Remington returned to spend a few days in San Antonio. Though he ignored the Alamo, which would have seemed to be a natural subject for his artistic interests, Remington became quite taken with John S. ("Rip") Ford, Bigfoot Wallace, and other former Texas Rangers that he encountered. *The Mier Expedition: Drawing of the Black Bean* (1896; Pl. 18) appeared as an illustration (entitled *Prisoners Drawing Their Beans*) for an article by Remington in *Harper's New Monthly Magazine* of December 1896, "How the Law Got Into the Chaparral." This canvas is one of three paintings and numerous

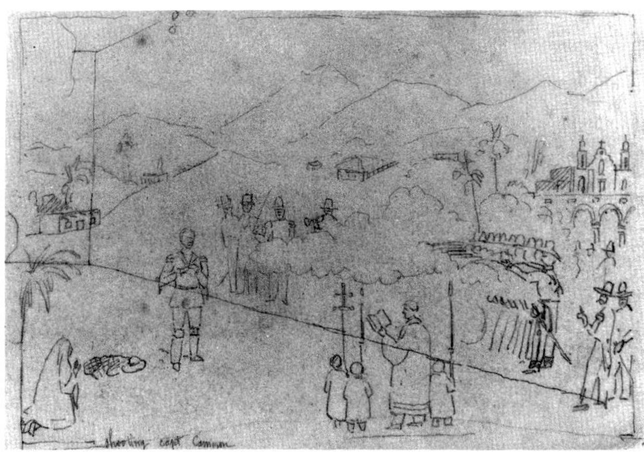

FIGURE 38. Theodore Gentilz, *Shooting Capt. Cameron*, n.d. Pencil. Daughters of the Republic of Texas Library at the Alamo, San Antonio, Texas.

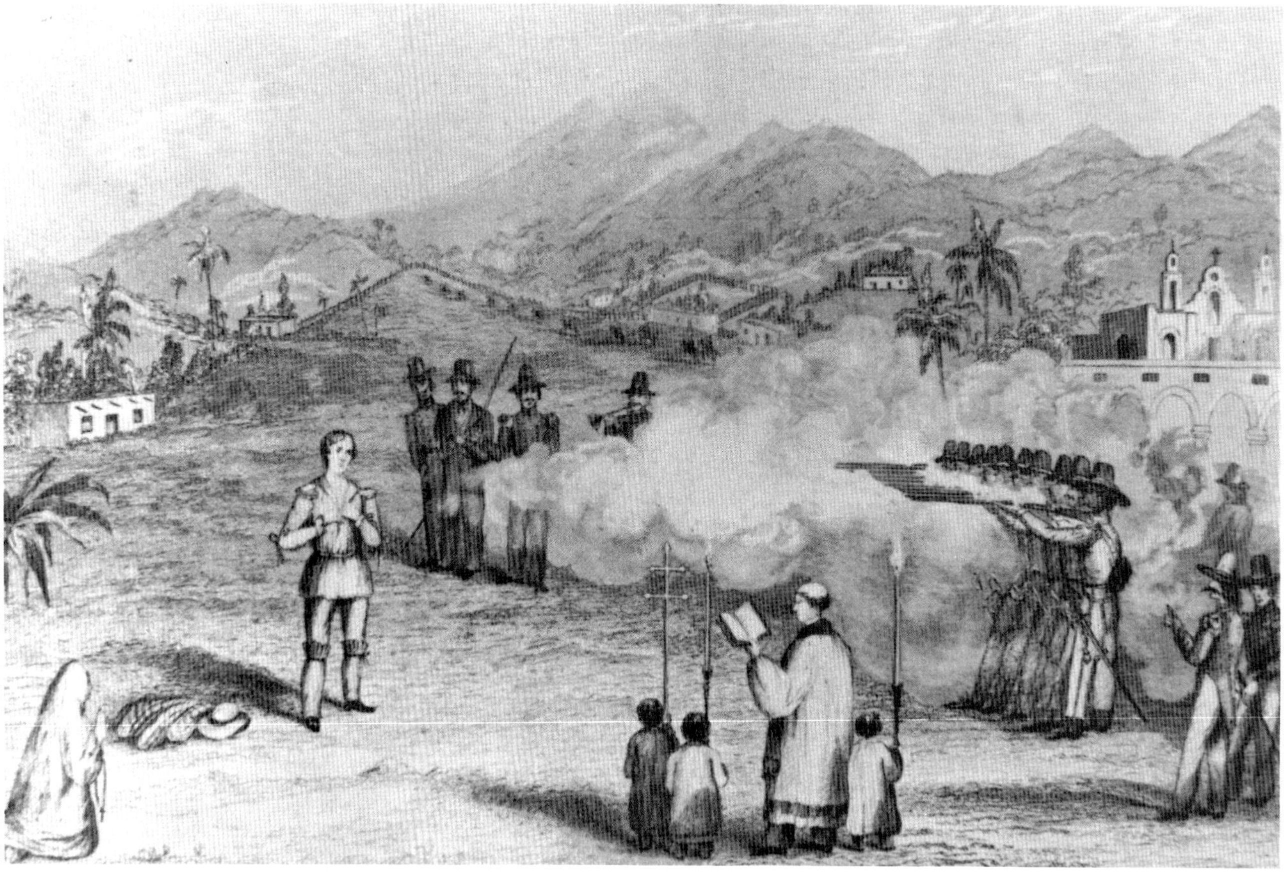

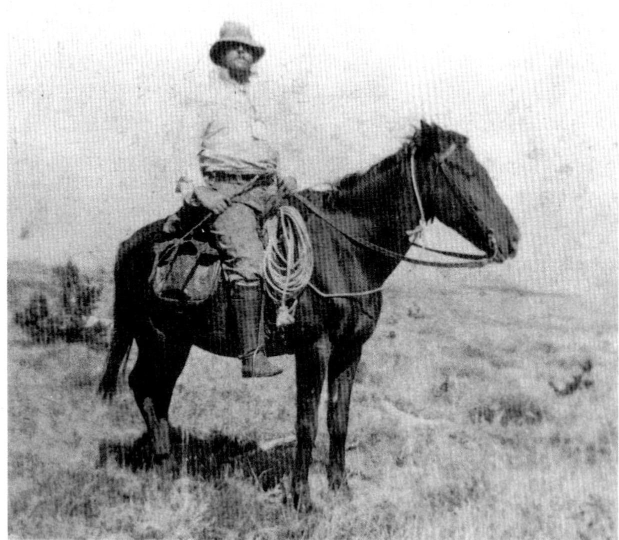

FIGURE 39. Charles McLaughlin, *Shooting of Captain Ewen Cameron*, 1845. Engraving. From Thomas J. Green, *Journal of the Texian Expedition Against Mier*. Photograph by King Douglas, Dallas, Texas.

FIGURE 40. Frederic Remington, ca. 1893. The Kansas State Historical Society, Topeka, Kansas.

sketches illustrating the article, which glorified the Texas Rangers and represented a continuation of Remington's fascination with the individuals he termed "men with the bark on" and their role in the Anglo-American opening of the West.[14]

Remington (Fig. 40) had made the first of his many journeys to the West in August of 1881 and sold a sketch from this trip to *Harper's Weekly*. His subsequent sojourns in the West and knowledge of the region served to impart an air of authenticity and authority to his art and writing, as did his interviews with such figures as Wallace. But "How the Law Got Into the Chaparral" summarized the activities of the Mier Expedition in a very few sentences, and, even then, Remington's understanding of this and other historical events seems muddled. Throughout the article, he obviously relied for his information on interviews with such individuals as Ford and Wallace, both of whom were notorious for their "exaggerations."[15]

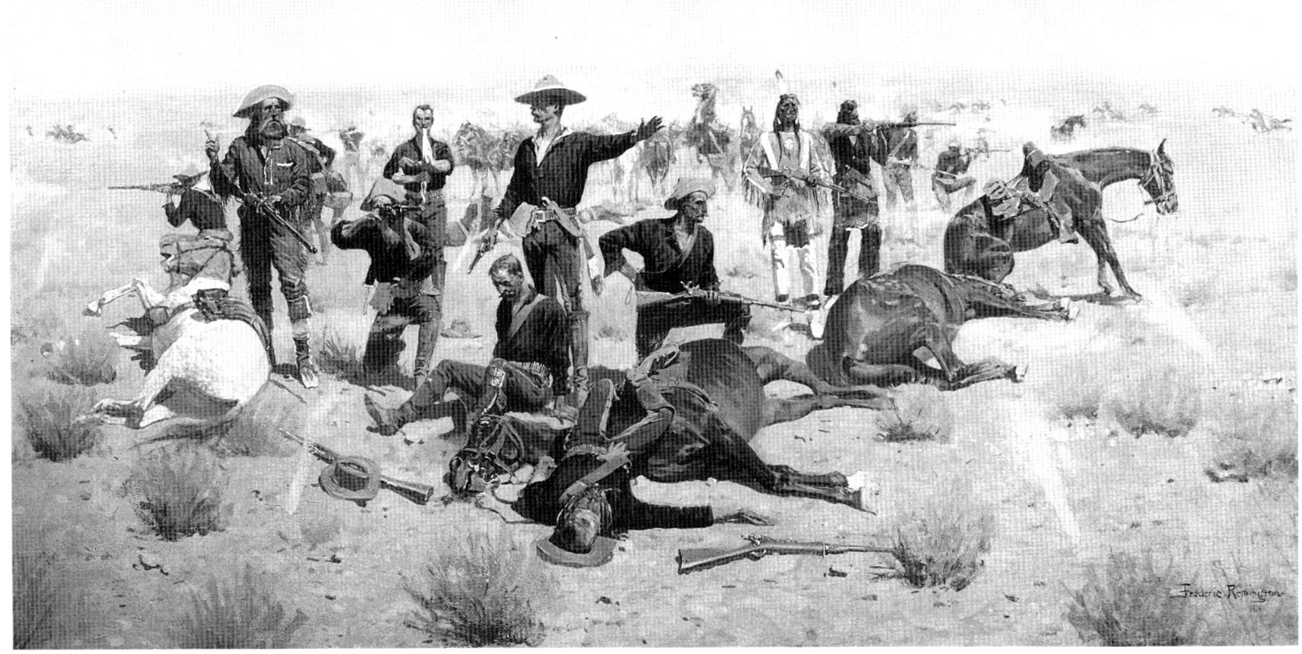

FIGURE 41. Frederic Remington, *Rounded Up, Custer's Last Stand*, 1901. Oil on canvas. Courtesy Sid Richardson Collection of Western Art, Fort Worth, Texas.

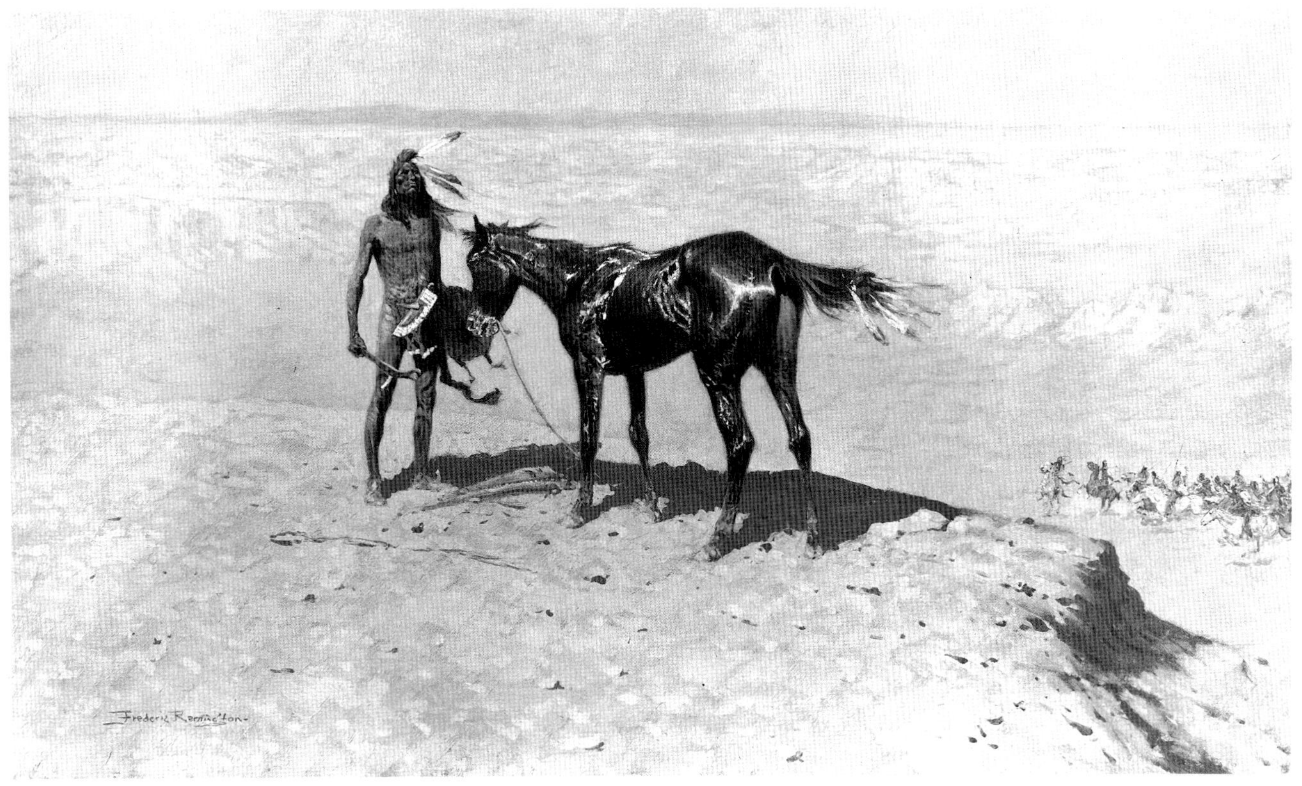

FIGURE 42. Frederic Remington, *Ridden Down*, 1905. Oil on canvas. Amon Carter Museum, Fort Worth, Texas. Acc. no. 1961.224.

But Remington's use of such sources was appropriate, since he had less interest in detailing the intricacies of Mexico-Texas relations and the facts of the expedition than in setting forth what he believed was symbolized by the drawing of the beans. The fate of the Mier Expedition fitted in perfectly with the artist's preoccupation with death and how various players in the panorama of Western history faced it in a noble fashion. Significantly, Remington did not choose to paint the execution, a moment of complete helplessness. Rather, he depicted the time when the prisoners' fate was determined. As in so many of Remington's paintings concerning death, the Texans play out this drama in the bright glare of the midday sun. The soldiers guarding them bear a marked resemblance to a figure in another of Remington's works,

Cavalryman of the Line, Mexico (1889; Pl. 19), and he simply may have transferred the same background of sky and architecture to *The Mier Expedition*. The members of the Mier Expedition join the cavalrymen of *Rounded Up, Custer's Last Stand* (1901; Fig. 41) and the Crow brave of *Ridden Down* (1905; Fig. 42) in the pantheon of Remington's westerners who display stoic courage in the face of certain, violent death.[16]

Two years after the liberation of the prisoners of the Mier Expedition, the United States Congress, by one vote, approved the entry of Texas into the Union. Most Texans believed that annexation would ensure protection of their state's borders and hoped that it would bring an end to the ongoing conflict with Mexico. However, within a year of the annexation of Texas, hostilities com-

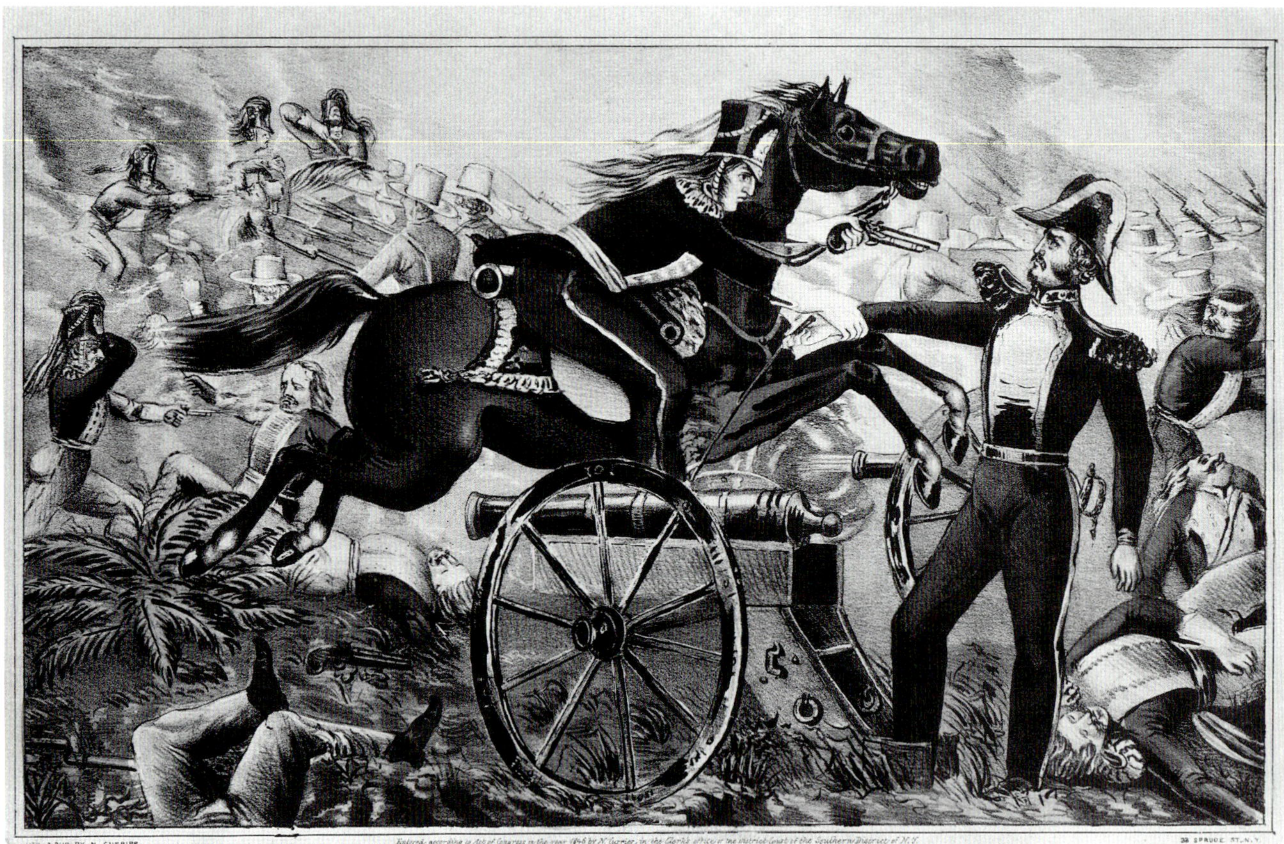

FIGURE 43. Lithography firm of Nathaniel Currier, *Battle of Resaca de la Palma, May 9th, 1846. Capture of Genl. Vega by the gallant Capt. May*, 1846. Hand-colored lithograph. Amon Carter Museum, Fort Worth, Texas. Acc. no. 1970.64.

menced between the United States and Mexico near the Rio Grande. These initial engagements of the battles of Palo Alto and Resaca de la Palma were the most important actions fought on Texas soil during the Mexican War. Lithography, a rapidly developing method of illustration, disseminated visual images of these and other engagements of the war to large numbers of Americans (Pl. 20 and Fig. 43).[17]

Aside from lithographs, the only known paintings of the war's Texas battles were executed by Samuel Emery Chamberlain (Fig. 44) (1829–1908), who served in the United States cavalry from the early days of the conflict through the conclusion of the American invasion and conquest of Mexico. During the last week of May 1846, as the Battle of Palo Alto was being fought in the southern tip of Texas, Chamberlain enlisted in the Alton Guards in St. Louis. After arriving in Texas, he was forced out of the army temporarily by a scarlet fever epidemic that swept through the American troops. Chamberlain subsequently reenlisted, this time as a cavalryman in Captain Enoch Steen's Company E, First U.S. Dragoons, under the command of Colonel William S. Harney. An untrained artist, Chamberlain did not have the technical skill to portray views of the war as did the popular lithographers of the 1840s. Instead of glorious, romanticized battlefield vistas, he offered up the view of the common soldier, the "grunt," as he would be termed in World War II.[18]

Despite these differences and the humorous touches and aesthetic shortcomings of his paintings, Chamberlain regarded the war as furnishing opportunities for heroism, as did the more accomplished artists who worked in lithography. Chamberlain's narratives of the incidents depicted in his paintings impute an often imagined drama and importance to these events. On 25 September 1846, Chamberlain's detachment, Harney's Dragoons, part of Brigadier General John Ellis Wool's division, departed San Antonio for the Rio Grande. In describing this incident, which he depicted in at least two paintings, including *Main Plaza, San Antonio* (n.d.; Pl. 21), Chamberlain noted the "imposing appearance" he and his fellow soldiers made to "a motley assembly" that included "wild looking Texans, Mexicans in their everlasting blankets, Negro Slaves, [and] a sprinkling of Lipan Indians in full dress of paint and feathers."[19]

Upon reaching the Rio Grande, General Wool ordered an immediate fording, despite rumors of a brigade of Mexican lancers and artillery entrenched on the other side that were prepared to blow the American troops

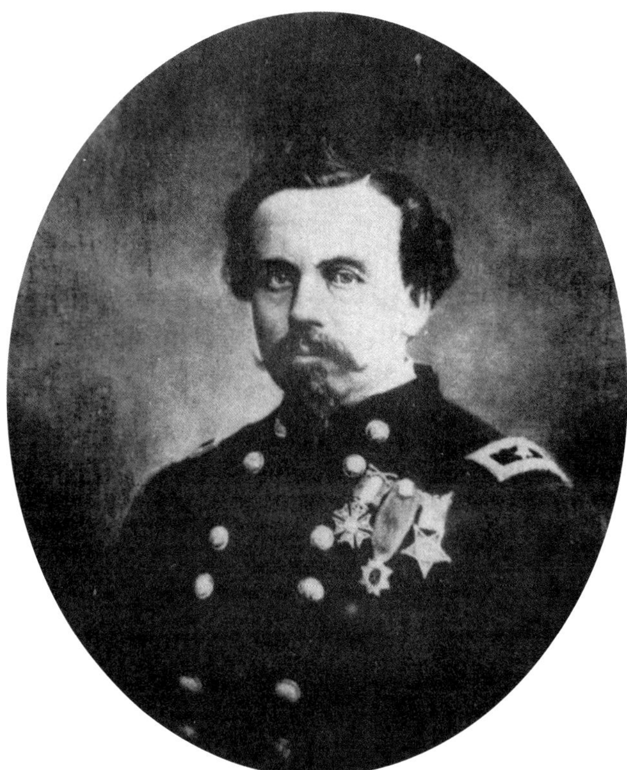

FIGURE 44. Samuel Chamberlain, n.d. The San Jacinto Museum of History Association, Houston, Texas.

out of the water. Chamberlain painted *Gen. Wool's Army Goes into Mexico* (n.d.; Pl. 22) to memorialize and emphasize his own role in helping to spearhead what he described as "the most difficult of all military operations: the *passage of a deep river in the face of the enemy*."[20] Inspired in his youth by reading the novels of Sir Walter Scott, Chamberlain reveled in being part of a potentially dangerous mission in the war against a nation of "Greasers," as he termed the Mexicans. He attempted to heighten the drama of what turned out to be an uneventful river crossing by remembering that "the passage was witnessed by the entire army which lined the Texas bank; all expected to see us fired on every moment, and when they saw us safe over their enthusiasm broke out in prolonged cheers."[21] Chamberlain portrayed the part played by Harney's Dragoons in a heroic light. But he conveniently omitted mentioning that Colonel Harney had led an unauthorized incursion into Mexico two months earlier (in which Chamberlain did not participate) and had been severely chastised by General Wool. Not surprisingly, Harney's aggressiveness was applauded by many Texans, who also thought favorably of him in his capacity as a cavalry commander in the state after the war.[22]

Although the Mexican War's conclusion secured the southern Texas border from invasion and effectively ended any further viable Mexican attempts to retake Texas, it did not bring an end to armed conflict in the new state. Since Austin's campaign against the Karankawas, Anglo settlers had been engaged in sporadic but frequently bloody armed conflicts with various Texas Indian tribes. Following the Texas Revolution, Mexico attempted to exploit these tensions in efforts to destabilize the government of the new nation. Throughout the existence of the Republic of Texas, this potential alliance had to be taken into account in Indian affairs, as Sam Houston did in his first days as president, insisting that all Texas Indian commissioners be able to speak "fluent Mexican."[23] Lamar was perpetually wary of Mexicans inciting the Indians during his term as president, suspecting them of creating unrest among tribes in Arkansas. In a letter to Lamar, one Texas farmer equated an Indian-free nation with the development of a small farmer society by relating, "All fears of an Indian invasion are dissapated [*sic*] and the people are actively employed in planting and landing their crops."[24] Advocates of this viewpoint, led by Lamar, maintained that Texas should keep a standing army in order to expel all Indian tribes from Texas before their continued depredations depopulated the frontier and weakened the nation. Houston's affinity for dependence upon short-term volunteer militia and sympathy with the land claims of some Indian tribes, such as the Cherokees, drew heavy criticism from Lamar and his supporters.[25]

As early as the summer of 1837, Mexican officials were promising certain tribes sovereignty over their traditional hunting grounds in exchange for a military alliance in order to destabilize the Texas frontier. During the winter of 1838–1839, self-styled "Commander of Mexican forces in Texas" Vicente Córdova led groups of Indians and Mexicans in numerous raids on Anglo-Texan settlements. On 18 May 1839, a detachment of Texas Rangers, after a skirmish with an Indian raiding party near Austin, discovered papers on the body of one of Córdova's agents, Manuel Flores, that indicated development of a Mexican plot to incite an uprising among several Texas Indian tribes, especially the Cherokees. In July, even though the Cherokees had not agreed to Córdova's and Flores's plan, Lamar used the Flores papers as a pretext for attacking the tribe, killing many of its members and driving the survivors across the Red River. Within six months, following other defeats of Indian bands by Anglo-Texans, Texas newspapers were exulting that "every friend of

Texas cannot but feel grateful at the flourishing condition of our frontier."[26]

This self-congratulatory air was soon supplanted by the fervor of another campaign against a tribe more formidable than the Cherokees. In attempting to deal with the Comanches, Anglo settlers had difficulties similar to those experienced by the Spaniards; by the winter of 1839–1840, Comanche bands held several captives taken during raids on Anglo-Texan settlements. On 19 March 1840, in San Antonio, a planned prisoner exchange and treaty session turned into a brief but extremely bloody battle, the Council House Fight, in which thirty-five Comanches and seven settlers were killed.[27]

During the ensuing spring and summer, Texas newspapers were filled with accounts of Indian depredations, ranging from horse theft to the killing of settlers. In August, approximately one thousand Comanches raided through the Texas Hill Country, then on to Victoria and the coastal town of Linnville, the tribe's deepest southeastern penetration into Texas. Flushed with their success, and laden with booty and a large herd of stolen horses, the Comanches carelessly began to return to their High Plains homeland in a single large band. On 10 August 1840, a group of two hundred armed Texans, composed of Rangers and volunteers, converged at Good's Crossing on Plum Creek, two miles from the present site of Lockhart. Commanded by Edward Burleson, Felix Huston, Ben McCulloch, and John Tumlinson, they routed the Comanches, liberated three of the four prisoners from the Linnville raid, and recovered most of the stolen herd of four thousand horses and mules.[28]

In *The Battle of Plum Creek* (n.d.; Fig. 45), Louis Eyth depicted this high-water mark of Comanche power in much of Texas. This painting is unlocated and, as in the case of Eyth's Alamo paintings, exists only in photographic reproductions. But even these inferior images attest that this work is more skillfully executed than *Death of Bowie* or *Speech of Travis*. In depicting a more action-filled scene in *The Battle of Plum Creek*, Eyth displays a slightly more "painterly" touch than is evident in his Alamo paintings, although the figures are posed with similar stiffness. Eyth's portrayal of a few Comanches clad in an ensemble of their native dress and clothing looted from Linnville stores and warehouses indicates that he drew on reports by participants in the battle. Other aspects of the painting are explained less readily; for example, the viewer can only speculate whether Eyth intended the central mounted figure, gesturing with his sword, to depict Texan commander Felix Huston.[29]

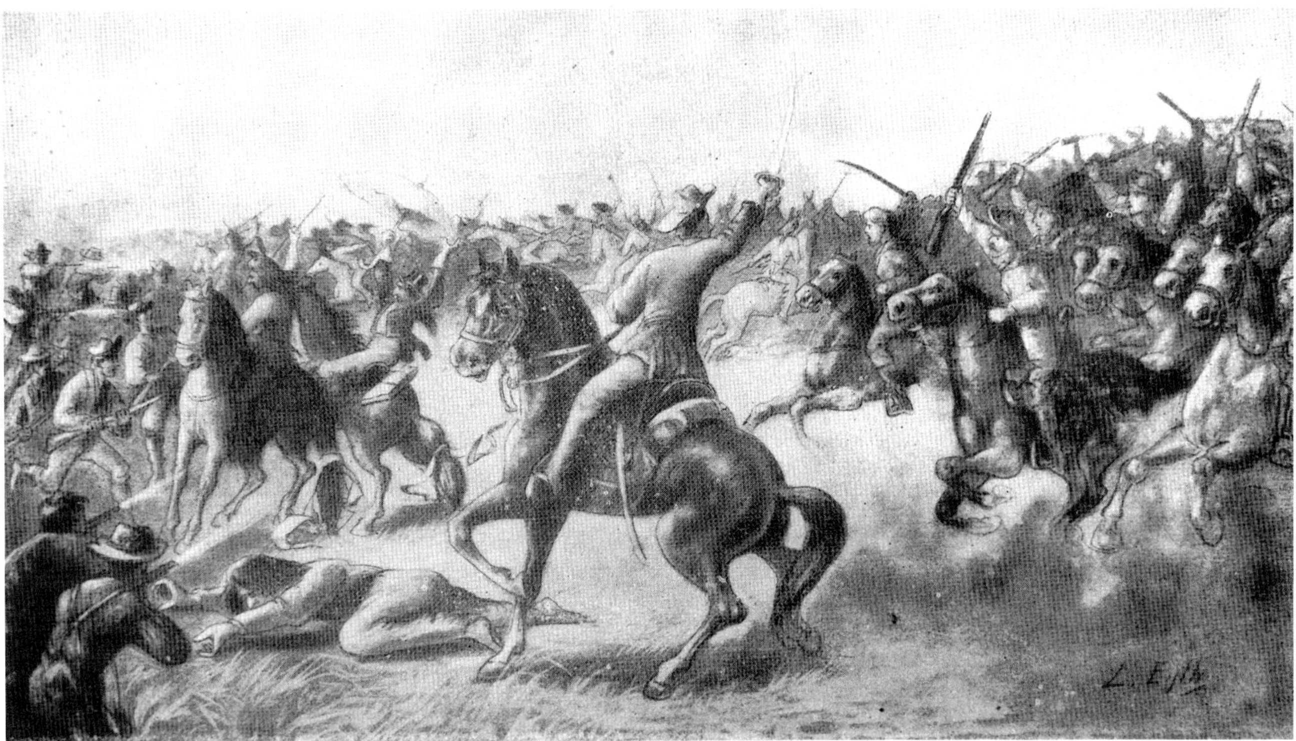

FIGURE 45. Louis Eyth, *The Battle of Plum Creek*, n.d. Medium unknown. Unlocated; reproduced in James T. DeShields, *Border Wars of Texas*, 1912. Photograph by King Douglas, Dallas, Texas.

Anglo-Texans celebrated Plum Creek as marking their deliverance from a Mexican-Indian alliance that they believed threatened to exterminate their settlements. Eyth undoubtedly drew on the many newspaper accounts of the battle, several of which included Felix Huston's official report of the encounter. Some newspapers also published accounts of cannibalism of dead Comanche warriors by the Texans' Indian allies and lists of Texan casualties and estimates of damages inflicted by the Comanches during their raid. But *The Battle of Plum Creek* is also surrounded by questions similar to those concerning Eyth's *Death of Bowie* and *Speech of Travis*. Possibly commissioned by James T. DeShields at the same time as the Alamo paintings, the work did not have a wide audience until several decades after the artist's death, when published as an illustration in DeShields's *Border Wars of Texas* in 1912. A 1930 newspaper story that reproduced the painting did not discuss its provenance, and it may well have fallen victim to the 1918 fire in the DeShields home.[30]

The Comanche raid of 1840 intensified the belief of many Texans that the surest hope of protecting their frontier lay in securing annexation to the United States and protection by its armed forces. However, following annexation in 1845, many Texans were dismayed when the United States government proved to be as concerned about the welfare of the Plains tribes as it was in protecting frontier settlers from Indian attack. In 1855, establishment of a Penateka Comanche reservation on the Clear Fork of the Brazos River fanned neighboring Anglo-Texans' fears of Indian attacks, despite assurances of this band's peaceful intentions by Indian agent Robert S. Neighbors. Over the next three years, settlers on the northwest Texas frontier blamed the Penatekas for complicity in raids by the Nokoni Comanche band. In order to supplement Texas frontier defense, the state legislature authorized creation of a regiment of Texas Mounted Volunteers under the command of Texas Ranger Captain Rip Ford. In the spring of 1858, Ford led this regiment on a punitive expedition against the Nokoni into the northeastern corner of the Texas Panhandle and across the Red River.[31]

At the time of Ford's expedition, Texas Rangers had not yet attained a reputation as invincible fighters and paragons of citizenship. During the Mexican War, Sam

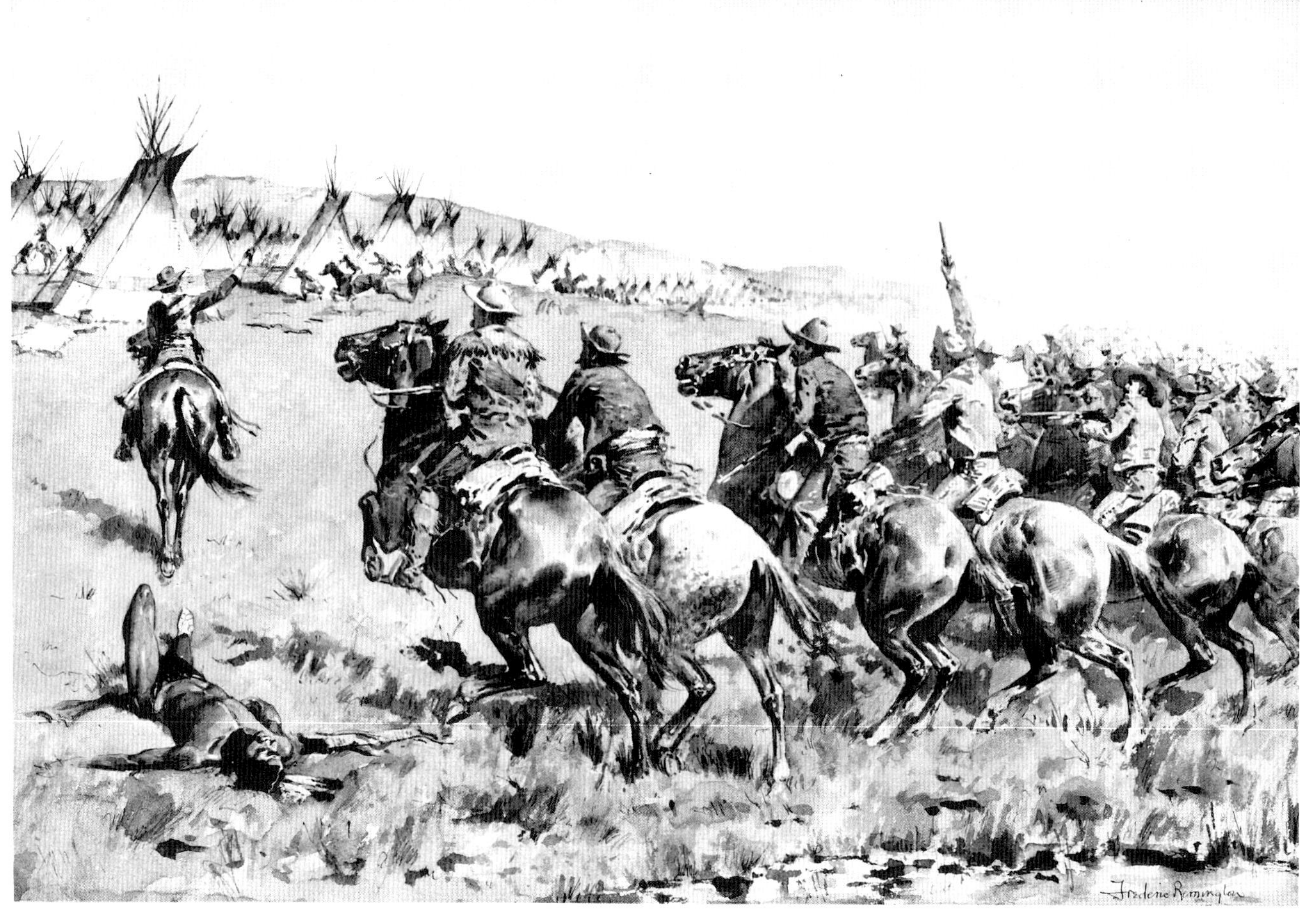

FIGURE 46. Frederic Remington, *"We Struck Some Boggy Ground,"* ca. 1896. Gouache. Courtesy of The R. W. Norton Art Gallery, Shreveport, Louisiana.

Chamberlain characterized the Rangers with whom he mingled in San Antonio's Bexar Exchange Bar as "fit representatives of the outlaws which made up the population of the Lone Star State." Soon after Chamberlain had entered this establishment, a Ranger challenged a gambler and was summarily dispatched with a single fatal stroke of a Bowie knife.[32] Four years prior to Ford's campaign, New York journalist Frederick Law Olmsted commented on the inadequacy of U.S. Army protection of the Texas frontier and concluded that the Rangers, "civilized white Indians," were far better suited for this task. But he went on to indict them for their haphazard appearance and organization, concluding with the tale of one Ranger killed near Sisterdale by a Comanche arrow that pierced the newspaper he was reading while on guard duty.[33]

During his 1896 San Antonio sojourn, Frederic Remington listened to Ford's account of the climactic battle of this campaign and quoted the interview at length in "How the Law Got Into the Chaparral." This opening vignette in the *Harper's* article also furnished the title for Remington's painting of the Ranger charge, *"We Struck Some Boggy Ground"* (ca. 1896; Fig. 46). On 12 May 1858, Ford's force of some 200 Texans and 100 of their Anadarko, Caddo, Delaware, Shawnee, Tahuanco, and Tonkawa allies advanced on a Comanche village consisting of eighty lodges and 350 warriors. Two surprised Comanche scouts had fled across the Canadian River to warn the village but, in so doing, led the Texans directly to the safest ford in the quicksand-laden riverbed. As the Rangers and their allies prepared to attack, Comanche Chief Po-bish-e-quash-o (Iron Jacket), so named due to his battle array of a full suit of Spanish armor, rode alone between the two hostile forces to demonstrate his "invincibility." Immediately, a volley of rifle fire brought down Iron Jacket, and Ford's Rangers charged: "At the river we struck some boggy ground and floundered around considerable but we got through," Ford recalled. "I never expect again to hear such a noise—I never want to hear it—what with the whoops of the warriors—the screaming of the women and children—our boys yelling—the shooting, and the horses just amixin' up and stampeding around."[34]

As he had with the Mier Expedition, Remington had stumbled upon an event well suited to one of his favorite themes, empire-building Anglos wresting the frontier from an ethnic enemy. He and a companion paid rapt attention to Ford as "through the veil of tobacco smoke the ancient warrior . . . gradually separated and arranged the details of countless fights. We saw through the smoke the brave young faces of the hosts which poured into Texas to war with the enemies of their race . . . impelled by Destiny to conquer, like their remote ancestors, 'the godless host of Pagan.'"[35] In Remington's eyes, Ford's tales made the Rangers eligible to join the ranks of the procession that the artist portrayed in *Last Cavalier* (1895), a painting that lionized numerous equestrian figures in world history.[36]

This description of Rip Ford anticipated Remington's characterization of another veteran of frontier life. In 1905, in an autobiographical sketch, Remington recalled a vision he allegedly had had during his first trip to the West in 1881 while engaged in conversation beside the Montana campfire of an aging freighter: "I saw men all ready [*sic*] swarming into the land. I knew the derby hat, the smoking chimneys, and cord-binders, and the thirty-day notes were upon us in a restless surge. I knew the wild riders and the vacant land were about to vanish forever . . . and the more I considered the subject, the bigger the forever loomed. Without knowing exactly how to do it, I began to try to record some facts around me, and the more I looked the more the panorama unfolded . . . I saw the living, breathing end of three centuries of smoke and dust and sweat."[37] In Remington's mind, Ford and the Montana freighter served the same function, that of the aged seer relating the story of a tribal conquest of the wilderness by Anglo-Americans. In 1896, the recollection of the former Texas Ranger prompted Remington to look backward in time; a decade later, reflecting on the reminiscences of a veteran frontiersman beside a Montana campfire caused the artist to dread the future direction of Western history and "development."

Ford's reminiscence and *"We Struck Some Boggy Ground"* represent the triumphalist aspect of Remington's deification of men who faced possible death with

courageous resignation, such as the members of the Mier Expedition. Remington characterized Ford's command as invaders but gave the event a curious twist: they went out "to war with the enemies of their race" in a defensive invasion of Indian country. In Remington's scenario, these warriors bore no personal responsibility for their actions, for they were "impelled by Destiny." Curiously, in depicting acts of individual heroism, Remington undercuts their significance by ascribing these actions to Destiny, reflecting the Social Darwinism of late nineteenth-century America that shaped much of his thinking. In this same vein, Remington also hinted at genetic determinism in his reference to the Rangers' "remote ancestors."[38]

Taken together, *The Mier Expedition* and *"We Struck Some Boggy Ground"* reflect Remington's double-edged philosophy of Western life, a life that he believed furnished a universal model and pattern of masculine bravery. The unifying force in both paintings is Remington's belief that an impersonal Fate finally determines men's actions and that a man attains heroism not by autonomously controlling his life but by fulfilling nobly the role that Destiny allots to him. The Mier prisoners had less direct control of their situation than did Ford's Rangers, but they were no less heroic, for they drew calmly their lots of life or death. In *"We Struck Some Boggy Ground,"* the attacking Rangers act as conquerors, aggressively overrunning the fallen Comanche brave in the painting's foreground. The rider to the right of center points his pistol skyward in a gesture employed often by Remington to signify a turning point or prelude to an overwhelming victory. Both works are best understood as celebrations of their subjects' importance in the history of Texas as well as subjects for a Romantic Realism that sought to interpret these incidents in the context of empire-building and the process of establishing Anglo-American institutions in the West.[39]

Despite campaigns such as that led by Ford in the quarter-century before the Civil War, the entire Indian and white populations of Texas were not perpetually warring against one another during these years. Even though the Texas Constitution had not recognized Indians as citizens of the Republic, some Anglo-Texans desired to forge military alliances with as many tribes as possible and allow these Indians to remain on their land as farmers, pending clarification of their citizenship status. Sam Houston, believing that human "natural reason" would lead at least some tribes to befriend the whites, promoted this Jeffersonian ideal of a society of small farmers that would incorporate the Indian. During his second term as president, Houston instructed Indian agent Stephen Slater to "advise [the Indians], as far as you can, to turn their attention to the cultivation of the soil . . . which will enable them to live much more comfortably."[40] Significantly, Indian trade and intercourse acts in Texas were passed only during Houston's administrations.

In addition to these laws, Texas officials actively pursued peace treaties with various tribes, hoping to thwart the Mexican strategy of building alliances with Texas Indians. In March 1843, John Mix Stanley (1814–1872) depicted a meeting of American and Texas representatives with members of the Anadarko, Caddo, Delaware, Hasinai, Keitsash, Shawnee, Tawakoni, Waco, and Wichita tribes. Stanley had been invited by the head of the United States delegation, Arkansas Governor Pierce M. Butler, to accompany the group from Fort Gibson, near the present site of Tahlequah, Oklahoma, to the treaty site near the confluence of the Brazos and Bosque rivers, in the vicinity of present-day Waco.[41]

Butler intended for Stanley to visually narrate the proceedings of the treaty session in a historical painting. But Stanley painted *Tehuacana Creek Indian Council* (1843; Pl. 23) before the council commenced. Since the fifteen-member military detachment arrived at the council grounds a few days early, Stanley chose that time to render his anticipatory version of the treaty session. After the session began, he occupied himself by painting six portraits of other participants, scouts, and interpreters as well as a portrait of each of the sixteen tribal representatives gathered for the three-day treaty session. Stanley evidently decided to finish the painting of the council itself before concentrating on executing the twenty-two portraits. Upon its completion, Stanley presented *Tehuacana Creek Indian Council* to Governor Butler. Unfortunately, all but one of these portraits were lost in an 1865 fire at the Smithsonian Institution that destroyed the bulk of Stanley's "Indian Gallery" of 152 paintings of members of forty-three tribes.[42]

Stanley had acquired an interest in Indians during his youth in Canadauga, New York, by viewing the paintings of an unknown artist on the walls of the Stanley family's tavern. In 1839, the young artist made his first excursion to the West, painting genre scenes and Indian portraits at Fort Snelling, Minnesota. The unprofitability of this trip prompted Stanley to move eastward in order to raise money for another, more extensive journey west of the Mississippi. For three years, he worked as a portrait painter and daguerrotypist, traveling throughout

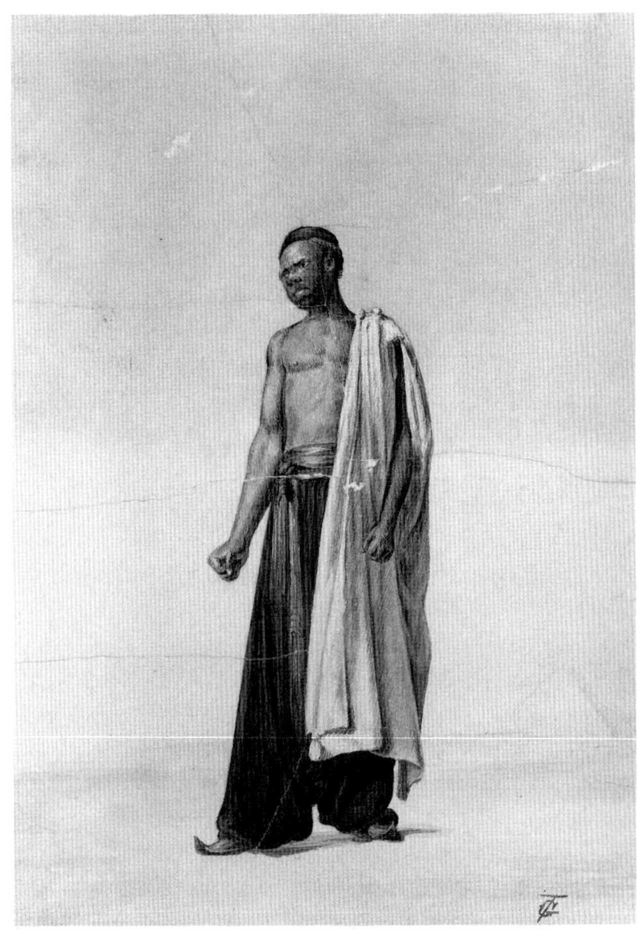

FIGURE 47. Theodore Gentilz, *North African*, 1878. Watercolor. Daughters of the Republic of Texas Library at the Alamo, San Antonio, Texas.

the northeastern United States before his 1842 arrival in Indian Territory. After his false start at Fort Snelling, Stanley's 1842 foray to Fort Gibson marked the actual beginning of an artistic career in the West that eventually would take him as far as Hawaii.[43]

In *Tehuacana Creek Indian Council*, Stanley portrayed himself in the right foreground, kneeling over a small field desk, painting the portrait of an Indian posed on the bough of a fallen tree at the upper right-hand edge of the canvas. Another Indian holds an errant tree limb out of the artist's line of sight. Stanley's meticulous attention to details of portraiture, such as his inclusion of a turban, characteristic of tribes in eastern Texas and Oklahoma, worn by the tiny, posed Indian, reflects his only known artistic training from James Bowman, a Detroit portraitist. Other aspects of this canvas are more puzzling. For example, the records of the council do not refer to the three white flags in the center of the meeting ground.

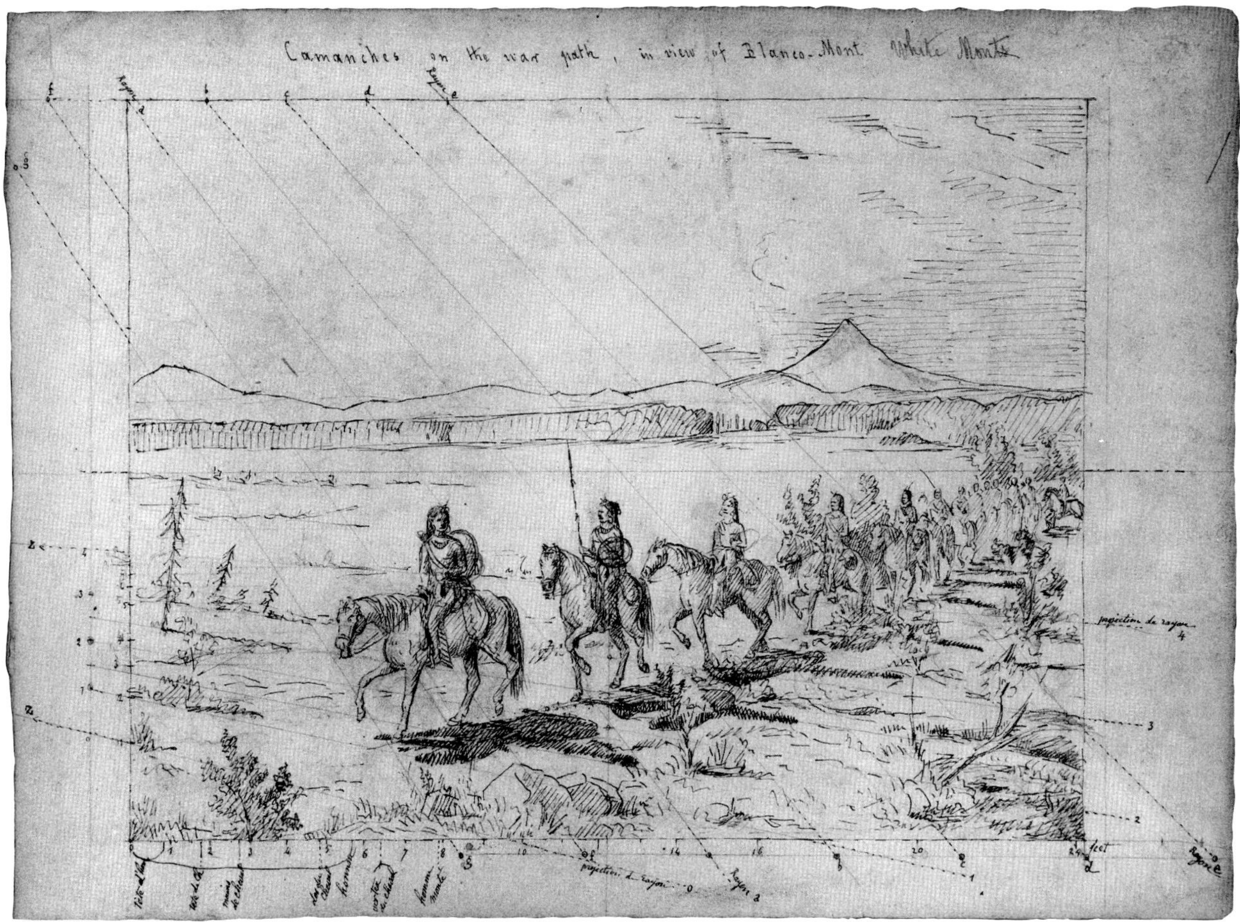

FIGURE 48. Theodore Gentilz, sketch for *Comanches on the Warpath*, n.d. Pencil. Daughters of the Republic of Texas Library at the Alamo, San Antonio, Texas.

Possibly, Stanley meant these banners to represent the Indian delegations, the United States, and Texas; the flag on the right does bear a single star in its center, a possible reference to Texas. However, Stanley's familiarity with Indian culture would seem to preclude any use of a flag to symbolize a tribe or group of tribes. But Stanley did anticipate accurately the amicable tone of the council by depicting representatives of the relatively tractable tribes placidly smoking pipes as two of their number parlay with a member of the United States/Texas delegation. Although Stanley may have added a few details to the canvas following the council, this painting cannot be characterized as a purely after-the-fact representational work. Rather, it becomes one man's "advance history" lesson as Stanley created his own version of what he felt *should* and, coincidentally, did happen at the Tehaucana Creek council.[44]

While John Mix Stanley's idyllic vision of Indian-white relations counterbalanced the viewpoint of Eyth, McArdle, and Remington, European emigrant painters, such as Theodore Gentilz and the German artist Friedrich Richard Petri (1824–1857), took an even more pacific and sympathetic view of Texas Indians. Gentilz and Petri matured during the years when Romanticism was deeply affecting European art and literature; by the mid-nineteenth century, this movement also had touched Europeans' perceptions of the American frontier and its native peoples. For example, almost immediately after attaining widespread popularity in the United States, the Leatherstocking novels of James Fenimore Cooper were being translated into several European languages. As did many Americans, Europeans held contradictory views of Indians, regarding them simultaneously as "noble savages" and as ignorant barbarians intent on lifting the hair of as many white scalps as possible. Europeans imbibed these perceptions not only from translations of Cooper but also from travel accounts, letters from European immigrants to the United States, and European authors who utilized frontier subjects for works of popular fiction.[45]

Many Europeans, especially intellectuals, feared what they perceived as the peculiarly American excesses of waste and materialism and looked to the Indian as an antidote to these attitudes allegedly engendered by a frontier society. Idealizing the "red man" as a Stoic philosopher living in harmony with Nature in an egalitarian, democratic utopia, some visitors from Europe hoped that the Indian's "example" somehow could serve as a reform mechanism for European cities that were falling prey to the problems of urbanization and worker discontent accompanying the Industrial Revolution. Since the effects of literature on specific individuals are difficult to pinpoint, any generalizations regarding the expectations of individual European immigrants regarding Indians would require extensive qualification. But Gentilz, Petri, and most other artists who came to Texas were of the European educated class and held at least some of its predominant attitudes toward the native peoples of the New World. Even though these attitudes may have been modified by actual contact with Texas Indians, the paintings of these Europeans constitute a distinctly different vision from that of their American counterparts in Texas.[46]

Theodore Gentilz took to the Texas Indian as an exotic subject in the same way that he had been drawn to the San Antonio missions, Mexican culture, and heroic episodes of Texas history. This flair for the exotic is manifested in other of his works unrelated to Texas subjects, such as his 1878 study of a black man clad in North African garb (Fig. 47). Gentilz first encountered Texas Indians while working as a surveyor in the 1840s, contacts that resulted in works such as *Comanche Chief* (n.d.; Pl. 24). In *Comanches on the Warpath* (1896; Pl. 25), Gentilz portrayed members of the tribe matter-of-factly, in contrast to Eyth's and Remington's more inimical depictions. Gentilz designed this canvas as a landscape as much as an ethnographic narrative, as indicated by the caption on the study sketch, "view of white mountains" (1896; Fig. 48).[47] The serenity of the scene causes the viewer to dissociate the horsemen from the purpose indicated by their weapons and the work's title.

Gentilz's *Camp of the Lipans* (1896; Pl. 26) has a similarly elegiac quality, as an Indian youth aims an arrow at an unseen fish and a mother restrains her child from wading into the stream. In the background, Gentilz's Indians are involved in the daily activities of any community: pairs of individuals are engaged in conversation, a woman

sits beside her cooking fire, and, behind the young archer, an apprehensive father stands by, watching his child demonstrate an ability to ride a horse bareback. In these paintings, each of which constitutes a small story, Gentilz depicted Indians forthrightly and avoided the extremes of "noble savages" or "bloodthirsty barbarians," just as his details in *Shooting of the 17 Decimated Texians* came together to give a balanced view of Mexicans.

While Gentilz respected Indians and painted several scenes of Lipan and Comanche life, he devoted more attention to the Mexican community in and around San Antonio. By contrast, Friedrich Richard Petri (1824–1857; Fig. 49) populated a large number of his works with Indian subjects and, even more than Gentilz, was a visual ethnographer of tribes that he encountered. Petri had been drawn into the upsurge of Romanticism sweeping Germany while studying at Dresden's Academy of Fine Arts under instructors J. C. C. Dahl, Adrian Ludwig Richter, and Julius Hübner. The Romantic movement had a primarily artistic and literary focus but also was linked closely to a growing sense of political nationalism and unrest. By 1848, this drive for political change had touched off riots in Dresden, in which Petri participated alongside Hermann Lungkwitz, his future brother-in-law, and, according to Petri family tradition, the composer Richard Wagner. As the revolution failed, the family decided to emigrate to Texas. The Lungkwitz-Petri family arrived late in 1851 in New Braunfels and, in July 1852, settled on a farm five miles southwest of Fredericksburg, a six-year-old village of five hundred people.[48]

By the time that Petri emigrated from his native Saxony, the American West was being popularized by a host of "blood and thunder" German fiction writers, including Baldwin Möllhausen, the "Cooper of Germany." As early as 1827, the West had caught the fancy of the leader of the Romantic movement in German literature, Johann Wolfgang von Goethe. Many German writers assumed the inevitability of the ultimate extermination of the "vanishing race" of Indians by the encroachment of white civilization and cast the Indian as a valiant, doomed representative of a life of close communion with the beneficial, regenerative natural world. Since Petri left behind only numerous sketches, drawings, and paintings, but no writings, his precise sentiments on any subject are only adduced through family reminiscenses and his art. One family legend recounted that Petri once pacified a threatening Comanche band at his cabin door by setting up his easel and beginning to paint the Indians. Whether or not this is true, it does indicate the generally cordial

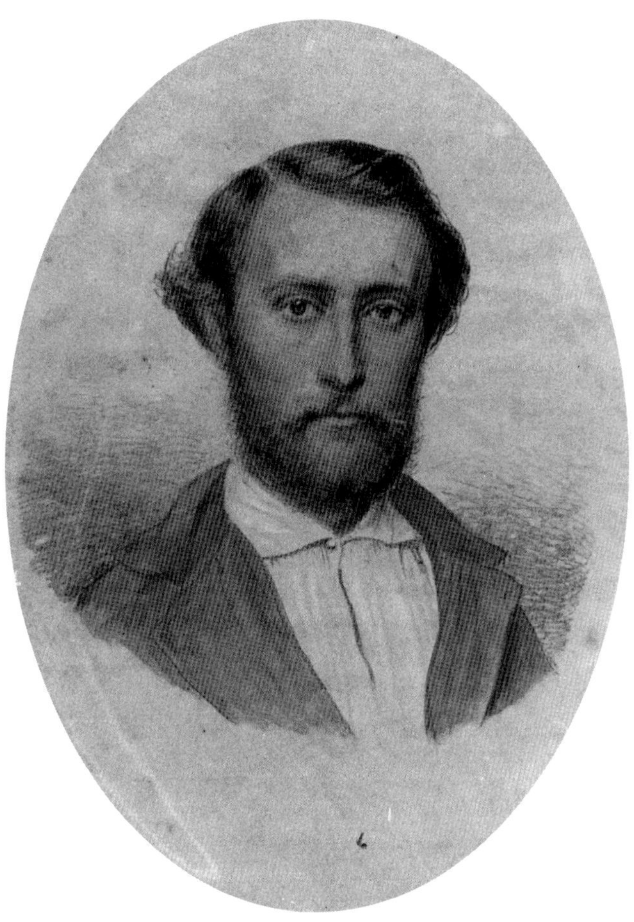

FIGURE 49. Friedrich Richard Petri, *Self-portrait*, n.d.
Watercolor. Courtesy of the Texas Memorial Museum,
Austin, Texas. TMM no. 2269-5.

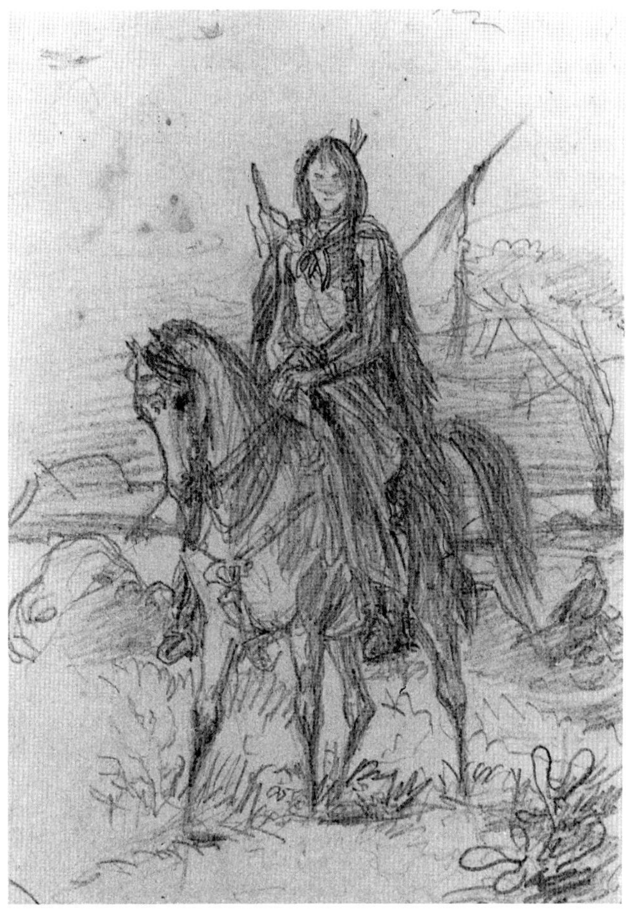

FIGURE 50. Friedrich Richard Petri, *Mounted Plains Indian
with Lance*, sketch for *Plains Indian Warrior in Blue*, n.d. Pencil.
Courtesy of the Texas Memorial Museum, Austin, Texas.
TMM no. 2319-1.

relationship that existed between many German settlers
and the Comanches. Another possible indicator of the
sympathy that Petri felt for the Indian is that he commenced no major works on any subject after the Penateka
Comanches were driven away from Fredericksburg.[49]

As did Gentilz, Petri captured the stern pride of Comanche warriors in works such as *Plains Indian with
Shield* (n.d.; Pl. 27) and *Plains Indian Warrior in Blue*
(n.d.; Pl. 28 and Fig. 50). The former work, an unfinished
watercolor, was composed with the same mathematical
precision as were Gentilz's sketches for *Death of Dickinson*
and *Fall of the Alamo*. With *Plains Indian Warrior in Blue*,
Petri became the first white artist to depict the hair-pipe
breastplate and silver pendant characteristic of the costume of Penateka Comanche warriors. This painting illustrated the Comanche and Lipan Apache practices of
facial and body painting and of male ornamentation. Petri's warriors in these and other canvases stand as repre-

sentative "noble savages" who would have incarnated the
expectations of the most romantic European.[50]

Despite Petri's skill in portraying Comanche warriors,
these works do not represent the only subject of his Indian paintings. Instead, Petri was drawn to these men as
they participated in the daily life of their tribe, and he
depicted them within that context. Petri was intent on
humanizing the Indian, on portraying him as being wor-
thy of equal consideration with white settlers. The theme
of *Indian Woman on Saddled Mule* (n.d.; Pl. 29) could
easily be adapted to a German street scene as an Indian
couple greet a passing acquaintance. Equally suggestive
of multiracial themes are Petri's sketches of an Indian
watering a horse (n.d.; Fig. 51) and of an Indian bartering
with a white man (n.d.; Fig. 52). The latter sketch bears
a figure that recurs throughout Petri's work, that of an
Indian mother and child. By repeating these themes,
Petri emphasized the importance of the institution of the

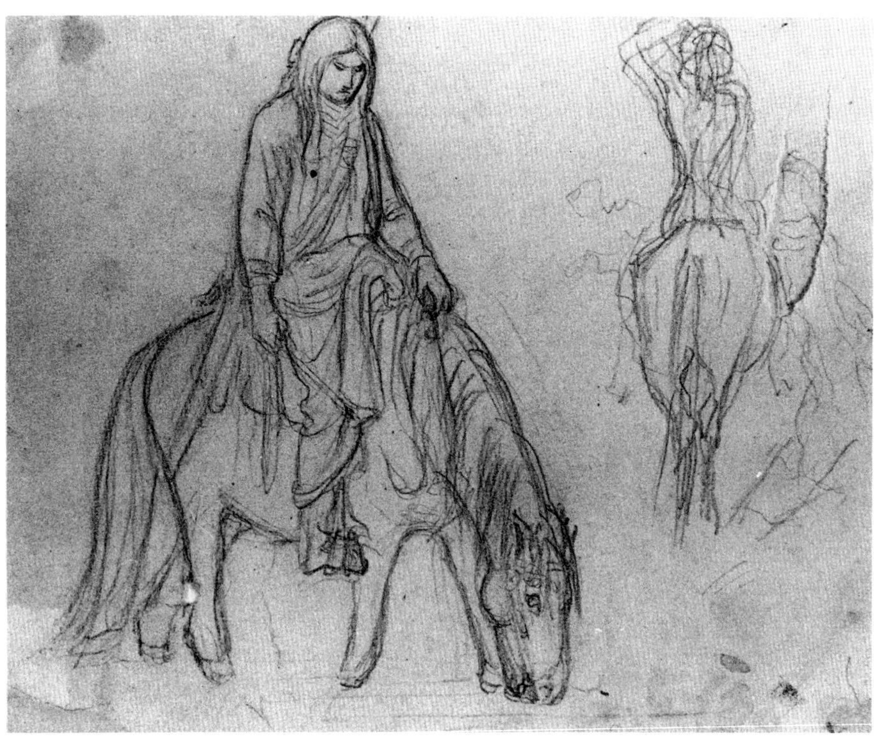

FIGURE 51. Friedrich Richard Petri, *Indian Watering Pony*, n.d.
Pencil. Courtesy of the Texas Memorial Museum, Austin, Texas.
TMM no. 2318-1.

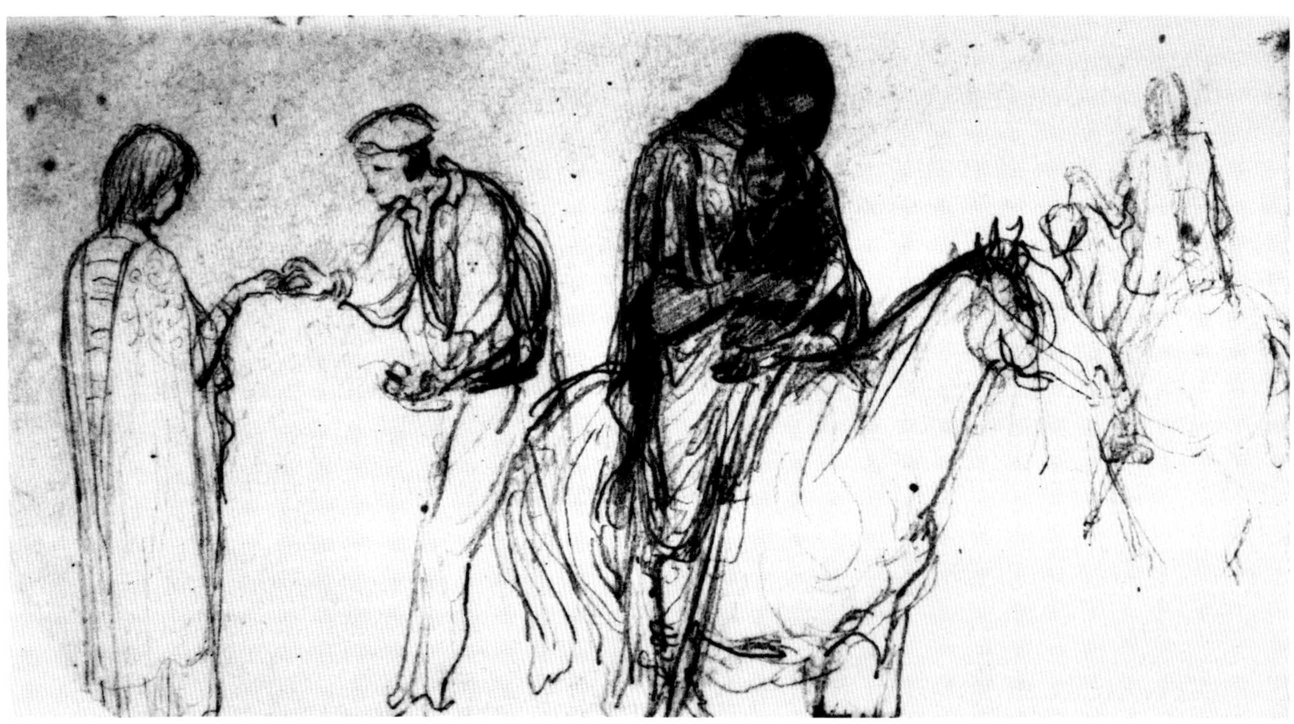

FIGURE 52. Friedrich Richard Petri, *Bartering with an Indian*,
n.d. Pencil. Courtesy of the Texas Memorial Museum, Austin,
Texas. TMM no. 2269-3-3.

family in Comanche culture, implying the similarity of this culture to that of white settlers. Petri's devotion to members of his own family is evident in the many works devoted to their portraits. When considered in the context of the tragic fate that soon befell the Penateka Comanches, Petri's sketches and paintings, portraying these people with the same dignity that he had treated subjects in his classes in Dresden, take on an especially bittersweet quality. Emerging from a cultural milieu that glorified the Indian as a unique child of Nature, Richard Petri actually pointed out fundamental similarities between Indians and whites in his portrayals of the everyday life of the "vanishing race."[51]

Theodore Gentilz and Richard Petri were forced to encounter a frontier that differed greatly from the romanticized West of European writers and opinion-makers of the early and mid-nineteenth century. Their canvases portrayed some of the fiercest tribes on the North American continent, and each man knew of atrocities committed by these tribes' members and, perhaps, by some of the same individuals who sat for their portraits. While Gentilz and Petri acknowledged the violent, warlike aspects of Indian life, they nonetheless strived to capture the totality of that life. In this attempt, they left behind not only a valuable ethnographic record but also a vision of Texas Indians that contrasted sharply with the perceptions expressed by Eyth, McArdle, and Remington. Some art historians have considered Gentilz and Petri as "culturally homeless," isolated in a remote wilderness.[52] Yet these painters were able to live and express their artistic vision in the midst of "Nature's noblemen" before the Indians relinquished their domains, an opportunity denied most Romantic painters and one that united for Gentilz and Petri the seemingly contradictory notions of Texas as a land of savagery and a land of promise.

CHAPTER FIVE

Realizing the Promise

UNLIKE THEODORE GENTILZ and Richard Petri, most Texas settlers could not reconcile the notion of what was at times a land of savagery with that of a land of promise. They would have wholeheartedly agreed with the farmer who wrote President Lamar that agricultural prosperity could only be achieved after the Texas Indian population was either conquered militarily or expelled. Annexation to the United States and the outcome of the Mexican War made the American government, especially the U.S. Army, an important partner in the enterprise of building an agrarian paradise. Paintings of this American military presence and of life in a land of farms, ranches, and in growing towns documented peaceful aspects of the transformation of nineteenth-century Texas.

Following the Mexican War, the Treaty of Guadalupe-Hidalgo endowed the United States with a tremendous amount of uncharted land west of the Mississippi. Since one of the catalysts of the conflict had been disagreement concerning the location of the Texas-Mexico border, both nations agreed on the urgency of mapping the entire international boundary line from Brownsville to San Diego, California. The treaty required each government to appoint a commissioner and a surveyor whose conclusions were to be considered as part of the text of the treaty. This responsibility cast the American survey team members in the role of de facto diplomats engaged in a cooperative effort with their Mexican counterparts and conferred wide-ranging powers on the office of boundary commissioner. This post was filled by John Russell Bartlett (1805–1886), a New York bookstore owner, who had actively opposed the annexation of Texas and United States involvement in the Mexican War; his primary qualifications for the position of commissioner were a great amount of scientific curiosity and a desire to travel in the West for health reasons (Fig. 53). Despite his lack of credentials, political connections as well as a rather ill-defined label as a "scientist" aided Bartlett in his quest to secure this appointment.[1]

Despite his earlier opposition to the war that had acquired the Southwest for the United States, the new commissioner pursued his duties zealously, including determining the most effective way to visually depict the expedition's efforts. Expedition members debated vigorously the most desirable medium for making a pictorial record of their activities. Their discussions centered around the relative merits of two recent technological breakthroughs for making pictorial records, the daguerreotype and the camera lucida. Bartlett finally resolved the dispute by deciding wisely that such cumbersome instruments would be less useful than his own drawings and paintings. As did many men of his day with a scientific bent, Bartlett had worked as an amateur artist for several years. But his paintings and drawings executed on the Texas leg of the boundary survey marked Bartlett's transition from a casual dabbler to a serious artist intent on documenting contemporary historical events.[2]

The expedition's route ran through some of the most forbidding terrain in Texas, including a three-day stretch between water sources, before fording the treacherous Pecos River at Horsehead Crossing. While the expedition members welcomed the sight of the river, its crossing of this stream was a harrowing experience that included the swamping and near loss of two wagons. Bartlett himself narrowly escaped drowning and was saved when two of his men pulled him from the stream. His *Crossing the Pecos* (1850; Fig. 54) was the first artistic depiction of a historical incident at Horsehead Crossing, an important ford for post–Civil War cattle drives. The painting was reproduced as one of several illustrations in Bartlett's account of the expedition.[3]

Bartlett's mission was one of several expeditions that pointed up the formidable obstacles to effective communication and transportation in Texas and the Southwest. These obstacles prodded American officials to explore unorthodox ways to overcome the problems presented by the region's aridity and distances. In the mid-1850s, Secretary of War Jefferson Davis, looking to Napoleon's use of camels during his Egyptian campaigns as an example, decided that the American military should experiment with a similar use of the beasts in the desert Southwest. Numerous prominent Americans with Western experience, including Bartlett, shared Secretary Davis's enthusiasm for the camel experiment, believing that camels would prove themselves to be superior to mules. In the summer of 1856, the U.S. Army transported a herd of seventy-one Tunisian camels to the Texas port of Indianola before herding them overland to San Antonio. On 17 June 1856, Theodore Gentilz may have been one of many curious San Antonians who lined the streets upon hearing the Army teamsters shout, "Get out of the way, the camels are coming."[4] He gave both his yen for the exotic and eye for humorous incidents full play in *Camel and Rider* (1856–1857; Pl. 30), depicting one of the five Middle Eastern camel trainers employed by the Army sitting atop a grinning, striding camel.

After eleven days in San Antonio, the camels were moved to Camp Val Verde, a permanent Army post sixty-five miles north of the city. Although Gentilz sketched the beasts and their handlers during their bivouac in San Antonio, the rough, open terrain of *Camel and Rider* suggests that he was portraying the area around Camp Val Verde in this painting. Richard Petri sketched the camels but never executed a finished painting concerning the experiment (1856; Fig. 55).

Over the next two years, outposts such as Fort Davis in far West Texas served as the proving ground for the camel experiment, which ultimately failed because the animals' padded feet could not withstand the sharp rocks of the Southwestern deserts. Few of the soldiers grieved over this failure; most of the men disliked the camels' odor and disposition, claimed that the beasts were unridable, that they scared the regiment's horses, and that

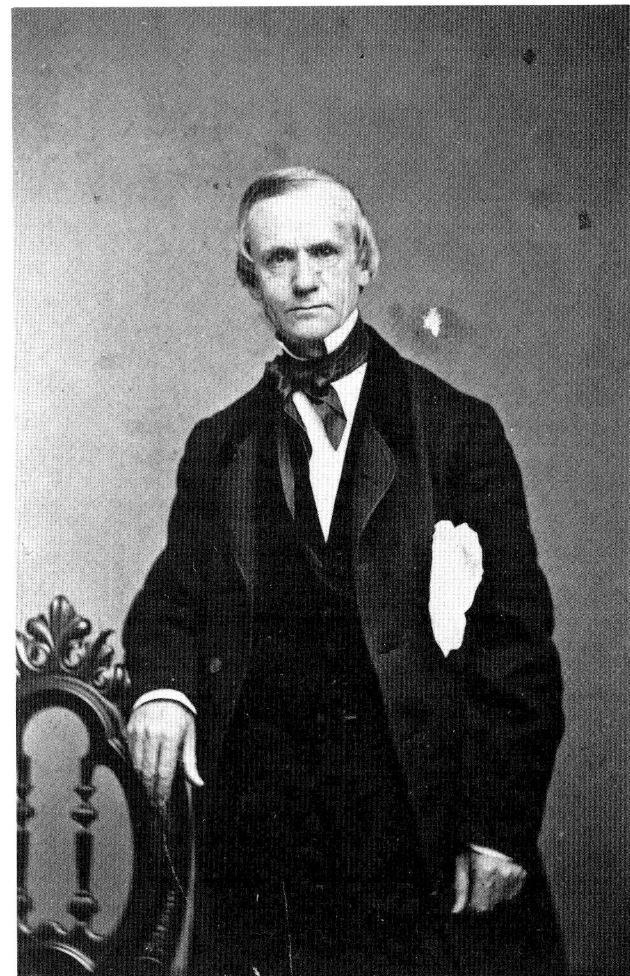

FIGURE 53. John Russell Bartlett, n.d. Courtesy of the John Carter Brown Library at Brown University.

their special saddles were too difficult to pack. Captain Arthur T. Lee (Fig. 56), Fort Davis's second-in-command and the officer in charge of many of the camels' endurance tests, concurred with his enlisted men in regarding the entire experiment with a somewhat jaundiced eye. An accomplished artist, Lee recalled that, while camel caravans in the Middle East might appear "picturesque and imposing," camels loaded with army equipment "are simply hideous in West Texas."[5]

Perhaps because they offended his aesthetic sensibilities, Captain Lee did not see fit, as Gentilz had, to depict camels in his art. Instead, during the twelve years he spent in Texas, Lee concentrated his artistic attentions on recording vignettes of daily life at Fort Davis and other Texas posts. Although many of these watercolors were composed as landscapes, the Fort Davis scenes are also historical narrative paintings, depicting work and leisure

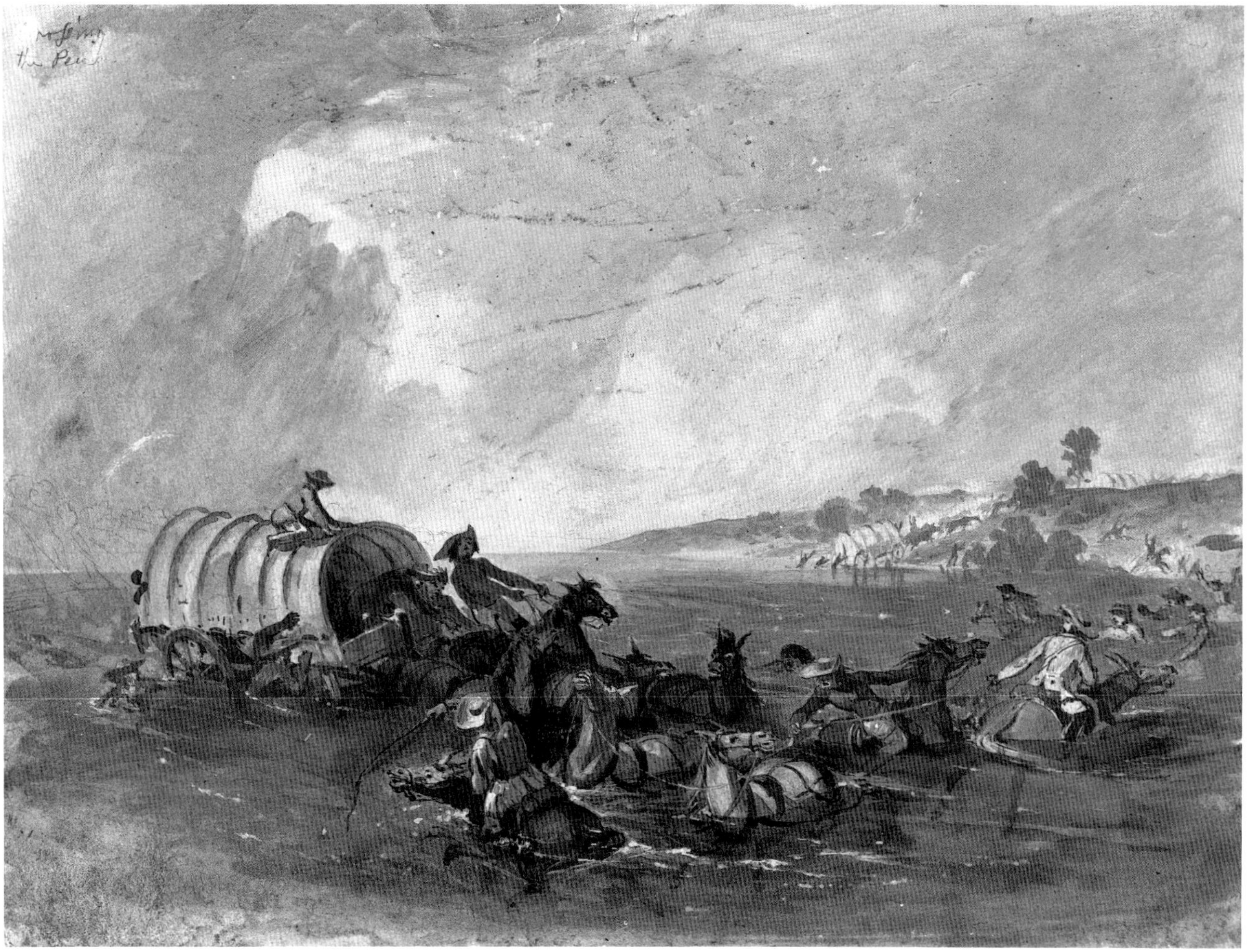

FIGURE 54. John Russell Bartlett, *Crossing the Pecos*, 1850. Sepia wash. Courtesy of the John Carter Brown Library at Brown University.

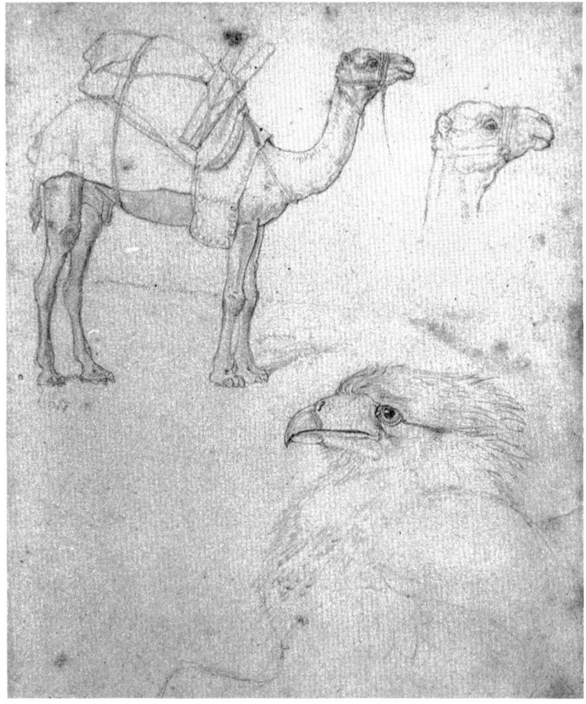

FIGURE 55. Friedrich Richard Petri, *Camp Verde Camel*, 1856. Pencil. Courtesy of the Texas Memorial Museum, Austin, Texas. TMM no. 2270-12-6.

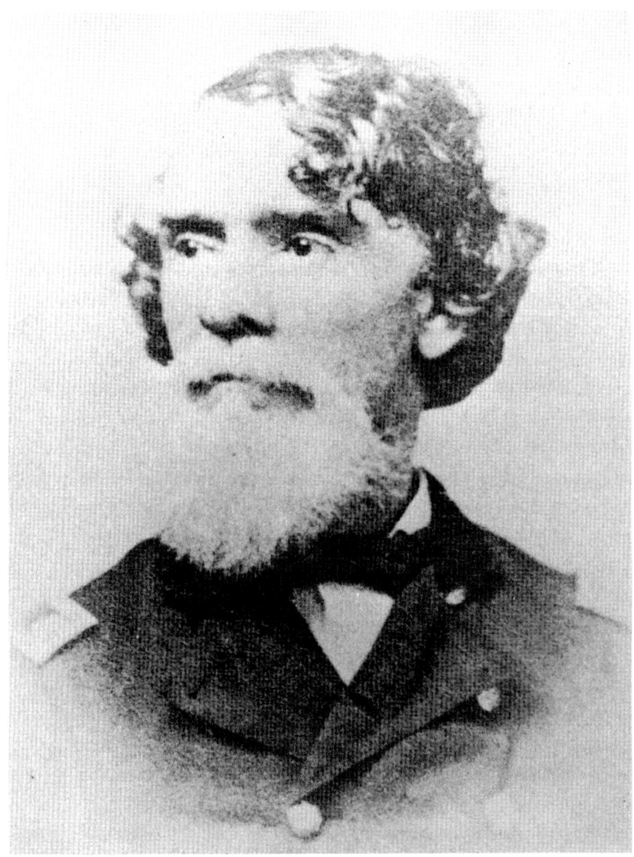

activities of civilians as well as soldiers. Careful examination of one scene set in the vicinity of Fort Croghan, site of Lee's first Texas assignment, reveals its tiny human figures to be Indians standing over a freshly killed buffalo. Lee was sympathetic to the plight of the Plains Indians, as was his fellow military artist and occasional sketching partner, Seth Eastman, and Lee's *View Near Fort Croghan* (ca. 1850; Pl. 31) is a quiet, poignant commentary on these tribes' impending loss of the material foundation of their way of life. Armed with lances and accompanied by their wives and children, the Indians seem more contemplative than triumphant and blend into the surrounding landscape. This mood contrasts sharply with Lee's *Buffalo Hunt* (n.d.) in which a mounted white man, brandishing a firearm and in pursuit of four buffalo, dominates the scene.[6]

Seth Eastman's (1808–1875) painstakingly detailed documentary sketches and drawings of Texas sites have little of Lee's poignant romanticism. Eastman's ability to include a number of details in an extremely small space re-flected his West Point training as a topographical engineer (Fig. 57). This beneficial attention to detail was evident in Eastman's work habits; he constantly sharpened his drawing pencils, which accounts for the long-lived clarity and distinctness of these images that enhance their value as a historical record. He also taught at West Point, and the military academy thought highly enough of Eastman's work to adopt his *Treatise on Topographical Drawing*, published in 1837, as a textbook. Eastman studied under Charles Robert Leslie and Robert W. Weir and gained some recognition as a minor Hudson River school landscape painter. But he is best known for his efforts to create and preserve a visual record of the tribes of the upper Midwest in hundreds of pencil and watercolor studies and for his illustrations for Henry Schoolcraft's six-volume study, *Historical and Statistical Information Respecting the History, Condition, and Prospects of the Indian Tribes of the United States*, published during the 1850s.[7]

Eastman came to Texas reluctantly in the autumn of 1848, after having been rejected in his initial attempt to be appointed as illustrator for the Schoolcraft study. Leaving his post of seven years at Fort Snelling, Minnesota, he executed numerous sketches on his voyage down the Mississippi to New Orleans. Eastman's initial encounter with Texas was not pleasant: he landed in Matagorda Bay "a day after the danger of being wrecked [in a] most severe storm," and his sketch of the shoreline includes a cluster of shabby buildings, one of which was upended by the storm (1848; Fig. 58).[8]

Upon reaching San Antonio, Eastman termed it "a wretched place, full of desperate characters."[9] Ironically, his Texas work is associated most with San Antonio, although one assessment of his drawings of the city as "the most authoritative and detailed ones known" must be revised in light of the work of Theodore Gentilz, examined later in this chapter.[10] As were most travelers of his day, Eastman was most taken with the area's missions, and he began his sketching efforts at Mission San José. He also sketched four views of the Alamo, noting in his journal that "it was in this building that Travis with his small band of Texians were all massacred by the Mexicans during the Texas Revolution" (1848; Fig. 59).[11]

Despite his extensive artistic activity in San Antonio, Eastman seemed happiest when on detail across the plains of Central and West Texas, areas that are portrayed in his correspondence as a bountiful, exotic, and sometimes dangerous wilderness. In December 1848, he wrote to his close friend at Fort Snelling, Colonel Henry Sibley, from "Near Fredericksburg, Texas: I have at last arrived

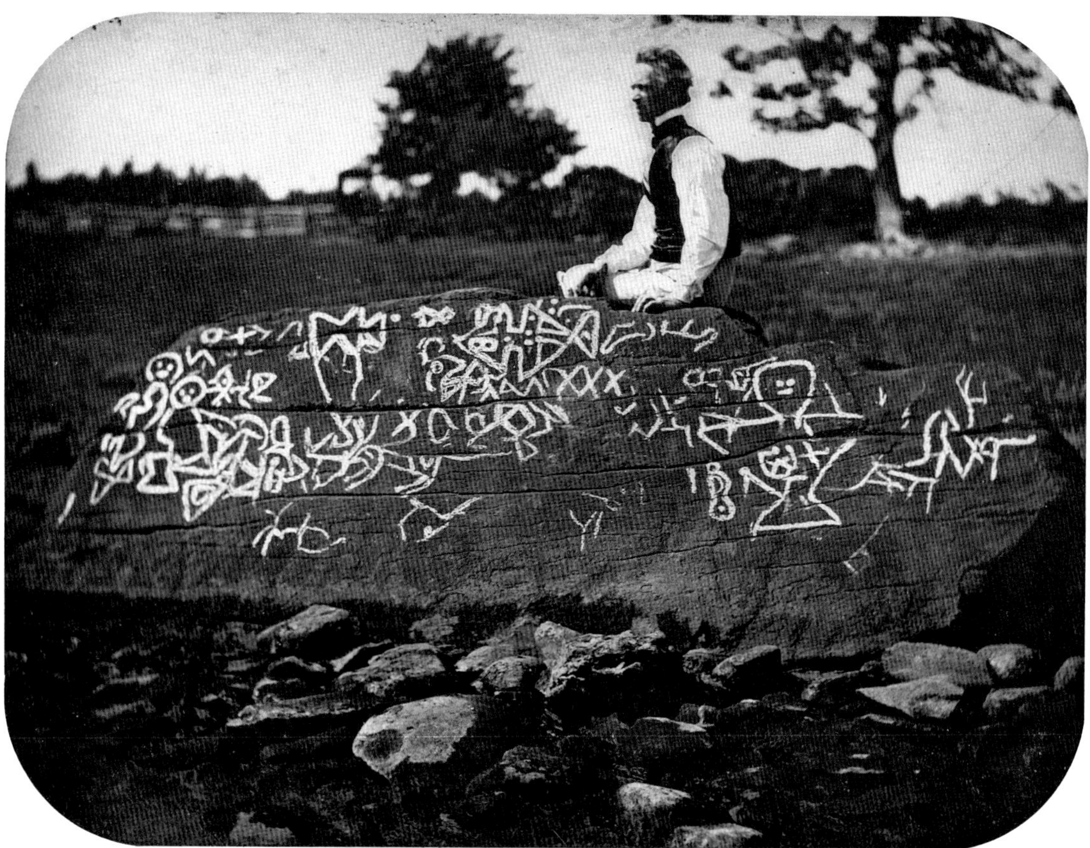

FIGURE 57. Horatio B. King, *Seth Eastman at Dighton Rock, Mass.*,
1853. Half plate daguerreotype. Collection of the J. Paul Getty
Museum, Malibu, California. Acc. no. 84.XT.182.1.

at my journey end and landed I know not where—but in
a very fine country, full of game and Indians. The Texians kicked up an Indian excitement. A dutch [German]
settlement . . . pretty well into the Cumanche [*sic*] country. Buffalo, Bear, Deer, Catamounts, Tigers, Turkies in
droves, a few quail and ducks. Deer . . . very tame and
easily killed. I wish you were here to go hunting with
me, it is rather dangerous, but very exciting."[12] His only
substantive complaint was that "I am 70 or 80 miles from
any mail route."[13] Eastman's several sketches and drawings made while on these expeditions serve as excellent
documents of military life on the trail (1848; Fig. 60).

In the spring and summer of 1849, Eastman probably
accompanied one or more U.S. Topographical Engineers
survey teams to West Texas. After receiving his description of one of these expeditions, his wife wrote to Henry
Sibley that her husband was "75 miles west of San Antonio—a post beautifully situated but extremely lonely."[14]
Eastman also noted the harsher aspects of Texas, ranging
from his account of a dog's death from a rattlesnake bite

to his observations on violence in Texas life, as evidenced
by Comanche intimidation of San Antonio's Mexican
population through tactics such as carrying off women
captives and the artist's recording of the story of the
bloody Council House Fight of 1840.[15]

Seth Eastman's tour of duty in Texas lasted a little over
one year. In early 1850, he departed for Washington,
D.C., to assume his long-desired assignment as illustrator
of Schoolcraft's study. Upon publication of the first volume two years later, a reviewer in the St. Louis *Missouri
Republican* praised one of the illustrations, a sketch of the
St. Peter's River valley near Fort Snelling, and hoped
that, in a future volume, Eastman would "let us have,
with all its monotony, a good prairie view."[16] But no
Texas scenes appeared in any of the volumes, the only
hint of the state being an illustration entitled *Emigrants
Attacked by Comanches*. Eastman's Texas subjects were an
anomaly in his body of work, consisting mostly of landscapes, architectural studies, and a few scenes of military
and farm life (1849; Fig. 61). Indians appear in only a very

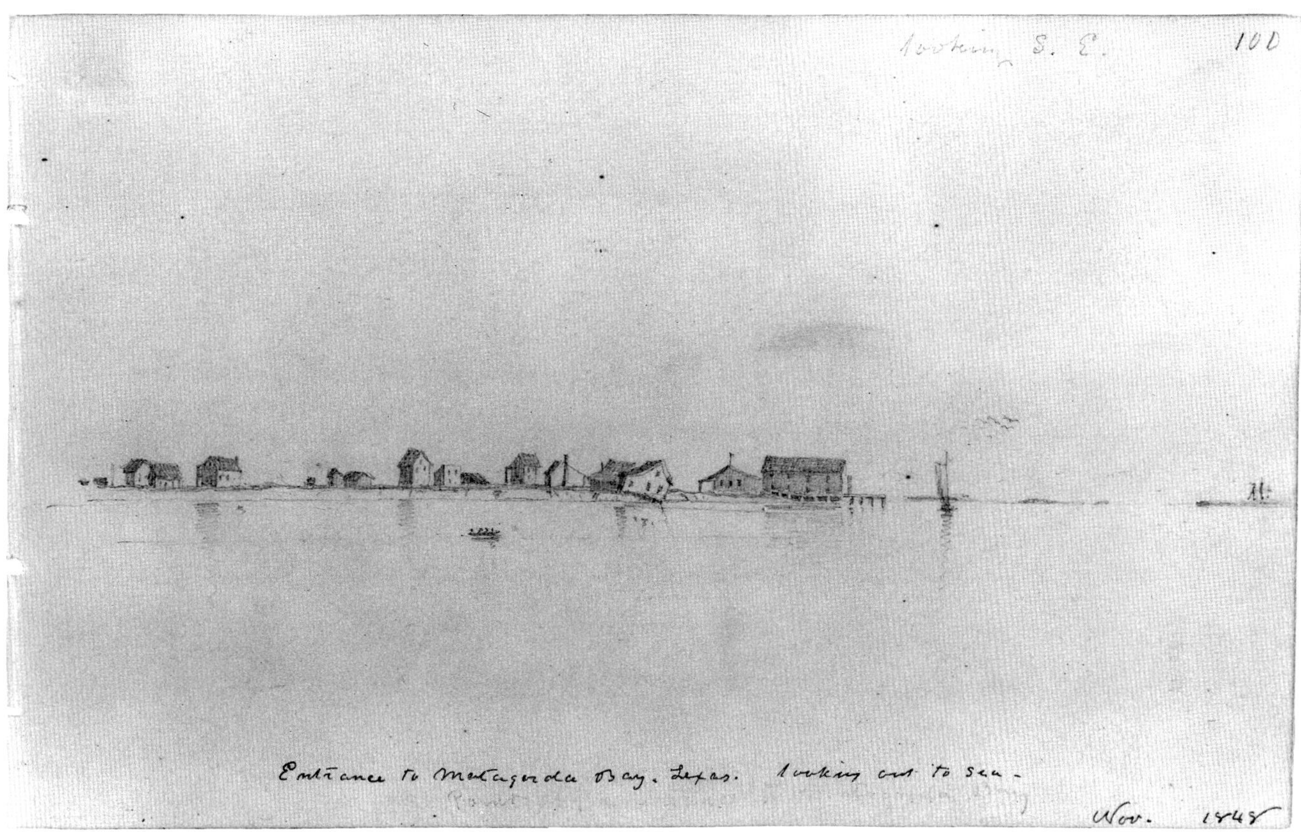

FIGURE 58. Seth Eastman, *Entrance to Matagorda Bay, Texas.
Looking Out to Sea*, 1848. Pencil on paper. Gift of the Pearl
Brewing Company. Marion Koogler McNay Art Museum,
San Antonio, Texas. No. 1961.5.

few scenes and then as small figures incidental to the
landscape.[17]

Despite the American military's involvement in exotic
transportation experiments and surveying activities, its
primary role in nineteenth-century Texas centered on
keeping the peace between Anglo settlers and Indian
tribes. Arthur T. Lee's station of Fort Davis was one
of eleven posts meant for this function, and Eastman's
encampment near Fredericksburg, Camp Houston, was
soon upgraded and renamed Fort Martin Scott, in memory of an American officer killed in the Mexican War.
Richard Petri's *Fort Martin Scott* (ca. 1853; Pl. 32 and
Fig. 62) depicts life at this outpost a few years after Eastman's stay. This unfinished work was Petri's only attempt
at oil painting in Texas. Although he worked primarily in
watercolor and various sketching media after emigrating
to America, Petri had painted extensively in oils during
his student days at Dresden. Preliminary sketches for this
work reveal Petri's extensive manipulation of the figures,
most of whom appear posed and artificial in the painting.

Was *Fort Martin Scott* an attempt to legitimize his work
in his own eyes by returning to a more formal, academic
style and subject? If so, it indicates that Petri actually succeeded most when trying least. Fort Martin Scott's inhabitants do not exhibit the animated qualities of *Plains
Indian Warrior in Blue* or of the subjects of Petri's scenes
of Texas farm life, discussed elsewhere in this chapter.[18]

While *Fort Martin Scott* has certain aesthetic shortcomings, it serves as a useful documentary of individuals
active on this portion of the Texas frontier during the
1850s. Major James Longstreet, the uniformed officer in
the center of the painting, went on to a Civil War career
as a famous Confederate general. Standing next to an un-
identified, mounted Indian and wearing a stovepipe hat,
Indian Agent George T. Howard converses with two
Delawares. John Conner, son of a Delaware woman and
a white trader and standing on Howard's immediate left,
served as a United States scout and later became chief of
the Kansas Delawares. Next to Conner, in the far right
portion of the canvas, stands John Taylor, a Delaware

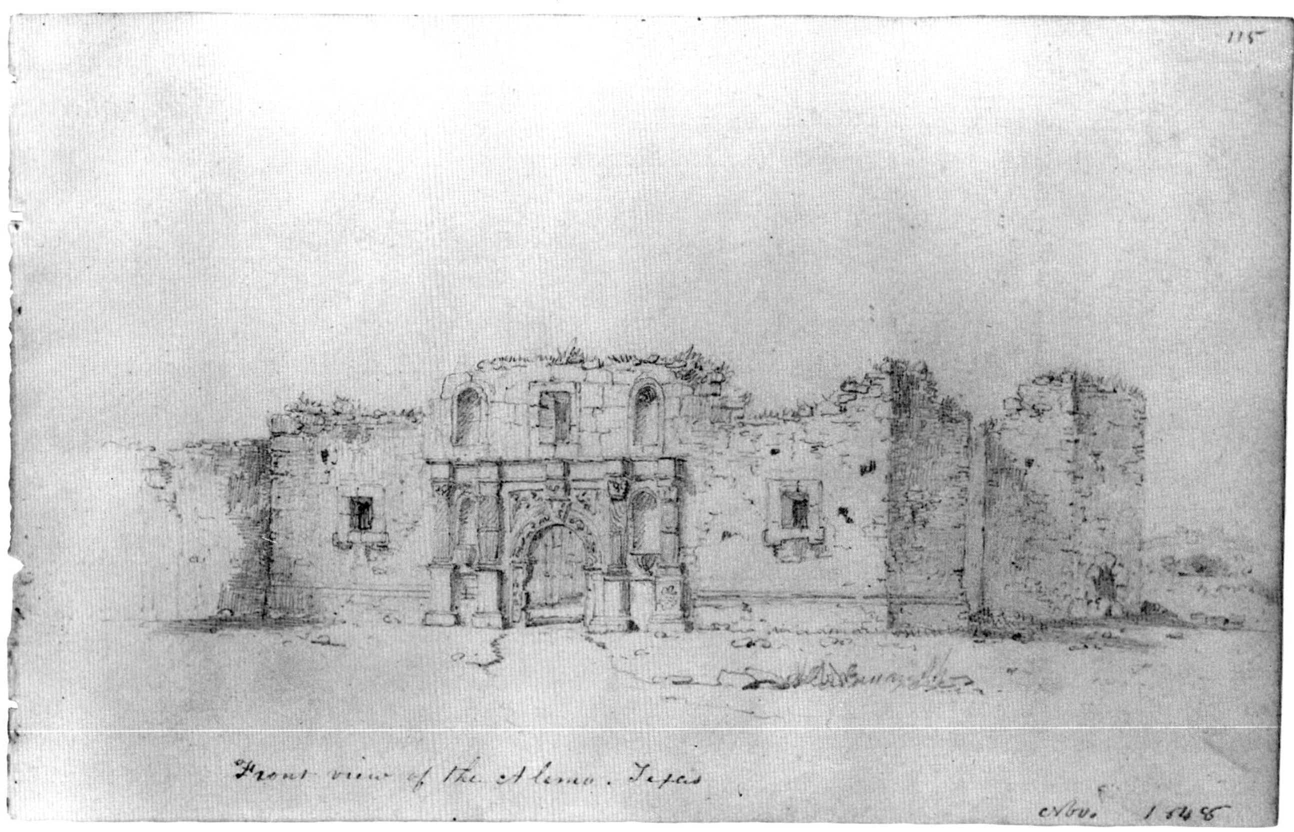

FIGURE 59. Seth Eastman, *Front View of the Alamo, Texas*, 1848.
Pencil on paper. Gift of the Pearl Brewing Company. Marion
Koogler McNay Art Museum, San Antonio, Texas. No. 1961.5.

guide and interpreter for the army. Quite possibly, another Delaware interpreter-guide, Jim Shaw, is the figure wrapped in a red blanket. Shaw was in the service of pioneer western military explorer Captain Randolph B. Marcy and Indian Agent Robert S. Neighbors.[19]

The identity of the unpainted figure of an Indian woman in *Fort Martin Scott* is a mystery, although Petri had previously painted a similar portrait on another canvas and identified the subject as a Lipan Apache. In the spring of 1853, several Lipans were brought to the fort, located two miles east of Fredericksburg, for negotiations with military authorities, and this Indian woman may well have been a member of that group. Depictions of other Indians in the painting reflected Petri's sense of humor: the cherubic Indian child, whose torn shirt at first glance resembles wings, crawls into the midst of this gathering while an Indian boy emerges from his tent in the lower left to wrestle with a dog for a bone. Of course, this last element is two-edged, illustrating Petri's disgust with the fact that Plains Indians had been reduced to such depths in order to eat.[20]

Other, less formal scenes provided Petri with a more suitable format for his artistic abilities. Two of Petri's most charming works, *The Pioneer Cowpen* (ca. 1853; Pl. 33) and *Going Visiting* (ca. 1853; Pl. 34), portrayed life on his family's farm. In *The Pioneer Cowpen*, Petri again exhibited an eye for humorous, realistic detail as a hen catches ticks near one of the cows and a calf nuzzles Marie Petri, the artist's sister, while she is milking. Petri also took care to render architectural details of the buildings, the curtains fluttering in the window, and cattle brands, a New World novelty that intrigued him. His brother-in-law, fellow artist Hermann Lungkwitz, rides across the yard in the background of the painting. *Going Visiting*, portraying the family in formal dress, complete with parasols, illustrates that not all Texas settlers lived in a totally primitive or rude environment. In this painting, Petri depicted himself as guiding the ox team that pulled the wagon bearing the rest of the family. The local mill, site of much of the social and business life of many nineteenth-century Texas communities, stands in the background.[21]

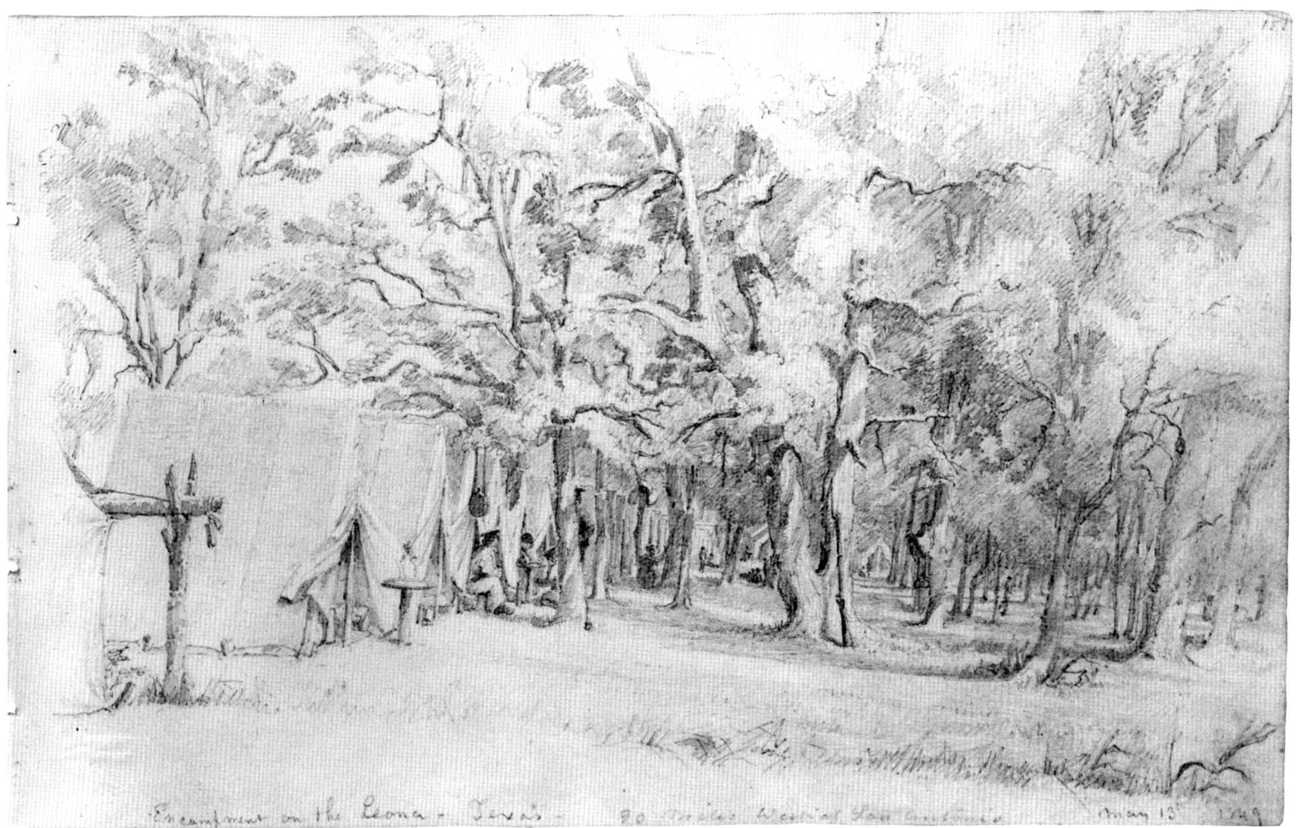

FIGURE 60. Seth Eastman, *Encampment on the Leona, Texas, 90 Miles West of San Antonio*, 1849. Pencil on paper. Gift of the Pearl Brewing Company. Marion Koogler McNay Art Museum, San Antonio, Texas. No. 1961.5.

The Petri-Lungkwitz family typified the overwhelming majority of all Texas settlers; living an undramatic existence engaged in mostly agricultural pursuits, their lives seemed to confirm the aspirations that Stephen F. Austin had held for Texas as an ideal haven for farmers. The American frontier pattern of having several occupations also held true in Texas, as a "farmer" might work as a blacksmith, school teacher, and mill owner at various times. Painters were not exempt from such a dual career, as demonstrated by the lives of Petri and two other German immigrant artists, Louis Hoppe (n.d.) and Carl G. von Iwonski (1830–1912).

Born and reared in Silesia, a province at various times part of both Germany and Poland, Iwonski emigrated to Texas with his family in 1846 (Fig. 63). *Log Cabin, New Braunfels* (ca. 1853; Pl. 35) portrayed his family's home in Guadalupe (later Comal) County near Hortontown, on a 320-acre farm that Iwonski's father had purchased sight unseen.[22] A few of young Carl Iwonski's initial artistic efforts in Texas dealt with these new surroundings. But Iwonski soon was drawn to town life rather than that of the farm; the largest group of his paintings depicted the activities of the German Theatre group of New Braunfels in the mid-1850s. In 1857 or 1858, Iwonski moved to San Antonio and, although he lacked extensive formal artistic training, began retouching portraits in oil and other media in the studio of William DeRyee.[23]

Although Iwonski enjoyed life in San Antonio more than in the country, he soon found himself to be in the minority as a member of San Antonio's strongly pro-Union German community when Texas became embroiled in the Civil War. At the outbreak of hostilities, Iwonski was teaching in San Antonio's German-American school and openly opposed secession. His accurately detailed sketch of a Confederate encampment near San Antonio was the first illustration of the war to appear in *Harper's Weekly* in its issue of 15 June 1861.[24]

Ironically, Iwonski executed one of the few paintings of Texan Confederate soldiers' activities in the state. *The Terry Rangers* (ca. 1862; Pl. 36), also titled *Sam Maverick and the Terry Rangers*, portrays Sam Maverick, Jr., son of a pioneer citizen of San Antonio, departing the city after

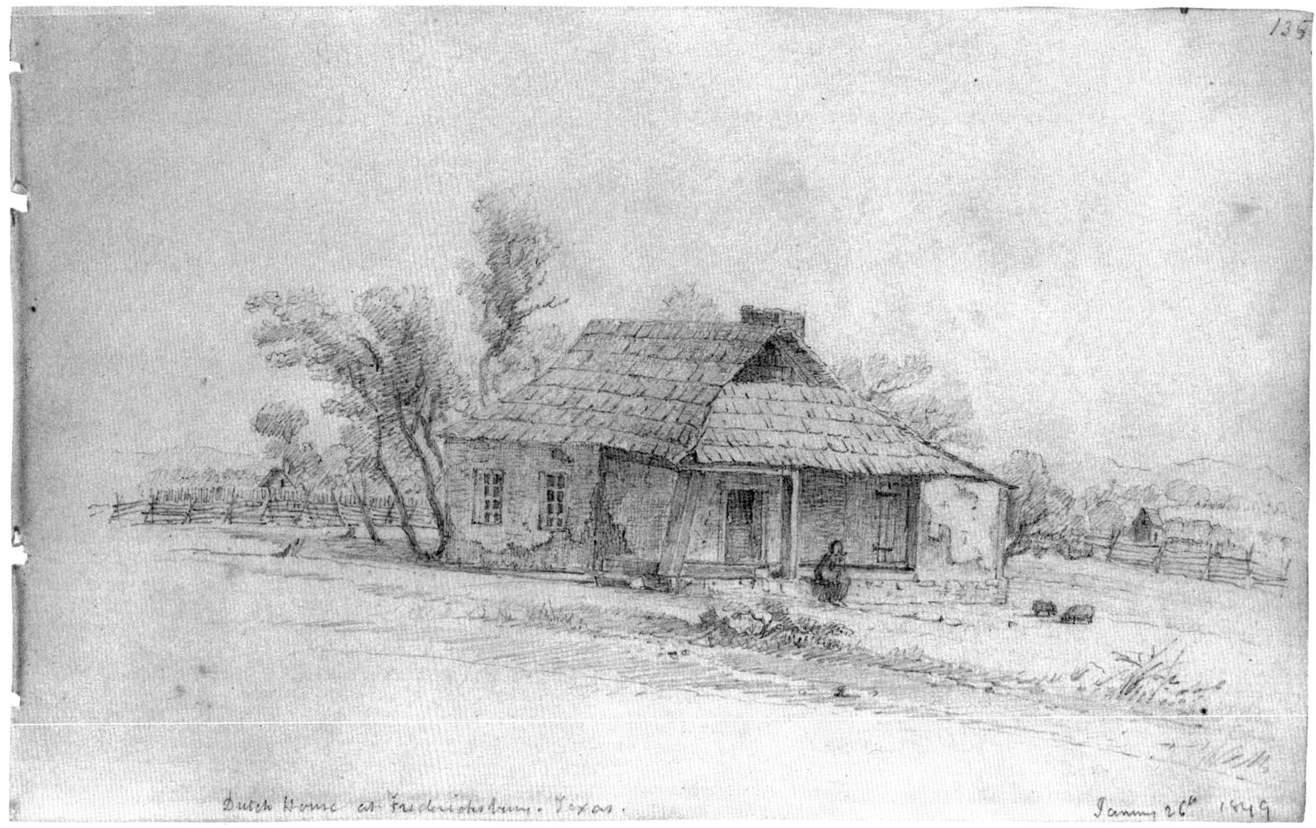

FIGURE 61. Seth Eastman, *Dutch House at Fredericksburg, Texas,* 1849. Pencil on paper. Gift of the Pearl Brewing Company. Marion Koogler McNay Art Museum, San Antonio, Texas. No. 1961.5.

enlisting as a private in the Confederate army in the spring of 1862. Young Maverick joined the Eighth Texas Cavalry, commanded by B. F. Terry, which became one of the most famous Texas units to fight in the Civil War. The origins of the painting are unclear; it does not depict a specific historical moment, and Iwonski likely worked from photographs, personal knowledge of the subject, and family accounts. Iwonski and the Maverick family apparently "agreed to disagree" concerning the war in order for one of the city's foremost artists and illustrators to render this portrayal.[25]

Certainly, Iwonski succeeded in capturing the dashing spirit of Sam Maverick, Jr., highlighted by the new private's bright red shirt. Maverick served in General Braxton Bragg's rear guard near Cumberland Gap and, during the battle for the strategically important post of Fort Donelson, swam to the middle of the Tennessee River and ignited an enemy boat. When word of this exploit reached his family, his father declared, "God Almighty save the noble boy . . . I shall write to him but I shall not oppress him, with a heavy load of advice and council."[26]

In the spring of 1864, Maverick served briefly with a "bushwhacking company" in Kentucky but returned to the Rangers, opting to stay in the war's heaviest combat in the eastern theater. Clearly, young Sam was the family's "lovable rogue," continually courting disaster but having a charmed life; he was the last member of the Terry Rangers to die, at age ninety-eight.[27]

Most of Iwonski's other artistic subjects in San Antonio consisted of portraits and cultural events, such as the activities of the city's Casino Club, a center of cultural activities and dramatic arts. Following the war, Iwonski and Hermann Lungkwitz opened a painting and photography studio. Also, at this time, Iwonski's experience and his cartoons in the local German language newspaper brought commissions to paint formal portraits of other members of Sam Maverick's family. His choice of subjects, aside from those of his portraits, indicates that Iwonski felt less comfortable in a rural, frontier setting than did other European artists in Texas and, indeed, he moved back to Germany following its unification in 1871.[28]

In contrast to Iwonski and Petri, very little is known

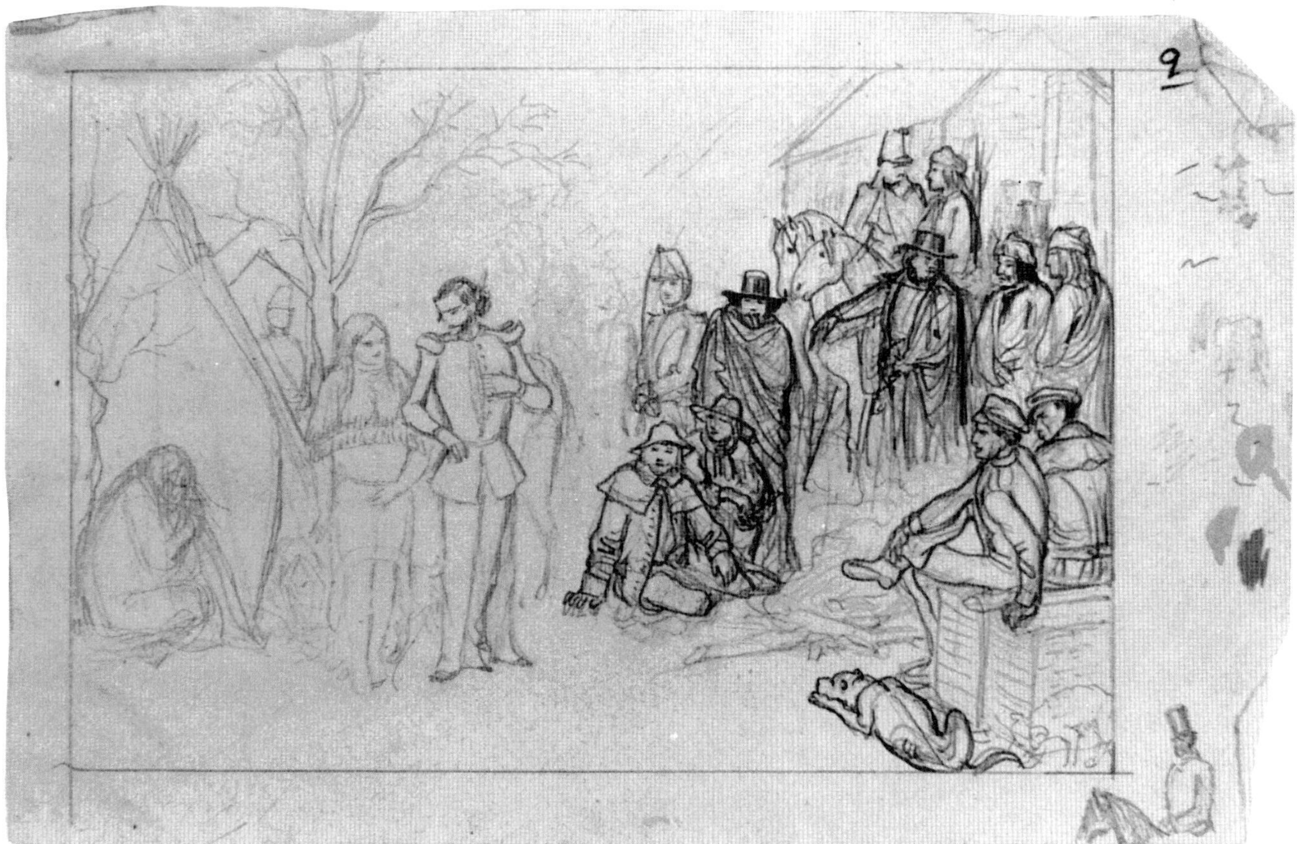

FIGURE 62. Friedrich Richard Petri, sketch for *Fort Martin Scott*, ca. 1853. Pencil. Courtesy of the Texas Memorial Museum, Austin, Texas. TMM no. 2270-12-1.

of the background of untrained German artist Louis Hoppe, an itinerant farm laborer in Central Texas. His *Joh[ann] Leyendecker's Farm-Haus bei Frelsburg, Colorado County, Texas* (ca. 1863; Pl. 37) is an accurate architectural rendering of the home on one of the farms that employed him. Hoppe includes the three architectural styles—log cabin, *fachwerk*, clapboard—of this residence of Johann F. Leyendecker, a prominent local official in Colorado and Lavaca counties. Leyendecker also was an accomplished horticulturist, and the flowers and shrubs in the yard still bloomed a century later. Hoppe's scene captures the front porch as the center of farm life as men in broadbrimmed hats lounge in the shade, women engage in conversation, and children play with a dog in the yard. In *Julius Meyenberg's Farm* (ca. 1864; Fig. 64), a slightly more skillfully executed work, Hoppe portrays another family that had employed him. Meyenberg arrived in Texas in 1845 and first bought a farm in the Frelsburg area, near that of Johann Leyendecker. Five years later, he moved to the Fayette County farm pictured in this scene. The pleasant atmosphere of the painting carries no

hint of the tragedy that struck the Meyenberg family shortly afterward when Mrs. Meyenberg and three of the children perished in a yellow fever epidemic in 1867.[29]

As a whole, the charming beauty of the rural scenes of Petri, Iwonski, and Hoppe belied the realities of life for farmers and other residents of the Texas frontier. Perceptions of Texas as an exotic, bountiful agrarian paradise suffused with "a pure atmosphere" coexisted with grumblings about food ("polecat is the worst meat I ever tasted"), transportation facilities, and the frequent mixing of alcohol and politics.[30] In 1845, one new resident of Tyler County, after delivering an inventory of complaints on a variety of subjects ranging from the Texas diet to the region's insect population, declared the place to be "the most perfect purgatory of any place on earth."[31] Travelers also offered schizophrenic assessments of Texas. In 1853, Frederick Law Olmsted, intent on demonstrating how Texas could become more prosperous by eliminating slavery, described parts of the state as a combination agrarian utopia/health resort. But he was appalled by what he regarded as the "degradation" of most Texans

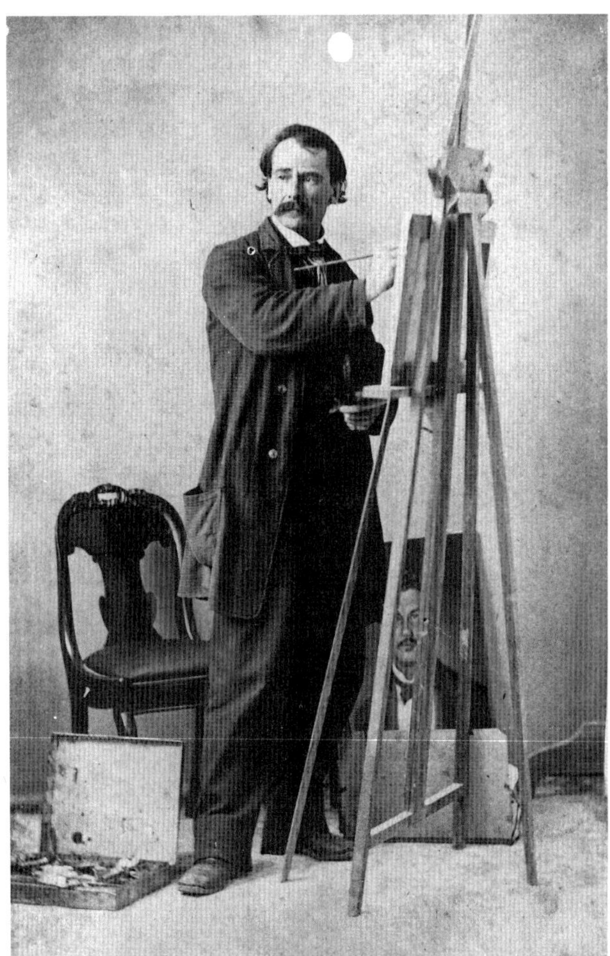

FIGURE 63. Carl G. von Iwonski at his easel, San Antonio, Texas, ca. 1866. The Institute of Texan Cultures, San Antonio, Texas. Acc. no. 72-1751.

FIGURE 64. Louis Hoppe, *Julius Meyenberg's Farm*, ca. 1864. Watercolor. Courtesy of the San Antonio Museum Association, San Antonio, Texas. Acc. no. 31-5360-255 P.

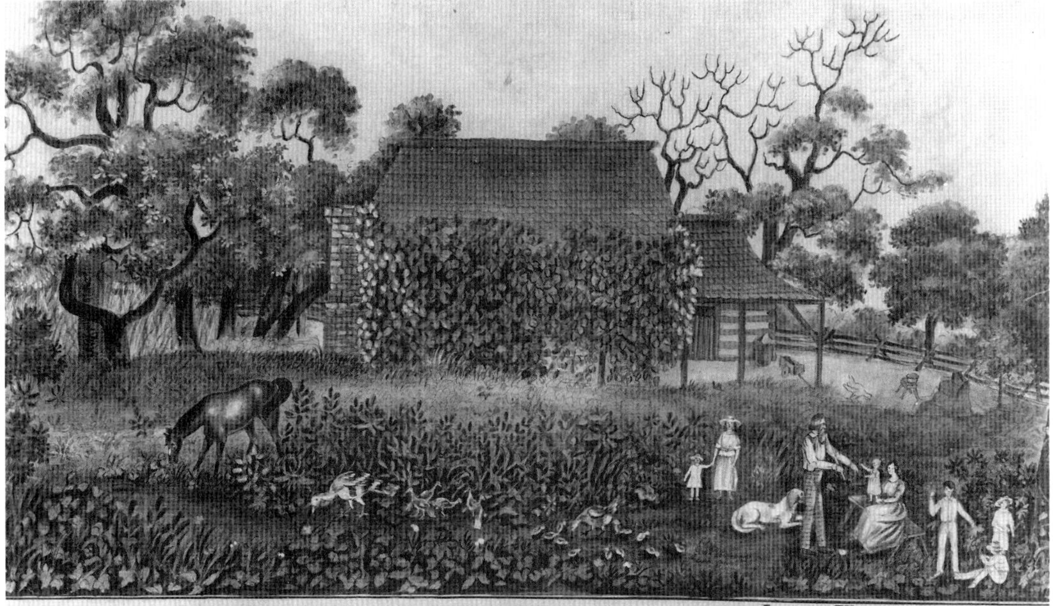

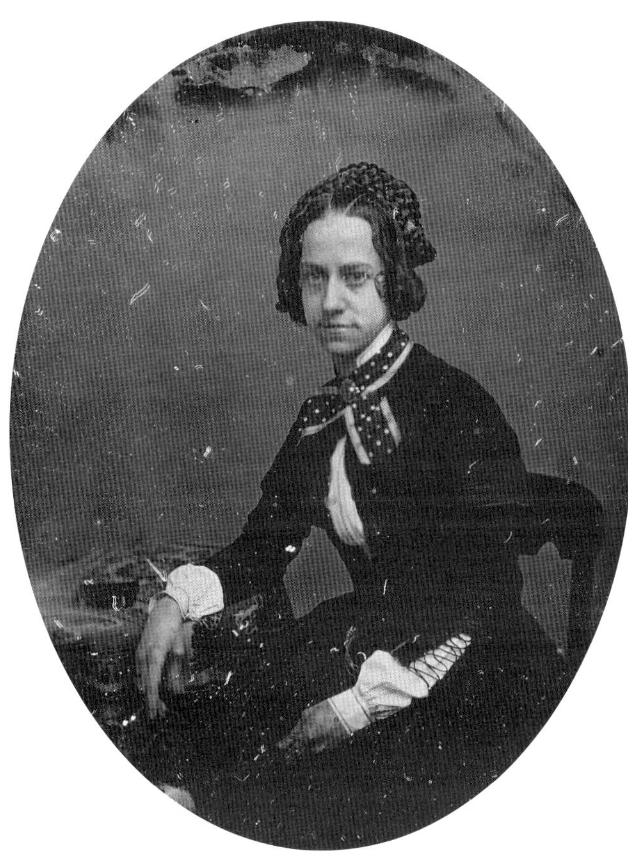

FIGURE 65. Sarah Hardinge, ca. 1850. Unknown photographer, one-sixth-plate daguerreotype with applied coloring. Amon Carter Museum, Fort Worth, Texas. Gift of Mrs. Natalie K. Shastid. No. P1988.26.

who lived a hand-to-mouth, seemingly unproductive existence yet were always eager to boast of the state's healthfulness and commercial potential.[32]

Olmsted's commentary on the abject conditions of life in Texas, especially for women, was borne out by the experiences of one New England woman who left a written journal and paintings chronicling her four-year stay in the state that overlapped the time of Olmsted's journey. Sarah Hardinge (1824–1913; Fig. 65) came to Texas in 1852 in order to claim and attempt to sell a land grant awarded to her deceased brother as compensation for his service in the Texas Revolution. Accompanied by her alcoholic husband, she worked out of necessity as a school teacher and gave lessons in drawing and painting in various locales. After undergoing a series of hardships, not the least of which were fears of Indian attacks and George Hardinge's increasingly frequent periods of drunkenness, the family returned to Boston, having been unable to sell the Texas land.[33]

Virtually every page of Sarah Hardinge's journal testifies to the truth of one of the favorite aphorisms of pioneer Texans: "Texas is great for men and dogs but hell on women and horses." Nevertheless, she left a series of striking watercolor scenes, composed primarily of landscapes, city views, and paintings of homes of prominent Texas settlers such as Jacob De Cordova and John Morrison (1853–1854; Pl. 38). Although an artist of only modest training and certainly not a professional, two of Mrs. Hardinge's most aesthetically pleasing paintings of architectural subjects portray missions San José and Concepción (1852–53; Pl. 39) in San Antonio. Others of her paintings convey the flavor of 1850s Texas, depicting such subjects as plantation life and operation of a ferry across the Guadalupe River (1853; Fig. 66).[34]

Sarah Hardinge's most important contribution to painters' narration of Texas history was a relatively minor element in a painting of one of the homes in which she had lived. The home pictured in *"Pleasant Grove." Residence of Mr. J. Morrison, Texas* had significance for the artist primarily as the birthplace of her second son, as she wrote in the border below the image. However, for subsequent generations, its importance is denoted by a tiny human figure, holding aloft a whip, mounted on a red horse in the lower right corner, the earliest known painting of a working Texas cowboy. This cowboy is driving a herd of horses from behind a well-kept picket fence and down the sloping river bank on the left to Morrison's Ferry. Ironically, this personification of what have been popularly considered as the definitive Texas qualities of machismo and fiercely defiant state pride was first painted by a "Yankee" woman artist who departed the state with overwhelmingly unhappy memories of her stay.[35]

Surprisingly, the cowboy's increased visibility after the Civil War in various American media, such as dime novels and Wild West shows, as well as in the work of a growing number of painters, prompted few artists to focus specifically on the Texas cattle industry as a subject. In the early 1850s, Richard Petri had sketched one rather humorous scene of a mounted German settler chasing three longhorn cattle, but even such minimal interest by painters in the Texas cattle industry was rare (n.d.; Fig. 67). During the remainder of the nineteenth century following the Civil War, only one artist of note focused specifically on Texas cowboys and ranching as artistic subjects. In the 1880s, Frank Reaugh (1860–1945) accompanied several cattle drives from Texas to Kansas that were led by cattlemen Frank and Romie Houston, with whom he remained friends and who later lent financial

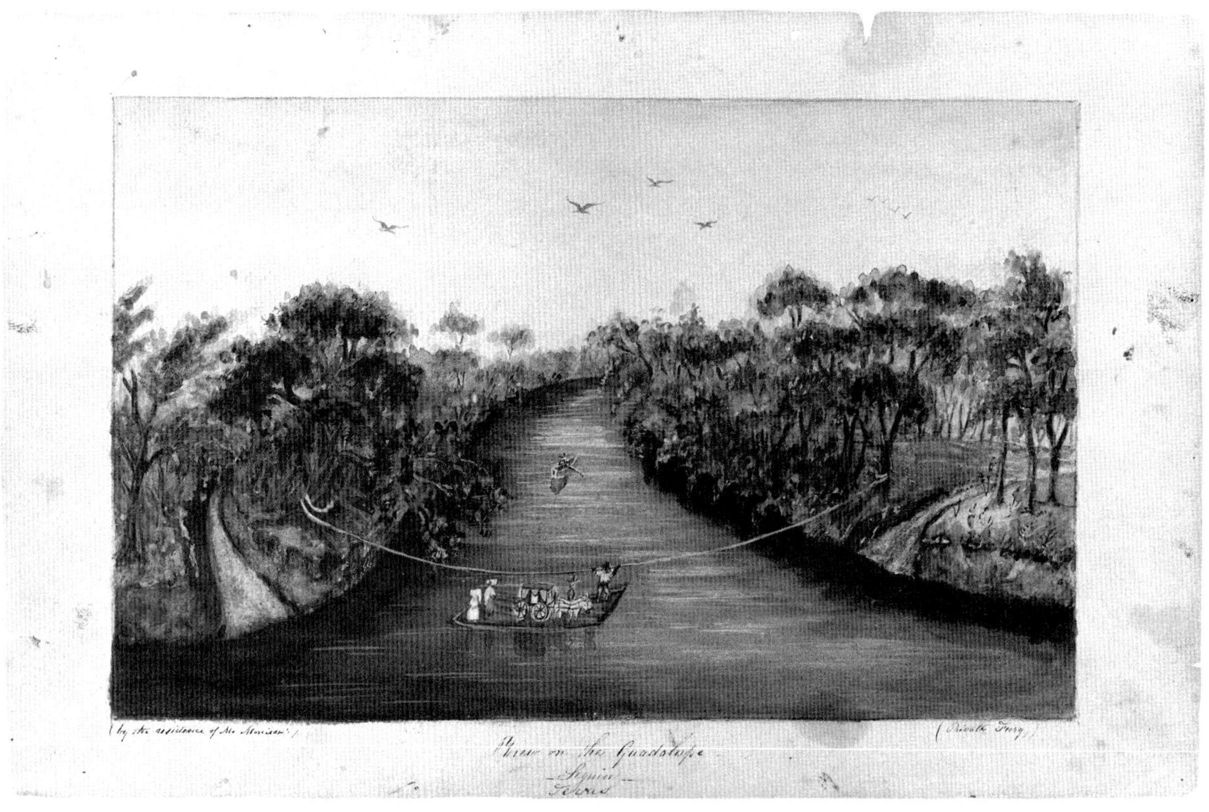

FIGURE 66. Sarah Hardinge, *View on the Guadalupe - Seguin, Texas*, 1853. Watercolor and gouache over graphite on paper. Amon Carter Museum, Fort Worth, Texas. Gift of Mrs. Natalie K. Shastid. Acc. no. 1984.3.14.

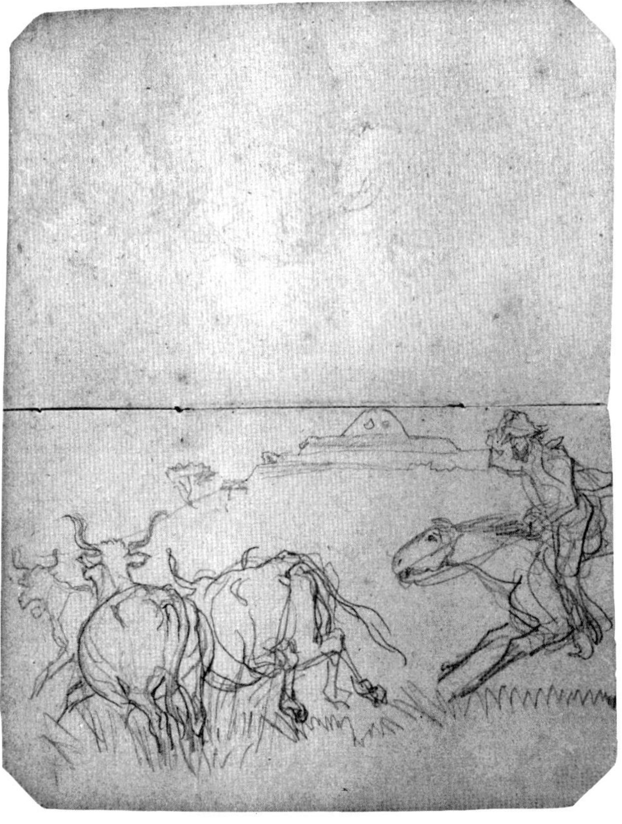

FIGURE 67. Friedrich Richard Petri, *Hazing Longhorns*, n.d. Pencil. Courtesy of the Texas Memorial Museum, Austin, Texas. TMM no. 2270-17-36.

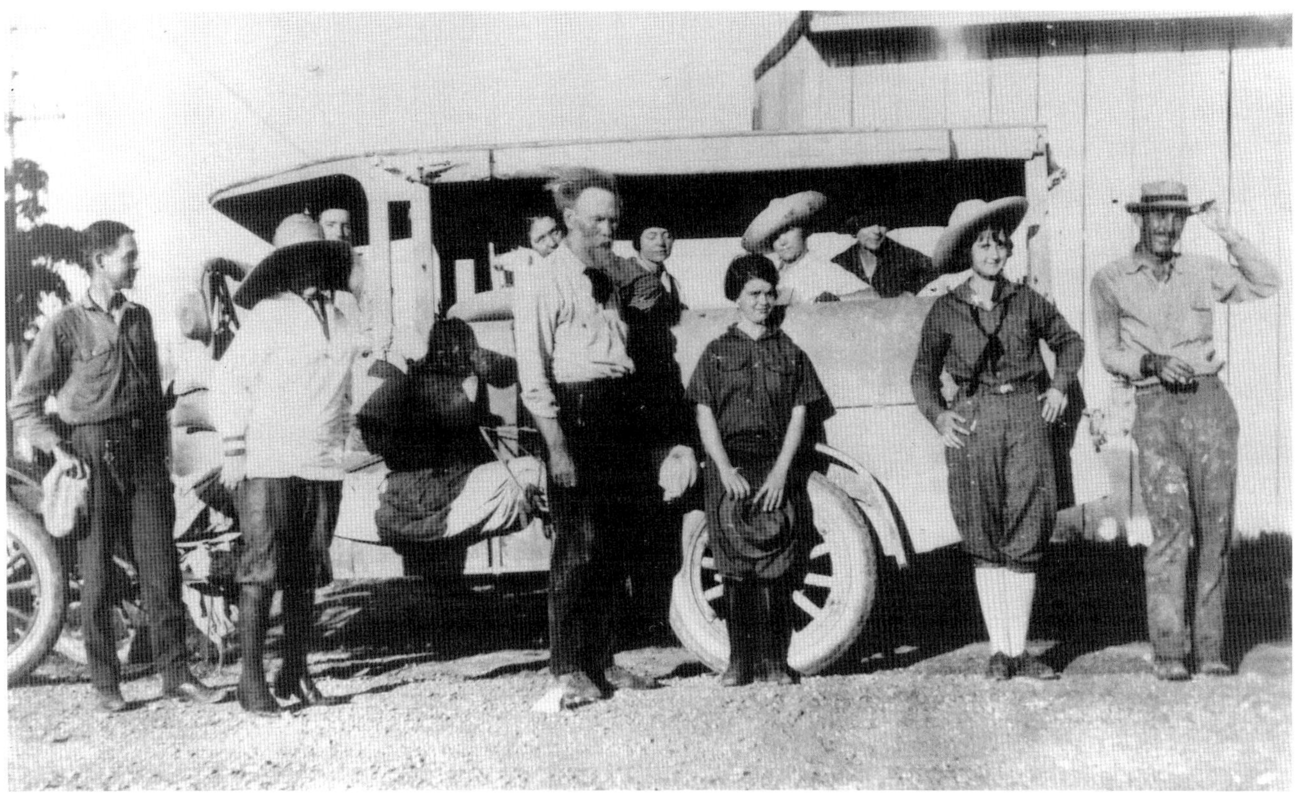

FIGURE 68. Frank Reaugh (*standing, third from left*) with students, including Reveau Bassett (*standing, far right*) ca. 1925. Jerry Bywaters Collection on Art of the Southwest, Hamon Arts Library, Southern Methodist University, Dallas, Texas.

support to his artistic career. Reaugh credited the Houston brothers with having given him an "exceptional opportunity to sketch and study the West and the range life of those early days."[36] He had spent the first fifteen years of his life in Illinois before moving with his family to a farm near Terrell, Texas, some forty miles east of Dallas. But Reaugh was not interested in a career as a cowboy, rancher, or farmer. He had honed a youthful interest in animal anatomy by studying several books on the subject and, while still in adolescence, set up his easel in a pasture to sketch cattle, which regarded him with mixed suspicion and curiosity. Reaugh saved these earliest sketches and worked from them throughout his life, confessing frankly, "My pictures have always been reminiscent."[37]

Frank Reaugh's life and character ran counter to stereotypical images of Texas and cowboys. In 1884, shortly after trail driving with the Houston brothers, he enrolled in the St. Louis School of Fine Arts. Within a few months, Reaugh returned to Terrell and launched a successful career as a private art instructor (Fig. 68); several of his female students soon formed a Frank Reaugh Art Study Club. At this time, he began to travel to West Texas on annual sketching trips, accompanied later by students, several of whom became well-known Texas artists.[38]

In November 1888, Reaugh decided that he needed further instruction and interrupted his budding career as an art teacher in order to study in Europe. Reaugh had been taken with published reproductions of the work of Jean Corot and J. M. W. Turner and wanted to learn to apply their uses of color, clouds, and atmospheric studies to Texas subjects. As had William Huddle, Reaugh knew that some European training would heighten his credibility as an artist in Texas. He enrolled in the Academie Julienne in Paris and took classes from Henri-Lucien Doucet, Jean-Joseph Benjamin-Constant, and Philip Bougereau. For over a year, he immersed himself in the pastel rooms at the Louvre and in private art galleries. He later cited the displayed works of Dutch landscapist Anton Mauve (Fig. 69) and French animal painter Rosa Bonheur as having had a greater impact on his own style than did any of his instructors. Before returning to Texas in the summer of 1889, Reaugh traveled through the galleries of Belgium and the Netherlands to become

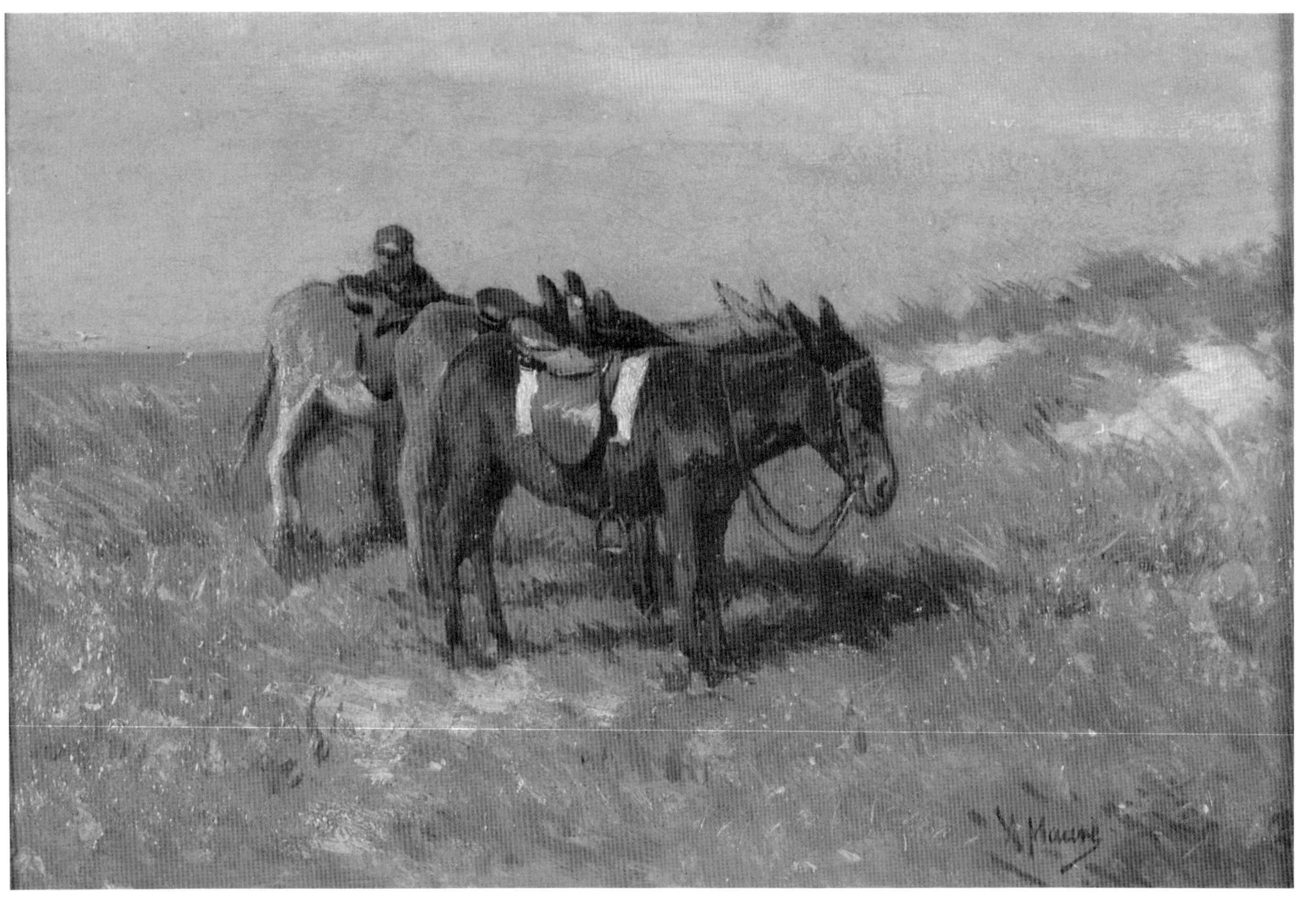

FIGURE 69. Anton Mauve, *Donkeys on the Beach*, 1874–1885.
Museum Mesdag, The Hague, Netherlands. Lent by
Rijksdienst Beeldende Kunst, The Netherlands.

more familiar with the work of Mauve, Paulus Potter, Willem Roelofs, and other northern European landscape painters.[39]

The art and life of Frank Reaugh present several paradoxes. While he deified the cowboy in his writings, cowboys played mostly minor roles in his paintings. An advocate of "roughing it" on sketching trips, Reaugh believed that art should be treated as "high" culture and that it should function with philosophy, literature, and music to "refine" the individual. While glorying in cowboy culture and in the West, declaring that he never wanted to live outside of Texas, Reaugh believed that the greatest benefit of his sojourn in Europe was that it had given him "contact with the world."[40]

The very reasons for Texas artists' neglect of the cowboy in the late nineteenth century are found in these characteristics and qualities of Reaugh's life and art. Though not a native Texan, he was intensely proud of his adopted state and believed cowboys, plains, and the cattle

industry to be the clearest expressions of its uniqueness. Yet Reaugh attempted to interpret these subjects in a decidedly "European" fashion, notions of which he first had absorbed in Texas by reading art magazines. He later sought to apply techniques he learned at Paris's Academie Julienne and by touring the galleries and museums of Europe. As did most Texans of his time, Reaugh believed these artistic conventions to be the proper expressions of "correct" art. Clearly, he worked throughout his career to present an idealized, softened view of cattle-raising that would be palatable to traditional patrons and audiences of the "fine arts." Reaugh was trying to counter such characterizations of cattlemen as that offered by one ranching historian as "wild, primitive, [with] no permanent improvements, families, scientific planning or adequate credit."[41]

Despite his attraction to the work of painters of the Low Countries, Reaugh did not incorporate their influences immediately into his own work. *Watering the Herd*

(1889; Pl. 40), based on a sketch executed a few months before he went to Europe (Pl. 41) but painted after his return, exhibits scant resemblance to the works of the Impressionists that had captivated Reaugh. Rather, the figures of cattle, cowboys, and landscape features were more clearly and sharply defined in this oil painting than in his works of a few years later. Reaugh's selection of subject matter for this canvas also differs slightly from his subsequent paintings in that it did not depict the open range. Instead, this scene could easily have been one that he witnessed on or near his family's farm at Terrell, as cattle drink from a man-made stock tank whose dam half-conceals three fenceposts.[42]

During and after the 1890s, as Reaugh spent more time in West Texas and other areas of the Southwest, he worked increasingly in pastels, a medium that enabled him to recreate atmospheric effects more similar to those of the European artists whom he admired. Reaugh's second version of *Watering the Herd* (Pl. 42), completed in 1932 and used as an illustration on his business cards, is part of the *Twenty-Four Hours with the Herd* series and reflects beautifully his European-derived dedication to pastels. For Reaugh, a devout Christian, painting the plains constituted a form of worship, for he believed that "Nature's church [is] the only one this ultra-modern world has left unspoiled."[43] He trusted the making of the instruments of this worship to no one but himself, compounding his own colors and molding pastel crayons of more than three hundred shades. Virtually all of his West Texas works were in this medium because pastels were dry, portable, and could reproduce effectively weather and atmospheric conditions. One former Reaugh student recalled that Reaugh's innovative uses of color in his West Texas scenes caused some of his students to dub him "the man who paints the purple cow."[44]

This exposure to the Great Plains and desert Southwest also increasingly turned Reaugh to a nostalgia for a time prior to that depicted in the 1889 version of *Watering the Herd*. Toward the end of his life, he harkened back to the days "of my first trips to the western plains . . . The barbed wire had not come yet; nor the nester; nor the sheep."[45] Reaugh also began to consider the cowboy as a heroic figure in that environment:

The cowboys that took the great herds across the country 50 years ago were different from any men that could be found today. Different, quite different, from the rollicking rodeo man, and different from the line rider on the ranch. Sober, hard, stern, generally middle age, they were men who could be trusted with thousands of dollars worth of cattle. Could be trusted (absolutely) to take them through hardship, storm and danger, and deliver them at destinations hundreds of miles away. There was no time for idling or fun while on the trail. It was work sixteen or eighteen hours, and in time of trouble, rain, cold or sleet, twenty-four hours per day. There were no houses or resting places on the trail. Only the open range, vast and wild. Fortune favored if there was good weather and time to sleep on the ground.[46]

Reaugh's nostalgia for the days of the open range echoed Frederic Remington's lamenting the passing of "the wild riders and the vacant land" and the "coming of the derby hat, the smoking chimneys, and cord-binders, and the thirty-day notes." Even though Reaugh was less dramatic in both his art and his writing, both men mourned the passing of untrammeled nature and of what each perceived as man's harmonious relationship with the natural order. Both artists valued nature on its own terms and as a stage for the enactment of a heroic drama. Although the two men were painting and writing from a genteel tradition, they expressed similar sadness at the "end of three centuries of smoke and dust and sweat" and "the open range, vast and wild." There is no evidence of any acquaintance between them, yet Reaugh and Remington would have understood perfectly each other's concern and sense of loss upon observing the closing of the open range. To juxtapose their eulogies for this world, they described the same "free-grass country . . . vacant land . . . [whose] wild riders . . . sober, hard, stern . . . men with the bark on" were being overwhelmed by "the derby hat, the smoking chimneys, the cord-binders, and the thirty-day notes . . . the barbed wire, the nester, and the sheep."[47]

A critically important step in the taming of the West of Frank Reaugh and Frederic Remington was town-building. One of Theodore Gentilz's first paintings in Texas depicted this process, with the artist working in his official capacity as the Castro colony's engineer during the survey of the future site of the town of Castroville, late in the summer of 1844. This painting constitutes a valuable first-hand record by a participant in surveying, a step often overlooked in assessing the process of cementing white settlers' hold on the Texas frontier. The artist's portrayal of himself sighting down the surveyor's line near the center of the painting explains his titling of the work, *Surveying in Texas before Annexation to the U.S.* or *Stick Stock* (1845; Pl. 43). Mounted on a white horse, John James, chief surveyor of the colony, supervises the party's laying out of town lots on one bank of the Medina River. Three years after this survey, Gentilz returned to Europe to recruit settlers for Castroville in Antwerp. In the first

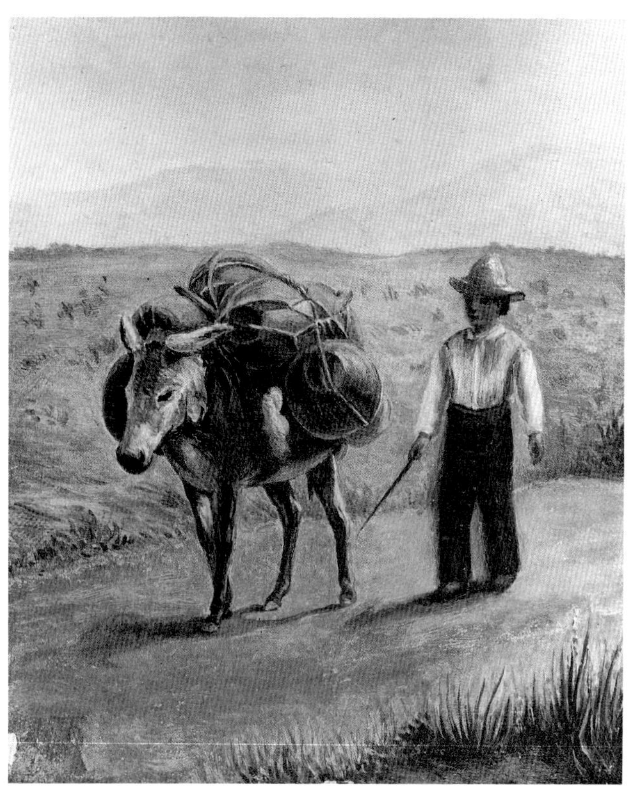

FIGURE 70. Theodore Gentilz, *Tinajera [Water Jar Seller]*, n.d. Oil. Daughters of the Republic of Texas Library at the Alamo, San Antonio, Texas.

FIGURE 71. Theodore Gentilz, *Fandango: Spanish Dance, San Antonio*, 1848. Oil. Daughters of the Republic of Texas Library at the Alamo, San Antonio, Texas.

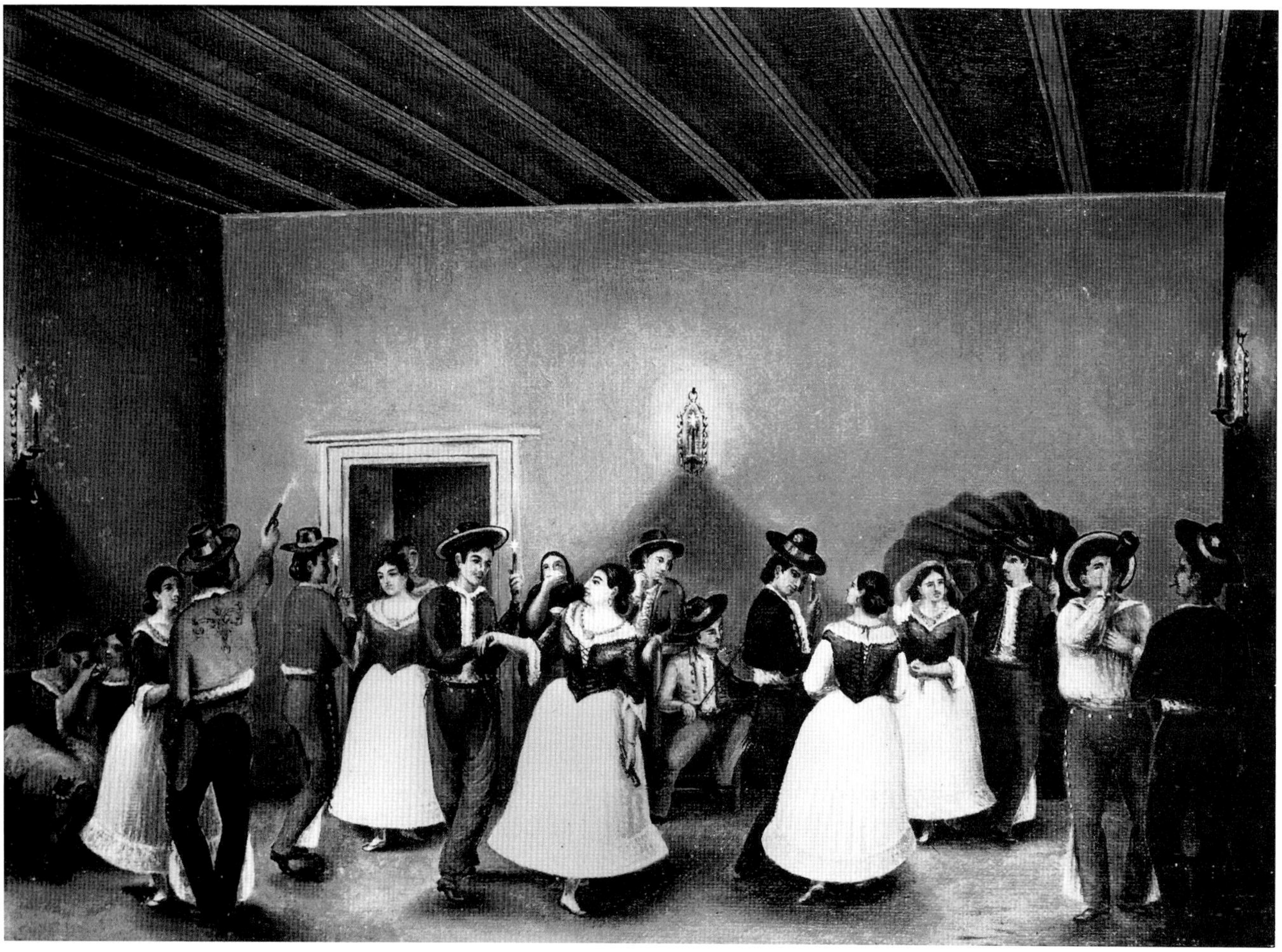

months of 1848, he moved back to Texas, establishing his residence in San Antonio, and began to sketch and paint the missions and Hispanic folk culture that had intrigued him since he first arrived in Texas.[48]

After moving to San Antonio, Gentilz portrayed the everyday activities of a water vendor in *Tinajera* (n.d.; Fig. 70) and the varieties of rituals associated with Hispanic feast days (*Corrida de la Sandía*, 1890; Pl. 44), dances (*Fandango*, 1848; Fig. 71, and *El Convite para el Baile*, n.d.), and funerals (*Entierro de un Angel*, n.d.; Fig. 72). Gentilz's sketches for each of these paintings indicate that many of them were set in specific places in San Antonio, as he included architectural details and noted the names of streets around the borders of the images. Gentilz plotted these works with the same mathematical precision that he devoted to more "monumental" subjects, such as the Alamo and the Mier Expedition, making complicated notes concerning lines of perspective and use of color in his intricate study sketches.[49]

Despite the charm of these scenes, the life of residents of San Antonio and other Texas towns was only marginally better, if at all, than that of the inhabitants of isolated Texas farms and ranches in the mid-nineteenth century. Often beset by near-squalid living conditions, these municipalities competed fiercely for primacy in population, trade, and transportation facilities. Local newspapers led these contests, playing up fears that rival towns had higher taxes, dishonest citizens, and epidemics of disease. Actually, most pre–Civil War Texas settlements shared such common problems as streets rendered impassable by mud that "sticks so confounded close," a dearth of cultural diversions, and chronic lawlessness.[50] Newspapers sternly criticized frequent attacks on property, including at least one instance in 1840 of vandalism of the modest capitol of the Republic of Texas, and a great number of towns passed strict regulations restricting the use of firearms.[51]

Appropriately, some of the earliest scenes of Texas

FIGURE 72. Theodore Gentilz, *Entierro de un Angel [The Funeral of an Angel]*, n.d. Oil. Daughters of the Republic of Texas Library at the Alamo, San Antonio, Texas.

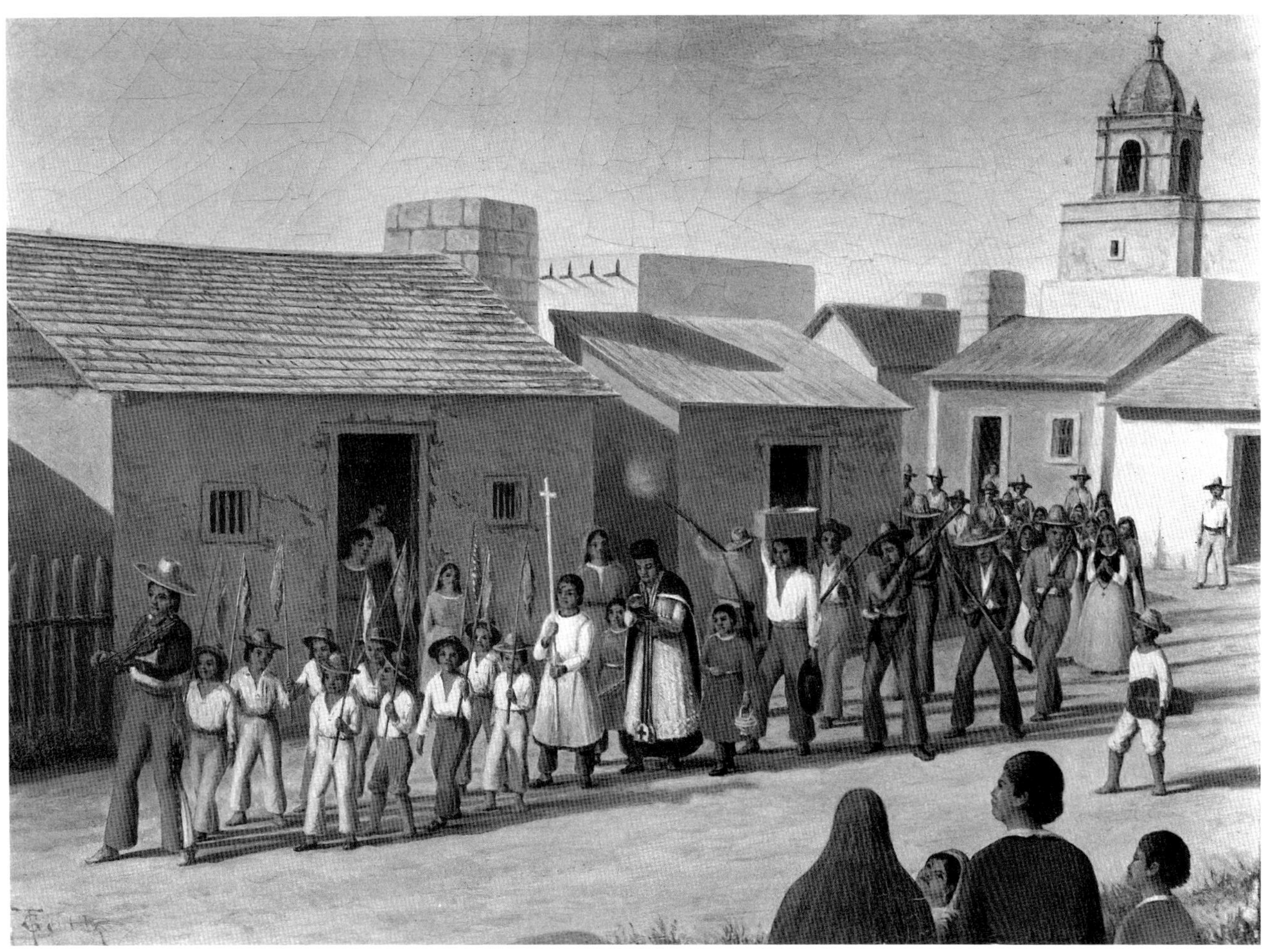

town life were painted by a deputy sheriff and former Texas Ranger. In 1849, W. G. M. Samuel (1815–1902) depicted the hub of San Antonio life, the Main Plaza, as viewed from the windows of the Bexar County Courthouse (Pls. 45–48). A Missourian who arrived in Texas shortly after the fall of the Alamo, Samuel fought under the command of Bigfoot Wallace in the Mexican War. He also executed portraits of several early Texas heroes, notably Wallace, Sam Houston, and Deaf Smith.[52]

Samuel titled his four paintings after the respective sides of the plaza depicted in each canvas. Even though Samuel had little or no formal art training, these street scenes serve as valuable architectural and sociological records. Several important San Antonio buildings were located on the Main Plaza and appear in these four works: the residences or former residences of prominent citizens Sam Maverick, Don José Erasmo Seguin, and Alejandro Treviño; the home believed to have been Santa Anna's headquarters during the siege of the Alamo; the landmark clock tower of Casas Reales, destroyed soon after Samuel completed these paintings; San Fernando Cathedral; and the residence later converted into the city's first U.S. Post Office.

Samuel did not paint San Antonio's Main Plaza with the sole intention of leaving an architectural record, however. The prominent and significant architectural features in each canvas frame vignettes similar to those found in Gentilz's paintings of San Antonio life. Taken together, the four paintings function as would home movies of a century later, as Samuel captured a cross section of the populace engaged in daily pursuits. Army freight wagons, their boxes marked "USA," crowd into the north side of the plaza, denoting the military presence that played a key role in the life of San Antonio (Pl. 45). The other three canvases are less crowded but populated by a diversity of individuals and activities. On the west side, a Butterfield stage rattles through the plaza as a horseman attempts to lasso a runaway cow and a brewer tows a barrel of his product behind a mule (Pl. 46). The mercantile establishments of Lewis and Groesbeck and of Bryan Callaghan dominate the south side (Pl. 47), while the plaza's east side is peopled by individuals engaged in conversation or transporting firewood and water (Pl. 48). Oxcarts appear throughout this series of paintings, attesting to their prevalence in Texas during this time. Samuel's sense of humor enlivens these works just as Gentilz's sympathy for his subjects breathed life into his genre scenes. In Samuel's *Main Plaza* vignettes, a boy and his dog attempt to stop a horse that has broken away, trailing a halter rope, a horseman gives chase to a colt

that has carried off a young boy's straw hat in his mouth, and another man wields a stick to break up a dog fight. Samuel manages to integrate these small, individually prosaic details and create a warm, human tapestry that could function as an entertaining "slice of life" for his contemporary audience as well as a useful historical document for future viewers.

A quarter-century later, Thomas Allen (1849–1924), a more accomplished artist than Samuel, also painted a number of San Antonio scenes. As did Gentilz and Samuel, Allen selected aspects of daily life as subjects of his paintings, the result of his long-standing interest in the American West. In 1869, an undergraduate sketching trip into the Colorado Rockies with Washington University Professor J. W. Pattison had encouraged Allen to pursue an art career, and Allen's visit to San Antonio was part of a lengthy stay in the West during 1878 and 1879. Aside from this sojourn, he resided in Paris after graduating from Dusseldorf's Royal Academy until 1882, when he moved to Boston and began the pursuit of twin careers in art and business.[53]

San Antonio captivated Thomas Allen just as it had Theodore Gentilz and, as did Gentilz, the St. Louis native concentrated his attention on the area's Tejano population. Instead of the Texas cowboy, Allen depicted less glamorous individuals in *Prairie Scene with Mexican Herdsmen and Cattle* (1878–1879, unlocated) and *Freighters from the Rio Grande* (1878–1879, unlocated). This most European of Texas cities must have reminded Allen of scenes he had witnessed during his years abroad. Certainly, he treated *Market Plaza, San Antonio* (1878–1879; Pl. 49) in the manner of a European street scene, and his *Old San Pedro Ford* (1878–1879; Fig. 73) has a flavor similar to that found in works by painters of European peasant life.[54]

The two decades following Thomas Allen's visit to Texas marked a dramatic change in the state's dominant way of life. While Allen was being charmed by scenes of San Antonio and the surrounding prairies, railroads were connecting Texas to the rest of the United States, an important step in eroding the indigenous character of the state's communities. But these railroad lines also represented the next logical step in Texans' attempts to be integrated into the mainstream of American culture.

Before the late nineteenth century, the shipping industry had been the primary means of solidifying ties between Texas and the outside world; in 1900, Galveston was still one of the five busiest seaports in the United States. The only deepwater port between New Orleans and Vera Cruz, the city had exported more cotton than

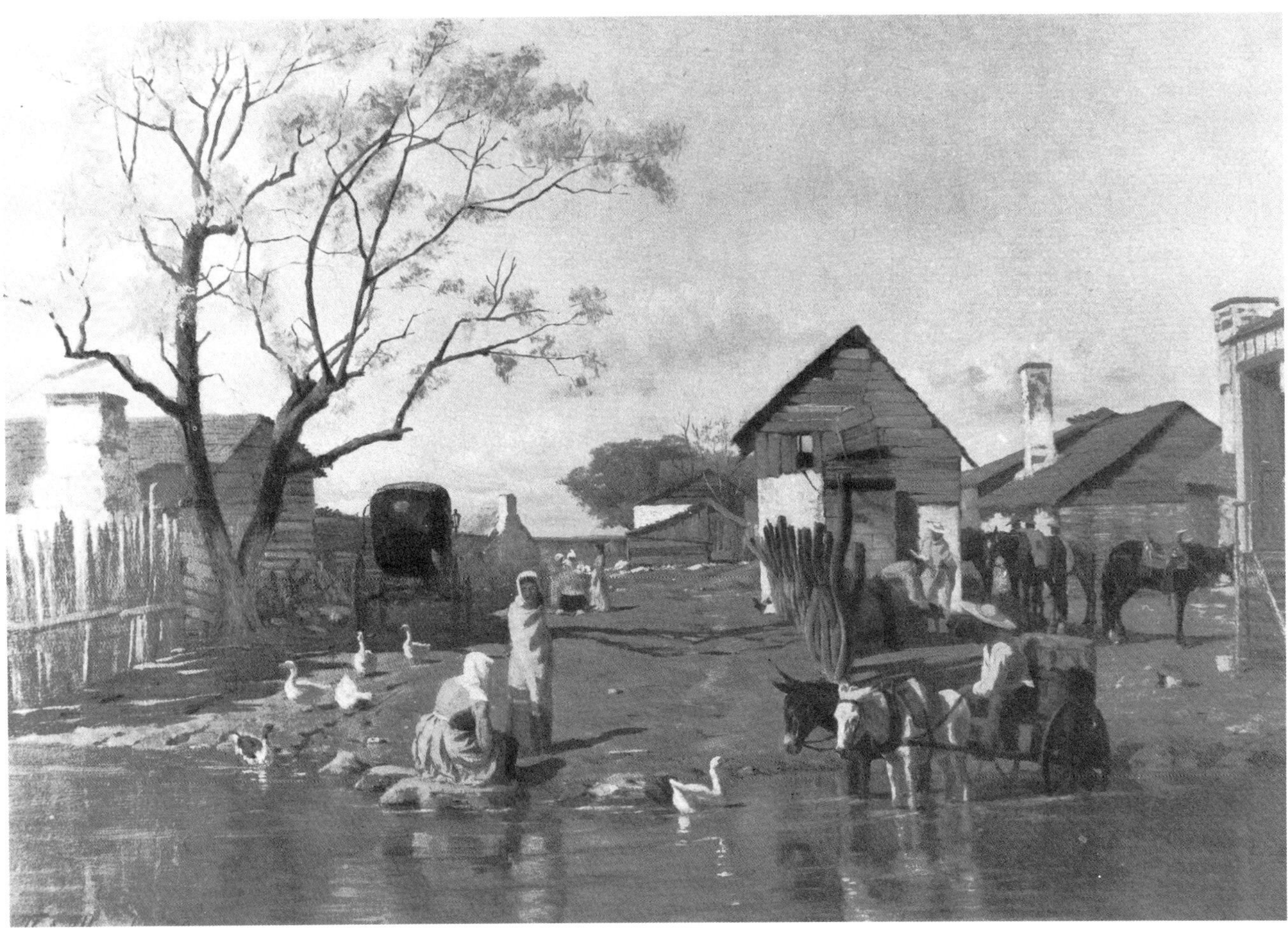

FIGURE 73. Thomas Allen, *Old San Pedro Ford*, 1878–1879.
San Antonio Public Library. Photograph by King Douglas,
Dallas, Texas.

any other American port during the 1890s. In this decade, its population had grown by 37,000 persons, or 30 percent, and Galveston had the second-highest per capita income in the nation in 1900.[55]

German immigrant Julius Stockfleth (1857–1935) was the only professional painter to depict the Texas Gulf Coast in Galveston's heyday (Fig. 74). Like the Gentilz, Petri, and Iwonski families, the Stockfleth family had been prompted to emigrate to the United States by hopes for greater economic and political opportunities. In 1883, Stockfleth followed his family in emigrating to Lake Charles, Louisiana. Two years later, the Stockfleths moved to Galveston, where Julius worked as a painter for the next twenty-two years. Although an apprenticeship to a village painter had been his only professional training before coming to America, Stockfleth painted numerous scenes of Galveston's bustling harbor in addition to portraits, landscapes, and architectural studies of Galveston residences.[56]

Stockfleth's works document commerce in the Texas Gulf between 1885 and 1907, years in which commercial sailing ships gave way totally to steam-powered vessels. Working from sketches executed from his perch on the beach or the seawall, Stockfleth documented the ships, wharves, and warehouses of the harbor district. *Galveston Wharf Scene* (n.d.; Fig. 75) is one of several Galveston harbor scenes by Stockfleth, the total number of which is unknown. Although his father had worked as a sailor, Stockfleth probably did not come to Galveston intent on focusing on maritime subjects but was willing to do any commissioned work. The artist viewed his role as that of a "topographical documentarian" of maritime shipping, working in a genre of painting that demanded depictions of ships and harbor life that would meet the exacting technical standards of shipmasters and owners.[57] Stockfleth succeeded in portraying the small ships resulting from a developing commerce that depended on decentralized shipbuilding rather than a few great shipyards.

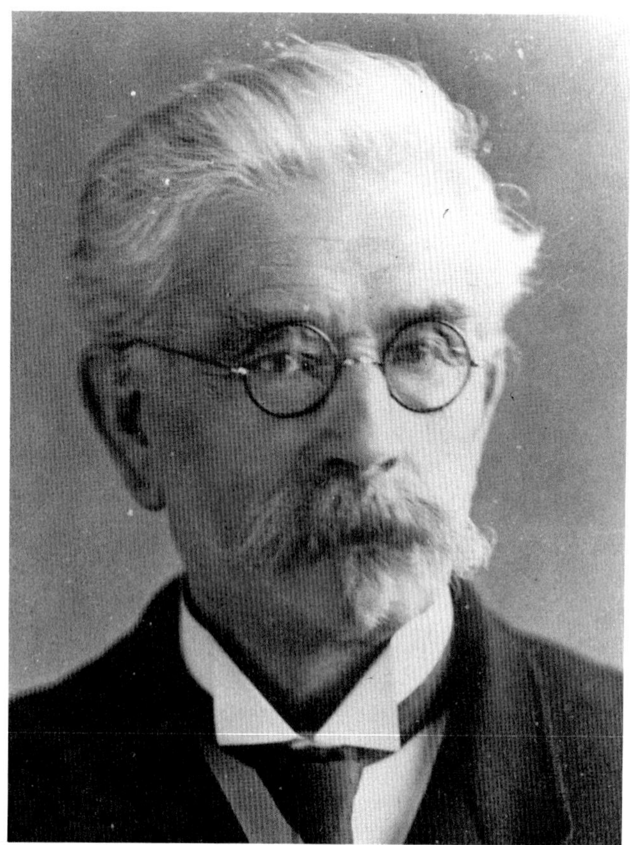

FIGURE 74. Julius Stockfleth, n.d. Courtesy Rosenberg Library, Galveston, Texas.

FIGURE 75. Julius Stockfleth, *Galveston Wharf Scene*, 1885. Courtesy Rosenberg Library, Galveston, Texas.

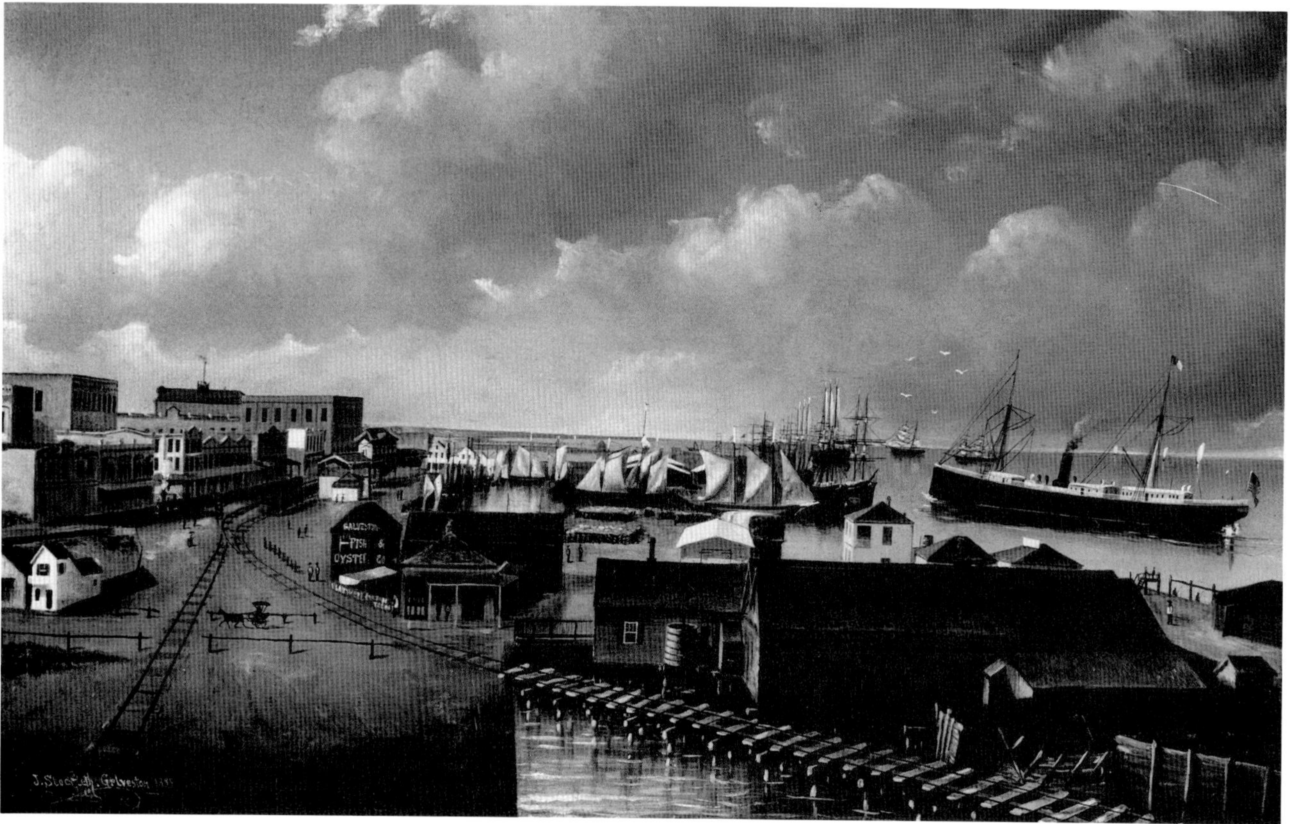

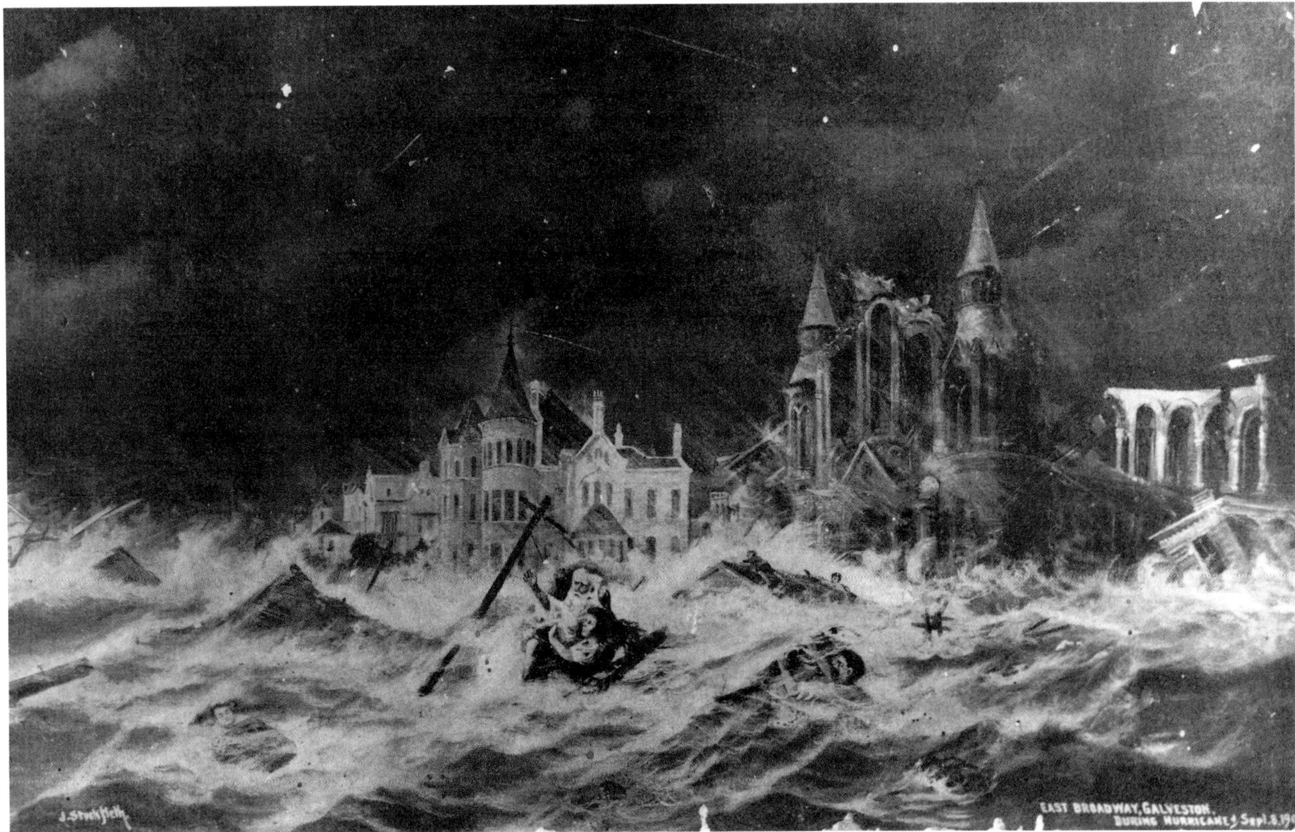

FIGURE 76. Julius Stockfleth, *East Broadway, Galveston During Hurricane Sept. 8th, 1900*, 1900. Unlocated; photograph courtesy Rosenberg Library, Galveston, Texas.

Galveston Wharf Scene captures this commerce, depicting a three-masted sailing ship, steam towboat, sailing schooner, fishing boats, and freighters in the harbor, and, along the skyline, elevators for storage of grain shipped by rail from the Great Plains.[58]

During the first week of September 1900, residents of Galveston read stories in the *Galveston Daily News* of a massive hurricane churning across Cuba and through the Gulf of Mexico. On the morning of 8 September, many townspeople, ignoring hurricane warnings, were attempting to proceed with business as usual despite a record downpour of rain. But, within the next twelve hours, flying slate from roofs filled the air, a tidal wave four to six feet high inundated the city, and the hurricane made landfall with winds of 110 to 120 miles per hour. The following afternoon, Colonel R. G. Lowe, operating head of the *Galveston Daily News*, wired Charles Diehl, New York general manager of the Associated Press, that "a summary of conditions prevailing at Galveston is more than human intellect can master."[59]

Julius Stockfleth left the only known paintings of the Galveston hurricane of 1900, the greatest natural disaster in the history of Texas. Twelve members of the artist's extended family were among the six thousand persons killed by the Galveston hurricane; only Stockfleth, his brother, and a sister were spared. All buildings on the beach, which comprised one-fourth of the city's land area, were swept into the Gulf; Stockfleth never found any trace of his missing relatives. He attempted to deal with his grief by painting a series of scenes from that weekend of terror.[60]

Despite their folk art naivete, Stockfleth's portrayals of the Galveston hurricane convey a stark sense of the devastation of the storm yet are also tinged with hope. In *East Broadway, Galveston During Hurricane Sept. 8th, 1900* (1900; Fig. 76), a spiritlike figure grasps at a telephone pole while holding a child in his other arm. Two Galveston landmarks, the Bishop's Palace and Sacred Heart Catholic Church, are visible above the surging flood waters. *Tremont Street, Galveston, During Hurricane Septem-*

ber 8, 1900 (1900; Pl. 50) also depicts a heroic vignette as members of the city's fire department rescue four men from the Tremont Hotel. But even this rescue scene is painted in somber tones and evokes the sentiment of many Galvestonians that the world was ending on that night.[61]

Although he was traumatized for life by the hurricane, Julius Stockfleth remained in Galveston for seven years following the storm. But his paintings did not sell well, despite their low prices; the present deteriorated condition of many of these works, due to poor canvas and thin paint, points up the artist's financial hardship. In 1907, finances drove Stockfleth and his widowed sister back to their native village on the North Sea island of Föhr. Until his death, he earned a meager living by painting for summer tourists, his neighbors commenting on his deep-seated fear of storms.[62]

In Texas, the year of 1900 marked both the beginning and end of changes that had a significance far deeper than the opening of a new century. The Galveston storm had done more than inflict unprecedented material and personal damage on the most important Texas port. The hurricane's effects forced Galvestonians to rethink both the physical and political structure of their city. In addition to building a seawall and taking other steps to guard against devastation from future storms, Galvestonians voted in America's first municipal city manager form of government, a system adopted by other American cities in the early twentieth century as they attempted to follow Galveston's lead in "modernizing" local government in the wake of the Progressive movement.[63]

The year after much of Galveston was destroyed, the first major oil discovery in Texas, at a salt dome dubbed "Spindletop," hastened tremendously the process of the state's transformation from rural to urban life. Cities such as Dallas and Houston, which depended less on agriculture and more on oil and financial industries, supplanted Galveston in importance during the twentieth century. Until 1900, Texas had been an agriculturally oriented, rural state with a recent past as a frontier region.[64] But the destruction of the cotton port of Galveston and the discovery of oil at Spindletop symbolized a fundamental change from a rural to an urban society; Julius Stockfleth's grief-motivated works had chronicled the final historically significant event in premodern Texas.

Heroism and the Common Man

SPINDLETOP MARKED the turning point of an economic and social transformation of Texas that had begun after Reconstruction and continued well into the twentieth century. Culturally, this transformation was accompanied by a mixture of an increasingly heightened sense of state pride and a desire to conform to perceived Eastern expectations and standards. This juxtaposition had surfaced as early as 1886; even as Texans were celebrating the fifty-year anniversary of their state's "uniqueness," they sought the approval of non-Texans by denying the realities of prominent aspects of Texas life. Uneasiness was evident in the pages of the state's newspapers, which often played down negative events such as drought and violent crime. This self-consciousness conflicted with a heightened interest on the part of other Texans in neglected aspects of the state's culture and history. A few years after the "Second Battle of the Alamo," the Texas Folklore Society was founded in order to further the preservation and study of Texas folkways and oral traditions. In 1910, John Lomax, one of the society's founders, published *Cowboy Songs and Frontier Ballads*, the first collection of American folk songs accompanied by published music. However, a few years before its publication, Lomax had had to endure dismissal of his work as "tawdry, cheap, and unworthy" by one of his professors at the University of Texas as well as unexpected derision from members of the Texas Cattlemen's Association.[1]

In the first decades of the twentieth century, this cultural identity crisis combined with national artistic trends to diminish the popularity of painting as a medium for the narrating of Texas history. During these years, an increasing number of artists, led by the Ashcan School, began to depict the realities of American city life instead of more romantic themes of farm life and heroic exploits. The Armory Show of 1913 accelerated this artistic trend toward mechanical, technological, and urban subjects, just as Spindletop hastened the urbanization of Texas. Cubism and other avant-garde art movements emphasized modernity, industrialization, and fragmentation. This focus struck directly at the presuppositions of historical narrative painting, which reveled in a more insular, rural past and heroic deeds and treated history as a flowing story comprehensible to the average citizen. Aside from a brief revival of interest in the 1930s, serious and academic painters increasingly left the work of visually narrating Texas history to film, a medium able to convey more effectively both sequential and simultaneous action.[2]

In describing *Fall of the Alamo* to James DeShields, Robert Onderdonk had hinted unwittingly at the ways in which film could improve on and refine the visual narrative of history. Onderdonk hoped that his combination of realistic approach, artistic talent, professional training, and scholarly research would enable the painting to "strike you with force all at once and keep your attention to the finish—that is, until you have seen it all and understand it all without words to help."[3] "To the finish" of what? Onderdonk seems to be describing a motion picture or a novel rather than a painting. McArdle's *Dawn at the Alamo*, depicting numerous simultaneous events, depended even more on conveying a sense of unfolding, sequential action than did Onderdonk's work. The subjects of these and other "pictorial history" paintings, in the terminology of Thomas Moran, proved well suited to film, the twentieth century's dominant form of visual narrative.

Although far removed in many ways from McArdle and Onderdonk and earlier grand style history painters such as Benjamin West, John Singleton Copley, and John Trumbull, filmmakers also began presenting "truth" in order to evoke emotion and nationalistic sentiment.[4] In dealing with Texas subjects, they found that painters had established the "central narrative structure" of Texas history in visual form for pre-twentieth-century viewers, just as Frederick Jackson Turner did for subsequent study of the history of the American West in 1893.[5] Painters codified this structure by exploiting the raw material of a folkloric oral tradition, legitimizing this tradition by transforming its tales into readily accessible cultural artifacts. Executed after the development of lithographic and offset printing, many of these paintings were in turn transformed through magazine, textbook, and newspaper reproductions into elements of a highly visible usable past. Setting forth images of military conflict, sacrifice and triumph, and the pivotal role of a Jacksonian Everyman in bringing American-style progress to Texas, these canvases reinforced visually the icons and stereotypes dominant in Texas by 1900. Feature films that have traditionally "defined" Texas demonstrate especially the primacy and power of nineteenth-century events and their accompanying stereotypes: *The Alamo*; *The Searchers*, one of several films depicting Indian-white relations in Texas; and *Red River*, the standard for the many films made concerning the Texas cattle industry.[6]

In addition to furnishing Texans with an outlet for emotions of state pride and patriotism, historical narrative paintings kindled an interest in art and history on the part of individuals who might well have remained apathetic otherwise. The most outstanding example is that of James DeShields, who transplanted to Texas a long tradition of painters furnishing illustrations for nationalistic literary efforts written for a popular audience.[7] The reception given these and other historical narrative paintings raises the question of the criteria for artists' professional success in late nineteenth-century Texas. While this question merits lengthy discussion beyond the limits of the present study, aspects of the careers of Henry McArdle and Robert Onderdonk provide telling glimpses of the poles of failure and success. McArdle was a stereo-

typical *artiste*, always striving in his painting to match an idealistically based standard of perfection. This intensity was matched by a business ineptitude that often threatened his ability to deal with the world outside his studio. In 1885, when Colonel Moses Austin Bryan could not pay McArdle for *Settlement of Austin's Colony*, the artist readily released Bryan from any financial obligations, thinking that he "could do better with the State."[8] And McArdle could never be deterred from bidding for state patronage with his scheme of executing a series of Texas history paintings and bronzes, despite state officials' obvious preference for the work of William Huddle. By contrast, Onderdonk exhibited more hard-headed business sense in such matters as keeping close watch on individuals who might violate copyright laws in making reproductions of *Fall of the Alamo*.[9]

Onderdonk, who served as the instructor and director of the state's first professional art organization and who labored to strengthen Texas art institutions, was one of a handful of Texas painters who lived long enough to bridge the gap from nineteenth- to twentieth-century art traditions. By the close of the first decade of the twentieth century, only a few of the artists who had been active during the heyday of Texas historical narrative painting were still living. In addition to Onderdonk, Frank Reaugh, who lived until 1945, served as a link from nineteenth-century painting to the generation of Texas artists who came to professional maturity in the wake of the effects of the Armory Show.[10]

While no single painter was wholly typical of Texas historical narrative painting, the work of Theodore Gentilz brought together the variety of what Octavio Paz would have characterized as its pre-twentieth-century "fragments." Gentilz's paintings had elements of several "Wests" that also found expression in the works of other painters of Texas historical scenes: the exotic West of early maps and woodcuts and depictions of Indian life; the heroic West of military and battle paintings; the pioneer West of scenes of farming, ranching, surveying, and town life; and, finally, the nostalgic West, evoked especially by European immigrant painters and such artists as Thomas Allen.

Gentilz approached Texas historical subjects as did many other painters of these scenes, synthesizing documentary and pictorial history in his art. But Gentilz also pursued the task of painting the totality of Texas life. He believed the funeral of an anonymous child to be as deserving of his meticulous artistic attention as were traditionally heroic events of Texas history. In painting the

Battle of the Alamo, Almeron Dickinson's execution, and the deaths of the Mier Expedition prisoners, Gentilz was working within the generally accepted tradition of historical painting. But Gentilz saw equal significance in the panoply of Texas life that followed these more spectacular events. In doing so, he made a statement regarding the nature of historical painting and, by inference, of history itself. Unlike such artists as Huddle, McArdle, and Remington, Gentilz did not regard Texas history as consisting primarily of a series of "freeze-framed" events to be enshrined for a people. In a frontier society that stressed egalitarian values, Gentilz believed that a painter also had to treat nonheroic, less dramatic aspects of life, for each of these aspects, whether surveying, selling water jars, or conducting funerals, enriched any culture struggling to hold fast in an often hostile environment. Gentilz knew that painting only these more mundane aspects of life or only the heroic exploits of Texas history would mean relating merely half of this history, a history that he, more than any other painter, succeeded in putting completely into visual narrative form. Gentilz's balanced inclusion of both the hero and the common man in his paintings reflected a belief that, in Texas, the two often were indistinguishable.

Notes

1. Gene Burd, "Texas: A State of Mind and Media," in *The Texas Literary Tradition*, ed. Don Graham, James Lee, and Thomas Pilkington, p. 154.

2. Herbert and Virginia Gambrell's *A Pictorial History of Texas* contains a wealth of visual images depicting events and individuals in Texas history. However, the text focuses on historical narrative, the only analysis of the many examples of architecture, cartography, lithography, and painting being confined to brief captions. Pauline A. Pinckney's *Painting in Texas*, while inadequate, remains the only attempt to bring together information on some of the most important portrayals of Texas history in painting. One of the more useful exhibition catalogs for a study of paintings with Texas history subjects is William H. Goetzmann and Becky Duval Reese, *Texas Images and Visions*. Relevant artists' biographies will be cited in conjunction with discussions of their works in subsequent chapters.

3. See Susan Prendergast Schoelwer, "The Artist's Alamo: A Reappraisal of Pictorial Evidence, 1835–1850," *Southwestern Historical Quarterly* 91 (April 1988): 408.

4. Recent interdisciplinary studies of American historical painting include William H. and William N. Goetzmann, *The West of the Imagination*; Mark Edward Thistlethwaite, *The Image of George Washington*; and William H. Truettner, "The Art of History: American Exploration and Discovery Scenes, 1840–1860," *American Art Journal* 14 (Winter 1982): 4–31. The Goetzmanns do incorporate some analysis of paintings having Texas history subjects, pp. 83–89.

Even Barbara Novak, an art historian who professes a desire to expand the boundaries of art criticism, hints at favoring discussion of "formal aspects" over what she terms "the nine-teenth-century concern with narrative meaning." See *American Painting of the Nineteenth Century*, p. 153.

5. John G. Cawelti, "The Frontier and the Native American," in Joshua C. Taylor, *America As Art*, p. 141. This essay is a general discussion of the various uses of elements of western life as visual symbols.

6. Quoted in Robert Taft, *Artists and Illustrators of the Old West*, p. 250. For further discussion of the composition of this work as well as of Moran's other experiences in Yellowstone and his aesthetic approach to watercolor painting, see Carol Clark, *Thomas Moran*, pp. 11–35; John C. Ewers, *Artists of the Old West*, pp. 194–197; and Goetzmann and Goetzmann, *The West of the Imagination*, pp. 176–178.

7. Octavio Paz, "Ceremonies in the Catacombs," *Chronicles: A Magazine of American Culture* 12 (April 1988): 11. This article is the reprinted text of Paz's acceptance speech on the occasion of receiving the Ingersoll Foundation's 1987 T. S. Eliot Award for Creative Writing.

8. Ibid., p. 10. Although Paz was speaking in the context of cubist painting and the poetry of T. S. Eliot and Ezra Pound, his thoughts are instructive in considering the relationship that can exist between other types of visual and written expression and how some painters also have functioned as storytellers. For the views of an artist and art historian on the role of art in a language-based culture and the differences between art and language as communication media, see Donald L. Weismann, *The Visual Arts as Human Experience*, pp. 10–13.

9. Frederick Jackson Turner, "The Significance of the Frontier in American History," *American Historical Association Annual Report for the Year 1893*, p. 208.

10. Jan Keene Muhlert, Peter H. Hassrick, and Linda Bantel employ this term in the preface to Ron Tyler et al., *American Frontier Life*, introduction by Peter H. Hassrick, p. 6. Martha Hutson points out that nineteenth-century genre and narrative painting were often so similar as to be indistinguishable, in "Narrative Painting: The Painters' America, Rural and Urban Life, 1810–1910," *American Art Review* 1 (November–December 1974): 94–109. Overlapping of these fields of painting is not confined to the United States. For example, R. H. Fuchs argues convincingly that, in the Netherlands, the boundaries between history, genre, and narrative painting blurred as early as the fifteenth century (see Fuchs, *Dutch Painting*, pp. 11, 18, 22).

11. All quotations are from Tyler et al., *American Frontier Life*, p. 14.

12. The scarcity of material concerning a painting of this importance is only one indication of the need for a comprehensive study of portrayals in all artistic media of pre-Anglo Texas. The most accessible source dealing with the history of the painting and its function as a historical document is Sam D. Ratcliffe, "'Escenas de Martirio': Notes on *The Destruction of Mission San Sabá*," *Southwestern Historical Quarterly* 94 (April 1991): 506–534. This painting is discussed in more detail in Chapter 1, below.

13. The glorification of the common man that had bloomed in Jacksonian America and continued to manifest itself in painting until the Civil War also had encouragement from literary figures. In 1845, South Carolina critic and novelist William Gilmore Simms urged painters to seek out "a story to burn upon the canvas." See "The Epochs and Events of American History, as Suited to the Purposes of Art in Fiction," in William Gilmore Simms, *Views and Reviews in American Literature, History, and Fiction*, p. 87. This quote also appears in Truettner, "The Art of History," p. 13. R. W. B. Lewis explores the presentation of the common man, the ideal American as a figure of heroic innocence, in fiction during these years in *The American Adam*.

Barbara Novak points out that Mount abandoned traditional history painting because he believed that "it had no root in the people," alluding to the received wisdom of Mount's day that approved only of classical and European subjects. Quoted in *American Painting of the Nineteenth Century*, p. 150. The most thorough biography of Mount, the leading genre painter of mid-nineteenth-century America, is Alfred Frankenstein, *William Sidney Mount*. See also James Flexner, *That Wilder Image*, pp. 19–33, 122–134, and Tyler et al., *American Frontier Life*, p. 13.

Perhaps because several of the Texas immigrant artists had fled European revolutions, they had little desire to paint the more violent side of the state's immediate past. Theodore Gentilz, the one prominent Texas painter who did take an interest in the Texas Revolution and subsequent conflicts with Mexico, is the exception who proves the rule in regard to the apathy of these artists. And even he delayed execution of *Battle of the Alamo* and *Shooting of the 17 Decimated Texians* until the mid-1880s, although he had begun to gather research material on these subjects soon after his arrival in Texas in 1844. See Dorothy Steinbomer Kendall and Carmen Perry, *Gentilz*, pp. 22–23. Virgil Barker comments on the isolation of these Texas artists in *American Painting*, p. 455.

14. Quoted in Joseph Leach, *The Typical Texan*, p. 28. The Davy Crockett Almanacs were one of the most widespread manifestations of this fascination with things Texan. See Michael C. Lofaro, "The Hidden 'Hero' of the Nashville Crockett Almanacs," in *Davy Crockett*, ed. Michael C. Lofaro, pp. 46–80; James A. Shackford, *David Crockett*, pp. 248–250; and Richard Slotkin, *Regeneration through Violence*, pp. 394–465. Frederick S. Voss examines visual aspects of the Crockett legend in "Portraying an American Original: The Likenesses of Davy Crockett," *Southwestern Historical Quarterly* 91 (April 1988): 457–482.

15. Pinckney's *Painting in Texas* constitutes the best single source on the role of painters in the cultural life of Texas during this time. William Ransom Hogan describes the crude conditions of Texas life between 1836 and 1845 in *The Texas Republic*.

16. Exhibition catalogs of the San Francisco Art Association for this decade as well as the organization's membership rolls and constitution are found in the Archives of American Art, Collection of Exhibition Catalogs, N-564, items 49–175. As in the case of Texas, some of the most reliable information concerning the development of an artistic tradition in the nineteenth century is found in exhibition catalogs. In addition to those noted above, see Christina Orr-Cahall, ed. and introduction, *The Art of California*; and *A Woman's Vision*, introduction by Raymond L. Wilson. For further biographical information on a wide range of the state's artists, see Edan Milton Hughes, *Artists in California, 1786–1940*; and Nancy Dustin Wall Moore, *Publications in Southern California Art: 1, 2 & 3*. I am grateful to Thomas Gates, Fine Arts Librarian, Hamon Arts Library, Southern Methodist University, for sharing his knowledge of California art history.

17. To suggest just one possibility, Bingham could have executed a canvas of Stephen F. Austin and his settlers that would have functioned as a companion piece to the artist's well-received *The Emigration of Daniel Boone*. Since Bingham was from Missouri, the state of origin of most of the Austin colonists, he undoubtedly was familiar with accounts of the colony's founding and development. The work of Bingham, Deas, Ranney, and Tait is treated in separate essays devoted to each artist in Tyler et al., *American Frontier Life*. See also Goetzmann and Goetzmann, *The West of the Imagination*, pp. 71–79. Barbara S. Groseclose has furnished an extensive discussion of Leutze's work in *Emanuel Leutze, 1816–1868*. For analysis of Leutze's best-known canvas with a western subject, *Westward the Course of Empire Takes Its Way*, see Flexner, *That Wilder Image*, pp. 163–169; and Dawn Glanz, *How the West Was Drawn*, pp. 77–81.

18. Quoted in Leach, *The Typical Texan*, p. 30.

19. Emily Fourmy Cutrer discusses this statuary in "'The Hardy, Stalwart Son of Texas': Art and Mythology at the State Capitol," *Southwestern Historical Quarterly* 92 (October 1988):

312–322. D. W. Meinig's *Imperial Texas* discusses the development of these ideological characteristics in the cultural, economic, and political expansion of Texas influences. In contrast to Meinig, and somewhat more tenuously, Frank Vandiver maintains that this type of regional nationalism is common to the entire Southwest in *The Southwest*, p. 39.

20. A clue to DeShields's view of Texas history is the fact that he approvingly quotes the characterization of Texas by "the versatile J. H. Beadle" as "the land of border romance," in the foreword to *Border Wars of Texas*, p. 5. Beadle owned the House of Beadle and Adams, the leading publisher of dime novels in the late nineteenth century. Not coincidentally, *Texas History Movies*, a lengthy comic-book version of Texas history published in the 1920s by the Magnolia Petroleum Company, also was flavored with DeShields's historical interpretations. For a study of DeShields's career, see Sam D. Ratcliffe, "For the Love of Texas—James T. DeShields: Art Patron and Historian," *Legacies: A History Journal for Dallas and North Central Texas* 2 (Spring 1990): 17–25.

21. The best source for the scant information on Eyth is found in Pinckney, *Painting in Texas*, p. 188. Cecilia Steinfeldt's *The Onderdonks* provides extensive biographical data on Robert Onderdonk. Although no comprehensive biography of McArdle exists, information concerning this prolific painter of Texas history scenes may be gleaned from numerous, though sometimes conflicting, sources. Pinckney furnishes the most information in *Painting in Texas*, pp. 190–195. See also Frances Battaile Fisk, *A History of Texas Artists and Sculptors*, p. 7; C. W. Raines, *A Yearbook for Texas, 1901–1903* 1: 50; Dorothy Renick, "The Eyes of Texas," *San Antonio Express*, 22 July 1923; and Peggy Samuels and Harold Samuels, *The Illustrated Biographical Encyclopedia of Artists of the American West*, p. 312.

Thousands of Southerners migrated to Texas during the years after the Civil War. Then, as would be true a century later, new arrivals could seek "instant Texan" status by identifying with the history of their adopted state. Undoubtedly, the fact that this history included a decisive military victory over another nation heightened its attractiveness for defeated Arkansans, Georgians, Louisianans, and other Southerners. See the reminiscences of Texas Ranger George Durham, who moved with his family from Georgia, concerning Reconstruction, in George Durham and Clyde Wantland, *Taming the Nueces Strip*, pp. 3–7.

22. Since William Huddle left few papers, scholars have had great difficulty in assembling facts concerning his career. See Pinckney, *Painting in Texas*, pp. 196, 201–203; and Skipper Steely, "Archives," *Dallas Times Herald*, 17 July 1983. Although DeShields never employed Huddle, he did use some of the artists' portraits for illustrations in *They Sat in High Place*.

23. Hassrick, introduction to Tyler et al., *American Frontier Life*, p. 13. These artists' focus on the Texas Revolution indicates that they shared with the popular Currier & Ives artist Arthur Fitzwilliam Tait a "taste for violence" and a perception that "the West was won by conflict and confrontation" (p. 20).

24. Truettner, "The Art of History," pp. 5–9. See also "American Art: The Need and Nature of Its History," *Illustrated Magazine of Art* 3 (1854): 262–263; E. Benson, "Historical Art in the United States," *Appleton's Journal of Literature, Science, and Art* 1 (10 April 1869): 45–46; Henry Steele Commager, "The Search for a Usable Past," *American Heritage* 16 (February 1965): 90–93; James Flexner, *The Light of Distant Skies, 1760–1835*, pp. 84–88; and Taylor, *America as Art*, especially Chapter 1, "America as Symbol," pp. 1–36. Barker points out that Trumbull's paintings determined the "popular visual imagery of the Revolution" and sparked demands for more such works in the Capitol in *American Painting*, p. 463.

25. Flexner discusses how American history painters at this time attempted to express community goals and values in *That Wilder Image*, pp. xi–xv. He also briefly surveys "amateur" history painting in *The Light of Distant Skies*, pp. 110–113. For a study of Bingham's work, see Maurice E. Bloch, *George Caleb Bingham*. David Levin examines the relationships between mid-nineteenth-century painters and historians in *History as Romantic Art* and concludes that although the romantic historian believed that "his job was to find documents that would enable him to paint an authentic and colorful picture that would add detail and correct earlier errors," he also believed that history had purposes that transcended mere entertainment and the celebration of selected events (pp. 12–13).

26. See Andy Adams, *Log of a Cowboy*, and Owen Wister, *The Virginian*. Henry Nash Smith delineates the nineteenth-century background of the cowboy's apotheosis in *Virgin Land*, pp. 99–135. Archie Green surveys both the historical framework of this process and its twentieth-century manifestations in "Austin's Cosmic Cowboys: Words in Collision," in *"And Other Neighborly Names,"* ed. Richard Bauman and Roger D. Abrahams, pp. 152–194.

Donald L. Weismann's *Frank Reaugh* is a useful, if brief, summary of the artist's career. The most accurate and thorough study of the formative years of Reaugh's career is Michael R. Grauer, "The Early Career of Frank Reaugh, 1860–1889" (Master's thesis, Southern Methodist University, 1990).

27. See Alwyn Barr, "The Semicentennial of Texas Independence in 1886," *Southwestern Historical Quarterly* 91 (January 1988): 349–360. Occasionally, DeShields's writings were excerpted for curriculum purposes in the Texas public schools. See "The Story of Warren Lions," in *Texas Literature Reader*, ed. Davis Foute Eagleton, pp. 78–82.

I. POPULATING THAT IMMENSE TERRITORY

1. William H. Goetzmann, *Exploration and Empire*, p. 231.

2. Forrest Kirkland and William W. Newcomb, *The Rock Art of Texas Indians*, p. 4. This volume includes biographical information concerning Kirkland, many of his reproductions of pictographs, and observations concerning their various meanings by Kirkland and anthropologist Newcomb. Despite his

lack of formal education, Kirkland was a charter member of the Dallas Archaeological Society and the Dallas Fossil and Mineral Club and exchanged ideas with the scholar who was doing the most work on Indian rock art during Kirkland's lifetime, A. T. Jackson. Jackson, a field archaeologist for the University of Texas, takes a slightly less interpretive approach than do Kirkland and Newcomb in his *Picture-Writing of Texas Indians*.

3. See Kirkland and Newcomb, *The Rock Art of Texas Indians*, pp. 3–6. Forrest Kirkland was a man uniquely suited for this task, which became a labor of love for him and his wife and, finally, an obsession. He was trained as a commercial rather than as a studio artist but considered himself to be equally qualified in both types of painting and turned out watercolor landscapes in his spare time. But his skill in advertising art, with its emphasis on working rapidly and accurately, proved more valuable in copying and preserving Indian pictographs. His copies of pictographs appealed greatly to the general public during their first showing in the Southwest at the Dallas Museum of Fine Arts, 28 February–28 March 1943. See Forrest Kirkland File, Jerry Bywaters Collection on Art of the Southwest, Hamon Arts Library, Southern Methodist University (hereafter referred to as JBC-SMU). Many of the pictograph sites discovered by Kirkland are now under the oversight of the National Park Service.

4. See Kirkland and Newcomb, *The Rock Art of Texas Indians*, pp. 17–18, 34–36. Anthropologist Newcomb briefly summarizes a wide range of findings concerning non-American rock art, pp. 23–33. See also Jackson, *Picture-Writing of Texas Indians*, pp. 1–6. Pictographs also serve as an indication of the existence of species of plant and animal life in a given time and place, pp. 405–428.

The narrative quality of Indian pictographs is emphasized by the fact that some scholars of Southwestern literature classify these paintings as "literary expression." See T. M. Pearce and A. T. Thompson, eds., *Southwesterners Write*, p. 1.

5. See Jackson, *Picture-Writing of Texas Indians*, p. 3. Kirkland discovered forty-three sites of rock art in Val Verde County alone, comprising one-quarter of the total number of sites of the Lower Pecos Style. Because rock paintings are better preserved in a semiarid or arid climate, the overwhelming majority of these works in Texas have been found in the drier areas of the state. See Kirkland and Newcomb, *The Rock Art of Texas Indians*, pp. 37–42, 60–64.

6. See Kirkland and Newcomb, *The Rock Art of Texas Indians*, pp. 43–57, 65. Although Jackson includes these shaman pictographs in his study, he makes little attempt to interpret the meaning of the figures. See Jackson, *Picture-Writing of Texas Indians*, pp. 176, 187, 192.

7. See Kirkland and Newcomb, *The Rock Art of Texas Indians*, pp. 65–80.

8. Ibid., pp. 84, 100, 107, 120–123. The Kirklands underwent tremendous hardships in copying these pictographs: in Rattlesnake Canyon, they had to endure a severe thunderstorm, bats, and a nocturnal visit from a panther, while at Meyers Springs they suffered extremely painful sunburns. On other occasions, following apparently promising leads resulted in a fruitless search for nonexistent paintings. See pp. 7, 9, 12.

9. Dan L. Flores speculated on this possibility as part of his commentary on the papers delivered in a session entitled "San Sabá in Retrospect" at the annual meeting of the Texas State Historical Association, Austin, 2 March 1990.

10. See Kirkland and Newcomb, *The Rock Art of Texas Indians*, pp. 143, 153, and 155; and Jackson, *Picture-Writing of Texas Indians*, pp. 270, 276, 280, 286. A half-century earlier, Hasinai Indians at one of the Spaniard's East Texas missions had painted similar representations of Satan, complete with horns and pitchfork. Jackson furnishes a general discussion of how the presence of missionaries affected the Indians' pictographic art, pp. 380–388. Quite by accident, Kirkland discovered a hillside "palette" near Breckenridge from which Indians dug clay, mixed it into usable thickness, and transported it 150 miles to Paint Rock.

11. See William C. Sturtevant, "First Visual Images of Native America," in *First Images of America*, ed. Fredi Chiapelli, 1:417–419. Ray Allen Billington discusses these early explorers' writings about the New World in *Land of Savagery, Land of Promise*, pp. 1, 3, 5. See also Antonello Gerbi, "The Earliest Accounts on the New World," in *First Images of America*, ed. Chiapelli, 1:37–44; and Goetzmann and Goetzmann, *The West of the Imagination*, pp. xi–xii.

12. James Snyder analyzes this painting in "Jan Mostaert's West Indies Landscape" in *First Images of America*, ed. Chiapelli, 1:495–496. See also Hugh Honour, *The New Golden Land*, pp. 22–24.

Herwig Guratzsch traces Mostaert's handling of nature to the influence of "the true founder of Dutch painting," Geertgen tot Sint Jans. However, he also criticizes Mostaert's use of "the most unlikely sources fraught with complicated significances." See his *Painting of the Low Countries*, pp. 53, 84.

13. See Honour, *New Golden Land*, p. 24; and Snyder, "Jan Mostaert's West Indies Landscape," pp. 497–500. For brief analyses of other works by Mostaert as well as discussions of his career, see Fuchs, *Dutch Painting*, pp. 18–20; and Guratzsch, *Painting of the Low Countries*, p. 280.

A translation of de Vaca's account of his journey is found in *The Journey of Alvar Nuñez Cabeza de Vaca*, ed. and trans. Fanny Bandelier. Although de Vaca and Fray Marcos both fixed the belief in the existence of these pueblos in the Spanish mind, de Vaca did not actually see walled dwellings. See Cleve Hallenbeck, *Alvar Nuñez Cabeza de Vaca*, pp. 282–283. Donald E. Chipman addresses the controversy concerning the precise course of de Vaca's wanderings in "In Search of Cabeza de Vaca's Route Across Texas," *Southwestern Historical Quarterly* 91 (October 1987): 127–148. Marcos's claim to have seen the pueblos also sparked a still unresolved debate. Hallenbeck discusses this claim in *The Journey of Fray Marcos de Niza*, with an introduction by David J. Weber, p. 40. Weber traces the development of the controversy surrounding Marcos's story, pp. xix–

xxvii. In two essays reprinted in John Francis Bannon, ed., *Bolton and the Spanish Borderlands*, Herbert Eugene Bolton evokes the romantic nature of this legend; see "The Borderlands in American History," p. 40, and "Preliminaries to 'The Spanish Occupation of Texas, 1519–1690,'" p. 97.

The lesser-known story of three Englishmen's wanderings across Texas is reprinted in Everette DeGolyer, *The Journey of Three Englishmen across Texas in 1568*. The author is grateful to Mrs. Robert F. Ryan of Dallas for calling this volume to his attention.

14. Quoted in Honour, *New Golden Land*, p. 39. Four centuries later, a writer much more familiar with the armadillo still resorted to the porcine comparison, observing that "he roots like a pig for his food." See Roy Bedichek, *Adventures with a Texas Naturalist*, p. 52. Bedichek goes on to describe the armadillo as "being neither game nor pest nor commercially valuable . . . marked for nothing more than accidental slaughter," pp. 52, 165.

Sir Walter Raleigh aided in furthering the idea that the armadillo was a large animal, writing that it "seemeth to be barred over with small plates somewhat like to a rhinoceros" (Honour, *New Golden Land*, p. 40).

15. See Honour, *New Golden Land*, p. 89. Artists frequently used the figure of a young woman, portrayed occasionally as an American Indian, to symbolize the New World. See Honour's discussion of Giovanni Battista Tiepolo's mural, *America*, in the grand staircase of the Bishopresidenz in Würzburg, Germany, pp. 112–114. See also Suzanne Boorsch, "America in Festival Presentations," in *First Images of America*, ed. Chiapelli, 1:503–515.

16. See James C. Martin and Robert S. Martin, *Maps of Texas and the Southwest, 1513–1900*, pp. 3–11; and Norman J. W. Thrower, "New Geographical Horizons: Maps," in *First Images of America*, ed. Chiapelli, 2:660.

17. Martin and Martin, *Maps of Texas and the Southwest*, pp. 13–14, 18, 71, 73. Often, cartographers working outside of Spain did not have access to official reports from Spanish explorers, and this secrecy meant that they had to rely on second- or even thirdhand information when mapping Spanish North America. Robert S. Martin clarified further questions regarding this map in a telephone conversation with SDR on 12 May 1992.

18. See Martin and Martin, *Maps of Texas and the Southwest*, pp. 19, 83. The map is reproduced on p. 82. See also *Mapping a Region: Texas, 1656–1857*.

19. See Martin and Martin, *Maps of Texas and the Southwest*, p. 21. For an excerpt of a first-person account of LaSalle's 1682 exploration of the Mississippi by Henri Tonty, a member of the expedition, see Ray Allen Billington and Martin Ridge, eds., *America's Frontier Story*, pp. 107–111. The most extensive account of how the Fort St. Louis settlement figured in the French-Spanish rivalry is Robert S. Weddle's *Wilderness Manhunt*.

20. See Martin and Martin, *Maps of Texas and the Southwest*, pp. 22, 91.

21. See Robert S. Weddle, *The San Sabá Mission*, pp. 7–10. One of the five East Texas missions, San Miguel de los Linares, was only approximately twenty miles from the French settlement of Natchitoches on the Red River. In 1721, the nearby Presidio de Los Adaes was founded and served as the Spanish capital of Texas for the next half-century.

Bolton summarizes how French activity in Texas affected the establishing of various missions in "Preliminaries to 'The Spanish Occupation of Texas, 1519–1690,'" pp. 114, 120–122, and "The Mission as a Frontier Institution in the Spanish American Colonies," in *Bolton and the Spanish Borderlands*, ed. Bannon, pp. 195–196. The latter article is also useful in placing the mission system in the larger context of Spain's North American experience. In the same volume, see also "Defensive Spanish Expansion and the Significance of the Borderlands," pp. 49–50.

22. The most detailed account of the massacre is found in Weddle, *The San Sabá Mission*, pp. 72–89, and will be examined in detail in conjunction with the painting, *Destruction of Mission San Sabá*, at a later point in the text.

23. Lesley Byrd Simpson, ed. and trans., *The San Sabá Papers*, pp. 85, 92. These quotations are taken from the deposition that Father Molina gave five days after the massacre to Colonel Diego Ortiz Parrilla, commander of Presidio San Luis de las Amarillas, whose garrison guarded the mission.

24. The most prolific writer on this painting assesses this "poetic composition" by Arroyo, preacher/orator of College of San Fernando, as being "not of high literary merit, [but it] at least reveals the impression the martyrdom of Fr. Alonso de Terreros caused among the brothers." See Manuel Romero de Terreros, Marques de San Francisco, *El Conde de Regla: Creso de la Nueva España*, p. 60. Fidel de Lejarza quotes the poem in full in "Escenas de martirio en el Río S. Sabá," *Archivo Ibero-Americano* 12 (October–December 1943): 479–495. An undated article from an unknown Spanish newspaper by one José Andres Vázquez, "Homaje de un Martir," refers to this poem, which was dedicated to Colegio de San Fernando, as well as to a memorial folio published in 1958 in conjunction with the bicentennial commemoration of Terreros's death, "Una Gloria de Cortegana."

I am grateful to Dorothy Sloan of Austin for sharing documentation concerning the provenance of this painting, as well as for furnishing copies of several of these sources, and to Marú Cueto, M.A. candidate in art history at Southern Methodist University, for the translation of many of the Spanish language sources.

25. For a complete discussion of the painting's execution, authorship, patronage, and art historical significance, see Ratcliffe, "'Escenas de Martirio': Notes on *The Destruction of Mission San Sabá*."

26. The complete texts of the shields are reproduced in Manuel Terreros, "La Misión Franciscana de San Sabás en la Provincia de Texas. Año de 1758," *Anales de Instituto de Investigaciones Estéticas* 36 (1967): 56–57. Father Terreros's figure is reproduced as a portrait and the text of his shield quoted en-

tirely in Terreros, *Los Condes de Regla: Apuntes Biográficos,*
pp. 18–20. Robert Stroessner observes that the priests' figures
lend a "surrealistic impact" to the painting in "*Destruction of
Mission San Sabá in the Province of Texas and the Martyrdom of
the Fathers Alonso Giraldo de Terreros, Joseph Santiesteban:* A Brief
Research Report on an Important Historical Painting of the
Same Subject with an Attribution to Its Artist," Report for
New World Department, Denver Art Museum, 15 January 1982,
p. 5, copy in possession of SDR.

27. Terreros, "La Misión Franciscana de San Sabás," p. 55.

28. The artist's inclusion of selected incidents of the massacre and the text of the scroll indicate that the painter had a
thorough knowledge of the deposition of Father Molina. The
full text of the alphabetized key is reproduced in Terreros, "La
Misión Franciscana de San Sabás," pp. 55–56, and translated in
Stroessner, "*Destruction of Mission San Sabás,*" pp. 6–7.

Stroessner's belief that the three hundred figures corre-
sponding to the number of attacking Indians constitutes "another example of the attempt at historical accuracy" is incorrect.
While three hundred Indians made their way into the stockade,
the painting depicts the area inside and outside of the mission
grounds, where approximately two thousand Indians were
massed, as pointed out in the most thorough recountings of the
attack. See "*Destruction of Mission San Sabás,*" p. 4; and Weddle,
The San Sabá Mission, p. 75.

Assessments of the quality of the landscape portion of the
canvas have varied. Manuel Terreros terms it "a realistic and
well done background," in "La Misión Franciscana de San
Sabás," pp. 54–55. By contrast, Stroessner describes it as a
"naturalistic and convincing but entirely contrived" landscape.
However, he also states that "the artist . . . did . . . represent
the hill country around Austin in a very acceptable way," even
though the mission was located some two hundred miles from
Austin, p. 4.

29. Simpson, *The San Sabá Papers,* pp. 73–76.

30. Simpson, *The San Sabá Papers,* p. 84. One contemporary
historian of the mission, Father Arricivita, asserted that the Indians approached under "a banner of peace" (Terreros, "La Misión Franciscana de San Sabás," p. 53).

31. Simpson, *The San Sabá Papers,* pp. 84–85; and Weddle,
The San Sabá Mission, p. 75. Manuel Terreros quotes an unnamed source as describing the commander of the attacking
force as wearing "the very coat of French uniforms" in "La Misión Franciscana de San Sabás," p. 55.

32. Lejarza, "Escenas de martirio en el Río S. Sabá," pp. 466–
467; Simpson, *The San Sabá Papers,* pp. 85–86; and Weddle,
The San Sabá Mission, p. 75.

33. Lejarza, "Escenas de martirio en el Río S. Sabá," p. 468;
Simpson, *The San Sabá Papers,* pp. 87–88; Terreros, *El Conde
de Regla,* pp. 57–58; and Weddle, *The San Sabá Mission,* p. 77.

34. Lejarza, "Escenas de martirio en el Río S. Sabá," pp. 469–
470, 472–473; Simpson, *The San Sabá Papers,* pp. 85, 87–88;
Terreros, *El Conde de Regla,* p. 59; and Weddle, *The San Sabá
Mission,* pp. 77–78.

35. Lejarza, "Escenas de martirio en el Río S. Sabá," p. 471;
Simpson, *The San Sabá Papers,* pp. 47, 81; and Weddle, *The San
Sabá Mission,* pp. 80–81.

36. Vásquez's deposition is quoted in full in Simpson, *The
San Sabá Papers,* pp. 80–83.

37. See Weddle, *The San Sabá Mission,* p. 84.

38. Lejarza, "Escenas de martirio en el Río S. Sabá," p. 474;
Simpson, *The San Sabá Papers,* p. 56; and Weddle, *The San Sabá
Mission,* pp. 84, 87–88.

39. *The Death of General Wolfe* was the first historical painting to appeal to all of the disparate elements of the modern
nation-state in its expression of patriotism in terms comprehensible to a middle-class audience. See Flexner, *The Light of Distant Skies,* pp. 34–37, and *America's Old Masters,* pp. 52–67; and
Roy Strong, *Recreating the Past,* p. 26. Lloyd Goodrich points
to *The Death of General Wolfe* as marking the beginning of
American history painting and the subsequent broadening of
history painting to include genre painting in "The Painting of
American History: 1775 to 1900," *American Quarterly* 3 (Winter
1951): 268–269, 285. See also Truettner, "The Art of History,"
pp. 6–9, 23–25. For a discussion of the uniqueness of the work
depicting the attack on Mission Santa Cruz de San Sabá, see
Stroessner, "*Destruction of Mission San Sabás,*" p. 1. I am grateful
to Professor Clara Bargellini of the Instituto de Investigaciones
Estéticas, Universidad Nacional de México, for sharing her insights on Spanish colonial painting in Mexico.

40. A. C. Greene, "The Importance of the Mission San
Sabá Massacre in Texas History and the Historical Value of
Paez' Depiction of that Event," report for Dallas Public Library,
p. 19. Copy in possession of SDR.

41. Greene, "The Importance of the Mission San Sabá Massacre in Texas History," p. 1.

42. Stroessner, "*Destruction of Mission San Sabás,*" p. 3.

43. See Weddle, *The San Sabá Mission,* pp. 118–128.

44. See ibid., pp. 167–175. An interesting sidelight to the
San Sabá tragedy is that Father Junípero Serra was appointed
to replace Father Terreros in an attempt to revive the mission.
The failure of the Ortiz Parrilla expedition caused Spanish authorities to abandon this plan. Instead, Father Serra was as-
signed to California and attained fame as the father of its mission system. See Bolton, "Defensive Spanish Expansion and
the Significance of the Borderlands," in *Bolton and the Spanish
Borderlands,* ed. Bannon, p. 63.

45. John Edward Weems treats the activities of Philip Nolan
in *Men without Countries.* Although Magee and Long have not
been the subject of full-length biographical studies, their fili-
bustering activities are examined in Odie B. Faulk, *The Last
Years of Spanish Texas, 1778–1821,* pp. 113–140; and Harris Gaylord Warren, *The Sword Was Their Passport.* For a discussion of
the Stephen H. Long Expedition, see Goetzmann, *Exploration
and Empire,* pp. 58–64. David J. Weber discusses Spain's last-
ditch efforts to populate Texas during this period in *The Mexican Frontier, 1821–1846,* pp. 158–160.

46. Quoted in Nettie Lee Benson, "Texas as Viewed from

Mexico, 1820–1834," *Southwestern Historical Quarterly* 90 (January 1987): 220.

47. Eugene C. Barker examines the institutional workings of the empresario system in *The Life of Stephen F. Austin*, pp. 138–139, 150, 154. See also Weber, *The Mexican Frontier, 1821–1846*, pp. 160–166. The most thorough biographical study of the man whose vision led to the formation of the Austin Colony is David B. Gracy II, *Moses Austin*.

48. Quoted in Benson, "Texas as Viewed from Mexico," p. 225. Andreas V. Reichstein discusses the younger Austin's involvement in the colonization project, after initial reservations, in *Rise of the Lone Star*, pp. 20–29.

49. McArdle to Governor Lawrence Sullivan Ross, 6 August 1888, quoted in James M. Day, ed., "Texas Letters and Documents," *Texana* 8 (Summer 1970): 300. In this letter, the artist states that he had begun work on studies of these subjects twenty years earlier.

Soon after McArdle moved to Texas, he had requested William Carey Crane, president of Baylor University, to aid him in the procurement of state patronage. See McArdle to Crane, 19 September 1871, and Governor Edmund J. Davis to Crane, 1 February 1873, William Carey Crane Papers, Texas Collection, Baylor University. I am indebted to Ellen Kuniyuki Brown of the Texas Collection for pointing out these and other pieces of correspondence from the Texas Collection cited elsewhere in this book.

50. The state purchased the work following an extended dispute concerning ownership of the painting between DeShields and Ruskin McArdle, the artist's son. Prior to purchase by the state, the House of Representatives Claims Committee determined that, although the Twentieth, Twenty-First, and Twenty-Second Legislatures had appropriated amounts varying between one thousand and three thousand dollars for purchase of the painting during the nineteenth century, no record of a final transaction between the state and the artist existed. See Walter Acker, Sr., Committee Chair to DeShields, 4 October 1926 and 6 October 1926, box 5, file 142, James T. DeShields Collection, Daughters of the Republic of Texas Library at the Alamo, San Antonio (hereafter cited as JTD-DRT); and "Texas State Library Inventory of Paintings in State Capitol," Texas State Archives, pp. 14–15. McArdle could not remember when he hung the painting in the Capitol, and, since the state did not formally acquire it at the time, a specific date for its placement in the Capitol cannot be determined. See McArdle to DeShields, "'Log Cabin' Picture,"[n.d., ca. December 1900], box 5, file 144, JTD-DRT, pp. 2–3.

Moses Austin Bryan, who had pledged to pay for the painting with a tract of land worth two to three thousand dollars, which was subsequently "tied up," attested to the accuracy of his uncle's portrait. See William W. Fontaine to Mrs. E. B. Brewster, 25 May 1888, quoted in Day, "Texas Letters and Documents," p. 296; and McArdle to DeShields, "'Log Cabin' Picture," JTD-DRT, pp. 2–3. Brenham real-estate dealer and amateur Texas historian Harry Hanes also praised McArdle's

accuracy, claiming that McArdle had painted each of the portraits from life, except for those of Bastrop and the anonymous scout, and felt that this "ought to commend the painting to the committee" (Hanes to L. L. Foster, 18 July 1888, quoted in Day, "Texas Letters and Documents," p. 298).

51. McArdle to DeShields, "'Log Cabin' Picture," JTD-DRT, pp. 2–3. This letter is also quoted in Pinckney, *Painting in Texas*, p. 195. DeShields also listed the title of this work as *Anglo-American Settlement of Texas (Stephen F. Austin & Associates)* in "List of Paintings," 25 July 1904, box 5, file 142, JTD-DRT. McArdle may have drawn inspiration for this explanation of the work from his close friend and supporter, President William W. Fontaine of William Carey Crane College, who wrote in 1888 that the painting "portrays the constant alarms, trials, and dangers through which Austin and his colony passed in order to make Texas what it is." Fontaine to Mrs. E. B. Brewster, 25 May 1888, quoted in Day, ed., "Texas Letters and Documents," p. 296.

52. All quotations are from Eugene C. Barker, ed., *The Austin Papers*: Moses Morrison to Robert Kuykendall, 3 August 1823, 2:676; J. Child to Austin, 1 February 1824, 2:736; and Austin to J. M. Guerra, ca. November 1823, 2:710. For a portion of Austin's diary of the Karankawa campaign, see 2:885–887. For requests by Austin and his colonists to Mexican authorities for protection from these Indians, see 2:876, 883, and 913. William W. Newcomb notes that Anglo settlers may have misinterpreted and exaggerated the Karankawas' reputation for cannibalism; see *The Indians of Texas*, pp. 59–81. For a discussion of Austin's campaign against the tribe, see pp. 347–348.

53. The text of this treaty, dated 13 May 1827, is quoted in full in Barker, *The Austin Papers* 2:1639–1641.

54. See Harry Hanes to L. L. Foster, 18 July 1888. The most extensive information on Williams is found in Margaret Swett Henson, *Samuel May Williams, Early Texas Entrepreneur*. In comparison, Chriesman is not as well known, although he is portrayed favorably by early Texas settler Noah Smithwick in a brief anecdote in *The Evolution of a State*, p. 23. For additional discussions of this painting, see Cutrer, "'The Hardy, Stalwart Son of Texas,'" pp. 301–302; and Pinckney, *Painting in Texas*, p. 195.

55. Smithwick, *The Evolution of a State*, p. 9.

56. See Meinig, *Imperial Texas*, pp. 23–37.

57. Mier y Terán to C. M. Bustamente, 14 November 1829, quoted in Benson, "Texas as Viewed from Mexico," p. 268. Benson also discusses efforts to create an "Anglo-free" zone, p. 222. Reichstein summarizes the report of General Mier y Terán and its impact on Mexican policy in *Rise of the Lone Star*, pp. 53–57. Although Mexican officials' fears had some justification, many of Austin's colonists were loyal to the Mexican Republic. See John Child to Austin, 1 February 1824, in Barker, *The Austin Papers* 2:736.

58. Quoted in Benson, "Texas as Viewed from Mexico," p. 281.

59. Margaret Swett Henson summarizes these attacks and

the reactions of the Mexican government and Texas residents in "Tory Sentiment in Anglo-Texan Public Opinion, 1832–1836," *Southwestern Historical Quarterly* 90 (July 1986): 3–11.

60. Barker gives an extensive account of these events in *Stephen F. Austin*, pp. 404–459; Reichstein offers a revisionist view, emphasizing economic motivations, in *Rise of the Lone Star*, pp. 61–74.

61. Quoted in Benson, "Texas as Viewed from Mexico," p. 291. This statement appeared in the newspaper *El telégrafo*, 16 August 1834. Michael P. Costeloe points out that by 1835, despite official denials, Santa Anna was doing little to discourage the growth of his napoleonic personality cult. See "Notes and Documents: The Mexican Press of 1836 and the Battle of the Alamo," *Southwestern Historical Quarterly* 91 (April 1988): 535.

62. Quoted in Henson, "Tory Sentiment in Anglo-Texan Public Opinion," p. 19. See also Barker, *Stephen F. Austin*, pp. 480–482, and Reichstein, *Rise of the Lone Star*, pp. 75–77. Costeloe observes that Mexico's "highly polemical and politicized press" often portrayed the Texas rebels "as weak, cowardly, and dishonorable adventurers" who would be no match for the Mexican army. ("Notes and Documents," pp. 533–534). Weber places the turmoil in Texas in the context of Mexican national politics in *The Mexican Frontier, 1821–1846*, pp. 167–178.

63. The most complete study of the siege is Alwyn Barr, *Texans in Revolt*. See also Sam Houston to J. W. Fannin, 13 November 1835, quoted in Donald Day and Harry Herbert Ullom, eds., *The Autobiography of Sam Houston*, p. 85; Barker, *Stephen F. Austin*, pp. 484–492; James T. DeShields, *Tall Men with Long Rifles*, pp. 1–50; Herman Ehrenberg, *With Milam and Fannin*, pp. 1–45; Walter Lord, *A Time to Stand*, pp. 38–56; James W. Pohl and Stephen L. Hardin, "The Military History of the Texas Revolution: An Overview," *Southwestern Historical Quarterly* 89 (April 1986): 285–287; and Reichstein, *Rise of the Lone Star*, pp. 133–135.

64. For accounts of Milam's challenge and the Texan taking of San Antonio, see Barker, *Stephen F. Austin*, pp. 492–498; Barr, *Texans in Revolt*, pp. 41–59; DeShields, *Tall Men with Long Rifles*, pp. 51–69; Ehrenberg, *With Milam and Fannin*, pp. 47–99; Lord, *A Time to Stand*, pp. 56–58; and Pohl and Hardin, "Military History of the Texas Revolution," pp. 287–288.

65. J. R. Milam to McArdle, 2 January 1901, "McArdle Companion Battle Paintings, Historical Documents, 1: *Dawn at the Alamo*," Texas State Archives, Austin, p. 79 (hereafter cited as "McArdle Companion 1"). Assembled by Ruskin McArdle from contents of his father's papers, the "McArdle Companion" includes letters, manuscripts, photographs, and clippings. Although most of the contents of this scrapbook concern *Dawn at the Alamo*, it also contains the only known extant information concerning McArdle's research and execution of *Ben Milam*. These papers include a typescript, "The Storming of San Antonio, December 5, 1835," p. 82, excerpted from Dudley G. Wooten's *A Comprehensive History of Texas*, pp. 556–560, which McArdle relied on for information concerning the taking of San

Antonio. The artist's notations on this typescript indicate that he agreed with Wooten's sympathetic treatment of Burleson's role. I am grateful to Jean Carefoot, Archivist of the Texas State Archives, for supplying information concerning this aspect of McArdle's research.

66. DeShields, *Tall Men with Long Rifles*, p. 55.

67. Ibid., pp. 25–28.

2. LET US BAND TOGETHER AS BROTHERS

1. Analysis of the military aspects of the Texas war for independence is found in Pohl and Hardin, "Military History of the Texas Revolution," pp. 269–308. For analyses of the cultural, economic, and political elements of the conflict, see William C. Binkley, *The Texas Revolution*; Reichstein, *Rise of the Lone Star*; and Weber, *The Mexican Frontier, 1821–1846*, pp. 251–255. One recent treatment of the Texas Revolution that devotes particular attention to the Battle of the Alamo is Jeff Long's *Duel of Eagles*. However, this volume falls into the realm of popular journalism and has extremely limited value as a work of serious historical scholarship. Mexican histories of the war include Carlos E. Castañeda, *The Mexican Side of the Texas Revolution*; and José Enrique de la Peña, *With Santa Anna in Texas*, an account from the viewpoint of a Mexican officer.

2. Of the Alamo's famous troika of heroes, Crockett has been the subject of the most extensive biographical studies. See Paul Hutton's introduction to David Crockett, *A Narrative of the Life of David Crockett*, pp. v–lvii; Lofaro, ed., *Davy Crockett*; and Shackford, *David Crockett*. The only full-length biographical study of the garrison's commander is Archie P. McDonald's *Travis*. For biographical information on Bowie, see Lord, *A Time to Stand*, pp. 26–28; Susan Prendergast Schoelwer, *Alamo Images*, pp. 141–144; and Lon Tinkle, *13 Days to Glory*, pp. 46–53.

3. See Pohl and Hardin, "Military History of the Texas Revolution," pp. 289–296.

4. William E. Green discussed this monument in "Alamobilia: 'Remembering the Alamo' with Silver Spoons and Chocolate Bars" (Paper delivered to the annual meeting of Texas State Historical Association, Fort Worth, 2 March 1985), pp. 5–6. Green notes that an Alamo relic was sent to at least one mother of a slain defender. I wish to thank Dr. Green for sharing a copy of this manuscript.

5. See Reuben Marmaduke Potter, *The Fall of the Alamo*.

6. See Green, "Alamobilia," pp. 2–4.

7. Ibid., p. 5.

8. These observations were made in 1879 and 1881, respectively, and are quoted in Edward Tabor Linienthal, "'A Reservoir of Spiritual Power': Patriotic Faith at the Alamo in the Twentieth Century," *Southwestern Historical Quarterly* 91 (April 1988): 520, 522. Informal veneration of relics also heightened the anger of disappointed pilgrims at the formal neglect of the site.

In 1877, the Alamo was converted to commercial use after

the U.S. Army abandoned it and the Catholic Church gave up the idea of reconsecrating the chapel. South of the church, a meat market and saloons dominated the urban landscape. See Schoelwer, *Alamo Images*, pp. 38–39. One San Antonian griped about "going to Alamo Market (within 40 steps of where the heroes fell) every morning at dawn, as we have to do, in all kinds of weather, and then see what kind of a steak you get for 15 cents." Untitled article, *San Antonio Daily Herald*, 27 January 1875, p. 3. See also Cecilia Steinfeldt, *San Antonio Was*, p. 52.

9. Schoelwer discusses the existence of three Alamo landscapes, the contemporary, historic, and symbolic in "The Artist's Alamo," pp. 403–405. She observes that these landscapes began diverging soon after the battle and, because the contemporary and historic landscapes were so different, idealizations of the symbolic landscape, as occurred in heroic battle paintings, became the only way to make the latter accessible.

10. The fire in the Deshields home is mentioned in Julian Onderdonk to DeShields, 1 August 1918, box 5, file 154, JTD-DRT; and Ann Bradshaw, "Panorama of Texas History in Unique Dallas Art Collection," *Dallas Times Herald*, 11 May 1930. For an inventory of works in DeShields's possession several years before this fire, see "List of Paintings," 25 July 1904, box 5, file 142, JTD-DRT. The fact that a photograph of *Speech of Travis* and an accompanying, highly detailed pencil sketch are still in the possession of DeShields' descendants lends credence to Pinckney's claim that the image was commissioned for use in *Tall Men with Long Rifles*. However, the illustration does not appear in this volume, which was not published until 1935. See Pinckney, *Painting in Texas*, p. 187. Further research sources must be uncovered before any definitive conclusions may be made concerning many aspects of Eyth's life and artistic endeavors.

For biographical information concerning Eyth, see Pinckney, *Painting in Texas*, p. 188; and Samuels and Samuels, *The Illustrated Biographical Encyclopedia of Artists of the American West*, pp. 160–161. For unknown reasons, DeShields chose not to use many of Eyth's paintings as illustrations. But eight of the artist's illustrations do appear in at least one other early twentieth-century work concerning Texas history. Among these are four scenes concerning the Battle of San Jacinto and *Bowie Being Carried over the Line*, which appears to have been intended as a companion piece to *Speech of Travis*. The size and quality of these illustrations do not indicate the original medium in which they were executed, and therefore they cannot be conclusively termed historical narrative paintings. See Georgiana Burleson (Jenkins), *The Life and Writings of Rufus C. Burleson*, pp. 750, 762, 765, 773, 775, 777, 791, and 816.

11. Quoted in W. P. Zuber, "An Escape from the Alamo," in *The Texas Almanac, 1857–1873*, comp. James M. Day, p. 693. Zuber's story was later published in *In the Shadow of History*, ed. Mody C. Boatright, J. Frank Dobie, and Harry H. Ransom, pp. 17–27; and as an appendix to his autobiography, *My Eighty Years in Texas*, pp. 247–255.

12. Bowie to Texas Provisional Governor Henry Smith, 2 February 1836, in *Papers of the Texas Revolution*, ed. John H. Jenkins, 4:238.

13. J. Frank Dobie, "The Line That Travis Drew," in *In the Shadow of History*, ed. Boatright, Dobie, and Ransom, p. 10.

14. Schoelwer, *Alamo Images*, p. 10. See also Linienthal, "'A Reservoir of Spiritual Power,'" p. 516; Lord, *A Time to Stand*, pp. 202–203; and McDonald, *Travis*, pp. 172–175.

The details of Zuber's method of composition of Travis's speech are found in "An Escape from the Alamo," in *The Texas Almanac, 1857–1873*, comp. Day, pp. 691, 696; and in the reprinted account in *In the Shadow of History*, ed. Boatright, Dobie, and Ransom, p. 27. The version reprinted in *In the Shadow of History* incorporates details added by Zuber for publication in the 1895 edition of Anna J. Hardwicke Pennybacker's *History of Texas for Schools*. For a brief account of Milam's challenge, published shortly after the incident, see Henry Stuart Foote, *Texas and the Texans* 2:164–165.

Amateur historian R. B. Blake claimed that Rose settled in Nacogdoches, where he died in the 1850s. In answer to queries about his departure from the Alamo, Rose allegedly replied emphatically that he simply was not ready to die. See "A Vindication of Rose and His Story," in *In the Shadow of History*, ed. Boatright, Dobie, and Ransom, p. 39. For further discussion of the controversy concerning the Rose legend and a discussion of the significance of the story of Travis's speech for the Alamo myth, see Lord, *A Time to Stand*, pp. 201–204; Schoelwer, *Alamo Images*, pp. 133, 135, 138; and Tinkle, *13 Days to Glory*, pp. 179–185.

15. In 1843, an "old Mexican woman" told English traveler William Bollaert of seeing "the Texas flag float over the poor old walls" of the Alamo, but his account does not make clear whether she was referring to the time of the siege and battle. See Bollaert, *William Bollaert's Texas*, ed. W. Eugene Hollon and Ruth Lapham Butler, p. 224. This quote also appears in Schoelwer, "The Artist's Alamo," p. 435.

Although the defenders did not know of the writing of the Texas Declaration of Independence, Travis demanded that the Texas provisional government take such a step in his letter of 3 March 1836. See Hutton, introduction to Schoelwer, *Alamo Images*, p. 8. Potter's description of the banner allegedly flown by the garrison is found in *The Fall of the Alamo*, p. 11. For further discussion of the Alamo flag, see Mamie Wynne Cox, *The Romantic Flags of Texas*, pp. 53–55; Lord, *A Time to Stand*, pp. 210–212; and Schoelwer, *Alamo Images*, pp. 8, 94.

16. Richard Penn Smith, *Col. Crockett's Exploits and Adventures in Texas*, pp. 189–190. Shackford discusses the authorship of this publication in *David Crockett*, pp. 273–281. A similar description of this incident is quoted in Frederick C. Chabot, ed., *Texas Letters*, p. 75. Eyth's inclusion of a regulation military snare drum in the canvas's lower right corner also may indicate a knowledge of this account.

17. Alexander E. Sweet, "San Antonio Siftings," *Galveston*

Daily News, 18 July 1879, in *Alex Sweet's Texas*, ed. Virginia Eisenhour, p. 35.

Crockett had disliked Chapman's initial attempt at executing his portrait, declaring that in it he appeared to be "a sort of cross between a clean-shirted member of Congress and a Methodist Preacher." See Curtis Carroll Davis, ed., "A Legend at Full-Length: Mr. Chapman Paints Colonel Crockett—And Tells About It," *Proceedings of the American Antiquarian Society* 69 (21 October 1959): 165. This quote also appears in Voss, "Portraying an American Original," pp. 472–473.

Despite Crockett's public image as an uneducated innocent who was most at home in the Tennessee hills, his active participation and assistance of Chapman in the execution of his portrait indicates that he consciously manipulated his image. As further evidence that Crockett was more sophisticated than his popular image indicated, some biographers point out that he favored formal dress in Washington, where he was known as one of the most eloquent members of Congress and strived to fit into "polite" society. See Stephen L. Hardin, "Gallery: David Crockett," *Military Illustrated, Past and Present* 23 (February–March 1990): 28–30; Richard Boyd Hauck, "The Man in the Buckskin Hunting Shirt: Fact and Fiction in the Crockett Story," pp. 5–7, and "Making It All Up: Davy Crockett in the Theater," pp. 118–120, in *Davy Crockett*, ed. Lofaro; Schoelwer, *Alamo Images*, p. 154; Shackford, *David Crockett*, pp. 241–250; and Voss, "Portraying an American Original," pp. 469–474, 482. However, the long-standing perception of Crockett as "untutored in the social graces but naturally aware of the virtues of liberty and democracy" persists in some quarters. See Cutrer, "'The Hardy, Stalwart Son of Texas,'" p. 306.

18. Mrs. Dickinson's oft-quoted description of Crockett's corpse first appeared in James M. Morphis, *History of Texas, from Its Discovery and Settlement . . .* , p. 177. Crockett's controversial opposition to Andrew Jackson combined with his image as the personification of America vis-à-vis Europe to enhance his attractiveness for portraitists. Crockett posed for six artists, and all of these portraits survive in some form. However, death marked a new stage in the "saga of his likenesses," as they began conforming to myth, especially in the Davy Crockett almanacs. See Hutton, introduction to Crockett, *A Narrative*, pp. xxxvii–xlv; Shackford, *David Crockett*, p. 289; and Voss, "Portraying an American Original," pp. 459–463, 475. For a detailed discussion of Crockett's accoutrements and clothing at the Alamo, see Hardin, "Gallery: David Crockett," pp. 30–34.

19. Several interviews with Mrs. Dickinson regarding the siege and fall of the Alamo were published during the nineteenth century and reprinted in the twentieth. In addition to the interview cited above in Morphis's *History of Texas*, see the *Telegraph and Texas Register*, 24 March 1836, and the *San Antonio Express*, 28 April 1881 and 24 February 1929. Mrs. Dickinson's reliability as an eyewitness is discussed in Lord, *A Time to Stand*, pp. 146, 156, 160, 175–176, 179–182; Schoelwer, *Alamo Images*, pp. 115–118; and Shackford, *David Crockett*, pp. 228–231, 234–235.

20. For discussions of Bowie's manner of death in the Alamo, see Lord, *A Time to Stand*, pp. 165, 205; Potter, *Fall of the Alamo*, p. 11; Schoelwer, *Alamo Images*, p. 144–149; and Tinkle, *13 Days to Glory*, pp. 139–140.

21. Edward G. Rohrbough, "How Jim Bowie Died," in *In the Shadow of History*, ed., Boatright, Dobie, and Ransom, pp. 48, 53, 55. See also Stephen L. Hardin, ed., "Notes and Documents—The Félix Nuñez Account and the Siege of the Alamo: A Critical Appraisal," *Southwestern Historical Quarterly* 93 (July 1990): 80 n. 44

22. John J. Bowie, "Early Life in the Southwest—The Bowies," *DeBow's Review* 13 (October 1852): 383. This quote also appears in Rohrbough, "How Jim Bowie Died," in *In the Shadow of History*, ed. Boatright, Dobie, and Ransom, p. 56.

23. Quoted in Rohrbough, "How Jim Bowie Died," in *In the Shadow of History*, ed. Boatright, Dobie, and Ransom, p. 49. Saldigna's story first appeared in the *Houston Daily Post*, 1 March 1882, and was soon reprinted in full in Andrew Jackson Sowell, *Rangers and Pioneers of Texas*, pp. 146–150.

24. Rohrbough, "How Jim Bowie Died," in *In the Shadow of History*, ed. Boatright, Dobie, and Ransom, pp. 50–52.

25. See Schoelwer, "The Artist's Alamo," pp. 406–408; and Schoelwer, *Alamo Images*, p. 143. For biographical information on Healy, see Matthew Baigell, *Dictionary of American Art*, p. 160; and Barbara Novak, *American Painting of the Nineteenth Century*, p. 198.

26. The strongest evidence that Gentilz completed *Fall of the Alamo* shortly before Texas celebrated the fiftieth anniversary of its independence is found in a letter to Henry McArdle from a San Antonio resident. Its author mentions that "an artist here, Mr. T. Gentilz" had recently completed a "painting of the attack on the Alamo" that was not yet for sale. See Edward Miles to McArdle, 15 October 1885, "McArdle Companion Battle Paintings. Historical Documents, vol. 2: *Battle of San Jacinto*," Texas State Archives, Austin, p. 141, (hereafter cited as "McArdle Companion 2"). See also Kendall and Perry, *Gentilz*, pp. 3, 14, 21; Pinckney, *Painting in Texas*, pp. 99–102; Schoelwer, "The Artist's Alamo," p. 437; and Eric von Schmidt, "The Alamo Remembered from a Painter's Point of View," *Smithsonian* 16 (March 1986): 57. However, a few other scholars hold to an earlier date for the execution of the painting. See Cutrer, "'The Hardy, Stalwart Son of Texas,'" p. 303; and Pinckney, *Painting in Texas*, p. 108. The painting was also used as the cover illustration for sheet music of "In the Shadow of the Sacred Alamo" (Galveston: Thomas Goggan & Bro., n.d.).

The painting was destroyed by fire in a San Antonio paint supply store in 1906. See "Artist Is Forty Years Finishing Picture of Alamo Battle," *San Antonio Express*, 21 June 1927; and "Story of Alamo Told in Picture," *San Antonio Express*, 6 March 1936.

27. Schoelwer, *Alamo Images*, pp. 35–36. Eric von Schmidt, who completed an enormous Alamo battle painting in 1986, termed the Gentilz soldiers "obedient toys," in his lecture, "Alamo Iconography: Painting the Battle of the Alamo" (Paper

delivered to the annual meeting of the Texas State Historical Association, Fort Worth, 2 March 1985), p. 2. The author is grateful to Mr. von Schmidt for sharing a copy of this address.

Gentilz's study sketches are found in the Gentilz Collection, box A, Daughters of the Republic of Texas Library at the Alamo, San Antonio, (hereafter referred to as GC-DRT). The artist also may have employed photographs of the Alamo. For example, see "Looking in North-East direction [a]cross Alamo Plaza," Grandjean Collection, Alamo Plaza Notebook, photograph AP5431. I am grateful to Craig R. Covner for calling this photograph to my attention and for sharing copies of his articles, "Before 1850: A New Look at the Alamo through Art and Imagery, Part 1," *Alamo Journal* 70 (March 1990): 1–8, and "Before 1850: A New Look at the Alamo through Art and Imagery, Part 2," *Alamo Journal* 73 (November 1990): 1–6.

28. See box A, folder 33, GC-DRT. Gentilz also noted the total number of figures that he felt should be included in the painting.

29. See Lord, *A Time to Stand*, p. 160.

30. See Potter, "The Fall of the Alamo," p. 11. The first mention of this version of Dickinson's death appeared in Sam Houston's letter of 11 March 1836 to James Fannin in Eugene C. Barker and Amelia W. Williams, eds., *The Writings of Sam Houston, 1813–1863*, 1:362–365. For further discussion of this account, see Hardin, ed., "The Félix Nuñez Account and the Siege of the Alamo," p. 79 n.40; Shackford, *David Crockett*, p. 230; and Tinkle, *13 Days to Glory*, pp. 144–145.

The Arrocha account appears to be excerpted from an interview by Gentilz, box SM-2, GC-DRT. I am grateful to Martha Utterback of the DRT Library for pointing out this interview and for furnishing a translation of Gentilz's French transcription of it.

31. Quoted in Schoelwer, "The Artist's Alamo," p. 435. Schoelwer also points out the popularity of these guided tours in *Alamo Images*, p. 29.

32. Quoted in Kendall and Perry, *Gentilz*, p. 22.

33. Ibid.

34. Box A, folder 1, GC-DRT. See also Schoelwer, "The Artist's Alamo," p. 436. The first public mention of the Thermopylae parallel appeared in a declaration of 26 March 1836 by the citizens of Nacogdoches commemorating the Alamo defenders. See Schoelwer, *Alamo Images*, pp. 5–6.

35. For a thorough analysis of the "Second Battle of the Alamo" over ownership and use of the site, see Schoelwer, *Alamo Images*, pp. 43–60. For discussions of the upsurge of interest and activity around Alamo Plaza and of commemorative ceremonies at the Alamo, see Green, "Alamobilia," p. 9; Linienthal, "'A Reservoir of Spiritual Power,'" pp. 513–515; and Steinfeldt, *San Antonio Was*, pp. 30, 54–56. This increased interest in San Antonio produced a spate of publications designed to capitalize on the growing tourist trade. In one such publication, William Corner discussed local history, a survey of civic organizations, and "the waters of San Antonio and San Pedro" (*San Antonio de Bexar: A Guide and History*).

36. See von Schmidt, "The Alamo Remembered," pp. 57–58. For an extensive discussion of Otto Becker's lithograph and the painting by Cassilly Adams that served as its model, see Don Russell, *Custer's Last*, pp. 29–35. During the last year of his life, DeShields gave the title of the work as *Crockett's Last Fight* and priced it at $10,000. See DeShields to Harriet V. Fowles, custodian of the Alamo, 10 May 1947, box 5, file 152, JTD-DRT. Onderdonk acknowledged receipt of DeShields's payment for *Fall of the Alamo* in a letter of 18 June 1903, box 5, file 157, JTD-DRT.

DeShields and Onderdonk occasionally had the problems that crop up in many patron-artist relationships. In 1905, DeShields requested a $25.00 discount off the $75.00 price of a painting in exchange for payment of shipping costs of $7.50. Onderdonk, bemoaning the fact that "no one cares for historical pictures," rejected the offer and asked for $52.50 for the painting along with a drawing of Sam Houston that he had previously sent to DeShields. He also asked DeShields not to photograph this drawing as the merchant had done before with a sketch sent by Onderdonk on approval, as the artist regarded this as an unwitting violation of his "sacred property." Onderdonk to DeShields, 17 January 1905, box 5, file 156, JTD-DRT.

37. Onderdonk to DeShields, 18 June 1903, box 5, file 157, JTD-DRT.

38. "Painting of the Alamo: The Art Association Exults Over the Acquisition of a Canvas by Onderdonk," clipping [n.d.], Robert Onderdonk File, JBC-SMU. Voss discusses the DeRose portrait and the artist's arrangement with Hudson River School painter and engraver Asher B. Durand to sell engravings of it at fifty cents per copy in "Portraying an American Original," pp. 479–480. For information on Edwards's role as the Crockett model, see Steinfeldt, *The Onderdonks*, p. 27; and "Art Sleuths Desire Whereabouts of Rare Davy Crockett Painting," *San Antonio Express*, 17 August 1955.

39. Travis to Houston, 25 February 1836, in Jenkins, *Papers of the Texas Revolution* 4:34. This quote also appears in Schoelwer, *Alamo Images*, p. 154.

40. Lord, *A Time to Stand*, p. 97. Reviewers praised Onderdonk for his accuracy in this aspect of Crockett's portrayal. See "Beautifully Realistic: Onderdonk's Great Picture Charms Those Who Have Seen It," clipping [n.d.], Mrs. Edwin Gaston, Scrapbook, "Early History of Texas," Gaston Collection, DRT Library, p. 105 (hereafter cited as Gaston Scrapbook).

41. Onderdonk to DeShields, 17 December 1901, box 5, file 155, JTD-DRT. The artist titled this explanatory letter, "THE ALAMO: The Story of a Great Painting." Portions of this letter are quoted at length in Pinckney, *Painting in Texas*, p. 207; and Steinfeldt, *The Onderdonks*, p. 27.

42. The Candelaria interview appeared in Corner, *San Antonio de Bexar*, pp. 117–119. For discussions of Madam Candelaria's reliability as an eyewitness to events of the siege and battle, see Lord, *A Time to Stand*, p. 208; Schoelwer, *Alamo Images*, pp. 119–121; and Shackford, *David Crockett*, pp. 229–234.

43. Isaac N. Jones to Mrs. David Crockett, ca. 11 March–

21 April 1836, quoted in Shackford, *David Crockett*, p. 236. Voss comments on Onderdonk's selective use of the Candelaria account in "Portraying an American Original," p. 481.

44. "Fall of the Historic Alamo," *Farmersville Sentinel*, 19 March 1906.

45. W. P. Zuber to Charlie Jeffries, 17 August 1904, "Inventing Stories About the Alamo," in *In the Shadow of History*, ed. Boatright, Dobie, and Ransom, pp. 46–47. Mexican officer José Enrique de la Peña reinforces Santa Anna's brutal image in *With Santa Anna in Texas*, p. 53.

Voss terms an 1837 Davy Crockett almanac's account of Crockett going down fighting at the Alamo "altogether false" but does not explain the basis of his dismissal of this version. See "Portraying an American Original," p. 476. For further discussion of Crockett's death and the controversy surrounding it, see Hardin, ed., "The Félix Nuñez Account," p. 81 n.46; Dan Kilgore, *How Did Davy Die?*; Lord, *A Time to Stand*, pp. 206–207; and Schoelwer, *Alamo Images*, pp. 13, 15, 159.

46. Onderdonk to DeShields, 17 December 1901.

47. Steinfeldt summarizes this process in an appendix, "The Onderdonks' Use of Photographs," in *The Onderdonks*, p. 229, and discusses Onderdonk's pictorial principle of "unity and balance," p. 222 n.91. Use of photography was quite common among painters of Onderdonk's day. For example, Frederic Remington employed the equine motion photographic studies of Eadweard Muybridge. See Goetzmann and Goetzmann, *The West of the Imagination*, pp. 243, 247; Peter Hassrick, *Frederic Remington*, p. 22; and Novak, *American Painting of the Nineteenth Century*, p. 198–199.

For further discussion of Onderdonk's instructors and their influence on his career, see Eliot Clark, *History of the National Academy of Design, 1825–1953*, pp. 90, 97, 129–130; Pinckney, *Painting in Texas*, p. 204; Katherine Metcalf Roof, *The Life and Art of William Merritt Chase*, pp. 38–40; and Steinfeldt, *The Onderdonks*, p. 13.

48. "Onderdonk's Great Painting," clipping [n.d.], Gaston Scrapbook, p. 105.

49. "Beautifully Realistic: Onderdonk's Great Picture," Gaston Scrapbook, p. 105. This showing resulted from the artist's offer to display the work during the association's annual Easter week exhibition. See Mrs. John Edwin Kiest to DeShields [n.d., ca. Winter 1904], box 5, file 159, JTD-DRT. Following the Dallas show, *Fall of the Alamo* was displayed in the Texas Building at the St. Louis World's Fair. Free-lance lecturer Nat M. Brigham saw the painting there and requested a lantern slide of it from DeShields for use in his lecture, "The Men Who Won the West," in the series, "Strange Corners of Our Country." See Brigham to DeShields, 14 September 1904, Onderdonk File, DRT Library.

50. Onderdonk to DeShields, 17 December 1901, box 5, file 155, JTD-DRT.

51. "Painting of the Alamo," clipping [n.d.], Robert Onderdonk File, JBC-SMU.

52. Quoted in "Onderdonk's Great Painting," Gaston Scrapbook, p. 105.

53. "Fall of the Historic Alamo," *Farmersville Sentinel*. This story also pointed out that the canvas was currently on display in the president's office of First National Bank in Farmersville, one of DeShields's many places of residence. For further discussion of the near-triumphal tone of the painting, see von Schmidt, "Alamo Iconography," pp. 2, 3, 9, and "The Alamo Remembered," p. 58.

54. Santa Anna to McArdle, 19 March 1874, translation by Dr. Plutarco Ornelas, Mexican Consul of San Antonio, "McArdle Companion 1," p. 59. Henry McArdle's notation appears in the margin of "Brief Description or Reading of the Painting," "McArdle Companion 1," p. 13. The title page of this scrapbook reads, "Correspondence from Santa Anna, Potter, and other prominent authorities."

55. Potter's initial letter to McArdle, dated 2 August 1874, refers to the artist's inquiry of 28 July 1874. McArdle's papers also contain a photostat of Potter's *Hymn of the Alamo* and an annotated copy of Potter's "The Fall of the Alamo," *Magazine of American History* 2 (January 1878): 1–21. A letter from Potter to McArdle of 27 May 1887 indicates that the two men became close friends; this correspondence mentions a rough draft of a biography of Potter written by McArdle and the fact that the artist had named one of his sons after his advisor. See "McArdle Companion 1," pp. 11, 18, 20, and 28.

56. Potter to McArdle, 13 August 1874, "McArdle Companion 1," p. 22.

57. Potter to McArdle, 1 September 1874, ibid., p. 42.

58. See McArdle to Dr. William Carey Crane, 19 September 1871; 24 September 1872; and 6 June 1873, William Carey Crane Papers, Texas Collection, Baylor University. See also Schoelwer, *Alamo Images*, p. 5.

59. Potter to McArdle, 18 November 1874, pp. 2, 10, "McArdle Companion 1," p. 30 (this is a ten-page letter glued onto p. 30 of the scrapbook). A copy of this manuscript may also be found in the Henry McArdle File, DRT Library.

60. Ibid., pp. 6–7.

61. Ibid., p. 7. Von Schmidt comments on the extensive use of symbolism in *Dawn at the Alamo* in "Alamo Iconography," p. 3, and "The Alamo Remembered," p. 58.

62. Potter, "Comment on McArdle Painting," "McArdle Companion 1," p. 3. Potter mentioned his lobbying efforts concerning the painting in a letter to McArdle of 3 October 1874, "McArdle Companion 1," p. 43.

63. Ibid., pp. 2–3.

64. Frank W. Johnson, manuscript on *Dawn at the Alamo*, 18 May 1876, "McArdle Companion 1," p. 86.

65. A photograph of this work is found in "McArdle Companion 1," p. 37.

66. Woodward to McArdle, 29 August 1889, ibid., p. 98. This quote also appears in Pinckney, *Painting in Texas*, p. 193.

67. Ibid. In 1878, Potter commiserated with McArdle that

the legislature "had not the liberality to patronize the noble work you had in contemplation." Potter to McArdle, 8 March 1878, "McArdle Companion 1," p. 24.

68. A letter written by Onderdonk after the painting was completed indicates that magazine offers for reproduction of the work had reinforced the artist's confidence in its superiority. See Onderdonk to DeShields, 18 June 1903, box 5, file 157, JTD-DRT.

69. "McArdle's Latest Historic Painting: 'The Dawn at the Alamo,'" *San Antonio Daily Express* [n.d.]. Another newspaper story noted McArdle's "years of study" in addition to the fact that the canvas was on display at the Alamo Plaza establishment of Barr and Cones. See "*Dawn at the Alamo*: Historic Painting of Famous Texas Battle to Be Seen by Texas Enthusiasts," *San Antonio Daily Express*, 16 February 1906; and "Twenty-Nine Years Required for Artist to Paint Picture of Battle of Alamo," AP story, Austin, 6 July 1906, clipping, Gaston Scrapbook, p. 106.

70. Potter to McArdle, 1 September 1874, "McArdle Companion 1," p. 42.

71. For these and other visual renderings of the Alamo consulted by McArdle, see "McArdle Companion 1," pp. 12, 15–16, 19, 21, and 24–25. See also McArdle, "Brief Description or Reading of the Painting," "McArdle Companion 1," pp. 13–14; Schoelwer, "The Artist's Alamo," p. 453; and Schoelwer, *Alamo Images*, p. 50.

72. Soon after the Mexican army withdrew from San Antonio, visitors to the Alamo noted that the Texan defenders had built a platform and ramp sloping from the chapel's back wall down toward the front door. See Hardin, ed., "The Félix Nuñez Account and the Battle of the Alamo," p. 78 n.38. Whether the Alamo defenders actually built such a platform in this location is questionable, but these reports led Potter, McArdle's advisor on such questions, to assert in 1878 that "all the guns were mounted on high platforms of stockades and earth" ("The Fall of the Alamo," p. 3). More recently, Cutrer has implicitly endorsed this aspect of *Dawn at the Alamo*, stating that the platform was of a lower height than in McArdle's painting ("'The Hardy, Stalwart Son of Texas,'" p. 308). However, after analyzing in detail the conflicting evidence furnished by the several diagrams, maps, and plans of the Alamo grounds, Schoelwer disagrees, arguing that McArdle mistakenly "inserted" the platform into a copy of the Giraud plat ("The Artist's Alamo," pp. 409–423, 452–454). See also Lord, *A Time to Stand*, pp. 77, 108. A century later, a less imposing cannon platform would serve as a point of view for Alamo battle painter Eric von Schmidt. See von Schmidt, "The Alamo Remembered," p. 59.

For differing views on the exact meaning of the Mexicans' scarlet banner and the Texans' interpretation of it, see Schoelwer, *Alamo Images*, pp. 81–82, 94; and Lord, *A Time to Stand*, p. 101.

73. Woodward to McArdle, 29 August 1889, "McArdle Companion 1," p. 98.

74. McArdle's observation on the 1824 flag appears in "Brief Description or Reading of the Painting," "McArdle Companion 1," p. 14. In reference to Mrs. Dickinson, he commented on the "Hell of slaughter" escaped by "one woman and her baby of Caucasian race" (p. 13). Mrs. Dickinson aided McArdle in his efforts and gave a photograph of herself to the artist in the course of his research. See "McArdle Companion 1," p. 102.

75. "*Dawn at the Alamo*," *San Antonio Daily Express*. For further information concerning the artist's research into the rendering of the chapel's architectural features, see McArdle, "Brief Description or Reading of the Painting," "McArdle Companion 1," p. 15; Potter, "Comment on McArdle Painting," "McArdle Companion 1," p. 4; and Schoelwer, "The Artist's Alamo," p. 453.

76. See Dayton Kelly, "Painter of Texas History," *Dallas Times Herald, SUNDAY Magazine*, 1 December 1968, p. 32; and Charlotte Phelan, "Painters, McPainter," *Houston Post*, 4 June 1961. Both articles include interviews with Ruskin McArdle. Military historian Tom Gläser notes that, as depicted by Onderdonk, many members of the Mexican army did, indeed, wear peasants' white cotton rather than uniforms. See Schoelwer, *Alamo Images*, p. 76.

77. Potter, "Comment on McArdle Painting," "McArdle Companion 1," pp. 5–6. Woodward praised McArdle for "the effect of light, heightened by the torch of Evans" in his letter to the artist of 29 August 1889, "McArdle Companion 1," p. 98.

78. Potter to McArdle, 1 September 1874, "McArdle Companion 1," p. 42.

79. Potter, "Comment on McArdle Painting," "McArdle Companion 1," p. 4.

80. McArdle, "Brief Description or Reading of the Painting," "McArdle Companion 1," p. 13. Thirty years after McArdle completed his second *Dawn at the Alamo*, James DeShields's *Tall Men with Long Rifles* included a vague recollection by "a Mexican gentleman," who had allegedly served as a captain in Santa Anna's army, of the tale of one Texan defender who rose from his sickbed to take part in the fighting, pp. 160–161. DeShields may have heard this story several decades earlier and related it to McArdle at that time.

81. Potter, "Comment on McArdle Painting," "McArdle Companion 1," p. 4. The wording of DeShields's description of the painting in a one-page document beginning with the phrase "Every school child of Texas . . ." indicates that he may have had access to Potter's manuscript, especially in his use of such passages as "Crockett, like a giant dealing death . . . clubbed rifle barrel raised." The only clue to the date of this unpublished description is that it is written on 1911 stationery from the DeShields Brothers Cash Store in San Marcos, Texas. See Henry McArdle File, DRT Library. For a fuller account by DeShields of Crockett's death, see *Tall Men with Long Rifles*, pp. 160–164.

82. Woodward to McArdle, 29 August 1889, "McArdle Companion 1," p. 98. See also Potter to McArdle, 13 August 1874, "McArdle Companion 1," p. 22.

Cutrer observes that, in order to illustrate the artist's "Manichean vision" of the battle, McArdle "emphasizes Crockett's whiteness . . . while his hair, which in reality was black, here appears as almost sandy." See "'The Hardy, Stalwart Son of Texas,'" pp. 307–308. Other factors may have influenced the artist's conception. For example, only one contemporary observer is recorded as referring to Crockett as having black hair, while a great number of other descriptions, including that of Crockett himself, portray him as having brown hair, blue eyes, and a fair complexion with "roses in his cheeks." See Shackford, *David Crockett*, pp. 282–290; and Voss, "Portraying an American Original," pp. 464, 467–468.

83. For discussions of Travis's historical image as well as the time, manner, and place of his death and the controversy surrounding it, see Lord, *A Time to Stand*, pp. 155–156, 205; McDonald, *Travis*, pp. 176–177; Schoelwer, *Alamo Images*, pp. 132–140; and Tinkle, *13 Days to Glory*, pp. 136–137. For McArdle's notations concerning Travis, see Potter, "The Fall of the Alamo," p. 11, in "McArdle Companion 1," p. 28. See also Potter, "Comment on McArdle Painting of the Battle of the Alamo," p. 4.

84. Potter to McArdle, 3 October 1874, "McArdle Companion 1," p. 43. Potter had expressed confusion concerning the placement of Travis in his third letter to McArdle, 1 September 1874, "McArdle Companion 1," p. 42.

85. DeShields, "Every school child of Texas . . . ," Henry McArdle File, DRT Library. See also Potter to McArdle, 13 August 1874, "McArdle Companion 1," p. 22, and "McArdle's Latest Historic Painting," *San Antonio Daily Express*. Schoelwer points out the artist's use of the McHenry photograph in *Alamo Images*, p. 143.

86. Travis's sentiments are quoted in Michael R. Green, "To the People of Texas & All Americans in the World," *Southwestern Historical Quarterly* 91 (April 1988): 486–487. Potter remarks on McArdle's portrayal of Mexican soldiers in "Comment on McArdle Painting," "McArdle Companion 1," p. 8. For further discussion of the allegorical and ideological aspects of McArdle's composition of the painting, see Cutrer, "'The Hardy, Stalwart Son of Texas,'" pp. 306–310; Hugh Nugent Fitzgerald, "Texas History Pictured," *Austin American-Statesman*, 6 March 1927; Sam DeShong Ratcliffe, "Texas History Painting: An Iconographic Study" (Ph.D. diss., University of Texas at Austin, 1985), pp. 62–63; and Dorothy Renick, "McArdle's Paintings Tell the Story of Immortal Heroes at the Alamo and San Jacinto," *San Antonio Express*, 22 July 1923.

87. Lord maintains convincingly that Travis did not wear a uniform of any kind in *A Time to Stand*, p. 205. Hardin concurs but disagrees with Lord's assertion that Travis wore "a homespun jacket of Texas jeans" in "The Félix Nuñez Account," pp. 68–69, 83 n. 52, and in a telephone conversation with SDR, 10 July 1991. For one recent opinion that McArdle depicted this aspect of Travis's appearance accurately, see Cutrer, "'The Hardy, Stalwart Son of Texas,'" pp. 306–307.

88. Linienthal, "'A Reservoir of Spiritual Power,'" p. 510.

89. Von Schmidt categorizes the artists in these terms in "The Alamo Remembered," p. 58.

90. "Beautifully Realistic: Onderdonk's Great Picture," Gaston Scrapbook, p. 105. Onderdonk expressed his reservations in his letter to DeShields of 17 December 1901.

91. DeShields, "Every school child of Texas . . . ," Henry McArdle File, DRT Library.

92. Quoted in Schoelwer, *Alamo Images*, p. 59. Schoelwer also notes that, as photographic depictions of the site became more prominent, the "modernized Alamo" attracted fewer artists, pp. 41, 47. See also Steinfeldt, *San Antonio Was*, pp. 31–32. Linienthal discusses twentieth-century attitudes toward the Alamo in "'A Reservoir of Spiritual Power,'" p. 511. The "reverence" and "reconstruction" sentiments were expressed by Edith Mae Johnson, chair of the Daughters of the Republic of Texas Alamo Committee, and Alamo reenactor and amateur historian Gary L. Foreman, respectively.

3 . FREEDOM'S LIGHT

1. For Houston's recounting of the San Jacinto campaign, see Day and Ullom, eds., *The Autobiography of Sam Houston*, pp. 99–120. Reuben Potter played an important role in shaping perceptions of the campaign well into the twentieth century in "The Battle of San Jacinto," *Magazine of American History* 4 (May 1880): 321–333. See also Llerena Friend, *Sam Houston*, pp. 68–70; Marquis James, *The Raven*, pp. 187–202; Pohl and Hardin, "The Military History of the Texas Revolution," pp. 300–303; and M. K. Wisehart, *Sam Houston*, pp. 173–234.

2. Accounts of the details of the battle include James, *The Raven*, pp. 203–213; Pohl and Hardin, "The Military History of the Texas Revolution," pp. 278, 285, 303–304; Potter, "The Battle of San Jacinto," pp. 334–350; and Wisehart, *Sam Houston*, pp. 235–245. For descriptions of the battle by Mexican combatants, including Santa Anna, see Castañeda, *The Mexican Side of the Texas Revolution*, pp. 24, 36, 76–83, 353–355.

3. Potter to McArdle, 18 November 1874, p. 9, "McArdle Companion 1," p. 30. For an account of Texan brutality toward their foes by one member of the victorious army, see Walter P. Lane, *The Adventures and Recollections of General Walter P. Lane*, pp. 11–12.

4. Potter, "The Battle of San Jacinto," pp. 336–338, 342–343. For a discussion of other compositional aspects of this painting, see Cutrer, "'The Hardy, Stalwart Son of Texas,'" pp. 297–298.

McArdle executed a painting of Smith's destruction of Vince's Bridge, which is unlocated. In 1904, James DeShields owned a painting entitled *Deaf Smith*, the title of which could have referred to either a depiction of this incident or to a portrait of Smith. The work's price of two hundred dollars was in the range of other battle paintings owned by DeShields, indicating that it probably was the canvas known as *Deaf Smith at*

Vince's Bridge. It may have been lost in the 1918 fire at the art patron's home. See DeShields, "List of Paintings," 25 July 1904, box 5, file 142, JTD-DRT.

5. James Patrick McGuire speculates on Lungkwitz's possible participation in the execution of this work in *Hermann Lungkwitz*, pp. 37, 42, 47, 205 n. 25. Conclusive evidence for resolution of this question has not yet surfaced, although painting conservators have discovered evidence of extensive retouching concentrated in the landscape portions of the canvas. I am indebted to Jay Krueger of the conservation firm of Perry Huston and Associates, Fort Worth, for sharing a copy of his firm's report of 6 January 1987 summarizing the findings of an examination of the painting.

6. Pinckney, *Painting in Texas*, p. 196.

7. See Goetzmann and Goetzmann, *The West of the Imagination*, p. 77.

8. Huddle claimed that he hit upon the idea of executing a gallery of portraits of prominent Texans within a year after he moved to Austin, in a letter to Commissioner of Insurance, Statistics, and History L. L. Foster, 25 November 1888, quoted in full, in Day, "Texas Letters and Documents," p. 302. See also Lois Hale Galvin, "Early Texas Artists," *Austin American-Statesman*, 16 May 1965; Pinckney, *Painting in Texas*, p. 196; Martha Shaw, "The Legacy of a Love Affair," photocopy in possession of SDR; Skipper Steely, "Archives," *Dallas Times Herald*, 17 July 1983; and "Notes on William Henry Huddle," unattributed ms., William H. Huddle File, JBC-SMU. I am grateful to Martha Shaw, great-grandniece of Nannie Carver Huddle, for sharing a copy of her ms. dealing with Nannie and William Huddle as well as her collection of William Huddle's papers.

9. Huddle to Nannie Carver, 24 October 1884, collection of Mrs. Martha Shaw, Pacific Palisades, California (hereafter cited as Shaw Collection). Although Huddle's name does not appear in the academy's enrollment records, this may be because he sometimes took evening classes. I am grateful to the staff of Munich's Academy for the Visual Arts for permitting me to examine the records of the now-extinct Bavarian Royal Academy. See also Huddle to Nannie Carver, 9 February [1885], Shaw Collection; McGuire, *Hermann Lungkwitz*, pp. 41, 43; and Pinckney, *Painting in Texas*, p. 196. Huddle booked passage from Bremen to New York on 6 April 1885. See "Norddeutscher Lloyd" ticket, Shaw Collection.

10. Huddle to Nannie Carver, 9 February [1885].

11. See Lane, *Adventures and Recollections*, pp. 15–16; and Potter, "The Battle of San Jacinto," p. 342. Pinckney's assertion that Huddle journeyed to Mexico City for "thorough research" to study records and documents concerning the battle and Santa Anna's subsequent capture cannot be verified. See Pinckney, *Painting in Texas*, p. 202.

12. For the legislature's instructions and appropriation, see H. P. N. Gammel, comp., *The Laws of Texas, 1822–1897* 10: 126. The original version of the painting, sans Bryan, was reproduced as the frontispiece of L. E. Daniell's *Personnel of the Texas State Government*. Walter Lane describes Moses Austin Bryan's participation in the surrender in *Adventures and Recollections*, p. 15. I am grateful to Jean Carefoot, Archivist of the Texas State Archives, for calling to my attention this and other information regarding this aspect of Huddle's composition of the painting and for furnishing copies of relevant documents. Certainly, Huddle regarded the Battle of San Jacinto in a heroic light. While on a hunting trip, he camped along the route of Santa Anna's march to the Alamo and wrote to his fiancée, "What ambitious thoughts & schemes must have filled his mind at this lonely spot to be realized at San Antonio and afterwards to be dashed to earth when he[,] 'the Napoleon of the West[,]' gave up all to the motl[e]y mob of [p]atriots led by our great Houston at San Jacinto." Unfortunately, this letter is dated only "Dec. 2" and may not have reflected the artist's thoughts while he painted *The Surrender of Santa Anna*. Huddle to Nannie Carver, Shaw Collection.

In 1892, Austin photographer S. B. Hill reproduced a photograph of the painting that numbered each of the figures and identified them with a numbered key, in the fashion of McArdle's battle paintings. Whether this identification system was devised by the photographer or based on earlier work by Huddle cannot be determined. Hill's photograph gained rapid popularity in Texas and was soon reproduced in history textbooks. In the early 1900s, one owner transferred the image to canvas and hired an unknown artist to hand tint the scene, simulating an original oil painting (complete with the key numbers). I am grateful to Mr. and Mrs. James Chappel of Fort Worth for allowing me to examine this item from their collection.

13. For correspondence pertaining to Huddle's appropriation, see McDonald to L. S. Ross, 30 June 1888, and Huddle to Commissioners, 25 November 1888, in Day, "Texas Letters and Documents," pp. 297, 301–303. In this correspondence, Huddle justified the amount of his commission by enclosing a copy of a catalog of his works and challenged the committee to compare his prices "with those of other artists of my standing." Huddle also noted that he had repainted twenty-three of the portraits before being satisfied with the finished versions. To buttress his arguments, Huddle enclosed a letter from C. V. Turner, a former fellow student and past president of the Art Students' League of New York City.

Another example of Huddle's amicable relations with influential Texans is his letter of introduction from Governor John Ireland, obtained shortly before departing for Munich. In this letter, Ireland "commend[s] him to those with whom he may be thrown." 18 September 1884, Shaw Collection.

14. One San Jacinto veteran recalled Houston as having been clad in a "black suit of broadcloth, badly worn . . . the other officers were badly drest [*sic*]." See John P. Ferrell to Henry McArdle, September 1885, in "McArdle Companion 2," p. 189. For Guillaume's lack of any link to Texas, see Mrs. Ralph

Catterall to Pauline A. Pinckney, 4 October 1962, L. M. D. Guillaume File, Valentine Museum, Richmond, Virginia. I am indebted to Shelley Jost of the Valentine Museum for sharing the contents of this file. For further biographical information on Guillaume, see George C. Groce and David H. Wallace, *The New York Historical Society's Dictionary of Artists in America, 1564–1860*, p. 279; Pinckney, *Painting in Texas*, p. 145; *Richmond Portraits*, p. 220; "Who Painted It?," *Atlanta Constitution*, 15 May 1890; and "Death of a Noted Painter," *Washington Post*, 17 April 1892.

15. See Henry Cohen, *Business and Politics in America from the Age of Jackson to the Civil War*, pp. 207–222.

16. For further discussion of Corcoran's involvement with the Texas debt, see Cohen, *Business and Politics in America*, pp. 128–143, and Reichstein, *Rise of the Lone Star*, pp. 102–103.

The first contact between Guillaume and Corcoran may have occurred in 1874, when Guillaume was one of fourteen Washington-area artists who signed a letter requesting Corcoran to build a studio near his gallery so that the public might "learn to discriminate between good and bad art." Guillaume et al. to Corcoran, 1 June 1874, L. M. D. Guillaume File, Archives of American Art, Smithsonian Institution, Washington, D.C. In 1875, Corcoran sat for a portrait by the artist. See Guillaume biographical summary, Guillaume File, Valentine Museum.

17. See Herbert R. Collins to Daniel J. Reed, 28 January 1966, National Portrait Gallery memorandum, "The Surrender of General Lee to General Grant," unattributed ms., Guillaume File, Archives of American Art; "Painting by Richmonder Offered for Appomattox," *Richmond Times-Dispatch*, 20 January 1952; and Guillaume biographical summary, Guillaume File, Valentine Museum. Guillaume first exhibited in the United States at the National Academy of Design in 1855, while residing in Richmond.

18. Norman D. Ziff, *Paul Delaroche*, pp. 2, 24. Delaroche exhibited many of these canvases in the Paris Salon showings of 1822–1837.

19. Ibid., p. 185. *Trocadero* commemorated the French Bourbons' 1823 restoration of Ferdinand VII to the Spanish throne. *Charlemagne Crossing the Alps* was the first of five paintings projected for King Louis-Philippe's new historical museum at Versailles, a commission that Delaroche accepted with great reluctance, which was evident in the quality of his work on the project.

20. Ibid., p. 19.

21. Goetzmann and Goetzmann use this designation in referring to these paintings in *The West of the Imagination*, pp. 85–87. For a photographic reproduction of *San Jacinto* with fifty-nine of its figures numbered and an explanatory key, see "McArdle Companion 2," p. 19. See also Raines, *A Yearbook for Texas, 1901–1902* 1:250.

22. McArdle's papers indicate that he made a futile attempt to obtain a photographic reproduction of *Storming of Chapultepec*, going so far as to request assistance from one of Texas's U.S. Senators. See Senator Richard Coke to McArdle, 29 August 1890, "McArdle Companion 2," p. 157. Artists James Walker and Carl Nebel each produced color lithographs of the battle, but this correspondence does not indicate which of these works McArdle considered. For discussions of these images, see Kelley, "Painter of Texas History"; and Ron Tyler, *The Mexican War*, pp. 41–48, 65, 67, 69–70.

23. See Dayton Kelley, "Search Turns Up Copy of Texas Artist's Work," *Dallas Morning News*, 4 March 1965. Harold B. Simpson gives a detailed account of this incident and the brigade's critical role in the battle in *Hood's Texas Brigade*, pp. 389–401.

24. See Kelley, "Search Turns Up Copy of Texas Artist's Work"; and McArdle to Beauregard, 13 May 1892, "McArdle Companion 2," p. 175.

25. McArdle, "Description of the Painting," "McArdle Companion 2," p. 13.

26. Ibid. This description also mentions the painting's "wealth of episode" and "that eternal variety and change demanded by a natural presentation."

27. See DeShields, "List of Paintings," 25 July 1904, box 5, file 142, JTD-DRT. Ruskin McArdle unsuccessfully mounted emotional attempts to purchase both canvases from their owners. See Ruskin McArdle to DeShields, 12 December 1928, box 5, file 145, JTD-DRT. I am grateful to the present owner of McArdle's repainted *Lee at the Wilderness* for sharing information concerning this work from his family's papers and in an interview on 18 November 1988. The owner wishes to remain anonymous.

A 1935 newspaper story mentioned that "two of the best known pictures of Mr. DeShields' collection are a large panorama of San Jacinto and a graphic representation of the fall of the Alamo." This raises the possibility that McArdle also repainted *Dawn at the Alamo* but more likely refers to Onderdonk's study for his Alamo battle painting. See Hilton Greer, "Prose Writers of Texas: James Thomas DeShields, Who Has Told of Tall Men," no. 15 in Wednesday series, newspaper clipping [n.d.], Henry McArdle File, DRT Library.

28. *Austin Daily Democratic Statesman*, 29 June 1873.

29. See *Austin Daily Democratic Statesman*, 27, 28, and 29 June 1873; 6 July 1873; and 16 October 1877. Also see "Hard Luck Artist," *Houston Post*, 27 March 1949. I am grateful to the owner of the repainted *Lee at the Wilderness* and to Dr. Kenneth Hafertepe, Director of Academic Programs at Deerfield Historical Park, Massachusetts, for calling these notices and reviews to my attention. The exact date of the hanging of *Lee at the Wilderness* in the Capitol cannot be determined.

30. *Austin Daily Democratic Statesman*, 29 June 1873.

31. See Marcelle Lively Hamer, "Anecdotes as Sidelights to Texas History," in *In the Shadow of History*, ed. Boatright, Dobie, and Ransom, pp. 63–64.

32. Taylor to McArdle, 8 March 1886, "McArdle Companion

2," p. 117. Reuben Potter details the controversy concerning Houston in "The Battle of San Jacinto," pp. 322–328.

33. Lane, *Adventures and Recollections*, p. 14.

34. McArdle, "Description of the Painting," "McArdle Companion 2," p. 13.

35. Potter, "The Battle of San Jacinto," p. 321.

36. Potter to McArdle, 13 August 1874, "McArdle Companion 1," p. 22.

37. Potter, "The Battle of San Jacinto," pp. 339, 346. Famous Texas Ranger John S. "Rip" Ford urged McArdle to feature prominently Captain Antonio Manchaca of Seguin's command (which he did), claiming that it would win friends for the artist in San Antonio, Manchaca's place of residence. See Ford to McArdle, 1 June 1893, "McArdle Companion 2," p. 254.

38. See "McArdle Companion 2," pp. 236, 240.

39. Woodward to McArdle, 20 October 1890, "McArdle Companion 2," p. 33.

40. McArdle, "Description of the Painting," "McArdle Companion 2," p. 13.

41. See Lane, *Adventures and Recollections*, p. 14.

42. "List of Contributors," "McArdle Companion 2," p. 90.

43. Woodward to McArdle, 20 October 1890, "McArdle Companion 2," p. 33. In his study of San Jacinto's topography and battle positions, McArdle relied primarily on his own measurements and correspondence with Ricardo de Zavala from 1890 to 1894. Evidently, the artist also executed a landscape painting of the battlefield and submitted it for approval to knowledgeable individuals. For this correspondence, photographs, and McArdle's several plans and diagrams, see "McArdle Companion 2," pp. 38–47. He also may have employed the son of Anson Jones, last president of the Republic of Texas, as a guide during one of his research expeditions. See Mrs. Mary Jones to McArdle, July 1891, ibid., p. 216.

44. Among McArdle's most helpful correspondents were veterans James M. Hill and William Taylor and the families of veterans Henry McCulloch and Sidney Sherman. For this and other veterans' correspondence, see "McArdle Companion 2," pp. 124–151, 156, 168–173, and 262. For McArdle's annotated copies of the Houston and Delgado reports, see ibid., p. 76.

Beauregard and Howard either obtained information from third parties or simply approved whatever information was sent to them by McArdle. See Beauregard to McArdle, 28 May 1892, p. 36; and Howard to McArdle, 4 April 1892, p. 168. In his letter, Beauregard admitted that he had no idea of the configurations or plans of the "Mescican [*sic*] fortifications." Texan army uniforms and accoutrements proved to be more difficult to research than those of the Mexican army, since Houston's force had been comprised of a motley assortment of volunteers and regulars, and only a few individual units wore uniforms that served to distinguish them from all other combatants. See Kelley, "Painter of Texas History"; Esse Forrester O'Brien, *Art and Artists in Texas*, p. 28; and Pinckney, *Painting in Texas*, p. 193.

45. Twelve veterans of the battle signed a document attesting to the painting's accuracy during a Texas Veterans Association San Jacinto Day Reunion, 21 April 1891. Two of the more notable signatories were Walter P. Lane and Moses Austin Bryan. A year later, the artist referred to this endorsement as proof of his artistic legitimacy when he asked Beauregard to lend a "helping hand to art struggling in a new and rugged home" and hinted at the possibility of financial assistance from the former general in terming Beauregard an "art patron." See "Endorsement of McArdle's Painting," "McArdle Companion 2," p. 32; and McArdle to Beauregard, 13 May 1892, "McArdle Companion 2," p. 175.

46. McArdle, "Description of the Painting," "McArdle Companion 2," p. 13.

47. Ibid.

48. McArdle recorded names of supporters and their subscription amounts, ranging from $10.00 to $150.00, in his "List of Contributors." This list took the form of a newsletter in which the artist explained the slow pace of his work by taking an indirect swipe at Huddle, asserting that McArdle was not "content to work as some do—from fancy—but in every part of my work I have aimed at natural action and historic truth." For veterans' criticisms, see Taylor to McArdle, 8 March 1886 and Hill to McArdle, 20 October 1895, "McArdle Companion 2." Although McArdle did not depict Santa Anna's surrender, his interest in the incident is evidenced by his notes on p. 23 of his personal copy of Houston's official report of the battle; see "McArdle Companion 2," p. 60. See also Z. M. Matthews to McArdle, 19 October 1885, p. 260; F. G. Roberts to McArdle, 27 May 1889, p. 70; and Taylor to McArdle, 8 March 1886, "McArdle Companion 2."

49. McArdle to Beauregard, 13 May 1892, "McArdle Companion 2," p. 175. McArdle also undoubtedly resented the public's occasional misattribution of his works to Huddle, as occurred in one review of *Dawn at the Alamo*. See "Twenty-Nine Years Required for Artist to Paint Picture of Battle of Alamo," Gaston Scrapbook, p. 106. For a discussion of the San Jacinto paintings that places less emphasis on these differences between the two artists' methods and motivations, see Cutrer, "'The Hardy, Stalwart Son of Texas,'" pp. 310–312.

50. Woodward to McArdle, 19 February 1896, "McArdle Companion 2," p. 34.

51. Quoted in Phelan, "Painters, McPainter." For the facts concerning the state's acquisition of McArdle's battle paintings, see "Texas State Library Inventory of Paintings in State Capitol," pp. 14–15, Texas State Archives, Austin. See also *Senate and Special Laws, 40th Legislature, 1st Called Session* (1927), p. 474; Senate no. 101–124, 18 May 1927; *Senate Petitions and Memorials*, p. 57; O'Brien, *Art and Artists in Texas*, pp. 27–28; and Pinckney, *Painting in Texas*, pp. 193–194.

One newspaper columnist mentioned the protracted negotiations as early as 1923. See Renick, "The Eyes of Texas." See also the *Dallas Morning News*, 10 July 1927, and *Austin Statesman*, 6 March 1927.

52. Alexander Sweet commented on a few of the canvases in Huddle's "Gallery of the Governors" as well as the Chapman portrait of Crockett in "Portraits at the Capitol," in *Alex Sweet's Texas*, ed. Virginia Eisenhour, pp. 33–35.

53. Quoted in Audray Bateman, "An Artist for the Capitol," *Austin American-Statesman* [n.d.], William H. Huddle File, Barker Texas History Center, University of Texas at Austin.

54. Wallace Stegner, *The Sound of Mountain Water*, p. 192.

4. MEN WITH THE BARK ON

1. Charles Adams Gulick, Jr., and Katherine Elliott, eds., *The Papers of Mirabeau B. Lamar*, 3:165. In his second annual message to Congress, Lamar justified his military campaigns against various Indian tribes with the assertion that "they inspire confidence in the energy of our government" (3:182). For biographical information on Lamar, see Herbert Gambrell, *Mirabeau Buonaparte Lamar, Troubador and Crusader*.

2. George Wilkins Kendall's *Narrative of an Expedition across the Great South-Western Prairies from Texas to Santa Fe* is an account of this quixotic undertaking by one of its participants. See also William Ransom Hogan, *The Texas Republic*, p. 258; Joseph Milton Nance, *After San Jacinto*, pp. 397, 423, 504–508, 519–523, and *Attack and Counterattack*, pp. 293, 336n; Smithwick, *The Evolution of a State*, p. 188; and John Edward Weems, *Dream of Empire*, pp. 198–202, 205–218.

3. Nance describes this episode and the other 1842 campaigns in exhaustive detail in *Attack and Counterattack*. Sam W. Haynes explores the political impact of the Somervell and Mier expeditions in *Soldiers of Misfortune*.

4. See Smithwick, *The Evolution of a State*, pp. 202–205; Walter Prescott Webb, *The Texas Rangers*, pp. 76–77; and Weems, *Dream of Empire*, pp. 236–245, 249–270.

One of the Mier prisoners, Edward Manton, wrote a letter concerning the escape attempt during his imprisonment. This letter is reproduced in Frederick Chabot, ed., *Texas Letters*, pp. 45–46.

5. McLaughlin's engraving was reproduced in Thomas J. Green, *Journal of the Texian Expedition against Mier*, p. 173.

6. For brief discussions of this painting, see Kendall and Perry, *Gentilz*, p. 23; and Pinckney, *Painting in Texas*, p. 108.

One of the condemned men, R. H. Dunham, penned a letter to his mother shortly before his execution:

Dear Mother,

I write to you under the most awful feelings that a son ever addressed to a mother, for in half hour my doom will be finished on earth for I am doomed to die by the hands of the Mexicans for our late attempt to escape. The o[rders of] G. Santa Anna [were] that every tenth man should be shot. We drew lots; I was one of the unfortunates. I cannot say anything more. I die, I hope, with firmness. Farewell, may

God bless you and may he in this my last hour forgive and pardon all my sins. A. D. Headenberge (?) will, should he be [able, do] all to informe [sic] you. Farewell.

> *Your affectionate son,*
> *R. H. Dunham*

Dunham File, DRT Library.

7. Green, *Journal of the Texian Expedition*, p. 172. Since McLaughlin's and, by extension, Gentilz's images were related most directly to Green's account, it is the version cited most frequently below. However, a full account of the incident, and the Mier Expedition in general, can be obtained only by consulting additional sources, such as Thomas W. Bell, *A Narrative of the Capture and Subsequent Sufferings of the Mier Prisoners . . .*; Joseph D. McCutchan, *Mier Expedition Diary*; William Preston Stapp, *The Prisoners of Perote*; and Samuel H. Walker, *Samuel H. Walker's Account of the Mier Expedition*.

8. Green, *Journal of the Texian Expedition*, p. viii.

9. Ibid., pp. 17–19. For a discussion of the reactions of some of Green's contemporaries to his book and of his running feud with Sam Houston, see Haynes, *Soldiers of Misfortune*, pp. 29–31, 179–180, and 207–209.

10. Green, *Journal of the Texian Expedition*. Gentilz's sketch is found in box A, GC-DRT.

11. Green, *Journal of the Texian Expedition*, pp. 284–285.

12. See ibid., p. 286; McLaughlin's illustration serves as the frontispiece of this volume.

13. Quoted in Peter H. Hassrick, "Remington in the Southwest," *Southwestern Historical Quarterly* 76 (January 1973): 306.

14. Frederic Remington, "How the Law Got into the Chaparral," *Harper's New Monthly Magazine* 94 (December 1896): 60–69. For further information on this painting, see *Bulletin of the Museum of Fine Arts of Houston, Texas* 7 (Spring 1944).

William H. and William N. Goetzmann discuss Remington's glorification of certain frontier types in *The West of the Imagination*, pp. 238, 244–245. Peggy and Harold Samuels recount briefly Remington's journey to Texas but do not mention the works used to illustrate this article in *Frederic Remington*, pp. 239–240. The most recent assessment of Remington's career also does not include lengthy discussion of his travels in Texas. See Michael Edward Shapiro and Peter H. Hassrick, *Frederic Remington*.

15. Ben Merchant Vorpahl examines Remington's philosophy of history and the various ways in which he selected its facts to conform to his preconceived notions in *Frederic Remington and the West*, pp. 200–202. See also Hassrick, *Frederic Remington*, p. 20.

Joseph Leach points out that Wallace's yarns comprised some of the earliest contributions to the image of Texans as tellers of tall tales and discusses the evolution of this image as part of a Southern oral tradition in *The Typical Texan*, p. 42.

16. See Goetzmann and Goetzmann, *The West of the Imagination*, p. 239. See also William H. Goetzmann, "No Teacup

Tragedies Here: The Art of Frederic Remington" (Paper delivered at Denver Art Museum, 11 July 1981, mss. available at Denver Art Museum), pp. 6, 9; and William H. Goetzmann and Joseph C. Porter, *The West as Romantic Horizon*, p. 26. Peter H. Hassrick discusses briefly Remington's fascination with the soldiers of various nations as representative of courage in the face of fate in *The Way West*, pp. 172, 177. A brief discussion of *Cavalryman of the Line* is found in Hassrick, *Frederic Remington*, plate 14. Hassrick notes that Remington only mastered a technique of dealing with the "white glare of the sun" in the Southwest after considerable frustration. See "Remington in the Southwest," pp. 299, 309.

17. Tyler surveys the development of this art form in its documentation of the war in *The Mexican War*. See also Goetzmann and Goetzmann, *The West of the Imagination*, pp. 94–95, 98–99; and Robert W. Johannsen, *To the Halls of the Montezumas*, pp. 222–230. For accounts of the battles of Palo Alto and Resaca de la Palma, see A. H. Bill, *Rehearsal for Conflict*, pp. 94–99; and Justin H. Smith, *The War with Mexico* 1:165–176.

18. See Samuel E. Chamberlain, *My Confession*, with an introduction by Roger Butterfield, pp. 12–18, 20–25, 32. The son of a New Hampshire stonecutter, Chamberlain had been raised in Boston after the family's move to that city during his childhood. By the age of sixteen, he was, in his words, "a muscular Christian," dividing his time between boxing lessons at Sheridan's Gymnasium and attending Bowdoin Square Baptist Church. Expulsion from school for fighting and the death of Chamberlain's father prompted him to set out westward in hopes of moving in with his uncle's family, who lived near Alton, Illinois.

Smith describes the hardships of the journey of Chamberlain's division in *The War with Mexico* 1:267–268. See also Bill, *Rehearsal for Conflict*, pp. 110, 191.

19. Chamberlain, *My Confession*, p. 46.

20. Ibid., p. 51.

21. Ibid. Johannsen places Chamberlain's attitude within the context of American perceptions of the war in *To the Halls of the Montezumas*, pp. 83–84. This volume furnishes a wealth of information concerning the war's impact on drama, literature, music, and the visual arts.

22. See Smith, *The War with Mexico* 1:268–270; and Webb, *The Texas Rangers*, p. 130. Bill discusses briefly the political fallout from the disciplinary action taken against Colonel Harney in *Rehearsal for Conflict*, p. 185.

23. Quoted in Ernest W. Winkler, ed., *Secret Journals of the Senate, Republic of Texas, 1836–1845*, p. 21.

24. W. J. Jones to Lamar, 15 April 1839, in *The Papers of Mirabeau B. Lamar*, ed. Charles Adams Gulick and Katherine Elliott, 2:530. See also Winkler, *Secret Journals of the Senate*, p. 185.

25. Texas reliance on volunteers is demonstrated by such legislative acts as that of 23 January 1838, in which the president was "authorized to accept the services of three companies of mounted volunteers for immediate service, on the frontier of Bastrop, Robertson, and Milam counties, for the term of six months, unless sooner discharged, to be mounted and armed and equipped at their own expense." See H. P. N. Gammel, comp., *Laws of Texas, 1822–1897* 1:178.

26. *Texas Sentinel*, 15 January 1840. For a thorough discussion of relations between the Cherokees and Texan settlers, including details of Lamar's campaign against the tribe, see Mary Whatley Clarke, *Chief Bowles and the Texas Cherokees*. For accounts of Mexican attempts to foment Indian unrest, see Nance, *After San Jacinto*, pp. 113–141; Newcomb, *The Indians of Texas*, p. 347–348; Webb, *The Texas Rangers*, pp. 47–50, 53–55; and Weems, *Dream of Empire*, pp. 151–156, 163–164.

27. Accounts of the Council House Fight were published soon after the battle. Two of the most detailed were a letter from Texas Inspector General H[ugh] McLeod to President Lamar, 20 March 1840, reproduced in full in the *Texas Sentinel*, 25 March 1840, and a follow-up story, "Events of the Comanche Treaty," that appeared in the same newspaper, 15 April 1840. See also Nance, *After San Jacinto*, pp. 291–292; Webb, *The Texas Rangers*, pp. 55–57; and Weems, *Dream of Empire*, pp. 170–180.

Houston's instructions to the commander of an expedition to the Red River to "flog those Indians" effectively summed up Texans' sentiments concerning the Indians on their northwestern frontier. See Houston to Colonel James W. Parker, 10 June 1837, in *The Writings of Sam Houston, 1813–1863*, ed. Eugene C. Barker and Amelia W. Williams, 4:32. Virtually every Texas Indian agent placed any news of the Comanches at the beginning of his report; agent Joseph Baker opined that "one successful campaign against them would be of more service than a million dollars against them expended in attempting to conciliate them by presents." Baker to Lamar, 12 January 1839, in *Papers of Lamar*, ed. Gulick and Elliott, 2:398. Newspapers further demonstrated Anglo Texans' shared hatred of the Plains tribes. For example, the *Clarksville Northern Standard* of 13 March 1845 referred to the "pirates of the prairie" in an article entitled "Indian Difficulties," which accused the "Wichetaw" tribe of stealing horses.

28. Donley Bryce furnishes a thorough account of this campaign in *The Great Comanche Raid*. See also DeShields, *Border Wars of Texas*, pp. 322–328; Rupert N. Richardson, *The Comanche Barrier to South Plains Settlement*, pp. 108–115; Smithwick, *The Evolution of a State*, pp. 183–184; and Webb, *The Texas Rangers*, pp. 47–50, 57–62. DeShields's account of the battle includes a full quotation of Felix Huston's report of the encounter to Branch T. Archer, Texas Secretary of War, in a letter of 12 August 1840. For an account focusing on the exploits of individual Texans during the battle, see Victor M. Rose, *The Life and Services of General Ben McCulloch*, pp. 55–65. For a briefer account that is more sympathetic to the Indian side, see Newcomb, *The Indians of Texas*, p. 350.

For contemporary accounts of Indian-settler conflicts during the spring and summer of 1840, see the *Colorado Gazette and Advertiser*, 28 March and 18 April 1840, and the *Texas Sentinel*, 25 May and 20 June 1840.

29. The most accessible reproduction of this painting is in DeShields, *Border Wars of Texas*, p. 320. For a brief discussion of the painting, see Pinckney, *Painting in Texas*, p. 188.

30. See E. L. Callihan, "The Battles That Whipped Mexico," *Dallas Morning News*, 10 August 1930. This account essentially summarizes that of Victor Rose and plays up the battle as a victory for Anglo settlers over a sinister conspiracy by their traditional enemies in Texas. Huston's report was first reproduced in full in the *Texas Sentinel*, 15 August 1840. For other newspaper stories concerning this campaign and battle, see *Colorado Gazette and Advertiser*, 29 August 1840; and *Texas Sentinel*, 12 and 26 September 1840.

31. Establishment of the Clear Fork Reservation and the subsequent controversy concerning Comanche raids are discussed in Richardson, *The Comanche Barrier*, pp. 211–232. See also John Salmon Ford, *Rip Ford's Texas*, pp. 219–221; J. Evetts Haley, *Charles Goodnight*, pp. 21–32; W. J. Hughes, *Rebellious Ranger*, pp. 129, 135, 157–158; and William W. Newcomb, *German Artist on the Texas Frontier*, pp. 148–150, and *The Indians of Texas*, pp. 352–354. In 1838, Houston had anticipated later Texan disillusionment with U.S. government Indian policy, observing that "men accustomed to frontier life can better devise plans for the safety of the frontier, if it is really threatened, than those at a distance." See Barker and Williams, *The Writings of Sam Houston* 4:350.

32. Chamberlain recounts the incident in San Antonio in *My Confession*, pp. 39–40.

33. Frederick Law Olmsted, *A Journey Through Texas Or, A Saddle Trip on the South-Western Frontier*, pp. 298, 300, 303.

34. Quoted in Remington, "How the Law Got into the Chaparral," p. 64. Ford's interview with Remington became the standard source for some of the subsequently published accounts of this engagement. For accounts of the battle and campaign, see Ford, *Rip Ford's Texas*, pp. 221–240; Hughes, *Rebellious Ranger*, pp. 137–149; Newcomb, *The Indians of Texas*, p. 357; Richardson, *The Comanche Barrier*, pp. 229–230, 234–238; and Webb, *The Texas Rangers*, pp. 154–158.

35. Remington, "How the Law Got into the Chaparral," p. 60. For a further interpretation of the significance of Remington's interview with Ford that utilizes devices of literary criticism, see Vorpahl, *Frederic Remington and the West*, pp. 212–213. This entire chapter, "Top of Speculation," pp. 203–219, is devoted to exploring Remington's manipulation of history.

36. For discussions of this work, see Goetzmann and Goetzmann, *The West of the Imagination*, p. 246; and Vorpahl, *Frederic Remington and the West*, pp. 193, 202.

37. This frequently quoted passage first appeared in Frederic Remington, "A Few Words from Mr. Remington," *Collier's* 34 (18 March 1905): 16.

38. See Goetzmann, "No Teacup Tragedies Here," pp. 1, 7; and Goetzmann and Goetzmann, *The West of the Imagination*, pp. 238–239.

39. Hassrick discusses Remington as a Romantic Realist in *Frederic Remington*, pp. 21, 24. For analyses of Remington's work as an expression of the artist's philosophy of fate, see Goetzmann, "No Teacup Tragedies Here," pp. 5–6, 8, 10; Goetzmann and Goetzmann, *The West of the Imagination*, pp. 239, 247; and Goetzmann and Porter, *The West as Romantic Horizon*, p. 27. Vorpahl comments on Remington's implicit acknowledgement that the triumph of white civilization over that of the native inhabitants also meant the death of the West in *Frederic Remington and the West*, p. 257.

40. Houston to Slater, 6 August 1844, in *The Writings of Sam Houston*, ed. Barker and Williams, 4:358. Presidents of Texas used the power to "appoint ministers and consuls, and all officers whose offices are established by this constitution, not herein otherwise provided for" to appoint agents for various tribes and commissioners to treat with the Indians. See Constitution of the Republic of Texas, art. 6, sec. 5. For the first seven years of the republic's existence, the president handled Indian affairs through these appointed agents and the Senate's Standing Committee on Indian Affairs. For a thorough examination of this aspect of the governing of the Republic of Texas, see Anna Muckelroy, "The Indian Policy of the Republic of Texas," *Southwestern Historical Quarterly* 26 (July 1922–April 1923): 1–29, 128–148, and 184–206.

Before he took office, Sam Houston had revealed his belief in the viability of the process of acculturation in his negotiations with the Cherokees on behalf of the Texas provisional government in February 1836. According to the treaty, Texas retained the "right of soil," or fee-simple ownership of the land on which the Cherokees were settled, but the Indians were allowed to retain the usufructary rights to enable them to live on this land's agricultural produce. The text of this treaty is reproduced in full in Dorman H. Winfrey, ed., *Texas Indian Papers, 1825–1843*, pp. 14–16.

41. I am greatly indebted to Governor Butler's great-great-grandson, Captain Pierce M. Butler, of Nashville, Tennessee, for sharing certain of his ancestor's recollections of this treaty council, including information concerning Stanley's role at Tehuacana Creek. See Butler to SDR, 7 June 1984 and 17 June 1984. See also David I. Bushnell, "John Mix Stanley, Artist-Explorer," in *Annual Report of the Smithsonian Institution for the Year Ending June 30, 1924*, p. 508; and Carolyn T. Foreman, "Pierce Mason Butler," *Chronicles of Oklahoma* 30 (Spring 1952): 7, 13. Julie Schimmel places Stanley's participation in this treaty council within the context of his entire career in "John Mix Stanley and the Image of the West in 19th Century American Art" (Ph.D. diss., New York University, 1983), pp. 38–40. See also Taft, *Artists and Illustrators of the Old West*, pp. 8–10.

42. For information concerning this treaty session, see Butler to SDR, 7 June 1984; Foreman, "Pierce Mason Butler," pp. 7, 13; and Grant Foreman, *Advancing the Frontier, 1830–1860*, p. 168. For a discussion of the disastrous Smithsonian fire and its impact on Stanley's career, see Schimmel, "John Mix Stanley," pp. 143–147.

43. See Samuels and Samuels, *Illustrated Biographical Encyclopedia of Artists of the American West*, p. 460 and Schimmel, "John Mix Stanley," pp. 8–37. Bushnell, one of the first scholars to explore Stanley's career, furnishes information concerning the artist's activities in Hawaii and the Pacific Northwest in "John Mix Stanley, Artist-Explorer," p. 509. See also Hassrick, *The Way West*, p. 56. Orphaned at the age of fourteen, Stanley was apprenticed to a coachmaker; six years later, he moved to Detroit in order to earn a living painting signs and houses.

44. See Foreman, *Advancing the Frontier*, p. 169. Proceedings and text of the Tehuacana Creek Treaty have been published in Winfrey, *Texas Indian Papers, 1825–1843*, pp. 156–163. A second council at Tehuacana Creek, on 9 October 1844, resulted in a treaty between the Republic of Texas and several tribes, notably the Cherokee and Comanche. See Dorman H. Winfrey, ed., *Texas Indian Papers, 1844–1845*, pp. 114–117.

George Catlin (1796–1872), Stanley's contemporary in recording the life of the American Indian, claimed to have entered Texas on an 1834 expedition with a detachment of U.S. Dragoons. The most recent evidence indicates that Catlin traveled only as far as present-day southwestern Oklahoma and that his Indian "cartoons" bearing titles that refer to Texas were executed between 1846 and 1848 during the artist's residence in Paris. Possibly, Catlin was attempting to capitalize on European admiration for American military successes of the Mexican War, which, of course, was closely identified with Texas. Catlin scholar William Truettner endorsed this interpretation in a telephone conversation with SDR on 2 August 1990. For the artist's account of his 1834 journey, see his journal, *Letters and Notes on the Manners, Customs, and Conditions of North American Indians* 1 : 36–95. For later assessments of Catlin's activities on this expedition, see John C. Ewers, *Artists of the Old West*, pp. 56, 64–71; and William H. Truettner, *The Natural Man Observed*, pp. 11, 15, 26, 31. William H. Goetzmann believes that Catlin at least looked across the Red River into Texas. See Goetzmann and Reese, *Texas Images and Visions*, p. 46.

45. See Billington, *Land of Savagery, Land of Promise*, pp. 31–34.

46. See ibid., pp. 14–18, 196–207, 217.

47. This sketch is found in box 2, folder 14-A, GC-DRT. See also Kendall and Perry, *Gentilz*, pp. 17–18; Pinckney, *Painting in Texas*, p. 117; and Utterback, *Early Texas Art in the Witte Museum*.

48. See Newcomb, *German Artist on the Texas Frontier*, pp. 5–8, 13–19. For other discussions of Petri's career, see W. J. Battle, "Art in Texas: An Overview," *Southwest Review* 14 (Autumn 1928): 53; Don Carleton, "Art as Regional History," *Discovery* 6 (Spring 1983): 11; McGuire, *Hermann Lungkwitz*, pp. xi–xvii, 1–5, 9–13; Pinckney, *Painting in Texas*, pp. 74–79; and Lonn Taylor, "Texas Painters of Romantic Frontiers," *Texas Homes* 5 (October 1981): 112.

49. See Newcomb, *German Artist on the Texas Frontier*, pp. 87, 115, 118–121, and 150. Billington discusses German perceptions of the West and the American Indian in *Land of Savagery, Land of Promise*, pp. 35, 53–56, 144–145, and 164. For a biography of the German leader who dealt with Texas Comanches most successfully, see Irene Marschall King, *John O. Meusebach*.

50. Newcomb, *German Artist on the Texas Frontier*, pp. 129–130.

51. Ibid., pp. 115–143.

52. Virgil Barker uses this term to describe Petri in *American Painting*, p. 455.

5. REALIZING THE PROMISE

1. See Goetzmann, *Exploration and Empire*, pp. 257–262; and Robert V. Hine, *Bartlett's West*, pp. 2–3, 7, and 29. Goetzmann discusses the political controversy concerning the map of the boundary and its impact on the selection of a transcontinental railroad route, pp. 262–263. For an examination of the negotiation of the Treaty of Guadalupe-Hidalgo and the problems concerning the boundary line, see William H. Goetzmann, *Army Exploration in the West*, pp. 153–169.

In 1836, Bartlett moved to New York City and, four years later, opened the B&W Bookshop in partnership with Charles Wellford in the Astor House Hotel. This enterprise brought him into contact with some of the nation's leading figures in literature and science, including art critic Henry Tuckerman, Edgar Allen Poe, and, possibly, painter Thomas Cole. Another customer of the bookstore, Henry C. Pratt, later served under Bartlett as an artist on the Mexican boundary survey. During the Mexican War, Bartlett had assisted Albert Gallatin, former secretary of the treasury under Thomas Jefferson, in writing several vitriolic attacks on U.S. involvement in the conflict. See Hine, *Bartlett's West*, p. 6.

2. See Goetzmann, *Army Exploration*, pp. 170–173; and Hine, *Bartlett's West*, pp. 9, 12, 14–15. The debate over visual recordings of the survey team's labors was one of many disagreements afflicting the expedition. From the time of his appointment, Bartlett had a poorly delineated relationship with the U.S. Army and its Topographical Corps of Engineers, which would do the bulk of the work of surveying and staking out the boundary line. Chief Astronomer and Head of the Topographical Scientific Corps, Lieutenant-Colonel John McClellan, believed his powers to be coequal with those of Bartlett and Surveyor A. B. Gray. In spite of this confusion, McClellan's assistant, Lieutenant A. W. Whipple, provided valuable support to Bartlett during the chaotic time of preparation for departure of the survey crew.

3. John Russell Bartlett related this incident in his *Personal Narrative of Incidents in Texas, New Mexico, California, Sonora, and Chihuahua, Connected with the United States and Mexican Boundary Commission, During the Years 1850, '51, '52, and '53* 1 : 98. He also describes the expedition's trek from Fredericksburg to Horsehead Crossing, 1 : 61–95. See also Goetzmann, *Army Exploration*, pp. 173–208; and Hine, *Bartlett's West*, pp. 26–27.

4. Quoted in Harlan D. Fowler, *Camels to California*, p. 38. For other accounts of the beasts' status as instant celebrities in San Antonio, which was selected as initial headquarters for the experiment due to its climate and the availability of provisions, see Thomas L. Connelly, "The American Camel Experiment: A Reappraisal," *Southwestern Historical Quarterly* 69 (October 1966): 443–445, 447; Chris Emmett, *Texas Camel Tales*, pp. 2, 11, 43; Kendall and Perry, *Gentilz*, pp. 44–45; and Frank Bishop Lammons, "Operation Camel: An Experiment in Western Transportation in Texas, 1857–1860," *Southwestern Historical Quarterly* 6 (January 1957): 23–25, 30. For discussions of Americans' ideas concerning "The Great American Desert" during the mid-nineteenth century, see essays by John L. Allen, David M. Emmons, and Herman R. Friis, in *Images of the Plains*, ed. Brian W. Blouet and Merlin P. Lawson, pp. 3–11, 125–136, 59–74; Goetzmann, *Exploration and Empire*, pp. 136–178; and Smith, *Virgin Land*, pp. 201–213.

5. Quoted in W. Stephen Thomas, *Fort Davis and the Texas Frontier*, p. 21. For discussion of Lee's part in this venture, see pp. 19–21. This immediate cause of failure demonstrated the overall lack of commitment, planning, and common purpose on the part of the parties involved. See Connelly, "The American Camel Experiment," p. 462; Emmett, *Texas Camel Tales*, pp. 45, 48–49, 52; Fowler, *Camels to California*, pp. vii, 40–42; and Kendall and Perry, *Gentilz*, p. 45. See also Newcomb, *German Artist on the Texas Frontier*, pp. 95, 108–109.

6. For further discussion of Lee's attitudes toward the subjects of these works and of influences on his art, see Thomas, *Fort Davis and the Texas Frontier*, pp. 14, 17, 26–28, 34. Some of Lee's paintings, such as *View Near Ft. Croghan*, may be dated approximately by comparing their subjects with dates of the artist's postings at various forts in the West.

7. See Lois Burkhalter, introduction to *A Seth Eastman Sketchbook, 1848–1849*, pp. xv, xxv; and John Francis McDermott, *Seth Eastman*, pp. 3–4.

8. Quoted in McDermott, *Seth Eastman*, p. 67. For an account of Eastman's journey down the Mississippi, see pp. 13–17.

9. Quoted in ibid., p. 68.

10. Burkhalter, introduction to *A Seth Eastman Sketchbook*, p. xvii.

11. Quoted in ibid., p. xxii.

12. Quoted in McDermott, *Seth Eastman*, p. 68.

13. Ibid.

14. Ibid., p. 70. See also Burkhalter, introduction to *A Seth Eastman Sketchbook*, p. xix.

15. See Burkhalter, introduction to *A Seth Eastman Sketchbook*, pp. xxiii–xxiv; and McDermott, *Seth Eastman*, p. 70.

16. Quoted in Burkhalter, introduction to *A Seth Eastman Sketchbook*, p. xxv.

17. Ibid., p. xviii; and McDermott, *Seth Eastman*, p. 70.

18. See Newcomb, *German Artist on the Texas Frontier*, pp. 7, 115–116, 121, 150. In *Fort Martin Scott*, Petri placed figures in theatrical groupings, as did the Nazarene painters of Austria and Italy, a school of artists who had influenced Julius Hübner, one of Petri's instructors in Dresden.

19. Ibid., pp. 141–142.

20. Ibid., pp. 116, 119–120, 138–142, 193. Although it is difficult to affix a certain date to the execution of *Fort Martin Scott*, analysis of the work indicates a date of around 1853. Longstreet was transferred to another command after 1854, and some of the other individuals portrayed in the painting had also left by that time. The uniform of Longstreet and that of the mounted dragoon also aid in dating the work.

21. Ibid., pp. 84, 88; and Taylor, "Texas Painters of Romantic Frontiers," pp. 114, 116. The erroneous notations "1849" and "Austin, Texas" were added to these canvases sometime after Petri's death.

22. See James Patrick McGuire, *Iwonski in Texas*, pp. 11, 13, 16; and Martha Utterback, *Early Texas Art in the Witte Museum*, p. 28. Iwonski's father, Leopold, resigned his commission as a lieutenant in the Prussian army and had discussed emigration with the Adelsverein, the group that had aided Petri's emigration and by 1847 had sent seven thousand emigrants to Texas. The Iwonskis, upon arriving in Galveston after a two-and-a-half month voyage from Bremerhaven, Germany, joined these German colonists.

23. See McGuire, *Iwonski in Texas*, pp. 16–20.

24. Ibid., pp. 24–25, 76, 78.

25. Ibid., p. 44; and Paula Mitchell Marks, *Turn Your Eyes toward Texas*, pp. 227–228.

26. Quoted in Marks, *Turn Your Eyes toward Texas*, p. 232.

27. See Marks, *Turn Your Eyes toward Texas*, pp. 235–236; and McGuire, *Iwonski in Texas*, p. 44.

28. See McGuire, *Hermann Lungkwitz*, p. 20; and *Iwonski in Texas*, pp. 14, 16–18, 20, 25–26, 28–32. Unlike Lungkwitz and Petri, Iwonski appears never to have become totally committed to staying permanently in Texas. On 18 March 1871, he departed San Antonio bound for Berlin, the capital of the newly united German Empire. In October 1872, Iwonski arrived in San Antonio soon after the death of his father. He and his mother then left America permanently, moving back to Breslau. I am grateful to the late James Patrick McGuire for clarifying these and other questions concerning Iwonski's career in a letter of 6 July 1987.

29. See Frank Lotto, *Fayette County*, pp. 276–277; and Cecilia Steinfeldt, *Texas Folk Art*, pp. 35–39.

30. *San Augustine Journal and Advertiser*, 18 July 1840, first quote; and Hogan, *The Texas Republic*, p. 33, second quote.

31. Quoted in Hogan, *The Texas Republic*, p. 34.

32. Olmsted, *A Journey through Texas*, pp. 113, 188, 244, and 432.

33. See Ron Tyler, *Views of Texas, 1852–1856*, pp. 11–13, 15, 19. Soon after the family returned to Boston, George Hardinge deserted his wife and children. For Olmsted's description of the lot of Texas women, see *A Journey through Texas*, p. 88.

34. See Tyler, *Views of Texas, 1852–1856*, pp. 26–29, 34–35, 42–45.

35. For a brief discussion of this work and of the Hardinges' relationship with John Morrison, see Tyler, *Views of Texas, 1852–1856*, pp. 13, 46.

36. Frank Reaugh, preface, "Twenty-Four Hours with the Herd," 1934, pamphlet, box 2H451, Frank Reaugh Papers, Barker Texas History Center, University of Texas at Austin, (hereafter cited as FRP-BTHC). Reaugh collaborated with Dallas author Clyde Walton Hill in writing this brief booklet intended to accompany an exhibition of this series of paintings. For further discussion of Reaugh's relationship with the Houston brothers, see Grauer, "The Early Career of Frank Reaugh, 1860–1889," pp. 50–54, and *Frank Reaugh: From the Panhandle-Plains Historical Museum*, pamphlet accompanying exhibition in Texas A&M University Memorial Student Center, 8 February–13 May 1989; and Weismann, *Frank Reaugh*, p. 13.

37. Reaugh, "Twenty-Four Hours with the Herd." Grauer discusses the artist's youthful study of cattle as well as his later use of these early sketches in "The Early Career of Frank Reaugh," pp. 18–30, 44–49, 113.

38. For further discussion of this phase of Reaugh's career, see Fisk, *A History of Texas Artists and Sculptors*, p. 53; Grauer, "The Early Career of Frank Reaugh," pp. 55–65; J. Evetts Haley, *Frank Reaugh*; O'Brien, *Art and Artists in Texas*, p. 177; and Weismann, *Frank Reaugh*, p. 14. In an interview of 1 March 1985, the late Dallas artist Otis Dozier related to this author the importance of Reaugh's sketching expeditions in the professional development of a generation of Texas painters. The artist's hand-drawn "Map of the Route," detailing the direction of his travels on these West Texas sketching trips, is found in folio 4N37, FRP-BTHC.

39. See Grauer, "The Early Career of Frank Reaugh," pp. 31–40, 88–114; Haley, *Frank Reaugh*; O'Brien, *Art and Artists in Texas*, p. 177; Samuels and Samuels, *The Illustrated Biographical Encyclopedia of Artists of the American West*, p. 391; and Weismann, *Frank Reaugh*, pp. 11–12, 15. This European sojourn was something of a gamble, since Reaugh quite possibly could have at least made ends meet in Terrell and was risking losing the student clientele that he had cultivated. Reaugh's meticulous, though often indecipherable, notes testify to his artistic debt to Corot, Turner, Frederick Church, and other American and European painters. See box 2H451, "Painting Lists" File, FRP-BTHC.

40. Quoted in Weismann, *Frank Reaugh*, p. 16. Since the scope of this study does not include twentieth-century Texas paintings, extensive discussion of Reaugh's works is limited to those executed before 1900. Dating Reaugh's canvases can be a daunting task, but those that can be attributed to the first two decades of his career do indicate its subsequent direction and emphasis.

41. Edward Everett Dale, *The Range Cattle Industry, 1865–1925*, p. 50. Similarly, contemporary newspaper accounts described an 1885 St. Louis convention of cattlemen as "characterized by the free and easy fashion of the West and vigorous, racy, Texas yells" for the benefit of eastern and English reporters. See the *Edinburgh Courant*, 8 May 1885, quoted in Maurice Frink, W. Turrentine Jackson, and Agnes Wright Spring, *When Grass Was King*, p. 226.

42. See Weismann, *Frank Reaugh*, pp. 15–16, 31–34.

43. Quoted in Haley, *Frank Reaugh*. See also Reaugh, "Art A Religious Duty," transcript of sixth lecture in first "El Sibil" series, n.d., and "Talk 2—Beauty for Enjoyment," box 2H451, "Drafts of Talks on Art" File, FRP-BTHC. Grauer analyzes this spiritual aspect of the artist's work and his use of pastels in "The Early Career of Frank Reaugh," pp. 34–37.

44. Florence McClung, interview by Sam Ratcliffe, 23 January 1987, transcript, Florence McClung File, JBC-SMU.

45. Reaugh, preface, "Twenty-Four Hours with the Herd." The booklet accompanying *Twenty-Four Hours with the Herd* makes clear that, while this painting is of "an hour of rest, peace, quiet," the cowboys are "resting, but ever watchful, ever mindful of duty to the herd." See Hill, "Watering the Herd," in "Twenty-Four Hours with the Herd"; and Fisk, *A History of Texas Artists and Sculptors*, p. 55.

46. Reaugh, "Some Dope That May Be of Use in Advertising," box 2H451, "Notes on Collections and Exhibits" File, FRP-BTHC. This three-page manuscript contains specific instructions from the artist concerning the display of the "Twenty-Four Hours with the Herd" series. Reaugh believed that the paintings should be presented as part of a complete aesthetic experience by the viewer and was extremely particular about the lighting and music accompanying an evening program of viewing the series. The musical selections included tunes as diverse as "Home on the Range" and the adagio movement from Beethoven's "Spring Sonata." Reaugh stated that the latter selection was intended to suggest the cry of a western meadowlark, even though, as Reaugh observed, "Poor old Beethoven never heard a meadow lark."

47. Reaugh grieved at encroaching modernity but nevertheless accommodated himself to it in his avocation as an inventor. One cryptic letter suggests that he developed an oil-pumping device that he hoped to sell to the Magnolia Petroleum Company. See Arthur L. Ayres to Reaugh, 2 September 1919, box 2H451, "Correspondence" File, FRP-BTHC.

48. See Kendall and Perry, *Gentilz*, pp. 10, 13. Henry Castro ordered this survey immediately after his arrival in San Antonio. In addition to the townsite, the surveyors marked out the remainder of Castro's grant as forty-acre farms for distribution under the Germanic *Hufendorf* system of land ownership. Bobby D. Weaver discusses this survey in *Castro's Colony*, pp. 50–51. For an account of another Texas surveyor's experiences during this time, see Susanne Starling, "A Surveyor's Saga: Warren Angus Ferris at the Three Forks," *Legacies: A History Journal for Dallas and North Central Texas* 1 (Spring 1989): 6–11.

49. These sketches are found in box 2, GC-DRT, and a few are described in "Alsatian Artist Pictures Early San Antonio," *San Antonio Light*, 7 October 1945.

50. *Houston Weekly Times*, 9 April 1840.

51. See the *Texas Sentinel*, 8 March 1840, and *San Augustine Journal and Advertiser*, 4 June 1840.

52. For biographical information on Samuel, see Pinckney, *Painting in Texas*, pp. 30–31; and Utterback, *Early Texas Art in the Witte Museum*, p. 1. Utterback discusses the details of each of these canvases, pp. 2–5.

53. The most complete account of Allen's career is found in "Thomas Allen, N.A. (1849–1924)," pp. 1–4, unattributed ms., Thomas Allen File, Witte Museum. See also Pinckney, *Painting in Texas*, pp. 184–185; Taft, *Artists and Illustrators of the Old West, 1850–1900*, p. 346; and Utterback, *Early Texas Art in the Witte Museum*, p. 49. Before graduating from Dusseldorf's Royal Academy in 1876 or 1877, Allen had already exhibited his *Bridge at Linnengen* at the National Academy of Design. In Boston, Allen served on several prestigious art juries and received honors from various Boston art organizations.

54. See "Thomas Allen," pp. 2–5.

55. For histories of pre-twentieth-century Galveston, see Charles G. Hayes, *Galveston*, and David G. McComb, *Galveston*, pp. 5–120.

56. See James Patrick McGuire, *Julius Stockfleth*, with an introduction by Eric Steinfeldt, pp. 1–5. These works are part of the slightly less than one hundred paintings by Stockfleth having Texas subjects.

57. Quoted in McGuire, *Julius Stockfleth*, p. 12. For further discussion of shipping along the Texas Gulf Coast during this period, see Steinfeldt's introduction, pp. ix–xi.

58. See McGuire, *Julius Stockfleth*, p. 40.

59. Quoted in Sam Acheson, *35,000 Days in Texas*, p. 211. For a brief summary of contemporary news coverage of the storm, see pp. 207–209. Acheson gleaned his information from extensive coverage of the hurricane by the parent paper of the *Dallas Morning News*, the *Galveston Daily News*. For accounts of the Galveston hurricane, see Herbert M. Mason, *Death from the Sea*; McComb, *Galveston*, pp. 121–149; and John Edward Weems, *A Weekend in September*.

60. See McGuire, *Julius Stockfleth*, p. 8.

61. Ibid., pp. 56, 102.

62. Ibid., pp. 10–13.

63. See McComb, *Galveston*, pp. 134–139.

64. John S. Spratt details economic and social conditions in Texas between the Civil War and the turn of the century in *The Road to Spindletop*. James Anthony Clark and Michel C. Halbouty furnish a general history of the earliest and most famous Texas oil strike in *Spindletop*. For detailed accounts of the day the well blew in, see Acheson, *35,000 Days in Texas*, pp. 216, 295; and Mody C. Boatright, *Folklore of the Oil Industry*, pp. 83–85. William A. Owens furnishes a fictional account of the effects of the southeast Texas oil boom on the area's rural population in his novel, *Fever in the Earth*.

CONCLUSION:
HEROISM AND THE COMMON MAN

1. Quoted in John A. Lomax, *Adventures of a Ballad Hunter*, pp. 32, 41. See also Richard Bauman, "The Transmission of the Texas Myth," in *Texas Myths*, ed. Robert F. O'Connor, p. 37. A comparison of one of Texas's leading newspapers with one prominent American paper illustrates the desire of late-nineteenth-century Texans to be accepted as "normal" by the rest of the United States. During the 1880s, the *New York Times* reported more extensively on the "negative" subjects of drouth and violent crime in Texas than did the *Dallas Morning News*. I am indebted to Mr. Stephen Blow of the *Dallas Morning News* for sharing a copy of his manuscript, "The Texas Image: The State as Portrayed in the *New York Times* and the *Dallas Morning News*, 1885–1887."

2. See Novak, *American Painting of the Nineteenth Century*, pp. 263–265. Rick Stewart gives the most extensive account of Texas painting in the 1930s in *Lone Star Regionalism*. For an overview of mural painting during the 1930s, see Karal Ann Marling, *Wall-to-Wall America*. Contemporary writings on Texas art during this decade include Jerry Bywaters, "Contemporary American Artists," *Southwest Review* 23 (April 1938): 297–306, and "The New Texas Painters," *Southwest Review* 11 (Spring 1936): 330–342; and Richard Foster Howard, "Art of Texas Presents an Epitome of Aesthetics of the Modern Age," *Art Digest* 10 (1 June 1936): 14. The literature concerning Texas art throughout the twentieth century consists primarily of reviews of specific exhibitions and exhibition catalogues. For discussion of twentieth-century Texas painting, see Goetzmann and Reese, *Texas Images and Visions*; and Susie Kalil, *The Texas Landscape, 1900–1986*.

3. Onderdonk to DeShields, 17 December 1901, box 5, file 155, JTD-DRT.

4. For discussions of traditional historical painters' definition and use of "historical truth," see Flexner, *That Wilder Image*, pp. xi–xv; Strong, *Recreating the Past*, pp. 24–29; and Thistlethwaite, *The Image of George Washington*, p. 12.

5. William Cronon, "Revisiting the Vanishing Frontier: The Legacy of Frederick Jackson Turner," *Western Historical Quarterly* 18 (April 1987): 165–166.

6. The only aspect of twentieth-century Texas history to be featured prominently by Hollywood has been the oil industry, chronicled in films such as *Giant, Boom Town,* and *Hud*. See Don Graham, *Cowboys and Cadillacs*, pp. 1–9; Marcelle Lively Hamer, "Anecdote as Sidelights to Texas History," in *In the Shadow of History*, ed. Boatright, Dobie, and Ransom, pp. 59, 74; and Schoelwer, *Alamo Images*, pp. 3–4. Adaptation of Moran's concept of "pictorial Nature" to film has been especially evident since the earliest movie versions of the Alamo story. A few of these bits of artistic license have included casting Mrs. Dickinson as a heroine warding off a bayonet, transferring the attempt to fire the powder magazine from Evans to Crockett, and, most obviously, retaining the post-1850s addition to the chapel roof. The most thorough discussion of Alamo movies is found in Graham, *Cowboys and Cadillacs*, pp. 40–53. See also Schoelwer, "The Artist's Alamo," p. 432; and Schoelwer, *Alamo Images*, pp. 14, 117. Eric von Schmidt makes direct comparisons between the composition of films and paintings dealing with the Alamo in "The Alamo Remem-

bered," p. 65. Some of these paintings provided inspiration and/or source material for later artists. For example, Dallas artist Jerry Bywaters utilized Onderdonk's *Fall of the Alamo* as a model for his design of the stage set for *We Are Besieged*, a 1941 play based on the story of the siege and fall of the Alamo. See Louise Long Gossett, "Stage Set for Play Designed from Alamo Battle Paintings," *Dallas Morning News*, 24 April 1941.

Bauman discusses the significance and use of this folkloric tradition in "The Transmission of the Texas Myth," pp. 23–24, 36–37.

7. For discussions of painters' work as illustrators for patriotic writings, see Flexner, *The Light of Distant Skies*, p. 12; Goodrich, "The Painting of American History," p. 288; Strong, *Recreating the Past*, p. 14; Taylor, *America As Art*, esp. Chapter 2, "The American Cousin," pp. 37–94; Thistlethwaite, *The Image of George Washington*, p. 8–9; and Truettner, "The Art of History," pp. 6–9, 23–25.

8. McArdle to DeShields, "'Log Cabin Picture,'" JTD-DRT, pp. 3–4. In this letter, the artist also acknowledges that, "as I have often admitted to you, I know nothing of business and even less of legislation." McArdle also could not remember how long the painting had hung in the House chambers.

Strong discusses how eighteenth-century English painters served as illustrators for popular authors in *Recreating the Past*, pp. 13–23.

9. See Onderdonk to DeShields, 6 July 1903, box 5, file 158, JTD-DRT. In giving DeShields permission to reproduce the painting, which Onderdonk had copyrighted, the artist noted, "There are people in San Antonio that [*sic*] would not hesitate to pounce on it and reproduce it in some cheap form for souvenirs of the place." His fear was justified, since artists' sketches of the Alamo were commonly borrowed, copied, and otherwise pirated. See Schoelwer, "The Artist's Alamo," p. 455.

10. In 1893, the Dallas Art Students' League hired Onderdonk as its first instructor. The contract, dated 15 February 1893, is in the Robert Onderdonk File, Witte Museum. See also Eleanor Onderdonk to Jerry Bywaters, 13 March 1951, Robert Onderdonk File, JBC-SMU; and Steinfeldt, *The Onderdonks*, p. 22.

Selected Bibliography

PRIMARY SOURCES

Archival Collections

Archives of American Art, Smithsonian Institution (Washington, D.C.)
L.M.D. Guillaume File
Collection of Exhibition Catalogs (File N-564)
Barker Texas History Center (University of Texas at Austin)
William H. Huddle File
Frank Reaugh Papers
Jerry Bywaters Collection on Art of the Southwest (Jake and Nancy Hamon Arts Library, Southern Methodist University)
William H. Huddle File
Forrest Kirkland File
Robert Onderdonk File
Daughters of the Republic of Texas Library at the Alamo (San Antonio)
James T. DeShields Collection
R. H. Dunham File
Mrs. Edwin Gaston Collection
Theodore Gentilz Collection
Henry McArdle File
Robert Onderdonk File
Texas Collection (Baylor University)
William Carey Crane Papers
Henry McArdle File
Texas State Archives (Austin)
"McArdle Companion Battle Paintings, Historical Documents. Vol. 1: *Dawn at the Alamo*"
"McArdle Companion Battle Paintings, Historical Documents. Vol. 2: *Battle of San Jacinto*"
"Texas State Library Inventory of Paintings in State Capitol"
Valentine Museum (Richmond, Virginia)
L. M. D. Guillaume File
Witte Museum (San Antonio)
Thomas Allen File
Louis Hoppe File
Robert Onderdonk File

Letters and Interviews

Anonymous owner of Henry McArdle, *Lee at the Wilderness.* Interview with SDR. Dallas. 18 November 1988. Tape recording in possession of SDR.
Butler, Pierce M. Letters to SDR, 7 June 1984 and 17 June 1984.
Dozier, Otis. Interview with SDR. Dallas. 1 March 1985. Notes in possession of SDR.
McClung, Florence. Interview with SDR. Dallas. 23 January 1987. McClung File, Bywaters Collection, SMU.

SECONDARY SOURCES

Books, Dissertations, and Theses

Acheson, Sam. *35,000 Days in Texas: A History of the Dallas News and Its Forbears.* New York: Macmillan, 1938.
Adams, Andy. *Log of a Cowboy.* Boston: Houghton Mifflin, 1903.
Baigell, Matthew. *Dictionary of American Art.* London: John Murray, 1980.
Bandelier, Fanny, ed. and trans. *The Journey of Alvar Nuñez Cabeza de Vaca.* New York: Allerton Book Co., 1922.
Bannon, John Francis, ed. *Bolton and the Spanish Borderlands.* Norman: University of Oklahoma Press, 1964.

Barker, Eugene C., *The Life of Stephen F. Austin: Founder of Texas, 1793–1836*. Nashville: Cokesbury Press, 1926.

Barker, Eugene C., ed. *The Austin Papers*. Annual Report of the American Historical Association for the Year 1919. 2 vols. Washington, D.C.: Government Printing Office, 1924.

Barker, Eugene C., and Amelia W. Williams, ed. *The Writings of Sam Houston, 1813–1836*. 8 vols. Austin: University of Texas, 1938.

Barker, Virgil. *American Painting: History and Interpretation*. New York: Macmillan, 1951.

Barr, Alwyn. *Texans in Revolt: The Battle for San Antonio, 1835*. Austin: University of Texas Press, 1990.

Bartlett, John Russell. *Personal Narrative of Incidents in Texas, New Mexico, California, Sonora, and Chihuahua, Connected with the United States and Mexican Boundary Commission, During the Years 1850, '51, '52, and '53*. 2 vols. New York: D. Appleton and Co., 1854. Reprint, with an introduction by Odie B. Faulk. Chicago: Rio Grande Press, 1965.

Bauman, Richard, and Roger D. Abrahams, eds. *"And Other Neighborly Names": Social Process and Cultural Image in Texas Folklore*. Austin: University of Texas Press, 1981.

Bedichek, Roy. *Adventures with a Texas Naturalist*. Austin: University of Texas Press, 1947.

Bell, Thomas W. *A Narrative of the Capture and Subsequent Sufferings of the Mier Prisoners in Mexico*. . . . De Soto Co., Miss.: Printed for the author at the Press of R. Morris & Co., 1845. Reprint. Waco: Texian Press, 1964.

Bill, A. H. *Rehearsal for Conflict: The War with Mexico, 1846–1848*. New York: Alfred A. Knopf, 1947. Reprint, New York: Cooper Square Publishers, 1969.

Billington, Ray Allen. *Land of Savagery, Land of Promise: The European Image of the American Frontier*. New York: W. W. Norton & Co., 1981.

Billington, Ray Allen, and Martin Ridge, ed. *America's Frontier Story: A Documentary History of Westward Expansion*. New York: Holt, Rinehart, and Winston, 1969.

Binkley, William C. *The Texas Revolution*. Baton Rouge: Louisiana State University Press, 1952.

Bloch, Maurice E. *George Caleb Bingham: The Evolution of an Artist*. 2 vols. Berkeley: University of California Press, 1967.

Blouet, Brian W., and Merlin P. Lawson. *Images of the Plains: The Role of Human Nature in Settlement*. Lincoln: University of Nebraska Press, 1975.

Boatright, Mody C. *Folklore of the Oil Industry*. Dallas: Southern Methodist University Press, 1963.

Boatright, Mody C., J. Frank Dobie, and Harry H. Ransom, eds. *In the Shadow of History*. Austin: Texas Folk-Lore Society, 1939.

Bollaert, William. *William Bollaert's Texas*. Edited by W. Eugene Hollon and Ruth Lapham Butler. Norman: University of Oklahoma Press, 1956.

Bryce, Donley. *The Great Comanche Raid: Boldest Indian Attack of the Texas Republic*. Austin: Eakin Press, 1987.

Burleson, Georgiana (Jenkins). *The Life and Writings of Rufus C. Burleson*. N.p. 1901.

Castañeda, Carlos E. *The Mexican Side of the Texas Revolution*. Dallas: P. L. Turner Co., 1928.

Catlin, George. *Letters and Notes on the Manners, Customs, and Conditions of North American Indians*. 2 vols. London: David Bogue, 1844. Reprint. New York: Dover, 1973.

Chabot, Frederick, ed. *Texas Letters*. San Antonio: Yanaguana Society, 1940.

Chamberlain, Samuel E. *My Confession*. Introduction by Roger Butterfield. New York: Harper & Brothers, 1956.

Chiapelli, Fredi, ed. *First Images of America*. 2 vols. Berkeley: University of California Press, 1976.

Clark, Carol. *Thomas Moran: Watercolors of the American West*. Austin: University of Texas Press for the Amon Carter Museum, 1980.

Clark, Eliot. *History of the National Academy of Design, 1825–1953*. New York: Columbia University Press, 1954.

Clark, James Anthony, and Michel C. Halbouty. *Spindletop*. New York: Random House, 1952.

Clarke, Mary Whatley. *Chief Bowles and the Texas Cherokees*. Norman: University of Oklahoma Press, 1971.

Cohen, Henry. *Business and Politics in America from the Age of Jackson to the Civil War: The Career Biography of W. W. Corcoran*. Westport, Conn.: Greenwood Publishing, 1971.

Corner, William. *San Antonio de Bexar: A Guide and History*. San Antonio: Bainbridge and Corner, 1890.

Cox, Mamie Wynne. *The Romantic Flags of Texas*. Dallas: Banks Upshaw & Co., 1936.

Crockett, David. *A Narrative of the Life of David Crockett*. Introduction by Paul Hutton. Philadelphia: E. L. Carey and A. Hart, 1834. Reprint. Lincoln: University of Nebraska Press, 1987.

Dale, Edward Everett. *The Range Cattle Industry, 1865–1925*. Norman: University of Oklahoma Press, 1930.

Daniell, L. E. *Personnel of the Texas State Government*. San Antonio: Maverick Printing House, 1892.

Day, Donald, and Harry Herbert Ullom, eds. *The Autobiography of Sam Houston*. Norman: University of Oklahoma Press, 1954.

DeGolyer, Everette. *The Journey of Three Englishmen across Texas in 1568*. El Paso: Peripatetic Press, 1947.

DeShields, James T. *Border Wars of Texas*. Tioga, Tex.: Matt Bradley, 1912.

———. *Tall Men with Long Rifles*. San Antonio: Naylor Co., 1935.

———. *They Sat in High Place: The Governors and Presidents of Texas*. San Antonio: Naylor Co., 1940.

Durham, George, and Clyde Wantland. *Taming the Nueces Strip: The Story of McNelly's Rangers*. Austin: University of Texas Press, 1962.

Eagleton, Davis Foute, ed. *Texas Literature Reader*. Dallas: Southern Publishing Co., 1916.

Eastman, Seth. *A Seth Eastman Sketchbook, 1848–1849*. Introduction by Lois Burkhalter. Austin: University of Texas Press for the Marion Koogler McNay Art Institute, San Antonio, 1961.

Ehrenberg, Herman. *With Milam and Fannin: Adventures of a German Boy in Texas' Revolution*. Edited by Henry Nash Smith. Translated by Charlotte Churchill. Austin: Pemberton Press, 1968.

Emmett, Chris. *Texas Camel Tales*. San Antonio: Naylor Co., 1932.

Ewers, John C. *Artists of the Old West*. New York: Doubleday & Co., 1965.

Faulk, Odie B. *The Last Years of Spanish Texas, 1778–1821*. London: Hague Paris Press, 1964.

Fisk, Frances Battaile. *A History of Texas Artists and Sculptors*. Abilene: Privately published, 1928.

Flexner, James. *America's Old Masters*. New York: Viking Press, 1939.

———. *The Light of Distant Skies, 1760–1835*. New York: Harcourt, Brace & Co., 1954.

———. *That Wilder Image: The Native School from Thomas Cole to Winslow Homer*. Boston: Little, Brown & Co., 1962.

Foote, Henry Stuart. *Texas and the Texans; or, Advance of the Anglo-Americans to the Southwest. . . .* 2 vols. Philadelphia: Thomas, Cowperthwait & Co., 1841.

Ford, John Salmon. *Rip Ford's Texas*. Edited, introduction, and commentary by Stephen B. Oates. Austin: University of Texas Press, 1963.

Foreman, Grant. *Advancing the Frontier, 1830–1860*. Norman: University of Oklahoma Press, 1933.

Fowler, Harlan D. *Camels to California: A Chapter in Western Transportation*. Stanford: Stanford University Press, 1950.

Frankenstein, Alfred. *William Sidney Mount*. New York: Harry N. Abrams, 1975.

Friend, Llerena. *Sam Houston: The Great Designer*. Austin: University of Texas Press, 1954.

Frink, Maurice, W. Turrentine Jackson, and Agnes Wright Spring. *When Grass Was King: Contributions to the Western Range Cattle Industry Study*. Boulder: University of Colorado Press, 1956.

Fuchs, R. H. *Dutch Painting*. New York: Oxford University Press, 1978.

Gambrell, Herbert. *Mirabeau Buonaparte Lamar, Troubador and Crusader*. Dallas: Southwest Press, 1934.

Gambrell, Herbert, and Virginia Gambrell. *A Pictorial History of Texas*. New York: E. P. Dutton & Co., 1960.

Gammel, H. P. N., comp. *The Laws of Texas, 1822–1897*. 10 vols. Austin: Gammel Book Co., 1898.

Glanz, Dawn. *How the West Was Drawn: American Art and the Settling of the Frontier*. Ann Arbor, Mich.: UMI Research Press, 1978.

Goetzmann, William H. *Army Exploration in the West*. New Haven: Yale University Press, 1959.

———. *Exploration and Empire. The Explorer and Scientist in the Winning of the American West*. New York: W. W. Norton & Co., 1966.

Goetzmann, William H., and William N. Goetzmann. *The West of the Imagination*. New York: W. W. Norton & Co., 1986.

Goetzmann, William H., and Joseph C. Porter. *The West as Romantic Horizon*. Omaha: Center for Western Studies, Joslyn Art Museum, 1981.

Goetzmann, William H., and Becky Duval Reese. *Texas Images and Visions*. Austin: University of Texas Press for the Archer M. Huntington Art Gallery, 1983.

Gracy, David B. II. *Moses Austin: His Life*. San Antonio: Trinity University Press, 1987.

Graham, Don. *Cowboys and Cadillacs: How Hollywood Looks at Texas*. Austin: Texas Monthly Press, 1984.

Graham, Don, James Lee, and Thomas Pilkington, eds., *The Texas Literary Tradition*. Austin: University of Texas Press, 1983.

Grauer, Michael R. "The Early Career of Frank Reaugh, 1860–1889." Master's thesis, Southern Methodist University, 1990.

Green, Thomas J. *Journal of the Texian Expedition against Mier*. New York: Harper & Brothers, 1845. Reprint. Austin: Steck, 1935.

Groce, George C., and David H. Wallace. *The New York Historical Society's Dictionary of Artists in America, 1564–1869*. New Haven: Yale University Press, 1957.

Groseclose, Barbara S. *Emanuel Leutze, 1816–1868: A German-American History Painter*. Ann Arbor, Mich.: UMI Research Press, 1975.

Gulick, Charles Adams, Jr., and Katherine Elliott, eds. *The Papers of Mirabeau B. Lamar*. 6 vols. Austin: Von Boeckmann-Jones, 1920–1927.

Guratzsch, Herwig. *Painting of the Low Countries*. London: Jupiter Books, 1981.

Haley, J. Evetts. *Charles Goodnight: Cowman and Plainsman*. Norman: University of Oklahoma Press, 1936.

———. *Frank Reaugh: Man and Artist*. El Paso: Carl Hertzog, 1960.

Hallenbeck, Cleve. *Alvar Nuñez Cabeza de Vaca: The Journey and Route of the First European to Cross the Continent of North America, 1534–1536*. Glendale, Calif.: Arthur H. Clark Co., 1940.

———. *The Journey of Fray Marcos de Niza*. Introduction by David J. Weber. Dallas: Southern Methodist University Press, 1987.

Hassrick, Peter H. *Frederic Remington: Paintings, Drawings, and Sculpture in the Amon Carter Museum and the Sid W. Richardson Foundation Collections*. New York: Harry N. Abrams, 1973.

———. *The Way West: The Art of Frontier America*. New York: Harry N. Abrams, 1977.

Hayes, Charles G. *Galveston: A History of the Island and the City*. 2 vols. Austin: Jenkins Garrett Press, 1974.

Haynes, Sam W. *Soldiers of Misfortune: The Somervell and Mier Expeditions*. Austin: University of Texas Press, 1990.

Henson, Margaret Swett. *Samuel May Williams, Early Texas Entrepreneur*. College Station: Texas A&M University Press, 1976.

Hine, Robert V. *Bartlett's West: Drawing the Mexican Boundary*. New Haven: Yale University Press, 1968.

Hogan, William Ransom. *The Texas Republic: A Social and Eco-

nomic History. Norman: University of Oklahoma Press, 1946.

Honour, Hugh. *The New Golden Land: European Images of America from the Discoveries to the Present Time*. New York: Pantheon Books, 1975.

Hughes, Edan Milton. *Artists in California, 1786–1940*. San Francisco: Hughes Publishing Co., 1986.

Hughes, W. J. *Rebellious Ranger: "Rip" Ford and the Old Southwest*. Norman: University of Oklahoma Press, 1964.

Jackson, A. T. *Picture-Writing of Texas Indians*. University of Texas Bureau of Research in the Social Sciences, Study no. 27. Austin: University of Texas Press, 1938.

James, Marquis. *The Raven*. Indianapolis: Bobbs-Merrill, 1929.

Jenkins, John H., ed. *Papers of the Texas Revolution*. 10 vols. Austin: Presidial Press, 1973.

Johannsen, Robert W. *To the Halls of the Montezumas: The Mexican War in the American Imagination*. New York: Oxford University Press, 1985.

Kalil, Susie. *The Texas Landscape, 1900–1986*. Houston: Museum of Fine Arts, Houston, 1986.

Kendall, Dorothy S. and Carmen Perry. *Gentilz: Artist of the Old Southwest*. Austin: University of Texas Press, 1974.

Kendall, George Wilkins. *Narrative of an Expedition across the Great South-Western Prairies from Texas to Santa Fe*. 2 vols. London: David Bogue, 1845. Reprint. Ann Arbor: University Microfilms, 1966.

Kilgore, Dan. *How Did Davy Die?* College Station: Texas A&M University Press, 1978.

King, Irene Marschall. *John O. Meusebach: German Colonizer in Texas*. Austin: University of Texas Press, 1967.

Kirkland, Forrest, and William W. Newcomb. *The Rock Art of Texas Indians*. Austin: University of Texas Press, 1967.

Lane, Walter P. *The Adventures and Recollections of General Walter P. Lane*. Marshall, Tex.: Tri-Weekly Herald Job Print, 1887. Reprint. Austin: Pemberton Press, 1970.

Leach, Joseph. *The Typical Texan: Biography of an American Myth*. Dallas: Southern Methodist University Press, 1952.

Levin, David. *History as Romantic Art*. Stanford: Stanford University Press, 1959.

Lewis, R. W. B. *The American Adam: Innocence, Tragedy and Tradition in the Nineteenth Century*. Chicago: University of Chicago Press, 1955.

Lofaro, Michael C., ed. *Davy Crockett: The Man, the Legend, the Legacy, 1786–1986*. Knoxville: University of Tennessee Press, 1986.

Lomax, John A. *Adventures of a Ballad Hunter*. New York: Macmillan & Co., 1947.

Long, Jeff. *Duel of Eagles: The Mexican and U.S. Fight for the Alamo*. New York: Morrow, 1990.

Lord, Walter. *A Time to Stand*. New York: Harper & Brothers, 1961.

Lotto, Frank. *Fayette County: Her History and Her People*. Schulenburg, Tex.: Sticker Steam Press, 1902.

McComb, David G. *Galveston: A History*. Austin: University of Texas Press, 1986.

McCutchan, Joseph D. *Mier Expedition Diary: A Texan Prisoner's Account*. Edited by Joseph Milton Nance. Austin: University of Texas Press, 1978.

McDermott, John Francis. *Seth Eastman: Pictorial Historian of the Indian*. Norman: University of Oklahoma Press, 1961.

McDonald, Archie P. *Travis*. Austin: Pemberton Press, 1976.

McGuire, James Patrick. *Hermann Lungkwitz: Romantic Landscapist on the Texas Frontier*. Austin: University of Texas Press, 1983.

————. *Iwonski in Texas: Painter and Citizen*. San Antonio: San Antonio Museum Association, 1976.

————. *Julius Stockfleth: Gulf Coast Marine and Landscape Painter*. Introduction by Eric Steinfeldt. San Antonio: Trinity University Press and the Rosenberg Library, Galveston, 1976.

Mapping a Region: Texas, 1656–1857. Waco, Texas: Texas Collection, Baylor University, 1987.

Marks, Paula Mitchell. *Turn Your Eyes toward Texas: Pioneers Sam and Mary Maverick*. College Station: Texas A&M University Press, 1989.

Martin, James C., and Robert S. Martin. *Maps of Texas and the Southwest, 1513–1900*. Albuquerque: University of New Mexico Press, 1984.

Mason, Herbert M. *Death from the Sea: Our Greatest Natural Disaster, the Galveston Hurricane of 1900*. New York: Dial Press, 1972.

Meinig, D. W. *Imperial Texas*. Austin: University of Texas Press, 1969.

Moore, Nancy Dustin Wall. *Publications in Southern California Art: 1, 2 and 3*. Los Angeles: Dustin Publications, 1984.

Morphis, James M. *History of Texas, from Its Discovery and Settlement . . . .* New York: United States Publishing, 1874.

Nance, Joseph Milton. *After San Jacinto: The Texas-Mexican Frontier, 1836–1841*. Austin: University of Texas Press, 1963.

————. *Attack and Counterattack: The Texas-Mexican Frontier, 1842*. Austin: University of Texas Press, 1964.

Newcomb, William W. *German Artist on the Texas Frontier: Friedrich Richard Petri*. Austin: University of Texas Press, 1978.

————. *The Indians of Texas: From Prehistoric to Modern Times*. Austin: University of Texas Press, 1961.

Novak, Barbara. *American Painting of the Nineteenth Century: Realism, Idealism, and the American Experience*. New York: Harper & Row, 1969.

O'Brien, Esse Forrester. *Art and Artists in Texas*. Dallas: Tardy Publishing Co., 1935.

Olmsted, Frederick Law. *A Journey through Texas Or, A Saddle Trip on the South-Western Frontier*. New York: Dix, Edwards, 1857. Reprint. Austin: University of Texas Press, 1978.

Orr-Cahall, Christina, ed. and intro. *The Art of California: Selected Works from the Collection of the Oakland Museum*. Oakland: The Oakland Museum Art Department, 1984.

Owens, William A. *Fever in the Earth*. New York: G. P. Putnam, 1958.

Pearce, T. M., and A. T. Thompson, eds. *Southwesterners Write: The American Southwest in Stories and Articles by Thirty-Two Contributors*. Albuquerque: University of New Mexico Press, 1946.

Peña, José Enrique de la. *With Santa Anna in Texas: A Personal Narrative of the Revolution*. Edited and translated by Carmen Perry. College Station: Texas A&M University Press, 1975.

Pennybacker, Anna J. Hardwicke. *History of Texas for Schools*. Palestine, Texas: P. V. Pennybacker, 1895.

Pinckney, Pauline A. *Painting in Texas: The Nineteenth Century*. Austin: University of Texas Press for the Amon Carter Museum, 1967.

Potter, Reuben Marmaduke. *The Fall of the Alamo: A Reminiscence of the Revolution of Texas*. San Antonio: Herald Steam Press, 1860.

Raines, C. W. *A Yearbook for Texas, 1901–1903*. 2 vols. Austin: Gammel Publishing Co., 1902–1903.

Ratcliffe, Sam DeShong. "Texas History Painting: An Iconographic Study." Ph.D. diss. University of Texas at Austin, 1985.

Reichstein, Andreas V. *Rise of the Lone Star: The Making of Texas*. Translated by Jeanne R. Willson. College Station: Texas A&M University Press, 1989.

Richardson, Rupert N. *The Comanche Barrier to South Plains Settlement*. Glendale, Calif.: Arthur H. Clark, 1933.

Richmond Portraits: In an Exhibition of Makers of Richmond. Richmond: William Byrd Press, 1949.

Roof, Katherine Metcalf. *The Life and Art of William Merritt Chase*. New York: Hacker Art Books, 1975.

Rose, Victor M. *The Life and Services of General Ben McCulloch*. Philadelphia: Pictorial Bureau of the Press, 1888. Reprint. Austin: Steck, 1958.

Russell, Don. *Custer's Last*. Fort Worth: Amon Carter Museum, 1968.

Samuels, Peggy, and Harold Samuels. *Frederic Remington*. New York: Doubleday & Co., 1982.

———. *The Illustrated Biographical Encyclopedia of Artists of the American West*. Garden City, N.Y.: Doubleday & Co., 1976.

Schimmel, Julie. "John Mix Stanley and the Image of the West in 19th Century American Art." Ph.D. diss. New York University, 1983.

Schoelwer, Susan Prendergast, with Tom W. Gläser. *Alamo Images: Changing Perceptions of a Texas Experience*. Introduction by Paul Andrew Hutton. Dallas: DeGolyer Library and Southern Methodist University Press, 1985.

Shackford, James A. *David Crockett: The Man and the Legend*. Chapel Hill: University of North Carolina Press, 1956.

Shapiro, Michael Edward, and Peter H. Hassrick. *Frederic Remington: The Masterworks*. New York: Harry N. Abrams for the Saint Louis Art Museum and Buffalo Bill Historical Center, 1988.

Simms, William Gilmore. *Views and Reviews in American Literature, History, and Fiction*. New York: Wiley & Putnam, 1845.

Simpson, Harold B. *Hood's Texas Brigade: Lee's Grenadier Guard*. Waco, Tex.: Texian Press, 1970.

Simpson, Lesley Byrd, ed. and trans. *The San Sabá Papers*. San Francisco: John Howell Books, 1959.

Slotkin, Richard. *Regeneration through Violence: The Mythology of the American Frontier, 1600–1860*. Middletown, Conn.: Wesleyan University Press, 1973.

Smith, Henry Nash. *Virgin Land: The American West as Symbol and Myth*. Cambridge: Harvard University Press, 1950.

Smith, Justin H. *The War with Mexico*. 2 vols. New York: Macmillan, 1919.

Smith, Richard Penn. *Col. Crockett's Exploits and Adventures in Texas*. Philadelphia: T. K. and P. G. Collins, 1836.

Smithwick, Noah. *The Evolution of a State*. Austin: H. P. N. Gammel, 1900. Reprint. Austin: University of Texas Press, 1983.

Sowell, Andrew Jackson. *Rangers and Pioneers of Texas*. San Antonio, 1884.

Spratt, John S. *The Road to Spindletop: Economic Change in Texas, 1875–1901*. Dallas: Southern Methodist University Press, 1955.

Stapp, William Preston. *The Prisoners of Perote*. Philadelphia: G. B. Zieber and Co., 1845.

Stegner, Wallace. *The Sound of Mountain Water: The Changing American West*. Garden City, N.Y.: Doubleday & Co., 1969.

Steinfeldt, Cecilia. *San Antonio Was: Seen through a Magic Lantern*. San Antonio: San Antonio Museum Association, 1978.

———. *The Onderdonks: A Family of Texas Painters*. San Antonio: Trinity University Press for the San Antonio Museum Association, 1976.

———. *Texas Folk Art: One Hundred Fifty Years of the Southwestern Tradition*. Austin: Texas Monthly Press for the San Antonio Museum Association, 1981.

Stewart, Rick. *Lone Star Regionalism: The Dallas Nine and their Circle*. Austin: Texas Monthly Press, 1984.

Strong, Roy. *Recreating the Past: British History and the Victorian Painter*. London: Thames and Hudson, 1978.

Sweet, Alexander E. *Alex Sweet's Texas: The Lighter Side of Lone Star History*. Edited by Virginia Eisenhour. Austin: University of Texas Press, 1986.

Taft, Robert. *Artists and Illustrators of the Old West*. New York: Charles Scribner's Sons, 1950.

Taylor, Joshua C. *America As Art*. Washington, D.C.: Smithsonian Institution Press for the National Collection of Fine Arts, 1976.

Terreros, Manuel Romero de. *El Conde de Regla: Creso de la Nueva España*. Mexico City: Ediciones Xochitl, 1943.

———. *Los Condes de Regla: Apuntes Biográficos*. Mexico City: M. León Sánchez, 1909.

Texas. *Constitution* (1836).

Texas. *Senate and Special Laws, 40th Legislature, 1st Called Session*. 1927.

Thistlethwaite, Mark Edward. *The Image of George Washington: Studies in Mid-Nineteenth Century American History Painting*. New York: Garland Publishing Co., 1979.

Thomas, W. Stephen. *Fort Davis and the Texas Frontier: Paintings by Captain Arthur T. Lee, Eighth U.S. Infantry.* College Station: Texas A&M University Press, 1975.

Tinkle, Lon. *13 Days to Glory.* New York: McGraw-Hill, 1958.

Truettner, William H. *The Natural Man Observed: A Study of Catlin's Indian Gallery.* Washington, D.C.: Smithsonian Institution, 1979.

Tyler, Ron. *The Mexican War: A Lithographic Record.* Austin: Texas State Historical Association, 1973.

———. *Views of Texas, 1852–1856: Watercolors by Sarah Ann Lillie Hardinge.* Fort Worth: Amon Carter Museum, 1988.

Tyler, Ron, Linda Ayres, Warder H. Cadbury, Carol Clark, Bernard Reilly, Jr., and Herman J. Viola. *American Frontier Life: Early Western Painting and Prints.* Introduction by Peter H. Hassrick. New York: Abbeville Press, 1987.

Utterback, Martha. *Early Texas Art in the Witte Museum.* San Antonio: Prompt Printers, 1968.

Vandiver, Frank. *The Southwest: South or West?* College Station: Texas A&M University Press, 1975.

Vorpahl, Ben Merchant. *Frederic Remington and the West: With the Eye of the Mind.* Austin: University of Texas Press, 1978.

Walker, Samuel H. *Samuel H. Walker's Account of the Mier Expedition.* Edited by Marilyn McAdams Sibley. Austin: Texas State Historical Association, 1978.

Warren, Harris Gaylord. *The Sword Was Their Passport.* Baton Rouge: Louisiana State University Press, 1943.

Weaver, Bobby D. *Castro's Colony: Empresario Development in Texas, 1842–1865.* College Station: Texas A&M University Press, 1985.

Webb, Walter Prescott. *The Texas Rangers.* Boston: Houghton Mifflin Co., 1935.

Weber, David J. *The Mexican Frontier, 1821–1846: The American Southwest under Mexico.* Albuquerque: University of New Mexico Press, 1982.

Weddle, Robert S. *The San Sabá Mission: Spanish Pivot in Texas.* Austin: University of Texas Press, 1964.

———. *Wilderness Manhunt: The Spanish Search for La Salle.* Austin: University of Texas Press, 1973.

Weems, John Edward. *Dream of Empire: A Human History of the Republic of Texas, 1836–1846.* New York: Simon & Schuster, 1971.

———. *Men without Countries: Three Adventurers of the Early Southwest.* Boston: Houghton Mifflin Co., 1969.

———. *A Weekend in September.* New York: Holt, 1957.

Weismann, Donald L. *Frank Reaugh: Painter to the Longhorns.* College Station: Texas A&M University Press, 1985.

———. *The Visual Arts as Human Experience.* Englewood Cliffs, N.J.: Prentice-Hall, 1970.

Winfrey, Dorman H., ed. *Texas Indian Papers, 1825–1843.* Austin: Texas State Library, 1959.

———. *Texas Indian Papers, 1844–1845.* Austin: Texas State Library, 1959.

Winkler, Ernest W., ed. *Secret Journals of the Senate, Republic of Texas, 1836–1845.* Austin: Austin Printing Co., 1911.

Wisehart, M. K. *Sam Houston: American Giant.* Washington: Robert B. Luce, 1962.

Wister, Owen. *The Virginian.* New York: Macmillan, 1902.

A Woman's Vision: California Painting into the 20th Century. Introduction by Raymond L. Wilson. San Francisco: Maxwell Galleries, 1983.

Wooten, Dudley G. *A Comprehensive History of Texas.* Dallas: Texas History Co., 1899.

Ziff, Norman D. *Paul Delaroche: A Study in Nineteenth Century French History Painting.* New York: Garland Publishing Co., 1977.

Zuber, W. P. *My Eighty Years in Texas.* Austin: University of Texas Press, 1971.

Articles

"American Art: The Need and Nature of Its History." *Illustrated Magazine of Art* 3 (1854): 262–263.

Barr, Alwyn. "The Semicentennial of Texas Independence in 1886." *Southwestern Historical Quarterly* 91 (January 1988): 349–360.

Battle, W. J. "Art in Texas: An Overview." *Southwest Review* 14 (Autumn 1928): 51–59.

Bauman, Richard. "The Transmission of the Texas Myth." In *Texas Myths.* Edited by Robert F. O'Connor, pp. 23–41. College Station: Texas A&M University Press for the Texas Committee for the Humanities, 1986.

Benson, E. "Historical Art in the United States." *Appleton's Journal of Literature, Science, and Art* 1 (10 April 1869): 45–46.

Benson, Nettie Lee. "Texas as Viewed from Mexico, 1820–1834." *Southwestern Historical Quarterly* 90 (January 1987): 219–291.

Bowie, John J. "Early Life in the Southwest—The Bowies." *DeBow's Review* 13 (October 1852): 378–383.

Bushnell, David I. "John Mix Stanley, Artist-Explorer." In *Annual Report of the Smithsonian Institution for the Year Ending June 30, 1924,* 506–519. Washington, D.C.: Smithsonian Institution, 1925.

Bywaters, Jerry. "Contemporary American Artists." *Southwest Review* 23 (April 1938): 297–306.

———. "The New Texas Painters." *Southwest Review* 11 (Spring 1936): 330–342.

Carleton, Don. "Art as Regional History." *Discovery* 6 (Spring 1983): 10–11.

Chipman, Donald E. "In Search of Cabeza de Vaca's Route across Texas." *Southwestern Historical Quarterly* 91 (October 1987): 127–148.

Commager, Henry Steele. "The Search for a Usable Past." *American Heritage* 16 (February 1965): 4–9, 90–96.

Connelly, Thomas L. "The American Camel Experiment: A Reappraisal." *Southwestern Historical Quarterly* 69 (October 1966): 442–462.

Costeloe, Michael P. "Notes and Documents: The Mexican Press of 1836 and the Battle of the Alamo." *Southwestern Historical Quarterly* 91 (April 1988): 533–544.

Covner, Craig R. "Before 1850: A New Look at the Alamo through Art and Imagery, Part 1." *Alamo Journal* 70 (March 1990): 1–8.

———. "Before 1850: A New Look at the Alamo through Art and Imagery, Part 2." *Alamo Journal* 73 (November 1990): 1–6.

Cronon, William. "Revisiting the Vanishing Frontier: The Legacy of Frederick Jackson Turner." *Western Historical Quarterly* 18 (April 1987): 157–176.

Cutrer, Emily Fourmy. "'The Hardy, Stalwart Son of Texas': Art and Mythology at the State Capitol." *Southwestern Historical Quarterly* 92 (October 1988): 312–322.

Davis, Curtis Carroll, ed. "A Legend at Full-Length: Mr. Chapman Paints Colonel Crockett—And Tells About It." *Proceedings of the American Antiquarian Society* 69 (21 October 1959): 155–174.

Day, James M., ed. "Texas Letters and Documents." *Texana* 8 (Summer 1970): 295–305.

DeShields, James. "The Story of Warren Lions." In *Texas Literature Reader*, ed. Davis Foute Eagleton, pp. 78–82. Dallas: Southern Publishing Co., 1916.

Foreman, Carolyn T. "Pierce Mason Butler." *Chronicles of Oklahoma* 30 (Spring 1952): 6–28.

Goodrich, Lloyd. "The Painting of American History: 1775 to 1900." *American Quarterly* 3 (Winter 1951): 283–294.

Grauer, Michael R. *Frank Reaugh: From the Panhandle-Plains Historical Museum.* Pamphlet accompanying exhibition in Texas A&M University Memorial Student Center, 8 February–13 May 1989.

Green, Michael R. "'To the People of Texas & All Americans in the World.'" *Southwestern Historical Quarterly* 91 (April 1988): 483–508.

Hardin, Stephen L. "Gallery: David Crockett." *Military History, Past and Present* 23 (February–March 1990): 28–35.

———, ed. "Notes and Documents—The Félix Nuñez Account and the Siege of the Alamo: A Critical Appraisal." *Southwestern Historical Quarterly* 93 (July 1990): 65–84.

Hassrick, Peter H. "Remington in the Southwest." *Southwestern Historical Quarterly* 76 (January 1973): 297–302.

Henson, Margaret Swett. "Tory Sentiment in Anglo-Texan Public Opinion, 1832–1836." *Southwestern Historical Quarterly* 90 (July 1986): 3–11.

Howard, Richard Foster. "Art of Texas Presents an Epitome of Aesthetics of the Modern Age." *Art Digest* 10 (1 June 1936): 14.

Hutson, Martha. "Narrative Painting: The Painters' America, Rural and Urban Life, 1810–1910." *American Art Review* 1 (November–December 1974): 94–109.

Lammons, Frank Bishop. "Operation Camel: An Experiment in Western Transportation in Texas, 1857–1860." *Southwestern Historical Quarterly* 6 (January 1957): 20–50.

Lejarza, Fidel de. "Escenas de martirio en el Río S. Sabá." *Archivo Ibero-Americano* 12 (October–December 1943): 441–495.

Linienthal, Edward Tabor. "'A Reservoir of Spiritual Power': Patriotic Faith at the Alamo in the Twentieth Century." *Southwestern Historical Quarterly* 91 (April 1988): 509–532.

Muckelroy, Anna. "The Indian Policy of the Republic of Texas." *Southwestern Historical Quarterly* 26 (July 1922–April 1923): 1–29, 128–148, and 184–206.

Museum of Fine Arts of Houston, Texas. *Bulletin of the Museum of Fine Arts of Houston, Texas* 7 (Spring 1944).

Paz, Octavio. "Ceremonies in the Catacombs." *Chronicles: A Magazine of American Culture* 12 (April 1988): 10–12.

Pohl, James W., and Stephen L. Hardin. "The Military History of the Texas Revolution: An Overview." *Southwestern Historical Quarterly* 89 (April 1986): 269–308.

Potter, Reuben Marmaduke. "The Fall of the Alamo." *Magazine of American History* 2 (January 1878): 1–21.

———. "The Battle of San Jacinto." *The Magazine of American History* 4 (May 1880): 321–333.

Ratcliffe, Sam D. "'Escenas de Martirio': Notes on *The Destruction of Mission San Sabá*." *Southwestern Historical Quarterly* 94 (April 1991): 506–534.

———. "For the Love of Texas—James T. DeShields: Art Patron and Historian." *Legacies: A History Journal for Dallas and North Central Texas* 2 (Spring 1990): 17–25.

Remington, Frederic. "A Few Words from Mr. Remington." *Collier's* 34 (18 March 1905): 16–17.

———. "How the Law Got into the Chaparral." *Harper's New Monthly Magazine* 94 (December 1896): 60–69.

Schmidt, Eric von. "The Alamo Remembered from a Painter's Point of View." *Smithsonian* 16 (March 1986): 54–71.

Schoelwer, Susan Prendergast. "The Artist's Alamo: A Reappraisal of Pictorial Evidence, 1835–1850." *Southwestern Historical Quarterly* 91 (April 1988): 403–456.

Starling, Susanne. "A Surveyor's Saga: Warren Angus Ferris at the Three Forks." *Legacies: A History Journal for Dallas and North Central Texas* 1 (Spring 1989): 6–11.

Taylor, Lonn. "Texas Painters of Romantic Frontiers." *Texas Homes* 5 (October 1981): 106–124.

Terreros, Manuel Romero de. "La Misión Franciscana de San Sabás en la Provincia de Texas. Año de 1758." *Anales de Instituto de Investigaciones Estéticas* 36 (1967): 51–58.

Truettner, William H. "The Art of History: American Exploration and Discovery Scenes, 1840–1860." *American Art Journal* 14 (Winter 1982): 4–31.

Turner, Frederick Jackson. "The Significance of the Frontier in American History." In *American Historical Association Annual Report for the Year 1893*, pp. 199–217. Washington, D.C., 1894.

Voss, Frederick S. "Portraying an American Original: The Likenesses of Davy Crockett." *Southwestern Historical Quarterly* 91 (April 1988): 457–482.

Zuber, W. P. "An Escape from the Alamo." In *The Texas Almanac, 1857–1873*, compiled by James M. Day. Waco: Texian Press, 1967.

Newspapers

"Alsatian Artist Pictures Early San Antonio." *San Antonio Light*, 7 October 1945.

"Art Sleuths Desire Whereabouts of Rare Davy Crockett Painting." *San Antonio Express*, 17 August 1955.

"Artist Is Forty Years Finishing Picture of Alamo Battle." *San Antonio Express*, 21 June 1927.

Austin Daily Democratic Statesman, 27, 28, and 29 June 1873; 6 July 1873; and 16 October 1877.

Austin American-Statesman, 6 March 1927.

Bradshaw, Ann. "Panorama of Texas History in Unique Dallas Art Collection." *Dallas Times Herald*, 11 May 1930.

Callihan, E. L. "The Battles That Whipped Mexico." *Dallas Morning News*, 10 August 1930.

Colorado Gazette and Advertiser, 28 March; 18 April; and 29 August 1840.

Dallas Morning News, 10 July 1927.

"*Dawn at the Alamo*: Historic Painting of Famous Texas Battle to Be Seen by Texas Enthusiasts." *San Antonio Daily Express*, 16 February 1906.

"Death of a Noted Painter." *Washington Post*, 17 April 1892.

"Events of the Comanche Treaty." *Texas Sentinel*, 15 April 1840.

"Fall of the Historic Alamo." *Farmersville Sentinel*, 19 March 1906.

Fitzgerald, Hugh Nugent. "Texas History Pictured." *Austin American-Statesman*, 6 March 1927.

Galvin, Lois Hale. "Early Texas Artists." *Austin American-Statesman*, 16 May 1965.

Gossett, Louise Long. "Stage Set for Play Designed from Alamo Battle Paintings." *Dallas Morning News*, 24 April 1941.

Houston Daily Post, 1 March 1882.

Houston Weekly Times, 9 April 1840.

"Indian Difficulties." *Clarksville Northern Standard*, 13 March 1845.

Kelley, Dayton. "Search Turns Up Copy of Texas Artist's Work." *Dallas Morning News*, 4 March 1965.

———. "Painter of Texas History." *Dallas Times Herald, SUNDAY Magazine*, 1 December 1968.

"McArdle's Latest Historic Painting: 'The Dawn at the Alamo.'" *San Antonio Daily Express* [n.d.].

"Painting by Richmonder Offered for Appomattox." *Richmond Times-Dispatch*, 20 January 1952.

Phelan, Charlotte. "Painters, McPainter." *Houston Post*, 4 June 1961.

Renick, Dorothy. "The Eyes of Texas." *San Antonio Express*, 22 July 1923.

———. "McArdle's Paintings Tell the Story of Immortal Heroes at the Alamo and San Jacinto." *San Antonio Express*, 22 July 1923.

San Antonio Daily Herald, 27 January 1875.

San Antonio Express, 28 April 1881; and 24 February 1929.

San Augustine Journal and Advertiser, 4 June and 18 July 1840.

Steely, Skipper. "Archives." *Dallas Times Herald*, 17 July 1983.

"Story of Alamo Told in Picture." *San Antonio Express*, 6 March 1936.

Telegraph and Texas Register, 24 March 1836.

Texas Sentinel, 15 January, 8 and 25 March, 25 May, 20 June, 15 August, and 12 and 26 September 1840.

Vazquez, José. "Homaje de un Martir." N.p. N.d. Photocopy in possession of SDR.

"Who Painted It?" *Atlanta Constitution*, 15 May 1890.

Unpublished Materials

Blackard, Sandra R. "Examination Report on William Huddle, *Surrender of Santa Anna*," 6 January 1987. Perry Huston and Associates, Fort Worth. Photocopy of in-house conservation report in possession of SDR.

Blow, Stephen. "The Texas Image: The State as Portrayed in the *New York Times* and the *Dallas Morning News*, 1885–1887." Photocopy of unpublished paper in possession of SDR.

Goetzmann, William H. "No Teacup Tragedies Here: The Art of Frederic Remington." Paper delivered at Denver Art Museum, 11 July 1981. Manuscript available at Denver Art Museum.

Green, W. E. "Alamobilia: 'Remembering the Alamo' with Silver Spoons and Chocolate Bars." Paper delivered to the annual meeting of the Texas State Historical Association, Fort Worth, 2 March 1985. Copy in possession of SDR.

Greene, A. C. "The Importance of the Mission San Sabá Massacre in Texas History and the Historical Value of Paez' Depiction of that Event." Report for Dallas Public Library, 1984. Copy in possession of SDR.

Schmidt, Eric von. "Alamo Iconography: Painting the Battle of the Alamo." Paper delivered to the annual meeting of the Texas State Historical Association, Fort Worth, 2 March 1985. Copy in possession of SDR.

Stroessner, Robert. "*Destruction of Mission San Sabás in the Province of Texas and the Martyrdom of the Fathers Alonso Giraldo de Terreros, Joseph Santiesteban*: A Brief Research Report on an Important Historical Painting of the Same Subject with an Attribution to Its Artist." Report for New World Department, Denver Art Museum, 15 January 1982. Copy in possession of SDR.

Index